D0712904

San Diego Christian College
2100 Greenfield Drive
El Cajon, CA 92019

The Mathematics of Behavior

Mathematical thinking provides a clear, crisp way of defining problems. Our whole technology is based on it. What is less appreciated is that mathematical thinking can also be applied to problems in the social and behavioral sciences. This book illustrates how mathematics can be employed for understanding human and animal behavior, using examples in psychology, sociology, economics, ecology, and even marriage counseling.

Earl Hunt is Professor Emeritus of Psychology at the University of Washington in Seattle. He has written many articles and chapters in contributed volumes and is the past editor of *Cognitive Psychology* and *Journal of Experimental Psychology*. His books include *Concept Learning: An Information Processing Problem*, *Experiments in Induction*, *Artificial Intelligence*, and *Will We Be Smart Enough?*, which won the William James Book Award from the American Psychological Association in 1996. His most recent book is *Thoughts on Thought*.

The Mathematics of Behavior

EARL HUNT

University of Washington, Seattle

 **CAMBRIDGE**
UNIVERSITY PRESS

CAMBRIDGE UNIVERSITY PRESS
Cambridge, New York, Melbourne, Madrid, Cape Town, Singapore, São Paulo

Cambridge University Press
32 Avenue of the Americas, New York, NY 10013-2473, USA

www.cambridge.org
Information on this title: www.cambridge.org/9780521850124

© Cambridge University Press 2007

First published 2007

Printed in the United States of America

A catalog record for this publication is available from the British Library.

Library of Congress Cataloging in Publication Data
Hunt, Earl B.
The mathematics of behavior/Earl Hunt
p. cm.
Includes bibliographical references and index.
ISBN 0-521-85012-6 (hardcover) – ISBN 0-521-61522-4 (pbk.)
1. Psychology – Mathematical models. 2. Social sciences – Mathematical models. I. Title.
BF39.H86 2006
150.1'51–dc22   2005030591

ISBN-13 978-0-521-85012-4 hardback
ISBN-10 0-521-85012-6 hardback

ISBN-13 978-0-521-61522-8 paperback
ISBN-10 0-521-61522-4 paperback

Contents

Preface

Many, many years ago, when I was a graduate student at Yale University, I attended Professor Robert Abelson's seminar on mathematical psychology. This was in the late 1950s, just as mathematical techniques were beginning to hit psychology. Subsequently I met Professor Jacob Marschak, an economist whose work on the economics of information was seminal in the field. After I received my doctorate in 1960 I had the great opportunity to work with Marschak's group at the University of California, Los Angeles. Marschak set a gold standard for the use of mathematics to support clear, precise thinking. It is now almost 50 years later, near the end of my own career, and I have yet to meet someone whose logic was so clear. I have had the opportunity to see some people come close to Marschak's standard, both in my own discipline of psychology and in other fields. This book is an attempt to let future students see how our understanding of behaviors, by both humans and non-humans, can be enhanced by mathematical analysis.

Is such a goal realistic today? Many people have deplored the alleged decline in mathematical training among today's college students. I do not think that that is fair. On an absolute level, students at the major universities arrive far better trained than they were 50 years ago. High school courses in the calculus are common today; they were rare even 25 years ago. It is true that on a comparative basis American students have slipped compared to their peers abroad, but on an absolute basis the better students in all countries are simply better prepared than they used to be. I have set my sights accordingly. This book should be easily accessible to anyone who has a basic understanding of the calculus, and most of the book will not even require that. It will require the ability (the willingness?) to follow a mathematical argument. I hope that the effort will be rewarded. Curious about the mathematics of love? Or how unprejudiced people can produce a segregated society? Read on!

And to those of you on college and university faculties, consider teaching a course that covers topics like this; mathematics used to analyze important issues in our day, or important issues in the history of science. Don't restrict it to your own discipline; think broadly. I hope you find this book helpful, but if you don't, get some readings and teach the course anyway. I have been fortunate to teach such a course in the University of Washington Honors Program for the past several years, and the discussions among students pursuing majors from philosophy to biology and engineering have been informative and enjoyable.

No one prepares a book without a great deal of support. I have had it. I thank the Honors Program and, most especially, the students in my classes, for letting me lead the course. I also thank the Psychology Department for letting me lead a predecessor of this course, focusing somewhat more on psychology. Cambridge University Press provided assistance in book preparation that was far superior to that of any other press with which I have ever worked. I thank Regina Paleski for production editing assistance, and I particularly thank Phyllis Berk for a superb job of copyediting a difficult manuscript. I also thank the editor, Philip Laughlin, for his assistance, and in particular for his obtaining very high-quality editorial reviews. Naturally, the people who wrote them are thanked, too! The final review, by Professor Jerome Busemeyer of the University of Indiana, was a model of constructive criticism.

Every author closes with thanks to family … or at least, he should. My wife, Mary Lou Hunt, has supported me in this and all my scholarly work. I could not accomplish any efforts without her loving aid and assistance.

Earl Hunt
Bellevue, Washington, and
Hood Canal, Washington
February 2006

1

Introduction

1.1. WHAT'S IN THE BOOK?

This book is about using mathematics to think about how humans (and other animals) behave. We are hardly surprised to find that mathematics helps us when we deal with physical things. Although relatively few people can do the relevant mathematics, no one is surprised to find out that buildings are built, airplanes are designed, and ships and cars fueled according to some mathematical principle. But people? Or, for that matter, dogs and birds? Does mathematics have a place in understanding how animate, sentient beings move about, remember, quarrel, live with a spouse, or decide to invest in one venture and not another?

I think it does, and I am going to try to convince you. To make things easier to read, I will use the term *mathematical modeling* to refer to the process of analyzing behavior using the rules of mathematics. Just what this means will be described in more detail later. For now, though, just think of "mathematical modeling" as a shorthand for the clumsier term "using mathematics to study behavior." I want to convince you, the reader, that mathematical modeling is often a very good thing to do.

I will proceed by example. The chapters in this book present problems in the social and behavioral sciences, and then show how mathematical modeling has helped us to understand them. Before plunging into the details, though, I want to step back and look at the bigger picture.

Mathematical modeling is a specialization of a bigger idea, using formal analyses to guide actions. This bigger idea has an opponent: the use of memory, pattern recognition, analogies, and informal argument to make a decision. This opponent is no straw person; it's the legendary 800-pound gorilla. Modern psychological research has shown that our brains, and hence our minds, are very well organized to recognize a new situation as "like what we've seen before," and then to use rough-and-ready reasoning to decide what to do. To be fair, we are much better than other animals in our ability to follow abstract, formal

1

arguments ... but compared to a computer program for deductive reasoning, we aren't all that good.

The reason computers don't run the world, yet, is that reasoning based on memory and analogy works quickly and often works well. This is especially true when we are dealing with concrete, perceivable situations. Formal analysis shows its strength when we deal with abstractions. It's roughly the difference between deciding which steak to buy at the grocery store and deciding whether or not to invest in beef futures on the Chicago Stock Exchange.

For most of human existence people dealt with beef, not beef futures. Until very recently people could spend their lives moving, lifting, cutting, and building things. While abstract ideas certainly were around, they were not part of very many people's daily affairs. In the Industrial Revolution abstract ideas began to be more important than they had been. The intellectual pace quickened further in the late twentieth century, so much so that the economist Robert Reich has called the modern era the age of the "symbol analyst."[1] What he meant by this is that today, an ever-increasing number of people earn their living by manipulating symbols standing for things rather than the things themselves. Issues are decided by analysis rather than memory and pattern recognition. It is becoming more and more important to understand formal analysis, and the ultimate of that analysis, mathematical modeling. A major purpose of this book is to help readers reach such understanding by looking at a variety of models, based on relatively simple mathematics, that have been used to explore social and behavioral issues.

To kick things off, let's take a quick look at some examples showing the advantages and disadvantages of mathematical modeling.

1.2. SOME EXAMPLES OF FORMAL AND INFORMAL THINKING

In the seventeenth century, shipbuilders relied on personal experience to guide ship design. They made drawings of what they wanted without analysis. Skilled laborers then put things together using the drawing as a guide. This method was used in Sweden in 1628 to build the 100-gun *Vasa*, the largest warship of its time. When the King of Sweden saw the plans he had the gut feeling that the ship would be still more powerful if it had an extra gun deck on top. In seventeenth century Sweden, what the king wanted, the king got. The extra gun deck went on forthwith. The *Vasa* sailed the seas, or to be precise, Stockholm harbor, for 30 minutes. Then it capsized. Apparently the king's idea wasn't all that good.

This example does not mean that "gut" ideas, based on experience, are always wrong. In classic times, the Romans built their buildings in

[1] Reich (1991).

very much the same way as the *Vasa* was designed. The magnificent Colosseum of Rome, built about A.D. 65, is standing today.

Today every large engineering project relies on mathematical analysis. Indeed, we are not bothered by a decision to let mathematical analysis override our intuitions. On the face of it, the idea that a modern jumbo jet could get off the ground is ridiculous. That was my reaction the first time I saw a Boeing 747, the first of the jumbo jets. Nevertheless, I was not surprised when I read that the 747's test flight went off without a hitch. Why wasn't I surprised? Because I knew that careful mathematical analyses had shown that the 747 would fly. I trusted the mathematics. So do the millions of people who fly every week.

On the other hand, sometimes we are a bit too smug about our abilities to analyze things. This is shown by examples from the ancient and modern art of barrel making.

Back in the seventeenth century, employees of the Prince-Bishop of Würzburg were entitled to a wine ration from His Eminence's cellars. There were complaints that the Prince-Bishop played favorites when he chose the quality of wine to be distributed. He decided to show that these rumors were untrue by constructing a single wine cask, with a diameter of more than 10 meters. Henceforth everyone drew their ration from the same barrel. The barrel still existed in 2000. (I've seen it.) That is impressive, as the Prince-Bishop's barrel makers worked by intuition and custom, just like the designers of the *Vasa*.

Since the nineteenth century, large barrels like this have been built to engineering design, using our knowledge of metal strength, expansion rates, and so forth. And ...

In the early years of the twentieth century, a massive tank, 15 meters high, was built to store molasses in a factory in Boston. In January 1919 the tank burst. It released a 10-meter wall of molasses, 2 million gallons, on the streets of Boston. Molasses is said to be slow, but if a stream has enough mass behind it, it can push right along. The initial speed of the molasses wave was probably around 50 km/hr. Sadly, 21 people died because they could not outrun it.

The problem was a design fault. The bolts and straps that held the barrel together were made of different metals. On the day of the accident the temperature went from $-17°$ to $+9°$ C ($2°$ to $48°$ F). Alas, the designers had forgotten to allow for different rates of expansion. The result was the stickiest mess in history. If it had not been for the casualties, this would have been just plain funny.

There are probably thousands of examples where some physical construction or manipulation was made possible by mathematical analysis, and for every thousand of these examples, possibly 10 or 12 where the analysis went wrong. Today the balance is clearly on the side of analysis for physical systems, provided that we use a bit of caution. This is the result of centuries of study in which some of the greatest minds of our species (Euclid, Leonardo, Galileo, Descartes, Newton, and Einstein, to mention a few) developed and applied mathematical analyses to the study of the physical world. Now what about the social world?

1.3. A BIT OF HISTORY

The idea of applying mathematical analyses to the social world is an old one. The very first recorded use of arithmetic, in ancient Assyria, was to solve an economic problem. Assyrian merchants wanted to keep track of goods that were not immediately accessible for inspection. A clay tablet recovered from Assyrian ruins, when translated, said roughly:

I have paid your agents three minas of silver, so that they may purchase lead for your activities here. Now, if you are still my brother, send me the money owed by courier.[2]

This is clearly mathematics, for it illustrates the use of a medium of exchange, silver, to equate the values of other goods and services. Other tablets from the same era refer to the use of precious metals to value sheep, cattle, and land.

The next example illustrates a more sophisticated use of business mathematics. About 2,000 years later, in the eleventh century, the Spanish hero Ruy Diaz de Bivar (El Cid) needed cash to finance a campaign against the Moors. He sent Martin Antolínez, a nobleman of Burgos, to negotiate a loan from two bankers of that city. Three of the topics for negotiation were, in modern terms, the appropriate surety that El Cid had to put up to secure a loan of 600 marks, the fee that the bankers were to receive for the use of their money, and, interestingly, the finder's fee to be paid to Antolínez. He got 5%, which in modern terms would not be a bad commission. We find the echoes of such activity in modern investment banking and arbitrage.[3]

The Moors against whom El Cid fought were representatives of the sophisticated Arab-Iranian-Mogul civilization that flourished from roughly the eighth until the fifteenth century. Classical Islam's contribution to mathematics was immense. The number system we use today, *Arabic numbers* (which they probably borrowed from India) is well known. Arabic and Iranian scholars also developed the modern concept of algebra. These ideas could be considered contributions to pure mathematics, although clearly much of our applied mathematics would be impossible without them.

---

[2] Gullberg (1997).
[3] Anonymous ([1100s] 1959), *El Poema de mio Cid*, trans. W. S. Merwin (London: Dent).

Arab scholars of this time also pioneered in introducing mathematical concepts into everyday life. They developed the concept of insurance, which extends investment to the assessment of risk. Insurance is, as we shall see, mathematically virtually identical to gambling, even though it is psychologically quite different. The latter topic caught the fancy of the Europeans. Some of the greatest mathematical minds of the Enlightenment, including Pascal and the Bernoulli brothers, were commissioned to explore strategies for winning gambling games.

In the last two centuries there has been an explosion in the use of modeling to guide our thinking about human affairs. Some of the most interesting cases occur when a mathematical model used to solve a problem in one field is adapted to solve problems in a totally different field. Diagnostic radiologists (physicians who specialize in the interpretation of physiological images, from X rays to magnetic resonance imaging) (MRI) are keenly aware that they can never be certain of a diagnosis, and so must consider both the image they see and the costs of two types of misdiagnoses: false positives (e.g., saying that an organ is cancerous when it is not) and false negatives (failing to spot a tumor). The analytic techniques used to evaluate how well a diagnostic radiologist is doing were developed during World War II as an aid in hunting submarines.

Now, let's take a very different example. In December of 2002 the *New York Times* published an article about the reintroduction of North American wolves into the Yellowstone Park area. According to this article, wildlife biologists believed that in the Yellowstone region a population of 30 breeding pairs of wolves would be sufficient to ensure continuation of the wolf population. Why did they believe that? Because mathematical modeling of wolf population dynamics established that if the number of pairs is greater than 30, the probability that the population level will ever go to zero is acceptably low.

I have been talking about "mathematical modeling" without saying exactly what it is. I will now illustrate modeling with a famous physical example, explain it, and look at the general principles it illustrates. In the following chapters the same principles will be applied to problems in economics, ecology, epidemiology, psychology, sociology, and the neurosciences. The topics differ, the models differ, the mathematics differ, but the principles remain the same.

1.4. HOW BIG IS THE EARTH? ERATOSTHENES' SOLUTION

The idea that Columbus showed that the world is round is simply bunk. Columbus conducted a long voyage into an unknown region, and returned. He could have made his voyage on a disk, if the end of the Earth was somewhere to the west of the Americas. The Spanish court never entertained this idea, for neither Columbus nor the Spanish court believed that the world was flat. Three hundred years before Christ was born, the Hellenic Greeks had argued for a spherical Earth, based on (among other things) the observation that ships disappear from sight hull first when they "sail over the horizon." If the ship were sailing on a flat surface its optical image might be diminished as it withdrew, due to limits on sight, and might eventually disappear, but it would do so symmetrically rather than hull first.

The Greeks went well beyond presenting a logical argument for a spherical Earth. Eratosthenes of Cyrene (274–196 B.C.E), the librarian of Alexandria, used a mathematical model to measure the circumference of the Earth. His reasoning and experiments are worth careful study, for they illustrate the principles behind our use of mathematics today. Furthermore, Eratosthenes' principles are as applicable to economic and psychological models today as they were to the geographic model he worked with 2,300 years ago.[4]

To understand what Eratosthenes did, we first have to look at what his predecessor Euclid (330–275 B.C.E.?) had done. Euclid dealt in pure mathematics. He postulated several properties of an abstract world composed of straight lines and points, our modern Euclidean space. Then, in one of the most famous exercises in logic ever written, he used his postulates to prove theorems about the relation of angles, lines, and arcs in that space.

On the basis of Euclid's work, Eratosthenes knew that if you bisect a sphere with a plane, then the cross section of the sphere that cuts the plane is a circle whose center is the center of the sphere. (There is a fancier way to say this; the locus of all points on both the sphere and the plane is a circle.) In the special case of the Earth (Figure 1-1), a subset of these circles consists of (a) all north-south *polar* circumnavigations of the Earth through the poles (i.e., along lines of longitude, switching lines only at a pole) and (b) the equator.

The resulting circle is shown in Figure 1-2, which also shows two points on the circumference of the circle. These correspond either to two points on the equator or two points on the same line of longitude (on the same north-south line from pole to pole.) Therefore, if you want to measure the length of the equator, it is sufficient to measure the length of a polar circumnavigation.

A mathematical model for doing this is shown in Figure 1-2. The figure shows two points, A and S, on the circumference, and a point C at

---

[4] Many books on the history of mathematics describe Eratosthenes' reasoning. Historians differ as to whether Eratosthenes was brilliant or lucky. His contemporaries seem to have had similarly mixed views of his accomplishments. My account is based largely on the account in Gullberg (1997).

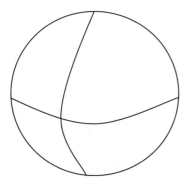

FIGURE 1-1. The first step in Eratosthones' reasoning. If the Earth is a sphere, the equator and any line of longitude can be thought of as points on a circle whose center point is the center of the Earth. All these circles have the same circumference.

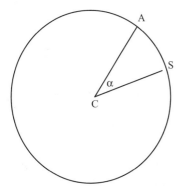

FIGURE 1-2. The second step in Eratosthenes' reasoning. Point C is the center of the circle. If the angle α, at point C, and the length of the arc AS are known, the circumference of the circle can be calculated, using equation (1-1).

the center of the circle, which is also the center of the Earth. Eratosthenes reasoned that the fraction of the circle's circumference that lies on the arc AS is equal to the fraction of the angular measurement of the circle ($360°$ in modern notation) contained in the angle α between lines CA and CS. Translated back into the original problem,

$$\frac{\alpha}{360°} = \frac{arc(AS)}{Cr.}$$

$$Cr = arc(AS) \bullet \frac{360°}{\alpha}$$

(1-1)

where *Cr* stands for circumference.

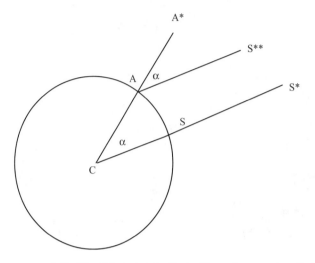

FIGURE 1-3. The third step in Eratosthenes' reasoning. Let lines AS** and SS* be parallel lines (rays of sunlight) and let A and S be two points on a circle with center C. Line SC is an extension of line SS* because the Sun is directly overhead at point S, and so the Sun's rays point directly down toward the center of the Earth. If A* is any point on a line perpendicular to the Earth's surface at point A, then line A*A can also be continued by line AC, which terminates at the center of the Earth. However, line A*A is not parallel to S*A because the Sun is not directly overhead at point A. Therefore, by Euclid's theorem for alternate angles, angle A*AS** = angle ACS = α. Angle A*AS** is on the Earth's surface, and so it can be measured.

Eratosthenes reasoned that if he could find appropriate points A and S on the same line of longitude, and measure angle α, then the length of the Earth's equator could be found. Unfortunately, angle α is at the center of the Earth, ruling out direct measurement. This brings us to the third step in Eratosthenes' reasoning.

The argument is shown in Figure 1-3, which should be examined carefully. Eratosthenes assumed that the Sun's rays are parallel to each other. (This is true if the Earth is much smaller than the Sun, as it is, or if the Sun is very far away, which it is.) Given this assumption, the angle between point A and S, measured at the center of the Earth, C, can be found if we can find two locations on the same longitude (i.e., one directly south of the other). If the Sun is directly overhead at one point, S, (at an angle of incidence of 0°) and the Sun strikes the other point, A, at an angle of incidence of α degrees at exactly the same moment, then the angle between the two, measured from the center of the Earth, is also α. The mathematical argument is shown in Figure 1-3. I urge the reader to examine it carefully.

At this point Eratosthenes had connected his model to reality by expressing it in measurements that could be taken. This can be contrasted with a measure that required, say, suspending an instrument in the sky at a known height, and then measuring the angle between locations using that instrument. We can do this today using satellites and radar-ranging techniques, but the technology was not available to Eratosthenes!

The problem now shifts from one of having a model identifying the measures that need to be made to actually making the measurements. Before Eratosthenes' solution is presented, let us take a look at another problem that he, and every mathematical modeler after him, had to deal with: measurement error.

In order to apply his model, Eratosthenes had to rely on measured values of α and arc(AS) rather than the actual values. Measurements inevitably contain a measurement error. Therefore, any application of equation 1-1 to measured values will be

$$\frac{\alpha + error(\alpha)}{360°} = \frac{arc(AS) + error(arc(AS))}{Cr} \qquad (1\text{-}2)$$

where *error(α)* and *error(arc(AS))* refer to errors in measuring the angle or the arc. The measurement errors have to be so small relative to their true values that equation (1-2) is close enough to equation (1-1) so that the discrepancy can be disregarded.

There is a general principle here. Application of a model is always limited by our ability to measure the relevant variables! We will meet this idea again, for it certainly is not unique to Eratosthenes' model. The instruments that he had to work with, in the way of measurements of angles and distances, were primitive compared to what we have today. Nevertheless, as will now be shown, he did pretty well considering that neither lasers and radar nor statistics had been invented.

Thought question. Why did I include statistics in that list?

There is another measurement problem, timing. In order for the model to work, the Sun has to be directly overhead at S; that is, the line CS must be a continuation of line SS*. This happens only when the sun is directly overhead at noon. Also, because the Earth and Sun move relative to each other during the day, it is essential that measurements be taken at A, at exactly the time at which the Sun is overhead at S. Unfortunately, a good clock would not be invented until about 1,800 years later (and there wasn't any radio time signal, either), and so Eratosthenes faced another problem. He solved it.

Noon, local time, is the point at which the Sun reaches its maximum height in the sky, at that point. Therefore, if points A and S are on the same longitude, we can make a measure at point A, at local noon, and be sure that the Sun will be at its highest point at S at exactly that time.

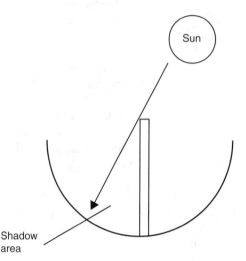

FIGURE 1-4. The straphe was a device used in the Hellenistic period to measure the angle of the Sun. The U-shaped base piece is marked in angular measures. The shaded area indicates how high the Sun is above the horizon. The point at which the Sun is at its height is always local noon. Whether or not the angle is zero, however, depends upon the day and the latitude. For all points on the tropic of Cancer, the Sun is immediately overhead at local noon on the summer solstice.

The device Eratosthenes used to measure angle α was called a *straphe*. It was basically a bowl with a needle sticking up from the middle. The bowl was planted in the ground, with the needle sticking straight up, so that it would be along line CA in Figure 1-3. When this was done, the shadow of the needle would measure angle α. This is shown in Figure 1-4.

Think about it. In Seattle, which is well north of the tropic of Cancer, at noon on the summer solstice (June 21–22) the Sun is always to the south. On the tropic of Cancer, however, the Sun is directly overhead at noon on the summer solstice. Today we know that this is due to the interaction of the Earth's path around the Sun, the angle of inclination of the Earth's axis of rotation to the Sun-Earth line, and the rotation of the Earth. Eratosthenes did not have to know this, although he may well have known of the heliocentric theory developed by Aristarchos of Samos (310–250 B.C.E.) a century earlier. All he needed to do was to know that there was a particular day that marked the solstice, and that this day was the same everywhere.

Eratosthenes next had to find two observation points for A and S. He learned that in the city of Syene (modern Aswan), on the Nile to the south of Alexandria, the Sun shone at the bottom of a vertical well at noon on the summer solstice. This implied that Syene was on the tropic of Cancer. Relying on dead-reckoning reports of travelers, Eratosthenes himself had previously constructed a map showing Syene directly south of Alexandria, and so he believed that the two were on the same longitude. (Precise determination of longitude was not possible until the mid–eighteenth century, 1,900 years later.) Eratosthenes concluded that Alexandria and Syene could serve as points A and S.

In modern terms, Eratosthenes was making assumptions about his *measurement model*, the way in which he was going to connect conceptual variables in his model of the Earth to physical measurements in the world. His assumptions about Syene and Alexandria were not too far off. Syene (Aswan) is on the tropic of Cancer, but it is about 3° east of Alexandria, which amounts to a constant error of 12 minutes of arc. This would not make any appreciable difference.

Eratosthenes measured angle α at Alexandria to be 1/50th of a full circle. Therefore, the Alexandria-Syene distance had to be 1/50th of the distance of a polar circumnavigation, and hence 1/50th of the length of the equator. How far was it from Alexandria to Syene?

Eratosthenes consulted travelers. They told him that it took 25 days by caravan, but that a fast camel could do the trip in 20 days. On the basis of this estimate, and some knowledge about how fast camels move, Eratosthenes decided that the distance between Alexandria and Syene was 5,000 stadia, where the *stadion* was the unit of distance used in Hellenic times.

Eratosthenes concluded that the distance around the Earth at both the equator and along a line of longitude was $50 \times 5,000 = 250,000$ stadia.

He then did something that we, today, regard as unacceptable, although it is not unknown! The figure 250,000 stadia was politically incorrect. Why? Because 250,000 is not evenly divisible by 60, and 60 was regarded as a magical number in ancient times, and even late as the Renaissance. In order to provide an estimate that was acceptable to the powers that be, Eratosthenes added 2,000 stadia, producing an estimate of 252,000 stadia. This can be divided by 60, and so it was acceptable. Or at least, to politicians. In Eratosthenes' own time he was criticized by other mathematicians.

Would we do this sort of thing today? I advise you to look at the political response to the results of using mathematical models to estimate the human role in global warming. But I digress.

How close did Eratosthenes get to the truth? In order to answer this question directly, we have to know how long a stadion is in modern units. The historical record is ambiguous. What we can do is to repeat his calculations, but this time using a modern, presumably more accurate, measure of the distance between Alexandria and Syene. The distance is 800 km. If we assume that Eratosthenes' estimate of the distance was correct, in stadia, we can convert to modern estimates using the equality

5,000 stadia = 800 km. Therefore, Eratosthenes' uncorrected estimate of the length of the equator was 40,000 km. His politically correct estimate, which he may have believed in himself, was 41,600 km.

The modern estimate is 40,076 km. Using primitive instruments, but far from primitive reasoning, Eratosthenes estimated the length of the equator with an error of measurement less than 1%.

1.5. A CRITIQUE OF ERATOSTHENES

It has been argued that Eratosthenes was just plain lucky. His model was based on an erroneous assumption. What Eratosthenes measured was the length of a polar circumnavigation, not the length of the equator. This, would make no difference if the Earth were a perfect sphere, but it is not. It is an oblate spheroid, which means that the poles are slightly squashed toward the equator. Therefore, the distance of a circumnavigation along a line of longitude is not exactly equal to a circumnavigation along the equator.

As we have noted, Syene was not exactly south of Alexandria, but this does not matter very much.

Eratosthenes' own contemporaries quarreled with his estimate of the distance between Alexandria and Syene. They claimed that the distance from Alexandria to Syrene was about 4,300 stadia. If you accept this measure, rather than 5,000, Eratosthenes' estimate is under by about 14%, providing you assume that he and his critics were talking about the same stadion. There was no Bureau of Standards in Hellenic times, and the discrepancy may have been because different authors used different lengths for the stadion. We have no way of knowing.

Frankly, none of these objections bother me. I am impressed that anyone could get as close to the modern estimate as Eratosthenes did, given the technology available to him. Mathematical reasoning stretched his technology almost beyond imagination.

Although Eratosthenes lived a long time ago and worked in the physical sciences, his story illustrates principles that are directly applicable to modern scientific reasoning, regardless of the field of application. They are as follows:

1. A mathematical model is a precise simplification of the pheno-
    menon being described. Eratosthenes' model was exactly correct
    for a sphere, which is a simplification of the actual shape of the
    Earth. When you apply a model, you hope that the simplification is
    close enough to the truth so that results in the model will be close
    approximations of results in the world itself. For instance, later on
    we will encounter models of the behavior of a perfectly rational
    decision maker. No such human being exists, but we try.

2. In order to make contact between the model and the world, you have to make a coordinating statement indicating that certain properties of objects or relations between objects in the model match other relationships and properties in the world. The statements "Syene is exactly south of Alexandria" and "Syene has the property of being on the tropic of Cancer" are examples. So is a statement in an economic model saying "We will represent executive compensation by salary and the value of exercised stock options." The geographic statements about Syene were not exactly correct. The economic statement ignores perks, such as a reserved parking slot and use of the executive bathroom.

    My economic example is glib, but other examples can be given that are more serious. Thousands of articles in psychology journals contain a paraphrase of the following remark: Intelligence will be represented by a person's score on the Wechsler Adult Intelligence Scale (WAIS). In fact, *intelligence* is an abstract concept and the WAIS is only one possible measure of it.

    The moral? Keep in mind the difference between the variables in a conceptual model and the variables in the measurement model that is used to apply the conceptual model. Many arguments about the use of scientific results become confused because the discussants do not make a clear distinction between the conceptual model and the measurement model. Both have to be justified.

3. Any measurement always contains an error! As a result, we do not expect the measurements that we take in an experiment to agree exactly with the values that are predicted by a model, even if a model is true. Therefore, instead of asking "Do the observed values agree with the predicted values?" we ask "Is the discrepancy between the observed and expected values greater than the discrepancy that would be expected given the reliability of our measurements?"

    To illustrate, suppose an intrepid contemporary of Eratosthenes had tried to test his model by actually traveling around the Earth. No one would have expected the traveler to report (honestly) that the voyage was exactly 252,000 stadia long, because the traveler would not have been able to keep track of his mileage that accurately.

    Some centuries after Eratosthenes, exactly this error occurred. The Venetian traveler Marco Polo wildly overestimated the distance between Europe and Cathay (China). This led Columbus to underestimate the distance that he would have to sail to the west to reach China from Spain. If the Americas hadn't been in the way, Columbus's voyagers would have had to turn back or would have perished from lack of fresh water.

    The measurement error problem puts every scientist, and most especially every social scientist, on the horns of a dilemma. Models are approximations of the truth, in exactly the same sense that a sphere is an approximation of the shape of the Earth. Understandably, scientists like to have their models accepted. But the more accurately a scientist measures a phenomenon, the more likely that scientist is to find a discrepancy between model and observation that cannot be accounted for by measurement error. Accordingly, the more sophisticated of modern scientists do not try to "accept" or "disprove" a model; they try to develop models whose predictions are very close approximations to the truth. Science does *not* advance by proving theories correct; it advances by developing models that are progressively more and more accurate.

Given the prominence of science in our society, it is surprising how many people do not seem to understand this very important point about scientific reasoning.

1.6. APPLICATIONS OF MATHEMATICS TO SOCIAL AND BEHAVIORAL ISSUES

Eratosthenes attacked a problem in geography by applying a particular type of mathematical argument, Euclidean geometry. This sort of pairing is the basis of mathematical modeling; the problem to be solved is combined with the type of mathematics used. I will now list briefly, and certainly not exhaustively, some combinations of problem and mathematical field that have been used in the social and behavioral sciences.

Psychophysics. Psychophysics refers to the relation between the physical stimulus imposing on an observer's sensors and the observer's perception of that stimulus. One of the simplest illustrations is the distinction between weight and heaviness. Does a 3-kilo weight feel exactly three times as heavy as a 1-kilo weight? (It does not.) The *psychophysical function* is the function that maps from physically defined stimuli to psychologically reported sensations. What is the mathematical form of this function?

Modern experimental psychology began when nineteenth-century German psychophysicists, notably Wilhelm Wundt, began to explore this issue mathematically. It is an active area of research today. The questions psychophysicists ask have to be answered if we are to know how we detect the world in which we live.

Psychometrics. Psychometrics attempts to determine the underlying dimensions of variations in human behavior. Suppose we confront a hundred people with a hundred different problems, including problems in mathematics, understanding political arguments, writing poems, and finding their way through a complicated building. Similarly, if we place people in social settings, we find that they choose to react in different ways. Some like to spend their weekends gardening; others play tennis or collect stamps. At professional conferences, some people will seek out large groups to go out to dinner; others prefer to have only one or two companions or even to dine alone. Can the huge variation in human behavior be explained by assuming that there are underlying dimensions of intelligence and personality, and if so, what are these dimensions?

Psychometricians have developed ways of answering this question, based on linear algebra. Psychometric investigation started in the mid–nineteenth century, but the really big breakthroughs came first in the 1930–50 period, when psychologists with mathematical training began to apply linear algebra to the analysis of data from intelligence and personality tests. Although the resulting models were clear conceptually, testing them required computations that were not remotely feasible prior to 1960. Because of advances in electronic computing, today we routinely evaluate models that simply could not be explored 50 years ago.

The Development of Interacting Systems over Time. Many problems in the behavioral and social sciences involve systems that develop over time. The systems involved vary greatly in scale, but the mathematical technique, linear systems analysis, remains the same. Applications include studying the relationship between predator and prey populations, the spread of knowledge (or rumors) through societies, and the exchange of positive and negative communications between individuals or nations.

Over the last 10 years, there has been increasing interest in the study of non-linear systems that evolve over time. These are systems that seem to be moving smoothly and then suddenly "explode" in some unexpected way. Because predicting the behavior of these systems sometimes seems impossible, names like "chaos theory" and "catastrophe theory" have caught the attention of the popular press. In fact, both chaos theory and catastrophe theory are quite understandable branches of mathematics. We shall take a look at these developments, paying particular attention to chaos theory.

How to Make Decisions. Mathematical models of decision making date back at least to the eighteenth century, when Daniel Bernoulli used a mathematical argument, plus a thought experiment, to demonstrate that the psychological value of wealth cannot be a linear function of money. In the 1940s, the study of decision making received a huge boost when John von Neumann and Oskar Morgenstern published *The Theory of Games.* Their work was firmly based on two mathematical approaches, axiomatic reasoning (just like Euclid!) and the probability calculus.

Von Neumann and Morgenstern's work both guided economic theory and inspired psychologists to study discrepancies between economic models of how decisions should be made and psychological models of how they are actually made. Daniel Kahneman, a professor at Princeton University, received the Nobel Prize in 2002 for his research in this area.

The Relation Between Models of the Brain and Models of Behavior. Clearly, the mind is the product of the brain. How does the brain do it? At one level, neurons are fantastically complicated machines. At another level, they are computationally rather simple. How might a collection of simple, abstract neurons produce the pattern recognition, classification, and reasoning behavior that we observe in human behavior? This topic is studied under the name *connectionism*, where linear algebra and computing power are used to produce some surprisingly flexible models of thought.

Learning and Memory. While all animals learn, humans are unusually flexible learners. Mathematical models of learning have been used to reveal surprising regularities underneath the learning process. Many of these models deal with probabilistic learning, and hence are based on the calculus of probabilities. Others are based on a branch of mathematics known as Markov chains. Learning and memory models are also closely related to connectionist models of pattern recognition and decision making.

And many more. The examples listed are certainly not exhaustive. In fact, we will go beyond this list in subsequent chapters. But first I want to make a brief comment about statistics.

1.7. STATISTICS

The social and behavioral sciences use statistics all the time. We are told about the average number of children born to families in Italy, the median income in the United States, and the distribution of Scholastic Assessment Test (SAT) scores for scholarship athletes, compared to the distribution of scores for the entering university students who do not have athletic scholarships. All such applications are important. Nevertheless, statistics will play only a small part in this book. Why?

There are two different ways to use statistics. *Descriptive statistics* summarize different aspects of large bodies of data. These summaries may be presented as single numbers, in tables, or in charts and graphs. Descriptive statistics will be used throughout the book as a way of demonstrating the phenomenon to be studied. From time to time, I may discuss how different pictures can be obtained when different statistics are used. However, I will spend almost no time discussing the merits of one or another summarizing measure, for its own sake. Such discussions are very interesting, but that's another topic.

Inferential statistics, all clustering around the famous *p value* featured in textbooks on statistics for the social sciences, are used to decide whether an observed phenomenon is "close enough" or "far enough" from those predicted by some model. If the statistics tell us the data are close enough, then we say that the data support the model. If the statistics tell us the data are too far from the model's expectations, then the model is rejected. By far, the commonest example of this sort of reasoning in the social sciences is use of statistics to reject the "null hypothesis," that the data arose "by chance." More sophisticated uses involve comparisons between different non-chance models. Very elaborate statistical procedures have been developed to answer these sorts of questions. We are not going to discuss them, except when they are relevant to evaluating a particular model. These are certainly interesting issues, but they are not the topic under discussion.

With all this said and done, we turn, in the next chapter, to our first substantive topic; the use of probability theory to understand behavior.

2

Applying Probability Theory to Problems in Sociology and Psychology

2.1. INTRODUCTION

Eratosthenes used geometry to solve a physical problem, measuring the circumference of the Earth. This chapter will deal with a different branch of mathematics, *probability theory*, and some very different problems, measuring the extent to which a social network is connected and measuring properties of conscious and unconscious memory. These two problems are different from each other, and very different from the geographic problem that Eratosthenes tackled. All three problems apply mathematics in the same way.

Probability theory deals with the likelihood that an event might happen. The notion of a probabilistic event is familiar to all of us, though perhaps not in those terms. For example, each autumn the Centers for Disease Control (CDC) urges Americans to receive an influenza vaccination. There is no claim that the vaccine will prevent you from getting the flu, nor is there any claim that you will, for sure, get the flu if you don't get the shot. The argument is that the probability that you will get influenza will be reduced if you receive the vaccine, compared to what it would be if you don't become vaccinated.

Examples like this are so familiar that they seem trite. Indeed, probabilistic reasoning is so common in our world that elementary courses in probability are part of the middle school mathematics curriculum. The first part of almost every introductory course in statistics contains a brief discussion of probability. These discussions often gloss over some important philosophical and practical issues in the application of the theory. Consider the following examples, all of which involve probabilistic reasoning:

Gambling with Dice. During the Renaissance and the Reformation periods, certain aristocrats asked court mathematicians to tell them what the best strategy was in order to win various games. Some of the greatest mathematicians of all time, including Pascal, Fermat, Huygens, and Jacob

Bernoulli, were among those who responded to the gamblers' challenges. In doing so they laid the foundations for the modern theory of probability Let us look at one of the simplest questions a gambler might ask.

Modern dice (singular, die) are cubes. Each of the six faces of a die is numbered, from 1 to 6. A *fair die* is a die that is constructed so that on a given throw no face is more likely to come up than any other one. In the typical game, two fair dice are thrown, and the score of the throw is determined by summing the numbers on the upper faces of the dice. Payoffs are determined by complicated formulae, which vary with the game being played. In all cases, though, the probability of a particular outcome is determined ultimately by the probabilities associated with different scores.

That describes honest gambling. The same mathematical rules apply to dishonest gambling. A die is *loaded* if one side has been weighted, so that the die is most likely to land with the weighted face down, and hence the opposite face up. A game is crooked if some of the players think the dice are fair when, in fact, they are loaded and the manner of loading is known to at least one other player. The knowledgeable player has an unfair advantage over other players because he/she has a better idea of the probabilities of different scores than do the other players.

Surveys. Bookstore owners have found that the way books are placed on tables influences which books are bought. Patrons are most likely to purchase a book that is on a table immediately in front of the door. A bookstore may wish to know the probabilities of purchase associated with each of the tables in the store, based upon a survey of customers' purchases.

This is typical of many other survey situations. For example, the CDC uses surveys to determine the probability that a person with/without a vaccination will catch influenza.

Probability of Future Unique Events. What is the probability that the next president of the United States will be a woman? Is it higher or lower than the probability that the next vice president will be a woman? These questions strike me, at least, as being reasonable ones.

The language of probability can be (and is) used in all these situations. But the language means something slightly different in each case. To understand the difference, we have to think more deeply about just what "probability" means.

2.2. DEFINING PROBABILITY AND PROBABILITY MEASURES

Some school systems introduce probability as early as middle school. On the other hand, if you really, really what to know about probability, you can take advanced courses in graduate school. The discussion here falls in between. It certainly is not the beginning of a graduate course on probability, but it does raise some issues that are always swept under the rug in middle school, and often not raised in courses on applied statistics.

The central concept of probability theory is the idea of a *random event*. A random event is one whose occurrence can be predicted only up to a degree of probability. Let *e* be an event, for example, that you roll a seven while playing dice or that the United States will elect a woman president in the year 2072. Just what do we mean when we say that these events have a probability associated with them?

The *classic* definition of probability appeals to the concept of equally likely events. Suppose that *n* possible events could occur, that each of them is equally likely to occur, and that *m* of them are designated as "favorable." The probability of a favorable event is

$$P(\textit{favorable}) = \frac{m}{n}. \tag{2-1}$$

This definition is suitable for events analogous to rolling fair dice. When a pair of fair dice are rolled, the set of possible outcomes is the set of sums of all possible combinations of the numbers 1–6 for the first die and 1–6 for the second. Therefore, any roll of the dice must produce one of the following sets:

$$E = \{(1, 1), (1, 2) \dots (1, 6), (2, 1), (2, 2) \dots \dots (6, 5), (6, 6)\}.$$

Let a favorable event be the event "The player rolls a 7," denoted E_7. This refers to the set of possible rolls

$$E_7 = \{(1, 6), (2, 5), (3, 4), (4, 3), (5, 2), (6, 1)\}$$

since there are six members of E_7 $P(E_7) = 6/36 = 1/6$, by the classic definition.

Two special cases are of interest. An event is *impossible* if there is no outcome that satisfies its definition. In a game of dice, there is no way that a player can roll a 13. Because E_{13} is the null set, $P(E_{13}) = 0/36 = 0$. The principle generalizes; any impossible event has a probability of zero.

An event is *certain* if the set of outcomes that satisfy its definition is equivalent to the set of all possible outcomes. What is the probability of a roll of the dice that has a value between 2 and 12, inclusive? In this case, $E_{2-12} = E$, so $P(E_{2-12}) = 36/36 = 1$. Any certain event has probability 1.

The classic definition is sensible for a game with fair dice, and for any situation that is analogous to such a game. But few situations are. This certainly is not the case for a game with loaded dice, or for the survey situation. Consideration of situations such as this has led to the *frequentist* definition of probability.

To understand the frequentist definition, we need to introduce the concept of a *trial* (equivalently, an observation or experiment). Each trial has an outcome that either does or does not satisfy some definition. For example, in rolling dice each roll is a trial, and the outcome may or may not be a seven, regardless of whether or not the dice are fair. In the book survey example, each person entering the store is a trial, and the outcome is defined by the table(s) from which books were selected, including the case where no book was selected.

Let E_* be the set of outcomes of interest, rolling a seven or buying from the table in front of the door. Assume that there are n trials, each conducted under exactly the same conditions, and let $N(E_*, n)$ be the number of times that a member of E_* was observed on these trials. The frequentist definition of probability is

$$P(E_*) = \frac{Lim}{n \to \infty} \frac{N(E_*, n)}{n}. \tag{2-2}$$

If the situation is one covered by the classical definition the frequentist definition will work as well. Impossible events have a probability of zero and certain events a probability of one under either definition.

This is as far as many textbooks go. The frequentist definition works well for many problems in the social sciences, including the ones considered in this chapter. It does fall down badly, though, when we want to reason about a unique event. This was illustrated by the third example, the probability that the next (or any specified future) president of the United States will be a woman.

The event "X is elected president of the United States in the next election" will be a unique event. My intuitions, at least, are that this event cannot be regarded as a selection from a set of other equally likely events, nor is it reasonable to think of the U.S. president as being drawn from a set of possible presidents, defined over an infinite set of parallel universes as they will exist at the time of the election. Neither the classic nor the frequentist definition of probability works. Looking at the relative frequency of elections of women as president in past elections is not appropriate. The frequentist definition requires that trials be conducted under exactly the same conditions. Each election takes place in the context of its own time. There may be occasions on which one election is a useful analog for another, but they are never randomly determined repetitions of equivalent trials.

Nevertheless, it does make sense to talk about the probability that a woman will be elected president. The problem is how to formalize this reasoning.

In the 1930s a Russian mathematician, A. N. Kolmogorov, offered a way to talk about probability without basing the argument on either the classic or the frequentist interpretations. Going into Kolmogorov's reasoning would involve an excessive detour, and so his results will be presented directly. (The detour is presented in Appendix 2A for those interested.)

Let $\mathbf{E} = \{e_1 \ldots \ldots e_n\}$ be the set of possible events that can happen in a trial, as in the frequentist definition. An event is a description of a concrete outcome, rather than the outcome itself, because the description specifies a set of outcomes. Events referring to the union, intersection, or complement of the sets defined by other events are also events. In the political example, the set of outcomes described by "the president is a woman" would be an event. So would the set of outcomes described by "the president is a woman or the president is a Republican."

A measure, $P(e)$, called the probability of e, is assigned to every event in E. The measure must satisfy the following restrictions:

All events have non-negative probabilities $P(e) \geq 0$.   (2-3a)

If an event S is certain (i.e., its description fits all possible
outcomes of a trial) $P(S) = 1$.   (2-3b)

If events $e_1, e_2, \ldots e_k$ are mutually exclusive in pairs (so that
if description e_i applies to an outcome description e_j does not,

for all i and j), then $P(e_1 \cup e_2 \cup \ldots \cup e_k) = \displaystyle\sum_{i=1}^{k} P(e_i).$ (2-3c)

The following *extended addition* axiom covers a situation in which exactly one of many events may occur.

If the occurrence of an event E is equivalent to the occurrence
of an arbitrary one of events $E_1 \ldots E_N$, and these events
are mutually exclusive in pairs, then $P(E) = \displaystyle\sum_{i=1}^{N} P(E_i).$ (2-3d)

Kolmogorov argued that we can assign *subjective* probabilities to a set of events of interest, and reason about them using the laws of probability, providing that the way the probabilities are assigned obeys the relations expressed by equations (2-3), and all inferences that can be drawn from them. We can reasonably say that "the probability that the next president is a woman is x," where x is some number between zero and one, inclusive, providing that we would also say "the probability that the next president is a man is $1 - x$."

This argument leads to a particular way of looking at scientific experimentation. We can regard a model as generating theoretical (*subjective*) probabilities for the outcomes of an experiment. We then conduct an experiment, to whose outcomes the frequentist definition of probability applies. Because the number of trials, n, must be finite, our observed frequencies of outcomes will be estimates of the actual (frequentist) probabilities. We then compare the subjective probabilities, from the model, to the frequentist estimates, from the experiment. If the estimates are too far from the values predicted by the model, the model is rejected. Otherwise the model is still worth considering. Deciding what "too far" means is the business of statistics.

Kolmogorov's axioms are the basis for the modern theory of probability. The major results are presented in the introduction to most statistics texts. As many of my readers will have had a statistics course, I will not present these results here. However, a brief summary of the concepts involved is included as appendix 2B.

Now let us look at the two examples of probabilistic modeling.

2.3. HOW CLOSELY CONNECTED ARE WE?

For about 95% of the time humans have lived on Earth, we lived in small hunting bands or agricultural and fishing villages. Everyone in the band knew everyone else. Today all the people in New York, or London, or even a relatively small city like Seattle, most emphatically do not know each other. But we have friends, and friends of friends. How closely connected is the world today? If you were to meet someone from the other side of the globe, how many links would you have to go through before you found that you had a mutual friend of a friend?

In the 1960s Stanley Milgram, a professor at Harvard University, proposed an experiment to answer this question.[1] Choose two people at random, a *sender* and a *target*. The sender's goal is to send a message to the target. Communication by mail or telephone is not permitted. The sender has to pass the message to a new sender, whom the first sender already knows, and who might either know the target or know someone else (whom the first sender may not know) who might know the target. This procedure is repeated, sender by sender, until the target is reached. How many links would there be in the chain of messages?

Jeffrey Travers and Milgram actually did this experiment.[2] They concluded that the average number of links between people is between five and six. The idea that we are so closely linked caught the public fancy. In 1993 it was the theme of an award-winning Broadway comedy, *Six Degrees of Separation* by John Guare.

Travers and Milgram's study was actually so restricted that it hardly represents a random sampling of the connections between humankind.

[1] Milgram (1967). [2] Travers and Milgram (1969).

There were just under 300 initial senders, all drawn either from Nebraska or Boston. All the targets lived in Massachusetts. Not surprisingly, senders from Boston were more successful in delivering a message to targets in Massachusetts than were senders from Nebraska. Only 18 of the successful deliveries were from outside the target's home city. Nevertheless, the idea caught on.

Thirty-some years after Travers and Milgram did their experiment, three Columbia University researchers, Peter Dodds, Roby Muhamed, and Duncan Watts, repeated it, but with a much larger sample of participants, recruited worldwide.[3] Dodds et al. placed an advertisement on the World Wide Web, asking people to volunteer for a search task similar to Milgram's, using electronic mail. Initial senders totaled 24,163, and more than 60 thousand people participated in the experiment. Eighteen targets were selected, including a professor at a prominent U.S. university, a policeman in Australia, a technology consultant in India, and a veterinarian in the Norwegian army. The rules were that a sender could only send a message to someone he or she already knew, and that senders had to let the researchers know (by copy of e-mail) when a message had been sent.

Of the 24,163 chains of messages that were started, only 384 reached their intended target. Nevertheless, Dodds et al. were able to estimate chain links for everyone on the basis of this data. How? Through mathematical modeling.

Dodds et al. assumed that there are no isolates in the e-mail system; any person can reach any other person if he or she tries hard enough. Chains terminate because people lose interest, not because people cannot think of anyone to send a message to. To check this assumption, the researchers sent follow-up e-mail to senders who had failed to pass the message along. Less than 1% of the people contacted said that they could not think of someone to send a message to. Apparently they just lost interest.

This is the point at which Dodds, Muhamed, and Watts applied their mathematical model. I will simplify it slightly and start my explanation by applying it to an overly simple network.

Figure 2-1 shows a network consisting of seven senders and a single target. Let individuals 1, 2, 3 in this network be initial senders. Inspection of the network shows that 1 can reach the target in two steps, while individual 2 has to use a four-step chain of messages, and individual 3 has a three-step chain. Therefore, the average link of the chain between the initial senders and the target is 3.

Assume that there is some probability, r, that a sender will decide not to forward a message. This will be called the *attrition rate*. The probability

---

[3] Dodds, Muhamed, and Watts (2003).

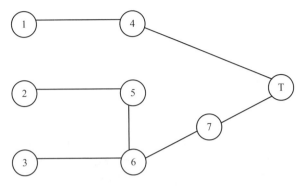

FIGURE 2-1. A hypothetical network consisting of seven senders (nodes 1–7) and a target (node T). Senders 1, 2, and 3 are chosen to initiate a message to be passed to T.

of completing the chain from 1 to 4 to T is the joint probability that sender 1 and sender 4 both transmit the message. This is $(1 - r) \cdot (1 - r) = (1 - r)^2$. In the general case, if we let $P(k)$ be the probability of completing a chain consisting of k links,

$$P(k|r) = (1 - r)^k. \tag{2-4}$$

To make the mathematics easy, let $r = .5$, so that a sender is as likely to forward a message as not. Then we have $P(2|r = .5) = .25$, $P(3|r = .5) = .125$, $P(4|r = .5) = .0625$.

We are now ready to estimate the lengths of the chains. To do this, imagine an experiment in which one hundred different, independent messages were started from each of the three initial senders, nodes 1, 2, and 3 in the diagram. Applying equation 2-4, we would expect, on the average, to have the following number of completed chains (rounding to the nearest integer):

25 chains of length 2
12 of length 3
6 of length 4.

The expected length of completed chains is just over 2.5. However, we know that the mean chain length is 3. What has gone wrong?

The problem is that the longer chains are underrepresented among completed chains because they are unlikely to be completed. However, the number of chains of any length can be calculated, providing that two parameters are known, the number of completed chains of length k and the value of r. To see this, let $N(k)$ be the number of chains of length k that exist, and let $O(k)$ be the number of chains that were observed. The two are related by

$$O(k) = N(k) \bullet P(k)$$

$$N(k) = \frac{O(k)}{(1-r)^k},$$
(2-5)

where the second line has been derived from the first by algebraic rearrangement, and then substituting (2-4) for $P(k)$. Doing this in our simple example produces an estimate of mean chain length of 2.99. The difference from the correct figure, 3, is due solely to rounding errors.

The Dodds, Muhamed, and Watts experiment was conceptually similar to the simple example, but much larger. Instead of passing many messages through each initial sender, they treated their initial senders as randomly chosen Internet users, and initiated one message from each of them. They then introduced two important technical considerations. First, they considered the possibility that the probability of dropping out of the chain (the r parameter) might vary with the number of links in the chain. By examining the attrition rates in their data, they calculated r_i, the probability that the ith sender in a chain would drop out. This changes Equation 2-4 to

$$P(k) = r_i \bullet r_2.. \bullet r_i.. \bullet r_k$$

$$P(k) = \prod_{i=1}^{k} r_i,$$
(2-6)

which was used to calculate $N(k)$. This makes a substantial difference, for the r_i values varied from an initial value of around .75 at the start of a chain to close to .5 later in the chain.

Dodds et al. point out that the accuracy depends crucially upon the accuracy of the estimates of attrition rate; small decreases in attrition rate could lead to very large increases in completion rate, especially for longer chains. Because relatively few long chains were observed, the estimates of attrition rate for i more than six were unstable. To compensate for this, Dodds et al. decided to report the median chain length rather than the mean. The median was 5 if the chain started in the same country as the target, and 7 if the chain had to cross countries. Six degrees of separation was not far off the mark, after all.

There are striking similarities between the approach that Dodds, Muhamed, and Watts took to the problem of estimating a property of social networks and the approach that Eratosthenes took to measure the length of the equator. In both cases, it was patently impossible to measure the desired quantity directly. Dodds et al. could no more calculate the actual number of links between everyone on the Internet than Eratosthenes could measure the length of the equator.

In both cases, the problem was attacked by constructing an abstract mathematical model to represent the actual situation: a network for Dodds et al. and a perfect sphere for Eratosthenes. In each case, the model was not exactly correct. The Earth is not the perfect sphere that Eratosthenes thought it was. In the sociological case, the problem is a bit more subtle.

The conclusions of Dodds et al. about connections on the Internet would be justified if the initial senders and the targets had been chosen randomly from the set of all Internet users. This would be impractical. What they actually analyzed were the 18 networks, each containing a single target and the initial senders assigned to send a message to that target. Furthermore, the senders were all self-nominated volunteers, and thus perhaps not representative of Internet users as a whole. This introduced an unknown amount of error.

The substance of the problems was different. Twenty-three hundred years separated Eratosthenes and Dodds, Muhamed, and Watts. The principles and problems of mathematical modeling were the same.

2.4. CONSCIOUS AND UNCONSCIOUS MEMORIES

We now turn to an elegant use of probability theory to measure the influence of "unconscious" memory upon behavior. First, though, a brief description of what we mean by conscious and unconscious memories is in order.

A conscious, or *explicit*, memory is a memory for an experience that a person is aware of. To illustrate, I have no trouble remembering that I had eggs for breakfast this morning; I explicitly recall fixing them. By contrast, an unconscious, *implicit* memory is a memory that I must have because it can be shown that it is influencing my behavior, but that I am not aware of. I would offer an example from my own life, but by definition, if I could, the memory would not be unconscious!

Historically, the idea of unconscious memory has played a prominent role in psychology. Sigmund Freud made implicit memories a major part of psychoanalysis. He believed that memories of traumatic or shameful experiences were often repressed. This included shameful thoughts, such as sexual attraction to a parent, sibling, or child. He further believed that the act of repression could lead to unhealthy and sometimes bizarre behavior, such as a fanatical desire for cleanliness.

Freud's ideas have been incorporated into many literary essays and appear to be widely accepted by the lay public. For instance, in the United States, several state legislatures have altered statute of limitation laws, which require that the prosecution of a crime must take place within a certain time period after the crime has occurred, to make special provision for situations in which memory of the crime (e.g., child molestation) may have been repressed.

Modern psychologists are split on this issue. Some clinical psychologists still hold to something very like the Freudian view of repressed memories. Most cognitive psychologists, who study memory scientifically, believe that Freud overstated the case. Cognitive psychologists believe that unconscious memories exist, but they do not believe that the unconscious is capable of the sort of complicated metaphorical reasoning that Freud ascribed to it. Instead, they think that the unconscious is limited to biasing people to interpret ambiguous stimuli in ways consistent with past experience, and to respond on the basis of responses made in the past. These biases can be overridden by conscious thought, although they often are not.[4]

The model that we will examine is in the tradition of scientific rather than clinical psychology. It was developed by a Canadian psychologist, Larry Jacoby, both to demonstrate that implicit memories exist in healthy young adults (college students) and to show that the way one attends to a situation will have major effect upon explicit recall of that situation, but have almost no affect on the implicit memory system.[5]

Jacoby and his colleagues showed college students a list of words. An abbreviated example might be

MOTEL
SCALP
SPOOF.

The actual lists were 72 words long, so that almost no one could recall the list completely after hearing it only once. The students were then asked to complete three-letter word stems, for example,

MOT__
SCA__
SPO__.

The word stems were chosen so that they could be completed either with a word that was on the original list (MOT__ – MOTEL) or with a common word not on the list (MOT__ – MOTOR). The word stems were printed in green or red. If the word was printed in green, the students were to complete it with a word from the list (MOTEL in the example), if they could remember one, or otherwise to complete it with "whatever popped into their head." This was called the *Inclusion* condition. The words printed in red were to be completed with words that were not on the original list. This was called the *Exclusion* condition.

---

[4] Greenwald (1992); Hunt (2002).   [5] Jacoby, Toth, and Yonelinas (1993).

These two conditions offer contrasting roles for explicit memory. If a person in the Inclusion condition explicitly recalls, say, that MOTEL was on the list, then he/she should make the response MOT__ -> MOTEL. On the other hand, if a person in the Exclusion condition recalls MOTEL, he/she should complete the word stem MOT__ with a response, like MOTOR, that was not on the initial list.

The role for implicit memory is the same in each condition. According to cognitive psychologists' view of unconsciousness, the word stem (MOT—) should be more likely to trigger an implicit recall of MOTEL than any other appropriate word, because the person's memory for the word MOTEL was activated in the recent past, when the word list was shown. Now suppose that the word stem reminds the person of MOTEL, but the person does not explicitly recall having seen MOTEL on the word list. The response MOTEL should be given in both the Exclusion and Inclusion conditions.

In order to measure these effects, Jacoby and his colleagues developed their *process-dissociation model*. Let

I = Probability of responding with a word on the list in the Inclusion condition.
E = Probability of responding with a word on the list in the Exclusion condition.
R = Probability of explicit recall.
A = Probability of implicit (automatic) recall.

I and E are observables. They can be estimated by the frequency of recall of words from the list, in the Inclusion and Exclusion conditions respectively. The process-dissociation model makes the unobservable recall probabilities, R and A, a function of the observables. The model equations are

$$I = \text{probability of explicit recall} + (\text{probability of no explicit recall})$$
$$\times (\text{probability of implicit recall}) \qquad (2\text{-}7)$$
$$I = R + (1 - R) \bullet A.$$

$$E = (\text{probability of no explicit recall}) \times (\text{probability of implicit recall})$$
$$E = (1 - R) \bullet A. \qquad (2\text{-}8)$$

Subtracting (2-8) from (2-7), and rearranging (2-8) produces

$$R = I - E$$
$$A = \frac{E}{1 - R} \qquad (2\text{-}9)$$

Equation (2-9) expresses the unobservable variables in the model in terms of the observable variables of the experiment.

This reasoning masks two assumptions. One is that when a word from the list is recalled in the Exclusion condition, the reason it popped into the person's head was that there was an implicit memory for the words just presented. This is not necessarily the case. A person might complete MOT__ with MOTEL without ever having seen the first list. Accordingly, the experimenters included an additional condition in which students completed the word stems without seeing the original list. This provided a measure of the frequency with which a word would be used. Call this estimate B. Equation (2-9) was augmented by subtracting B,

$$A^* = A - B \tag{2-10}$$

and using the A^* value to estimate implicit recall.

The second assumption is more involved. The process-dissociation model assumes that the outputs of the conscious and unconscious memory systems are statistically independent. One could imagine alternative models, in which the probability of unconscious recall depended upon whether or not the conscious recall system succeeded or failed. Such models have been developed, but evidence that we will not deal with indicates that these models are no more accurate than Jacoby's model. One of the well-established principles of mathematical modeling is that less complicated models are to be preferred to more complicated ones.

Up to this point, Jacoby's reasoning paralleled Eratosthenes' reasoning. Both of them set up a model of the system they were interested in, the Earth as a perfect sphere or recall of a word as the result of two independent processes. They then used different, but appropriate, mathematics to express variables in the model as a function of observable values. What was missing was that neither of them offered any proof that their model was correct. Eratosthenes would have obtained an estimate of the length of the equator if the Earth were shaped like a football; the estimate just would have been wrong. Jacoby and his colleagues could always obtain an estimate of explicit and implicit memory functioning, even if all recall was from a single memory system. So they went beyond measurement.

Jacoby and his colleagues used their measurement model to show that different conditions of memorization had different influences on conscious and unconscious recall of information. Their argument, which was based on a good deal of prior research, was as follows:

1. Anything that causes people to pay attention to a piece of information increases the probability that it will be stored in the explicit memory system. Therefore, the probability of explicit recall

depends upon the extent to which a person attends to information at the time it is presented.

2. Whenever a piece of information impinges on the sensory system it is stored in the unconscious system. The amount of attention paid does not matter. Therefore, implicit recall should not be influenced by the amount of attention paid at the time that a memory is laid down.

It follows from these assumptions that the probability of explicit recall (R) should be reduced if people are distracted as they read a list of words, but that the probability of implicit recall (A) should remain constant.

Jacoby and his colleagues then conducted two experiments using the same paradigm. In one condition, the participants read a list of words aloud, one by one. At the same time, half the participants, in the *divided attention* condition, heard a sequence of digits presented as they were reading. They were told that they should press a key on a computer keyboard whenever they heard three odd digits in a row (e.g., 9, 7, 5). It was stressed that detecting a sequence of odd digits was more important than remembering the words, although they were still to read the words aloud. This ensured that the participants saw the words, even though they did not pay much attention to them. The other participants, in the *full attention* condition, simply read the words and tried to remember them.

After the lists had been read, participants completed word stems, under either Inclusion or Exclusion instructions. The process-dissociation model was used to estimate explicit and implicit recall. The resulting estimates are shown in Table 2-1. Dividing attention effectively

TABLE 2-1. *Estimates of Explicit and Implicit Recall When People Memorized a Word List under Full or Divided Attention Conditions*

Attention	Explicit Recall Estimate	Implicit Recall Estimate
	Experiment 1a	
Full attention	.20	.21
Divided attention	.00	.27
	Experiment 1b	
Full attention	.25	.47
Divided attention	.00	.46

Source: *Table 2 from Jacoby, L. L., Toth, J. P., and Yonelinas, A. P. (1993).* Separating conscious and unconscious influences on memory: Measuring recollections. *Journal of Experimental Psychology: General,* 122(2): 139–54. (© American Psychological Association. Reprinted with permission.)

eliminated explicit recall but had no influence on implicit recall. This provides striking evidence that there are two memory systems.

2.5. SOME FINAL COMMENTS

The studies by Dodds et al. and by Jacoby et al. provide simple, elegant illustrations of how probability theory can be used to study questions in sociology and psychology. There are many similar models, although the mathematical reasoning is often more complicated than in these examples.

The logic of the modern social science studies is surprisingly close to Eratosthenes' reasoning about geography 2,300 years ago. In each case, the investigators wanted to measure properties of a system that could not be observed directly. They then constructed a model of how they thought the system worked, in which unobservable parameters of the model could be expressed in terms of observable values. The observations were then used to estimate the unobservables.

Eratosthenes and Dodds and his colleagues stopped there. In these two cases, the model was of the structure of a system, how things were built rather than how things worked. Jacoby and his colleagues had to go a step further. They wanted to measure how things worked, the processes of memory storage and retrieval rather than the structure of information within memory. Therefore, they followed the strategy of manipulating external conditions that they thought would influence each process in a different way, and showing that the parameters of their model changed in the way that they had expected. This is a common experimental strategy.

The rest of this book will deal with different phenomena to be modeled, and generally with different mathematics. The strategies of measurement and experimentation presented here will remain the same throughout.

APPENDIX 2A. THE BASIS FOR KOLMOGOROV'S AXIOMS

Kolmogorov departed from the frequentist and classic definitions by defining probability as belonging to a set of events, rather than to a single event.

Let **S** be a set of elementary events. It helps to think of these as all possible readings of a measuring instrument. Thus, the 36 possible outcomes of a set of dice, all possible readings of a stop watch, or all possible responses to questions in an opinion survey would qualify as elementary events in appropriate studies.

The system B consists of the subsets of **S**. The elements of B are the random events to which a probability measure will be assigned. B is called a *Borel Field* if it satisfies these conditions:

1. **S** and its members are members of **B**.
2. If two sets, E_1 and E_2, are elements of **B** then their unions, intersections, and complements are also elements of **B**.
3. If sets E_1, E_2, ..., E_n are elements of **B**, then the union and intersection of sets E_1 ... E_n are also elements of **B**.

Because **S** contains all possible outcomes of a trial, every observation must result in some member of **S** being observed. Therefore, **S** is called the *certain event*. By requirement 2, the complement of **S**, the empty set **O**, must also be a member of **B**.

Kolmogorov's axioms are as follows:

1. For every event E in **B** there is a non-negative real number, $P(E)$, called the probability of E.
2. The probability of **S** is 1.
3. If the events E_1, E_2, ..., E_n are mutually exclusive in pairs, the probability of their union is equal to the sum of the probabilities of the individual events.

Kolmogorov's axioms and definitions apply to any imaginable set of events, without appeal to any physical setting that might justify the classic or frequentist interpretations. For example, Kolmogorov's axioms apply to throws of a die, for which a frequentist interpretation is appropriate. They also permit us to talk about probabilities of unique, non-random events like the event "A woman will be elected president of the United States in 2040." Why? In this case, the set of events in *S* is {Woman is elected president in 2040, Man is elected president in 2040, No one is elected president in 2040}. Kolmogorov's axioms make sense, even though the concept of randomness does not.

APPENDIX 2B. SOME IMPORTANT PROPERTIES OF PROBABILITY MEASURES

This section describes a few of the derivable properties of probability measures. The actual derivations will not be given, as this would be another detour. The concepts involved are used both in this chapter and in later ones. This appendix is certainly not intended to be a brief course in statistics, as many important topics in that field have not been addressed.

Joint, Conditional, and Complementary Probability

Suppose that we conduct two observations, one that could result in events drawn from $\mathbf{E} = \{e\}$ and another where observations are drawn from $\mathbf{F} = \{f\}$, with associated probability distributions. The *conditional probability of e, given f* is the probability that event *e* will be observed given that *f* has been observed. This is written $P(e|f)$.

Example. The 2004 U.S. presidential election was between the incumbent, George W. Bush, and Senator John Kerry. Bush won the election, capturing 51% of the vote to Kerry's 48%. The remaining votes were split over a variety of minor candidates, who will not be considered. Therefore, the probability that a voter, selected at random from the entire electorate, was a Bush voter would be .51. This satisfies both the classic and frequentist definitions of probability.[6]

Analyses of the election results showed that voting was heavily concentrated in certain blocs, such as labor union members or evangelical Christians, who either went heavily for Bush or for Kerry. According to the *New York Times*, 63% of voters with annual incomes in excess of $200,000[7] voted for Bush. Therefore, the conditional probability *P(Bush Voter|income over $200,000) = .63*.

The *joint probability* of observing *e* in one experiment and *f* in another is written $P(e \cap f)$. Joint probability is derived from probability and conditional probability by the relation

$$P(e \cap f) = P(e)P(f|e)$$
$$P(e \cap f) = P(f)P(e|f) \tag{2B-1}$$

Continuing with the election example, what is the probability that a randomly selected voter would both have an income over $200,000 and vote for Bush? According to the *New York Times*, 3% of the electorate had incomes over $200,000. Combining this estimate with the voting information:

Probability (income over $200,000 ∩ vote for Bush)
$$= (.03) \times (.63) = .0189.$$

Slightly less than 2% of the voters both were rich and voted for Bush.

This example can be extended to make a very important point. *Conditional probabilities are not inherently symmetrical*; that is, it is possible that $P(e|f) \neq P(f|e)$. This is easy to see, algebraically, by rearranging equation (2B-1) to produce

$$P(e|f) = \frac{P(e \cap f)}{P(f)}$$
$$P(f|e) = \frac{P(e \cap f)}{P(e)}. \tag{2B-2}$$

---

[6] The statistics used for the 2004 presidential election example were taken from polling results reported in the *New York Times* Week in Review section for Nov. 7, 2004, p. 4.
[7] In 2004 dollars.

In the election example, we have already seen that Probability (vote for Bush|income over 200,000) = .63, which could be used to justify the statement "Wealthy people voted for Bush." On the other hand, the statement "Bush voters were wealthy people" cannot be justified. This statement depends upon the conditional probability that a person who voted for Bush was a wealthy person. Apply 2B-2, and using our earlier values:

Probability (Income over 200,000|voted for Bush)
$$= .0189/.51 = .0371$$

Slightly less than 4% of the people who voted for Bush had incomes over $200,000. The principle is an important point to keep in mind, for there are many cases in which people erroneously assume that $P(e|f) = P(f|e)$.

Two events e and f are said to be *statistically independent* if the probability of observing e does not change depending upon whether f is observed or not. If two events are statistically independent,

$$P(e \cap f) = P(e)P(f). \tag{2B-3}$$

If two events are statistically independent, the conditional probability of observing f when e has been observed must be equal to the conditional probability of observing f when e has not been observed. Writing e for "e was not observed," (2B-3) implies that

$$P(f|e) = P(f|\neg e). \tag{2B-4}$$

A good deal of science is devoted to showing that in some case, equation (2B-4) is not true. For example, medical studies have shown that a diet including antioxidants (e.g., fruit, vitamin E) reduces the probability of occurrence of certain types of cancer. The evidence for this rests on studies that show, with rather more sophisticated statistics than this, that if we write "Cancer" for the phrase "person has cancer" and "Antioxidants" for "person takes some form of antioxidants".

$$P(Cancer|Antioxidants) < P(Cancer|noAntioxidants). \tag{2B-5}$$

This discussion has referred to the "event" that an event was not observed. This is called a *complementary event*. As a consequence of the definition of a probability measure,

$$p(\neg e) = 1 - P(e). \tag{2B-6}$$

This is useful because there are occasions when it is easier to calculate the probability of the complement of event than to calculate the probability of the event directly.

Probability Distributions

Assume that there are a finite number of outcomes to a trial, $\{e_1, e_2, \ldots e_j \ldots e_k\}$, each occurring with probability $P(e_j)$. When this is the case, the set of probabilities, $\mathbf{P} = \{P(e_j)\}$ is a *probability distribution*. As an example, it is clearly possible to calculate the probability of the 11 possible outcomes (2–12) of rolls of a pair of fair dice, as defined in section 2.1. If you had reason to question whether or not the dice were fair, you could throw them a large number of times and compare the observed relative frequencies to the probabilities of the outcomes, on the assumption that the dice were fair.

In many cases instead of observing events that have discrete values we are interested in observing a continuous measurement. For instance, there are literally thousands of psychology experiments in which the researcher measured the speed with which someone did something. This requires timing a movement, and exact timing is impossible. All we can do is measure to within the accuracy of our timing device.

More formally, let X be the measure of interest and let x be a specific value of this measurement. If X is truly continuous, the probability of occurrence of observing an exact value of x (written $X = x$) is zero. For instance, it is not possible to measure exactly when 2 P.M. is because time is continuous, and so a point in time has no dimension. What we measure is the interval over which our clock reads 2 P.M.

On the other hand, we can deal with the probability that a measurement will fall within the interval defined by two values, x_1 and x_2, $P(x_1 \leq X \leq x_2)$. The statement "It's 2 P.M." really means that "2 P.M. is somewhere in the smallest interval that I can distinguish, given the accuracy of my clock and my ability to read it."

We may also talk about the probability that a continuous measure does not exceed a certain value, $P(X < x)$. This is a continuous function, $F(x)$, which ranges between zero and one. The derivative of this function, $f(x) = \frac{d(F(x))}{dx}$ is the *probability density function*. Alternatively, $F(x)$ is the *cumulative density function* for $f(x)$.

The probability density function is the continuous analog of $P(x)$ when x is a discrete measure. The following relations hold:

$$\int_{x_1}^{x_2} f(x) \geq 0 \qquad\qquad\qquad\qquad (2B\text{-}7)$$

$$\int_{-\infty}^{+\infty} f(x) = 1. \qquad\qquad\qquad\qquad (2B\text{-}8)$$

Take the case of height. Heights for men in North America approximate the normal distribution. If we denote a specific value of height by x,

$F(70) = P(X \leq 70)$ is the probability that a randomly chosen male is equal to or less than 70 inches (5'10") tall. In fact, 5'10" is approximately the median height of North American men. Therefore, in this case $F(70) = .50$. Now suppose that 30% of North American men are above 72 inches (6') in height. Then $F(72) = .70$.

More generally, for any distribution, the median is the point x at which $P(X \leq x) = .5$. This is sometimes written $P_{50}(X) = x$ to indicate that 50% of the observations are expected to fall at or below x. The first and third quartiles mark the 25% and 75% of the observations and are denoted $P_{25}(X)$ *and* $P_{75}(X)$. Other percentile values are defined using the same notation.

The median is a measure of location; in a sense it is the center of a probability distribution. An alternative measure is the *expected value*, or *expectation*. If the variable of interest is a discrete value, the expected value of a randomly chosen observation, x, is

$$E(X) = \sum_x P(X = x) \bullet x \qquad (2B\text{-}9)$$

where the sum is taken over all possible values, $\{x\}$ that the observation might take. $E(X)$ is the average value one would expect after taking a large number of observations. For that reason, the sample mean is often regarded as an estimate of the expectation. Note that the value of $E(X)$ may not correspond to any possible value of x. As of 2004, the expected number of children born to a randomly selected woman in the United States was approximately 2.3, although obviously no woman had 2.3 children.

The expectation is similarly defined for continuous distributions, except that probability density functions and integration are used:

$$E(X) = \int_{x \in \{X\}} f(x)x \qquad (2B\text{-}10)$$

where integration is over all possible values of X.

When dealing with distributions it is often useful to have some estimate of dispersion, the extent to which a measure is likely to lie away from the expected value. Two frequently used measures are the *standard deviation* and the *interquartile range*. The definition of the standard deviation for discrete distributions is

$$\sigma(X) = \left(\sum_{X \in \{X\}} P(X = x) \bullet (X - E(X))^2 \right)^{\frac{1}{2}}, \qquad (2B\text{-}11)$$

and for a continuous distribution

$$\sigma(X) = \left(\int\limits_{x \in \{X\}} f(x) \bullet (x - E(X))^2 \right)^{\frac{1}{2}} \tag{2B-12}$$

the interquartile range is

$$IQR(X) = P_{75}(X) - P_{25}(X). \tag{2B-13}$$

In words, the standard deviation is the square root of the expected squared deviation of a value from the expected value. That is a mouthful, but if you parse it carefully, it makes sense as a measure of variability.

To illustrate, consider the following two sets of numbers: $A = \{6, 7, 8, 9, 10, 11, 12, 13\}$, $B = \{2.5, 4.5, 6.5, 8.5, 10.5, 12.5, 14.5, 16.5\}$.   If you sample a number randomly from either of these sets, the expected value is 9.5. However, the values in set **B** are clearly more widely dispersed than in set **A**. This is reflected in the standard deviations, which are 2.45 for set **A**, and 4.90 for set **B**.

The interquartile range is the width of the interval between the lowest score in the top 25% of a distribution and the highest score in the bottom 25%. A slightly different way to look at this is to say that 50% of all scores will lie between $P_{.25}(X)$ and $P_{.75}(X)$. In the case of the examples, the interquartile range of set **A** is $12 - 7 = 5$, while the interquartile range for set **B** is $14.57 - 4.5 = 10$.

Intuitively, the meaning of the interquartile range is easier to understand than the meaning of the standard deviation. Therefore, one might think that the interquartile range would be the normal way of expressing variability. In fact, the opposite is true! The reason has to do with the mathematical properties of most commonly observed probability distributions and density functions. Unfortunately, this leads to two dialogues. People who are conversant with statistics usually prefer to indicate variability by the square of the standard deviation, which is called the *variance*. People who are not conversant with statistics are likely to find the interquartile range more useful.

Standard Scores

The number used to represent something depends upon the scale used. This means that the choice of a scale will influence the mean, variance, and standard deviation. To illustrate, suppose that the U.S. weather service reported that on eight consecutive summer days, the temperatures at a given point on the U.S.-Canadian border were, in degrees Farenheit, 65, 70, 75, 80, 85, 90, 75, 72. The mean of these temperatures is 76.5 and the standard deviation is 7.6. The Canadian weather service would report the identical observations in degrees Celsius, as 18, 21, 24,

27, 29, 32, 24, 20, with a mean of 20.5 and a standard deviation of 4.5.[8] Within rounding errors, these are the same temperatures, related by different scales using the conversion formula,

$$Degrees\,Farenheit = (9/5) \times Degrees\,Celsius + 32$$
$$Degrees\,Celsius = (5/9) \times (Degrees\,Farenheit - 32).$$
(2B-14)

The example is a special case of a common linear relationship between two scales, X and Y:

$$Y = BX + A; B \neq 0.$$
(2B-14)

It is easy to prove that when scale Y is a linear transformation of scale X the variances are related by

$$\sigma^2(Y) = B^2 \sigma^2(X).$$
(2B-15)

It is often desirable to have a common metric that represents the extent to which an observation is different from the expected observation, without having to state the scale. This is done by expressing the extent to which an observation differs from the expectation, relative to the variability in the observations. Let x and y be the same observation, but expressed in two different, linearly related scales. The *standard score*, z, of the observation is

$$z = \frac{x - E(X)}{\sigma(X)}.$$
(2B-16)

By substituting (2B-14) and (2B-15) into (2B-16), it is easily proven that the standard score for an observation is the same regardless of the scale used. Note that when standard scores are used, the expectation is always zero and the standard deviation is identically one.

The Normal (Gaussian) Distribution

Statisticians have explored a number of different probability distributions and probability density functions. By far the most widely used of these is the *Gaussian* or *normal* probability density function. Expressed in standard scores, the Gaussian density function is

$$f(z) = \frac{1}{\sqrt{2\pi}} e^{-\frac{z^2}{2}}$$
(2B-17)

---

[8] The numbers referring to temperatures have been rounded to the nearest whole number; means and standard deviations are reported to the nearest decimal. This introduces some inexactness because a Fahrenheit unit covers a smaller range of temperatures than does a Celsius unit.

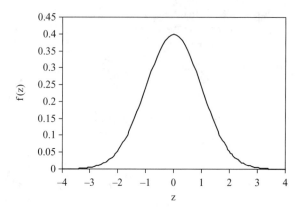

FIGURE 2-2. The standard normal distribution.

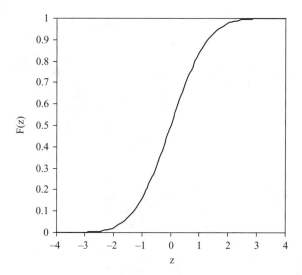

FIGURE 2-3. The cumulative normal distribution.

where e is the Naperian constant. This gives rise to the famous "Bell Curve," shown in Figure 2-2. Figure 2-3 shows corresponding cumulative probability distribution, $F(z)$.

There are three reasons for being interested in the normal distribution. Empirically, many variables studied in both the natural and social sciences turn out to approximate the normal distribution. Theoretically, the distribution could be produced by a simple, intuitively appealing process. Suppose that some phenomenon is produced by (a) establishing a central value and (b) adding to that central value a large number of random, statistically independent modifications. The modifications may be either positive or negative. As an example, consider height. Height is produced by a combination of genetic potential and health effects, especially early childhood nutrition. The genetic potential itself depends upon multiple genes. As a result, adult stature is approximately normally distributed.

There is also a pragmatic reason for being interested in the normal distribution. Scientists are frequently interested in comparing the values of a variable across two or more groups, for example, comparing earnings of equivalently educated men and women. Other, much more complex, examples abound. There are many statistical procedures for making such comparisons. Some of the most useful of these procedures are based on the assumption that the data follow the normal distribution. When non-normal distributions are found, scientists sometimes use a non-linear transformation of the original scores to produce a normal distribution, and then analyze the transformed data. For instance, in industrial societies, earnings typically are not normally distributed because some very high earnings skew the distribution toward the right, in comparison to Figure 2-2. Therefore, it is a common practice to compare the logarithm of earnings in order to apply statistical analyses that assume a normal distribution.

A discussion of when it is appropriate to take such transformations would lead us much further into a discussion of scaling and statistics than we want to go. We will return to this point in later chapters, when it becomes important in context. See especially Chapter 3.

Because of the ubiquity of the normal distribution, it pays to be familiar with some of its characteristics. The distribution is symmetric, as Figure 2-2 clearly shows. This means that if data are distributed normally, the probability of an observation x units above the mean is identical to the probability of one x units below the mean. As a consequence, the probability of an observation falling below (above) the mean is identically $1/2$. This can be seen in Figure 2-2, which is symmetric about a standard score of zero, and in Figure 2-3, which shows that at the mean $(z = 0)$ $F(0) = .5$.

When data are distributed normally, approximately two-thirds of the observations lie within one standard deviation of the mean, that is, between standard scores of $+1$ and -1. Approximately 90% of the observations will lie between standard scores of $+2$ and -2, with about 5% of all observations below -2 and 5% above $+2$. One in a hundred observations will be above 2.33 in standard score units, and one in a thousand above 3.0 standard score units.

To take a concrete illustration, scores on the widely used Wechsler Adult Intelligence Scale are approximately normally distributed, with a mean of 100 and a standard deviation of 15. Half the people who take the test score over 100, about one out of every six scores over 115, approximately one out of twenty scores over 130, and one in a thousand has a tested IQ of 145 or more.

3

From Physics to Perception

3.1. THE PSYCHOPHYSICAL PROBLEM

According to Shakespeare, "The world is much upon us." In fact, the world is always upon us. If we pick something up, gravity tries to make us put it down. Sometimes there is so much heat that we strip to bathing suits; sometimes there is so little that we pile on coats. Light energy falls on our eyes; if there is enough of it we can see. When air pressure fluctuations transfer energy to our eardrums, we hear. Just what is the mapping from the energies that impinge on us to our sensations of the world around us?

The field where this issue is explored is called *psychophysics*. It is one of the oldest and one of the most mathematically oriented fields of scientific psychology. It is also one that has a substantial practical application. Consider the following example, the case of machinery-generated noise.

Anything with a moving part generates air pressure waves. These waves cause fluctuations in listening devices, including the ear. The energy per unit area in the fluctuations is measured in decibels (db). To give some content, ordinary speech is conducted at about 60–70 db. The pain threshold for the ear is in the 115–125 db range, varying somewhat with frequency. Obviously, then, machinery noises must be held to 110 db or less.

But how much less? Muffling sounds can be an expensive process. Determining how much it will cost to reduce sound emissions by 10 db is often a straightforward problem in engineering. But what are the benefits in terms of the psychological sensation of loudness? In order to answer that question we have to know the function relating sound intensity to loudness. This is a tricky issue because we have no independent measure of loudness.

There are two issues here: How would we measure loudness and, once we had decided upon a measure, how would we use that measure to relate loudness to sound intensity? The same questions can be raised about relating brightness to luminosity, heaviness to weight, or pitch to frequency. Mathematical analysis has greatly clarified the issues. The sort of reasoning involved will be illustrated here for the relation between heaviness and weight, but this is for purposes of illustration only. The same argument could be developed for loudness and sound, brightness and light, or any other relation between a dimension of sensation and a dimension of the external physical world.

It is safe to assume that heaviness is a non-decreasing function, f, of weight:

Heaviness $= f(w)$.

Therefore, for any two weights, w_1, w_2 $f(w_1) \geq f(w_2) \Leftrightarrow w_1 \geq w_2$, where the double arrow indicates double implication, "if and only if." But this is hardly enough. How can we say more?

The problem lies in the measurement of heaviness. There is no reliable heaviness meter, analogous to scales for weighing objects. We have to ask a judge (an *observer* for consistency with other psychophysics problems) to do something that indicates how heavy the object feels. And that is the rub. What is the "something" that the observer has to do, and what can we infer about the observer's sensation of heaviness when something is done?

More formally, we can present an observer with a weight, w, and record the response, $R(w)$. Given enough values for w, we can establish an empirical mapping, $w \to R(w)$, but this is not the end of the endeavor. We assume that the response is mediated, in some unknown way, by the observer's internal sensation of heaviness, $f(w)$. That is,

$$R(w) = g(f(w)). \tag{3-1}$$

What we want to determine is the function $f(w)$ from an analysis of the $w \to R(w)$ mapping. In order to do this, we have to make some assumption about the sensation-to-response mapping, $g(f(w))$.

Two approaches have been taken. One is to make only the minimal assumption that an observer can discriminate between degrees of intensity. For instance, in a weight discrimination experiment you might assume that the observer can tell you which of two objects feels heavier, but cannot (reliably) tell you how much heavier one object feels than the other. I will call this the *minimalist* constraint. The other possibility is to make some very strong assumption about the sensation-to-response mapping. Perhaps the strongest that could be made is that the observer can discriminate ratios of heaviness. If you believe this you should take seriously a statement like "The first weight feels two and one-half times heavier than the second."

My own intuition is that the truth lies somewhere in between. I think people can tell more than the order of intensities of heaviness, loudness, and brightness. But how much more? I am uncomfortable with the notion that people can report ratios of intensity. The exploration of this issue has generated a great deal of discussion about what measurement is, what sorts of measurement scales there are, and how they can be used.[1] We are only going to touch the tip of the iceberg.

We will first look at two well-known examples of psychophysical scaling, Weber-Fechner and Stevens' magnitude estimation scaling. The first approach sticks tightly to the minimalist constraint; the second tosses it out the window. Following a discussion of these methods, a brief description will be given of two intermediate positions.

3.2. WEBER'S LAW

Inquiries into psychophysical functions began in German university laboratories early in the nineteenth century. Around 1830 Ernst Weber, a professor at the University of Leipzig proposed an answer to the measurement problem that is still in use today.

Weber argued that the way to measure a sensation was to determine how sensitive an observer was to changes in the physical stimulus that produced the sensation. In the case of heaviness, he asked people to compare two weights, a standard w and a comparison weight $w + \Delta(w)$, where $\Delta(w)$ is always positive. Typically, each person would make a hundred or more comparisons at a given increment, $\Delta(w)$, over the standard. Weber then calculated the frequency of correct choices at that weight. Write this as

$$P(\Delta(w) + w | \Delta(w) + w, w) = \pi, \tag{3-2}$$

which is interpreted as "When a judge is presented with two objects of mass w and $w + \Delta(w)$ respectively, the judge correctly identifies the larger object with probability π." Note that π is an observable.

In terms of the preceding section, what Weber did was to use as his response measure a discrimination between two weights, w and $w + \Delta(w)$. He implicitly assumed that the observable judgment "heavier" would only occur if the related sensations were heavier, that is, if $f(w + \Delta(w)) > f(w)$. Weber used a probabilistic definition for "heavier" because he believed that the perception of heaviness of an object may vary from time to time.

---

[1] Anderson (1996), Falmagne (1985), and Luce and Krumhansl (1988) provide discussions from somewhat different perspectives.

Not surprisingly, the larger $\Delta(w)$ is (i.e., the greater the difference in weight between the test and the standard), the higher the value of π, until $\Delta(w)$ is so large that the discrimination is trivial and π reaches its maximum at 1. If $\Delta(w)$ is zero, then $\pi = .5$, for the judge has no basis for judgment.

It is possible to turn Weber's procedure around, by choosing some value of π and w and varying $\Delta(w)$ until $\Delta(w)$ is found such that $P(\Delta(w) + w | \Delta(w) + w, w) = \pi$ for the chosen π value. For instance, suppose the standard, w, is 300 grams and the desired π value is .75. Weber would have people compare 300 grams to 310 grams, 320, and so on (not necessarily in ascending order) until he found the smallest weight, w_π, that could be correctly identified as "heavier than w" three times out of four. Suppose that this was 330 grams. Then $\Delta_{.75}(w) = w_{.75} - w = (330 - 300) = 30$ grams. In a more general notation, the function

$$\Delta_\pi(w) = w_\pi - w \qquad (3\text{-}3)$$

is called a *Weber function*.

Weber decided that three out of four correct judgments, which corresponds to $\pi = .75$, would be an acceptable level of accuracy. He called the increment in weight $\Delta_{.75}(w)$ a *just noticeable difference*, abbreviated jnd. He proposed that the jnd be accepted as the unit of the sensory scale.

In doing so, Weber made the first move toward establishing a correspondence between an observable scale, weight (or loudness or light intensity, etc.) and a psychological scale. Imagine that Weber had found that at a standard weight of 300 grams $\Delta_{.75}(300) = 30g$, and that at standard weight of 600 grams $\Delta_{.75}(600) = 60g$. He would have argued that an increment of 30g to a weight of 300g was psychologically equivalent to adding 60g to a 600g weight. The logic is shown in Figure 3-1.

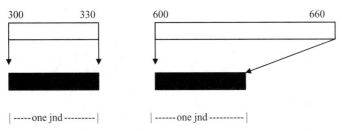

Sensory scale in jnds.

FIGURE 3-1. Weber defined the jnd as the unit of the sensory scale. A jnd is the change in the sensory scale corresponding to an increment in a standard physical stimulus (e.g., weight) sufficiently large so that when the increased weight is compared to the standard, a person makes a correct judgment on three out of four trials, $\pi = .75$. The physical increment required to produce a one-jnd difference in the sensory scale varies with the intensity of the standard stimulus.

Upon examining the data from a large number of experiments Weber noticed a relation that has become central in psychophysics:

$$\frac{\Delta_\pi(w)}{w} = c_\pi, \tag{3-4}$$

where c_π is a constant that depends upon π, but not w, and that, not surprisingly, varies over different sensory dimensions. The value of c at an accuracy of .75, $c_{.75}$, is known as the *Weber fraction*. In the illustration of Figure 3-1, the "Weber fraction" would be .1 ($30/300 = 60/600 = .1$), but that was only to make the mathematics obvious. In fact, the Weber fraction for lifted weights in the range of 300 grams is about .019, and for pressure on a spot on the skin at 5 grams/mm^2 is .136.[2]

A rearrangement of equation (3-4) produces

$$\Delta_\pi(w) = c_\pi w. \tag{3-5}$$

This equation is known as *Weber's law*. It states that the jnd at weight w is proportional to w, with the constant of proportionality determined by the accuracy required to define the jnd. Weber drew analogous conclusions for other physical-to-sensory judgments, such as warmth, loudness, and brightness.

Further studies of sensory discrimination have shown that Weber's law does not always hold, but that the failure is systematic. The Weber fraction is usually relatively large for small physical intensities (e.g., very light standard weights), then drops to an approximate constant.

It makes sense that Weber's law would fail at low intensities. Consider the following argument.

Obviously there is some lightest noticeable weight (or softest sound, etc.) that can be detected with accuracy π. Let this be w_0. By definition, $w_0 = \Delta_\pi(0)$. If equation 3-5 were to be applied literally, the Weber fraction would be $c_\pi = w_0/0 = \infty$, which is silly. On the other hand, we would expect w_0 to be fairly small. For the purpose of illustration, suppose it is 1 gram. We can then use w_0 as the standard, and try to find how much weight has to be added to w_0 to distinguish between w_0 and $w_0 + \Delta_\pi(w_0)$. We expect $\Delta_\pi(w_0)$ also to be small, but not quite as large as w_0. Suppose we find that $\Delta_{.75}(w_0)$ is .5 grams. Then the Weber fraction $\Delta_{.75}(w_0)/w_0$ would be the large value .5. If the same Weber fraction applied to distinguishing weight at the $w = 1$ kilogram level, a person should be less than 75% accurate in distinguishing between weights of 1,000 and 1,300 grams. In fact, this would be very easy to do. It follows that Weber's law has broken down over this range, and that the Weber fraction must fall over the range 1–1,000g.

---

[2] Luce and Galanter (1963), quoting earlier sources.

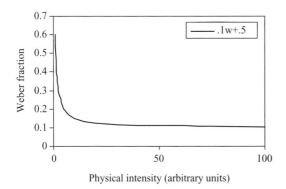

FIGURE 3-2. Variation in the Weber fraction under the generalized Weber law. This form has been found in many psychophysical experiments, using physical dimensions as different as weight and sound pressure.

Gustav Fechner, a retired professor of physics at Leipzig[3] who had studied with Weber, corrected for this problem by defining the *generalized Weber's law*,

$$\Delta_\pi(w) = c_\pi w + C_\pi. \tag{3-6}$$

According to the generalized law, the value of the Weber fraction, $\Delta_\pi(w)/w$, approximates C_π/w for small values of w, but approaches c_π as w increases without limit. An example, using the "made up" values of $C_\pi = .5$ and $c_\pi = .1$ is shown in Figure 3-2. This function seems to describe the data from many experiments on psychophysical discrimination.

3.3. FECHNER'S LAW[4]

Weber summarized experimental results. His findings, published in a lengthy treatise in 1860, represent the first attempt to go from finding laws summarizing data to testing models of mechanisms that underlie the data. Fechner took the next step. He presented a model of how a sensory discrimination takes place, including a discussion of why an observer will sometimes make an incorrect discrimination, such as judging weight a to be heavier than weight b when a is actually lighter than b. He then combined his model with Weber's law to define the *psychophysical function* $s = f(w)$, where s is the strength of a sensation, in unknown sensation units, and w is the strength of the impinging physical stimulus.

---

[3] Fechner retired from his professorial chair in his middle age, due to health problems. Nevertheless, he lived until he was 86! His research on psychophysics took place after his resignation.

[4] My treatment is based on discussions of Fechner's work by Link (1994) and by Luce & Krumhansl (1988).

Fechner thought of sensory systems as being conceptually analogous to measuring devices. For instance, the eye and a camera are both devices for measuring light. In the late eighteenth century, about 50 years before Fechner began his work, Friedrich Gauss had developed a theory of measurement that applied to such devices.[5] Gauss had argued that all measurements are the sum of two terms, a constant term representing the true value of whatever is being measured and an error that is distributed normally, with a mean of zero and an unknown standard deviation, σ, that is inversely related to the accuracy of measurement. Fechner applied Gauss's reasoning to the sensory system.

Fechner assumed that when a physical stimulus with intensity w is presented to the sensory organ, the resulting sensation is

$$\psi_t(w) = s_w + e_t, \tag{3-7}$$

where ψ_t is the perception of the stimulus on the tth presentation, s_w is the true sensation associated with the stimulus, and e_t is an error ("noise") term introduced by the sensory system. In a Weber-type experiment, a judge is asked to compare two weights, of masses a and b ($a < b$) whose true sensory values are s_a and s_b. Fechner made the minimalist assumption that the sensory experience is ordinally related to the physical values, that if $a \le b$, $s_a \le s_b$.

Following Gauss, Fechner assumed that the noise term, e_t, was distributed normally, with a mean of zero and an unknown standard deviation, σ.[6] Because the standard deviation represents a measure of the extent to which scores are spread apart, the inverse of the standard deviation, $1/\sigma$, is a measure of the sensitivity of the sensory system. Higher scores (lower σ values) represent greater accuracy. An important part of the theory is the assumption that σ does not depend upon w. This means that the variability in sensing a constant stimulus does not depend upon the intensity of the stimulus.

Consider a Weber-type experiment in which weights a, b ($a < b$) are presented for judgment. According to Fechner's model, the probability of correctly judging that b weighs more than a is

$$\begin{aligned}
P(b|a, b) &= P(\psi(a) < \psi(b)) \\
P(b|a, b) &= P(s_A + e_a < s_B + e_b) \\
P(b|a, b) &= P((e_a - e_b) < (s_b - s_a)) \\
P(b|a, b) &= P((e_a - e_b) < (f(b) - f(a))),
\end{aligned} \tag{3-8}$$

where f is the psychophysical function.

---

[5] Gauss's theory of measurement is a central part of modern statistics.

[6] Readers not familiar with what the normality assumption implies might review the discussion of the normal distribution, in Chapter 2, Appendix 2B.

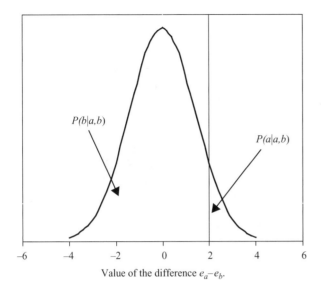

Value of the difference $e_a - e_b$.

FIGURE 3-3. A graphical representation of the decision situation. Assume that the difference in sensory units is $f(b) - f(a) = 2$, at the vertical line. Assume also that the standard deviation of the difference, $e_a - e_b$ is 1. The probability of a correct response, choosing b in the pair (a, b) is proportional to the area under the normal curve to the left of the vertical line, which is placed at $f(b) - f(a) = 2$. All values are in unobservable sensory units, but as explained in the text, these need not be known if $P(b|a, b)$ can be observed.

By hypothesis, the error terms are distributed normally with zero means and unknown standard deviations σ. (This is written $e_a, e_b \in N(0, \sigma)$) It follows that the difference, $e_a - e_b$, is a random variable, with distribution $e_a - e_b \in N(0, \sqrt{2}\sigma)$.[7] The situation is shown graphically in Figure 3-3. The probability that the correct response will be made is equal to the probability that $e_a - e_b$ is less than the difference between the values of the psychophysical function, $f(b) - f(a)$, for the two weights.

The contemporary psychophysicist Steven Link remarked that Fechner's reasoning anticipated modern theories of signal detection (Chapter 7) by about a century![8]

Fechner's model is stated in terms of unobservable sensory scale units. In order to calculate the probability of a correct judgment for any actual

---

[7] This is a special case of the following assertion, which is proven in virtually all introductory statistic texts. If two random variables, x and y, have expectation $E(x)$ and $E(y)$ and variances σ_x^2 and σ_y^2 respectively, then the variable $x + y$ has expectation $E(x + y) = E(x) + E(y)$ and variance $\sigma_{x+y}^2 = \sigma_x^2 + \sigma_y^2$. If $\sigma_x = \sigma_y = \sigma$, then $\sigma_{x+y} = \sqrt{2}\sigma$, as stated in the text.

[8] Link (1994). Link was correct insofar as signal detection is concerned. However, Fechner's approach to discrimination was also used by L. L. Thurstone (1927).

pair of weights, we have to know the psychometric function, f, which is what we are trying to find out! Fechner realized that this could be done by working backward. The probability of a correct judgment, $P(b|a,b)$, is an observable. Weber's law (equation 3-5) provided an important clue as to how it should be treated.

Recall that in Weber's studies the experimenter adjusted the difference $\Delta = b - a$ until the observer made correct discriminations on some fraction π of the trials. Let $\Delta_\pi(a)$ be the required difference in weights (or intensity, if the judgment is on some other dimension). In words, $\Delta_\pi(a)$ is the amount that has to be added to a standard of weight a in order to identify the heavier weight with accuracy π. According to Weber's law the ratio of the increment to the standard, c_π, depends only upon the accuracy level and not upon the intensity of the standard. Therefore, the last line of equation (3-8) can be written

$$P(a + c_\pi a | a + c_\pi a, a) = P(e_a - e_{a+c_\pi a} < f(a + c_\pi a) - f(a))$$
$$\pi = P(e_a - e_{a+c_\pi a} < f(a + c_\pi a) - f(a)) \tag{3-9}$$

Because $e_a - e_{a+c_\pi a}$ is distributed normally with zero mean and standard deviation $\sqrt{2}\sigma$, equation (3-9) can be expressed in terms of standard deviation units,

$$\pi = P\left(\frac{e_a - e_{a+c_\pi a}}{\sigma\sqrt{2}} < \frac{f(a + c_\pi a) - f(a)}{\sigma\sqrt{2}}\right)$$
$$\pi = P\left(z_\pi < \left(\frac{f(a + c_\pi a) - f(a)}{\sigma\sqrt{2}}\right)\right), \tag{3-10}$$

where z_π is the standard normal deviate corresponding to a probability value π. As defined in Chapter 2, Appendix B, $\pi = F(z_\pi)$, where F is the cumulative normal distribution function. Writing the last line of (3-10) using F,

$$F(z_\pi) = F\left(\frac{f(a + c_\pi a) - f(a)}{\sigma\sqrt{2}}\right)$$
$$F^{-1}(F(z_\pi)) = F^{-1}\left(F\left(\frac{f(a + c_\pi a) - f(a)}{\sigma\sqrt{2}}\right)\right) \tag{3-11}$$
$$z_\pi = \frac{f(a + c_\pi a) - f(a)}{\sigma\sqrt{2}}$$
$$f(a + c_\pi a) - f(a) = z_\pi\sqrt{2}\sigma.$$

This shows that the difference in sensory units required to produce a level of accuracy of discrimination π is a constant that does not depend upon the intensity of the stimulus, a. The problem is to find a function f that satisfies this requirement.

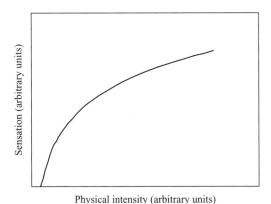

FIGURE 3-4. Fechner's law: The intensity of a sensation is a logarithmic function of the intensity of the physical stimulus. Fechner showed that this relation is a consequence of Weber's empirical observations. This was the first example of the derivation of an explicit psychophysical relationship between a variable in the physical world and one in the psychological world.

Fechner showed that equation (3-11) is satisfied by the function $f(x) = A \log(x)$, where $A > 0$ is a constant of proportionality that establishes a scale. Substituting $A \log(x)$ into equation (3-11),

$$A \log(a + c_\pi a) - A \log(a) = z_\pi \sqrt{2} \sigma$$
$$A[\log(1 + c_\pi) + \log(a) - \log(a)] = z_\pi \sqrt{2} \sigma . \qquad (3\text{-}12)$$
$$A \log(1 + c_\pi) = z_\pi \sqrt{2} \sigma$$

shows that the value of a does not matter to the relation.

Starting with Weber's law and a model of the discrimination process, Fechner had deduced that when a pure physical stimulus, such as a light or tone, impinges on the sensory system, the perceived intensity is proportional to the logarithm of the physical intensity of the stimulus. The form of this relation is shown in Figure 3-4.

Fechner used his law to study how different conditions of observation, such as time of day or temperature, might influence the accuracy of the sensory system. The logic of Fechner's approach, although not exactly what he did, is illustrated by a simple example.

According to the theory, accuracy is determined by σ, the standard deviation of the distribution of errors. The larger σ is, the less accurate the sensory system is. There is no way to measure σ directly, but it is possible to measure the relative values of σ under two different conditions. Rearranging equation (3-12) produces

$$K\sigma = \frac{\log(1 + c_\pi)}{z_\pi \sqrt{2}}, \qquad (3\text{-}13)$$

where $K = 1/A$. The value of π is set by the experimenter, and this in turn implies z_π. The value of c_π is determined by observation. Therefore σ is known up to a scaling constant.

Suppose that a discrimination experiment involving exactly the same physical intensities is conducted under two different conditions (e.g., daytime and nightime). The same level of accuracy is required under both conditions, while c_π is determined by observation. The relative values of σ, the measure of sensory error, can be determined by calculating

$$\frac{\sigma(day)}{\sigma(night)} = \frac{\log(1 + c_\pi(day))}{\log(1 + c_\pi(night))}. \tag{3-14}$$

The smaller the value of σ, the more accurate the observer is. Therefore, if accuracy is greater in the day than in the night, equation (3-14) should be less than one.

Did Fechner discover the true form of the psychophysical law, good for all stimulus intensities and all conditions? If he had it would have been the end of psychophysics, for all questions would have been answered. As you might expect, the situation is not quite that clear.

The derivation of Fechner's law relies on two assumptions, his model of sensory discrimination and the truth of Weber's law. As Fechner himself observed, Weber's law fails at small values of stimulus intensity, that is, for very small weights, very dim lights, and very soft tones. Fechner's generalization of Weber's law (equation 3-6), which covers the low intensity situation reasonably well, can be used to derive a generalization of Fechner's law,

$$f(w) = A \log(w + \gamma) + \alpha. \tag{3-15}$$

However, the derivation requires some additional assumptions that are hard to justify.[9] This leads us to question Fechner's law at low levels of intensity.

Fechner's argument depends upon the generality of Weber's law. While Weber's law is roughly valid in a wide range of situations, there are discrepancies. It has been suggested that Weber's law, $\Delta_\pi(w) = c_\pi w$ should be replaced by

$$\Delta_\pi(w) = c_\pi w^{1-\varepsilon}, \tag{3-16}$$

where ε is a positive number less than one. If ε is quite small, as has been found, this function approximates Weber's law except at high stimulus intensities, where it is more accurate. For that reason, equation (3-16) is sometimes referred to as the near-miss to Weber's law.

---

[9] Luce and Galanter (1963), p. 212–13.

We are left with the conclusion that Fechner's law does a pretty good job of modeling psychophysical functions that are derived from sensory discriminations within the "normal" range of weights, sounds, and lights. It does break down at high and low intensities. There is nothing wrong with putting limits on the range of a scientific model. Newton's laws apply under normal living conditions, but break down for things going unimaginably fast or in the range of massive gravitational forces!

None of these qualifications on Fechner's law should detract from his intellectual contribution. He was the first person to establish an explicit mathematical relationship between attributes of the physical and psychological world. According to Link, when that happened, "Psychology became a science."[10]

3.4. STEVENS'S SCALING TECHNIQUE: DERIVING THE PSYCHOPHYSICAL FUNCTION FROM MAGNITUDE ESTIMATION

Weber and Fechner worked within the minimalist constraint. All they asked of the observer was that he or she respond "*b* is heavier (or louder or brighter) than *a*" when the sensation associated with *b* was greater than the sensation associated with *a*. Observations of people's ability to discriminate increments at different levels of intensity were then used to infer a psychophysical function that applied over a wide range of intensities. Approaches of this sort are called *local psychophysics,* because actions in local regions of the intensity scale are used to infer a global relation between stimulus intensity and sensation.

There are two objections to local psychophysics. One is that it is time-consuming. In order to have enough data points to determine the parameters of Fechner's law (*A* and *c* in the previous section), the value of the increment in *a* required to produce discriminations that are, say, 75% accurate has to be determined for many values of *a*. This can be tiring to both the experimenter and the observer.

A second, conceptually deeper, objection to local psychophysics is that Fechner's law does not accord with a number of observations outside of the laboratory. One of these is brightness constancy. A bright sweater seems bright whether the wearer is indoors or outdoors, in spite of changes in the intensity of light reflected from the sweater to the observer. Experimentation has shown that the brightness of an object is strongly influenced by the relative luminance between the object and other objects in the visual field. This suggests that the ability to perceive ratios of intensities may be central to perception.

---

[10] Link (1994). I have also drawn from Falmagne (1985) and Luce and Krumhansl (1988).

About a hundred years after Fechner began his studies a Harvard professor, Stanley Smith Stevens, proposed a radically different approach to psychophysics. Beginning in the 1930s, Stevens conducted experiments in which he determined how well people judged the ratios between two stimulus intensities, for example, how well they could identify a weight that was twice as heavy as a 300 gm weight. Stevens's observers turned out to be surprisingly accurate. Furthermore, they could give numerical estimates that reflected this invariance. Accordingly, Stevens developed a technique that he called *magnitude estimation*. In a book published in 1975,[11] he provided an elegant description of an experiment conducted on one of his colleagues some 20 years earlier:

I turned on a very loud tone at 120 decibels, which made my colleague jump, and which we agreed to call 100. I then turned on various other intensities in irregular order, and he called out a number to specify the loudness. I plotted the numbers directly on a piece of graph paper in order to see immediately what course was being followed. (Stevens (1975), p. 23)

Because magnitude estimates are required across wide ranges of stimulus intensity, Stevens's procedure is an example of *global psychophysics*.

Stevens obtained magnitude estimates for the heaviness of weights, brightness of lights, and loudness of pure tones. When he plotted the judgments on log-log coordinates, he found that they fell on a straight line. Algebraically, he found that

$$\log(g(x)) = \beta \log(x) + \gamma, \tag{3-17}$$

where x is the physical intensity of the stimulus and $g(x)$ is the numeral that the observer assigns to indicate the sensation produced by intensity x. Note that I have written $g(x)$ to indicate that this is a relation between a response and a stimulus intensity, not necessarily a relation between a sensation and an intensity.

Equation (3-17) produced a good fit to the data relating sensation to objective measures, across all modalities. Not surprisingly, each modality had its own values for the β and γ parameters.

Stevens then took a controversial step. He decided to treat the observer's response, that is, the magnitude estimate, as if it was proportional to the unobservable internal sensation. This amounts to an assumption that $g(x) = \alpha f(x)$, which is a strong assumption indeed.

---

[11] Stevens (1957, 1975). Stevens died in 1973. His book *Psychophysics*, which reviews much of his work, was published posthumously two years later.

However, it is useful because it leads directly to a psychophysical function relating sensation to intensity. Taking the antilogarithms of equation (3-17),

$$f(x) = \alpha x^{\beta}. \tag{3-18}$$

The constant $\alpha = \text{antilog}(\gamma)$ can be thought of as a scaling constant, used to convert from one magnitude estimation procedure to another, as in converting from an experiment in which the observer was told to assign a 100 to the initial stimulus to one in which the initial stimulus had been assigned a value of 10.

Equation (3-18) is *Stevens's power law* for psychophysics. Qualitatively, the relation between sensation and intensity depends upon the value of β. If $\beta = 1$, sensation is proportional to intensity. For values less than one, sensation increases less rapidly than intensity; for values larger than one, sensation increases more rapidly than intensity. These two relations are sometimes referred to as *compressive* and *expansive* relations between sensation and stimulus intensity.

Like Fechner, Stevens explored the form of the psychophysical function in different modalities. Among other things, he determined empirical relationships between perceived loudness and sound intensity ($\beta = .67$), perceived and actual length of a line ($\beta = 1.0$), and rated discomfort to the amplitude of an electric shock through the fingers ($\beta = 3.5$). Because equation (3-18) contains a scaling constant, these functions can be plotted on the same graph, as is done in Figure 3-5. Loudness is a compressive scale, perceived length is a ratio scale, and perceived discomfort to shock is an expansive scale of their respective intensities.

Stevens thought that he had discovered a fundamental psychological relationship. He was buttressed in this belief by an interesting extension of his method, called *cross-modal matching*. In a cross-modal matching experiment the observer is presented with a stimulus in one dimension, say weight, and asked to adjust another dimension, say luminance, so that each matches the other in psychological intensity. Continuing the example, an observer might be asked to "make the light as bright as the weight is heavy." At first, this seems to be a silly task. Stevens's theory, though, makes very strong predictions about the outcome of a cross-modal experiment.

Let x and y be two physical stimuli in different modes, for example, amplitude of vibration of the fingers and intensity of a noise. The observer is asked either to match the vibration intensity to the noise intensity or vice versa. Let α_x and β_x be the Stevens law parameters for mode x and α_y and β_y be the parameters for y. Stevens's law implies the following relations between matching intensities.

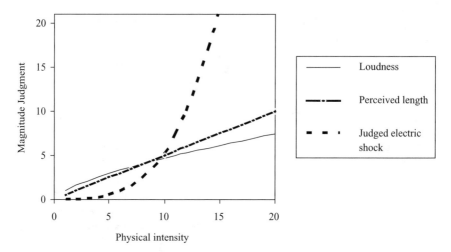

FIGURE 3-5. An illustration of Stevens's psychophysical laws, using loudness, perceived length of a line, and discomfort due to electric shock through the fingers as examples. These scales are, respectively, compressive $\beta < 1$, linear $\beta = 1$, and expansive, $\beta > 1$. Scaling constants have been chosen so that magnitudes are approximately equal at a physical intensity of 10 in arbitrary units. Therefore, the illustration properly conveys the shape of the functions but does not relate magnitude judgment to intensity in any concrete situation.

$$f(y) = f(x)$$
$$\alpha_y y^{\beta_y} = \alpha_x x^{\beta_x}$$
$$\beta_y \log(y) + \log(\alpha_y) = \beta_x \log(x) + \log(\alpha_x) \tag{3-19}$$
$$\log(y) = \frac{\beta_x}{\beta_y} \log(x) + \frac{1}{\beta_y} (\log(\alpha_x) - \log(\alpha_y)).$$

To take a concrete case, suppose we are matching vibration intensity at the fingers (y) to noise level (x). This is done for several values of x and y. According to equation (3-19), the logarithm of the vibration intensity will be a linear function of the logarithm of the noise intensity. It also says something much more specific. The model predicts that the slope of the vibration-noise function will be equal to the ratio $\beta_{noise}/\beta_{vibration}$. The β parameters can be estimated independently, by conducting separate magnitude estimation studies for vibration and for noise. When these estimates are obtained, the ratio for the cross-modal matching study can be predicted. For the particular case of vibration and loudness, in one of Stevens's experiments the predicted value of the ratio was 1.5 and the observed value was 1.6. Not bad.[12]

---

[12] Stevens (1975), p. 116.

Most of psychophysics has to do with relating basic sensory dimensions, such as heaviness and brightness, to basic dimensions of the physical world, such as weight and brightness. Stevens thought that psychophysical principles applied much more broadly. One can regard a sensation of intensity as an impression that is, internally, on the same scales as our impressions of much more complex stimuli. Stevens contended that scaling methods developed to map from stimulation to intensity could be applied to evaluate reactions to social judgments.[13]

As an illustration of his ideas, Stevens analyzed data from a study in which police officers had rated the severity of punishment appropriate for different crimes. He saw this as a method of magnitude estimation. But what would serve for intensity? Stevens represented intensity by the maximum penalty for the crime, as stated by the state penal code.[14] The judgments and the penalties were converted to logarithms and correlated. The value of the correlation coefficient was .94, indicating very strong agreement with equation 3-11. Converting back to the original units, we find that

Rated severity = (sentence length)$^{.7}$.

The form of this function is shown in Figure 3-6. The chart appears to indicate a rise in severity, followed by an almost linear relationship between severity and length after 10 years. However, the relation is not quite linear. The increase in severity associated with adding 10 years to a sentence of 30 years is about three-quarters of the increased severity of adding 10 years to a 10-year sentence.

If Stevens's power law was universally true, both theoretical and applied psychophysics would be easy. To see this, let us look again at the example of an engineer trying to establish the trade-off between the annoyance produced by a piece of machinery and the cost of noise abatement.

Establishing the function relating the cost in dollars to the reduction in noise intensity could be a straightforward problem in engineering. But this misses the point. What is needed is the relation between annoyance and the psychological cost of the dollars spent (*utility*, to be discussed in Chapter 7). If the engineer takes Stevens's law literally, all that is needed are separate rating experiments relating noise level to annoyance and relating the utility of money to costs in dollars. The cross-modality matching law could then be applied to determine the trade-off between

---

[13] Stevens (1966).

[14] The penalties were based on the Pennsylvania penal code, as of the 1960s. In the case of homicide, penalties of death or life imprisonment were set equal to the difference between the life expectancy and the median age of the offenders.

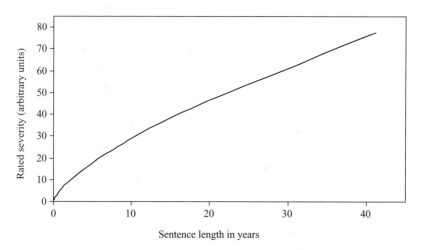

FIGURE 3-6. Rated severity of a sentence as a function of length of sentence, as calculated by Stevens's law with $\beta = .7$.

the psychological concepts of annoyance and psychological loss of wealth.

   Unfortunately, things are not that simple. There are several arguments against accepting Stevens's laws quite as literally as he did. Stevens based his analyses on a group statistic: the geometric mean of estimates made by several observers.[15] Stevens's law is often a rather poor fit to data from a single person, even when good fits are obtained for the group data. This is bothersome, for the idea that an observer converts a physical intensity to an internal sensation is clearly a model of individual behavior. Most psychophysicists plot the data for individual observers, and require that the same function fit the data for each observer, except for a change in parameters.

Logically, local and global psychophysical methods ought to produce the same or similar psychophysical functions. They do not. The heaviness-weight relation provides a clear example of the contrast. Fechner's law states that heaviness increases logarithmically with weight. Stevens's power law would approximate Fechner's law if magnitude estimation experiments produced a β value less than 1. However, Stevens reported a value of 1.45, which means that according to magnitude estimation, the heaviness function is expansive rather than

---

[15] Assume that N observers have made estimates $y_1 \ldots y_N$ at some value of stimulus magnitude. In this situation, psychologists typically use the mean value to summarize the data. This is valid if the distribution of the data is symmetric. Stevens noted that distributions of judgments were markedly skewed. In order to keep single large judgments from dominating the group data, he took as his measure the geometric mean $(\Pi y_i)^{1/N}$.

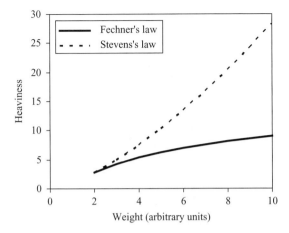

FIGURE 3-7. The heaviness-weight relationships predicted by Fechner's and Stevens's laws do not resemble each other.

compressive.[16] The difference between the two functions is illustrated in Figure 3-7. It is hard to see how these two different estimates of the same psychophysical relationship could differ more.

A third objection to Stevens's approach is that the magnitude estimate obtained for a physical quantity depends upon the context in which the judgment is made. The *frequency effect in psychophysics* provides a good example.

Suppose an observer is asked to judge the width of squares by assigning the numbers 1 ... 9 to squares of varying width. Suppose further that the judgments are made by presenting one square at a time and that the experimenter varies the frequency of presentation of different-sized squares. Thus, in condition (A), small squares are presented more often than big squares, while in condition (B), big squares are presented more often than small squares. A middle-sized square will be assigned a higher number if it is presented in a sequence in which small squares are more frequent than it will be if the middle-sized square is presented in a sequence in which large squares are more frequent.[17]

Given these problems, where are we with respect to Stevens's law? The answer depends more than a little upon how you view science.

---

[16] Stevens (1975), p. 15.
[17] Parducci and Wedell, (1986). This is only one of several studies in which Parducci and his colleagues have demonstrated how the context in which judgments are made can influence apparently simple psychophysical judgments.

The biggest problem, conceptually, is that Stevens's assumption that people can make ratio judgments of intensity seems to be too strong. The assumption was initially justified as a way of summarizing the data. Subsequently, Stevens made some remarks about a possible connection to neural firing, but this was not proposed seriously. The fact that people are bothered by the assumption, even though it produces reliable data, is a lesson for mathematical modelers in general. It is always interesting to observe mathematical regularities in scientific data, but ultimately, summarization alone is not enough. Some sort of explanation of the cause of the regularity is required.

An alternative to a causal explanation is to show that regularities found under an initially strong assumption, such as Stevens's ratio assumption, can be derived from weaker assumptions that are close to, though not quite at, the minimalist assumption. This has been done; it has been shown that Stevens's law can be derived from the assumption that an observer can detect the difference between two ratios of intensities. That is, given stimulus intensities x_1, x_2, x_3, x_4, Stevens's law follows from the assumption that the observer can tell when $x_1/x_2 \geq x_3/x_4$.[18]

The issue of individual differences is more serious. To my mind, one of the strongest arguments against Stevens's law is that it is often a poor fit to data taken from one person, even though it may fit statistical summarizations of the data from several observers. This suggests that the law is an artifact of the data summarization process, rather than a description of what is going on inside the mind of each observer.

Context effects are equally serious. Context effects cannot be explained by any theory that assumes that the psychophysical function is solely a property of the nature of the stimulus. Both Fechner's and Stevens's approaches fall down here. Psychophysical theories that consider context effects have been developed, but considering them would take us too far into a discussion of the field of psychophysics, rather than the mathematics used by psychophysicists.

Nevertheless, within a non-trivial range of situations, Stevens's law works. Stevens and his followers found that in many situations, there is a strikingly invariant relationship between physical intensity and reported magnitude of sensation. At the empirical level, this sort of information can be useful in human engineering, as in our acoustical engineering example. At a more scientific level, two things are important. First, science often deals with laws and models that apply only within a certain range of situations. Newton's laws of motion provide a case in point; they work very well in our normal world, even though Einstein and others showed that they break down for motions and gravitational fields

---

[18] The argument is fairly involved. See Narens (2002) for a discussion of this and other issues relating Stevens's law to other psychophysical approaches.

that are quite outside of everyday experience. Second, scientists are supposed to understand why invariant relationships exist. The ubiquity of Stevens's law is something to be explained, not explained away.

3.5. JUDGING COMPLEX OBJECTS

The nineteenth century psychophysicists tried to understand the mind by understanding how we form unidimensional sensations, like loudness, from unidimensional variations in physical intensity, like sound pressure levels. Most of the objects that we encounter outside of the laboratory vary on more than one dimension. Can the mathematics of psychophysics be applied to our judgments about multidimensional things? Two attempts have been made to do this. I will mention them only briefly.

Conjoint measurement is an extension of the minimalist constraint to the task of judging multidimensional objects. The idea is to extract information from judgments of stimuli defined by combinations of values on each of the two dimensions. Thus, in a conjoint measurement study, the observer might be asked which of two rectangles had the largest area.

Conjoint measurement is applied to judgments in a *factorial experiment*, in which the objects to be compared are defined by combinations of levels of the individual dimensions. In a conjoint measurement study of perception of the size of rectangles, an observer might be asked to judge the relative sizes of rectangles that were 5 cm by 2 cm, 5 cm by 6 cm, 8 cm by 2 cm, and 8 cm by 6 cm. This is analogous to the local psychophysics approach, for all the observer is asked to do is to make a discrimination between two areas. If the resulting data fall into certain patterns, it is possible to derive scales of the observer's internal reaction ("sensation") to variations in the length of vertical and horizontal lines from judgments of the relative size of rectangles. Similar studies can be done of stimuli constructed from other dimensions. Unfortunately, if the data do not fit into the required patterns, as it often does not, very little can be said.

The mathematical details of the conjoint measurement technique are too involved to present here. However, anyone seriously interested in psychophysics should be aware of it.[19]

Norman Anderson, a professor at the University of California, San Diego, has taken an approach to the judgment of multidimensional stimuli that resembles Stevens's global approach to scaling.[20] Like Stevens, Anderson uses numerical estimates of intensity as his observed response. However, these estimates are obtained by asking people to rate an object on an experimenter-provided scale (e.g., "rate from 1 to 10"), rather than

---

[19] Luce and Krumhansl, op. cit., provide a succinct discussion of conjoint measurement.
[20] Anderson (1996).

asking them to rate relative magnitudes. Anderson assumes that the ratings are a linear function of internal sensation:

$$g(f(x)) = K(f(x)) + C, \tag{3-20}$$

where both K and C are constants and K is positive. Stevens's assumption about the response-sensation relation is a special case of Anderson in which $C = 0$.

Anderson has focused on the rules that people use to combine unidimensional judgments into their impression of a multidimensional object. Let $h(x, y)$ be the impression formed of an object defined by two separate sources of information, x and y, and let $f_x(x)$ and $f_y(y)$ be the impressions of x and y separately. An overall impression of the multidimensional object might be formed in one of the following three ways:

Addition

$$h(x, y) = f_x(x) + f_y(y).$$

Multiplication

$$h(x, y) = f_x(x) \times f_y(y).$$

(Weighted)Averaging

if

$$x, y > 0$$

$$h(x, y) = \frac{w_x \, f_x(x) + w_y \, f_y(y)}{w_x + w_y} \tag{3-21}[21]$$

if

$$y = 0$$

$$h(x, 0) = f_x(x)$$

if

$$x = 0$$

$$h(0, y) = f_y(y)$$

If the assumption of response linearity (equation 3-20) holds, each of these integration rules implies a unique pattern of responding.

In order to demonstrate just what these patterns are, we consider a somewhat frivolous problem, rating restaurant meals. This example is very much in the spirit of the sort of things that Anderson has studied.

---

[21] The averaging rule given here is a simplification of Anderson's (op. cit, p. 56–7) averaging rule. I have used the simplification as a way of illustrating the mathematical principles involved. Anderson's own rule contains an additional term reflecting an impression of the stimulus prior to being given any information during an experiment. This does not make a great deal of sense in a psychophysical experiment using weights or sizes, but does make sense for socially relevant objects, such as those considered by Anderson in most of his work.

While Stevens was primarily interested in conventional psychophysical judgments of intensity-sensation relations, but dealt with social judgments as an aside, Anderson has tried to use psychophysical methods to understand social judgments.

Think of a newspaper food columnist rating a restaurant's soup-and-sandwich luncheon specialties. Component x (the soup) may be absent (0) or may take on values A, B, C, or D, where we assume only that the internal responses are ordered, that is, $f(A) \geq f(B) \geq f(C) \geq f(D)$. Component y (the sandwich) may also be absent (0) or take on similarly ordered values E, F, G, and H. The purpose of the exercise is to determine the rule that the columnist uses to combine his or her separate judgments of the soup and the sandwich into an overall rating of the meal.

Suppose further that, unknown to the experimenter, the columnist's rating of soup (x) is expansive over the A–D interval so that the intervals between internal judgments obey the relationship

$$f_x(B) - f_x(A) \leq f_x(C) - f_x(B)$$
$$f_x(C) - f_x(B) \leq f_x(D) - f_x(C),$$

while for the sandwich (y) component the scale is compressive in the E–H range,

$$f_y(F) - f_y(E) \geq f_y(G) - f_y(F)$$
$$f_y(G) - f_y(F) \geq f_y(H) - f_y(G).$$

To see what these suppositions mean, examine Figure 3-8. When the curve parameter y is zero, the curve represents the effect of changes in x alone, better and better soups without a sandwich. The curve is positively accelerating. When the abscissa parameter, x, is zero the points at which the different curves begin represent the effect of changes in y alone, better and better sandwiches without soup. The points are spaced closer together as y increases, reflecting a negatively accelerated scale.

Figure 3-8 shows the pattern of judgments that would be obtained if the food columnist used an additive combination rule. Although the curves are decidedly non-linear, they are parallel, in the following sense. The vertical distance between any two curves representing y values is the same, no matter what the value of the x variable is. Colloquially, going from a miserly to a generous sandwich improves the meal's rating by the same amount, no matter how good the soup is.

Figure 3-9 shows the pattern that would be obtained if the combination rule was multiplicative. Instead of the curves being parallel, they "fan out." The difference between various levels of the y (sandwich) variable increases as the x (soup) variable increases.

Figure 3-10 shows the relations that can be obtained if the averaging rule is used to combine component ratings. Of the three rules Anderson

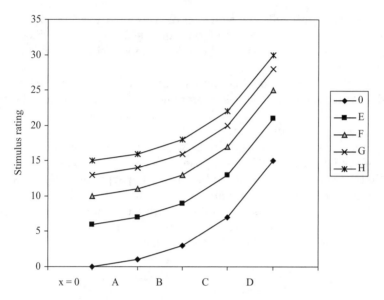

FIGURE 3-8. The linear rating curves for stimuli composed of an x component that takes on values 0 (absent) or A, B, C, or D and a y component that takes on values 0, E, F, G, H. The psychophysical function for the x component is expansive. The function for the y component is compressive. If the overall rating (on the ordinate) is determined by adding the psychological responses to x and to y, the curves will be parallel throughout the range of x.

proposed, only the averaging rule can produce curves that intersect. The reason for the intersection is that the rate of change in the stimulus, as a function of changes in the x component, is greater when the y component is absent than when it is present.

Anderson has found evidence for all the different types of combination rules, depending upon the variables being combined. In one experiment participants were told a story about how one person had damaged another's property. The stories varied in the extent of the damage, the intent of the individual who did the damage, and the compensation offered to the victim. Respondents (the term "observer" does not seem appropriate) rated the extent to which the perpetrator should be punished. The data supported an averaging rule for integrating information about the incident. By contrast, in another experiment respondents were asked how much they would pay for a drink of warm water, cold water, Coca-Cola, or beer, when they either were slightly thirsty, moderately thirsty, or parched. Here the data supported a multiplicative integration rule.

The reaction to Anderson's work is very much like the reaction to Stevens's research. On the one hand, the research seems to be based on

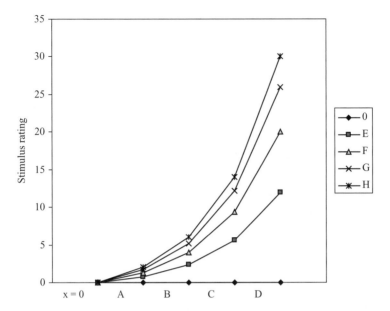

FIGURE 3-9. The curves that would be obtained in a rating experiment in which the x and y components are combined in accordance with the multiplicative rule. The curves are no longer parallel, as they were in Figure 3-8. Instead, the difference between any two levels of the y variable increases as the x variable increases.

assumptions about the response-sensation relationship that are just too strong. On the other, the approach works; orderly data are obtained. Data are to be explained, not explained away.

3.6. A COMMENT ON MEASUREMENT

Psychophysics offers, in microcosm, a look at a problem that has plagued the social and behavioral sciences. We want to know what is going on "inside the head," but all we can observe are actions of the body. What we are willing to assume about a person's response has a great deal to do with what we can infer about a person's psychological reaction to the stimulus.

Within what has traditionally been the province of psychophysics, mapping the sensation-intensity relation, there is an alternative to these elegant analyses. Conceivably, advances in the brain sciences will tell us more about the neural mechanisms underlying perceptions of heaviness, loudness, and brightness. When we know how these mechanisms act we will be able to specify the relevant psychophysical laws, because we will know how the behavior that they describe was constructed.

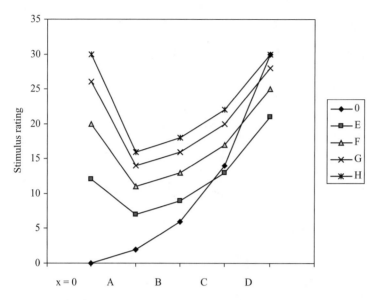

FIGURE 3-10. The rating curves that are produced using the averaging rule. The fact that the curves can intersect reflects the intuitively understandable finding that in some cases, combining a high level of the x component with a low level of the y component may actually produce a decrement in the overall rating. Think of the rating of a meal that consisted of a fine soup and a poor sandwich. If the food columnist uses an averaging rule, this combination will receive a lower rating than a meal consisting of the soup alone.

It seems unlikely that we will have similar success in explaining reactions to complex social stimuli, such as those studied by Anderson and, to some extent, by Stevens. It is true that we are beginning to identify the brain locations that are involved in social and cognitive activities, but that is a far cry from saying that we know how the neural circuits work. So we have to rely on measurements of behavior. Mathematical modeling has played, and will play, a major role in determining just what we can make of these measurements.

4

When Systems Evolve over Time

4.1. SYSTEMS OF VARIABLES

The social and behavioral sciences often deal with situations in which many variables interact over time. The term *system* is used to refer to such situations. Systems are ubiquitous. In psychotherapy, poor health may be a cause for depression, and the physiological effects of depression may, in turn, produce poor health. In economics price, production cost, and consumer demand vary together over time. In evolutionary biology, the rabbit and the fox evolved together. Time lags may be introduced. In manufacturing, production costs at time t fall as a result of capital investment at time $t - k$. When system behavior is being studied, the object of the game is to find how the simplest process that can describe the system is evolving. To do this, we develop a mathematical description of the process and compare the resulting numbers to the data. The mathematical description is called a *(model) system*, an idea that will now be described.

Imagine a system that consists of variables $x, y,$ and z and in which the change in each variable over time depends entirely upon the values of the other variables. This sort of system is called a *closed* system. The solar system, for example, can be treated as a (nearly) closed system because the positions and motions of the Sun and the planets are almost entirely determined by their current position and motion. The alternative to a closed system is an *open* system, in which the value of each variable in the system is determined partly by the other variables, and partly by variables outside the system (*exogenous* variables). A good example are the relations among a nation's gross domestic product, its literacy rate, and its investment in public education. It is generally agreed that these are positively related; "other things being equal," high literacy rates lead to increases in the gross domestic product, which translates into increased investment in public education and a higher literacy rate. However this is very much an open system. Many things other than literacy rate influence gross domestic product, and literacy rate does not depend solely upon the level of investment in education.

Most of the systems studied in the social and behavioral sciences are open rather than closed. Nevertheless, it often pays to treat a system as if it were closed, understand its idealized behavior, and then consider the influence of possible shocks to the system introduced by exogenous variables. When we do this we say that we are studying a *model* system that, we hope, behaves in a way that will enlighten our understanding of the messier open system that is being modeled. In fact, there are many cases in which the interesting thing is how a real-world system departs from the predictions of a model. This tells us, in a systematic way, what we do not understand. Identifying gaps in our knowledge is one of the most important steps in science.

I will start with a bit of mathematics, and then proceed with a series of case studies illustrating how widespread systems that evolve over time are.

4.2. DIFFERENCES AND DIFFERENTIATION

This section contains an introductory discussion to the concepts of differences and differentials. Readers familiar with these mathematical topics could skip it without loss of continuity.

Consider a simple, one-variable system in which the system changes in discrete time intervals and the value of the system at one time period is determined (largely) by the value at the previous time period. Two examples are the number of migratory birds returning to a nesting ground each season and the number of skiers returning to the slopes each year. Let time take on discrete values, $t = 0, 1, 2, \ldots$, and write the value at the next time period as a function of the current value;

$$x_t = f(x_{t-1}). \tag{4-1}$$

It is often useful to focus on the change in the value at each time period:

$$\Delta_t = x_t - x_{t-1}. \tag{4-2}$$

We do this because we may have a model of the change process. In the case of migratory birds, we would expect some loss of the population due to deaths during the winter, plus an increase due to the survival of birds born in the previous year. Let p be the fraction of birds that perish during the winter, and b the rate of increase due to the survival of birds born in the previous year. The change in the migratory population is

$$\begin{aligned} \Delta_t &= -px_{t-1} + bx_{t-1} \\ \Delta_t &= (b - p)x_{t-1}. \end{aligned} \tag{4-3}$$

Equation (4-3) is an example of a *difference equation*. These have the general form

$$\Delta_t = g(x_{t-1}) \tag{4-4}$$

for a system consisting of a single variable.

The notation readily generalizes to larger systems, in which each variable is a function of all variables in the previous time period. For a three-variable system, $\{x, y, z\}$ we have

$$x_t = f_x(x_{t-1}, y_{t-1}, z_{t-1})$$
$$y_t = f_y(x_{t-1}, y_{t-1}, z_{t-1}) \tag{4-5}$$
$$z_t = f_z(x_{t-1}, y_{t-1}, z_{t-1})$$

and

$$\Delta_{t,x} = g_x(x_{t-1}, y_{t-1}, z_{t-1})$$
$$\Delta_{t,y} = g_y(x_{t-1}, y_{t-1}, z_{t-1}) \tag{4-6}$$
$$\Delta_{t,z} = g_z(x_{t-1}, y_{t-1}, z_{t-1}).$$

These are called *difference equations* for the system of variables $\{x, y, z\}$.

A difference equation for a function implies the function itself, up to a constant. This is because the value of variable x_t is equal to the starting value plus the summation of the differences,

$$x_t = x_0 + \sum_{\tau=1}^{t} \Delta_\tau. \tag{4-7}$$

Derivatives and Difference Equations

Some systems change their states continuously, or at least at very short intervals relative to the total time of observation. In physical systems, gravity exerts a continuous accelerating force at all times. In social and behavioral systems change is not literally continuous, as it is in the case of gravity, but changes over a long time interval may best be modeled by a process of continuous change. In the stock market, for instance, changes in the price of a stock are determined by discrete sales. However there are so many sales, and each takes so little time, that it often makes sense to model the rate of change of a price as if it were actually a continuous variable. Let $g(x)$ represent the rate of change of variable x over time period h. Then

$$x_{t+h} - x_t = h * g(x)$$
$$\frac{x_{t+h} - x_t}{h} = g(x)$$

$$\frac{Lim}{h \to 0}\left[\frac{x_{t+h} - x_t}{h}\right] = g(x)$$

$$\frac{dx}{dt} = g(x),$$

(4-8)

providing that the limit exists. The quantity dx/dt is the *derivative* of x with respect to time t.

The ideas generalize to larger systems in the same way that the idea of a difference did. For a three-variable system $\{x,y,z\}$ we have a system of differential equations,

$$\frac{dx}{dt} = g_x(x, y, z)$$

$$\frac{dy}{dt} = g_y(x, y, z)$$

$$\frac{dz}{dt} = g_z(x, y, z).$$

(4-9)

Finally, as in the case of the difference equation, a differential equation implies the form of the function relating x to t; for any value t^*

$$f_x(t^*) = x_0 + \int_{=0}^{t^*} g(x)dt.$$

(4-10)

These ideas are applied in the next section, where we examine models of exponential growth and decay.

4.3. EXPONENTIAL GROWTH AND DECAY

Exponential growth (or decay) models are used to analyze single variable systems where the rate of change in a variable over time is proportional to the value of the variable:

$$\frac{dx}{dt} = ax.$$

(4-11)

This implies that

$$x_t = x_0 e^{at},$$

(4-12)

where x_0 is the starting value, and e is the Naperian constant. (In general, the derivative will be expressed without the time subscript, whereas the subscripted variable, x_t, refers to the value of the variable at time t.) Equation 4-12 is called the exponential growth (or decay, if $a < 0$) function. A proof of 4-12 will be found in Appendix 4-A.

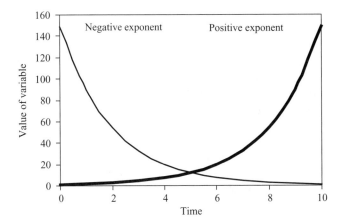

FIGURE 4-1. A depiction of exponential growth and decay. The units on the ordinate and abscissa are arbitrary. The important thing to note is the form of the rise (positive exponent) or decay (negative exponent).

Figure 4-1 provides a graphic view of exponential growth and decay. If the exponential term is positive (growth), the value of the variable will increase over time, at an ever-increasing rate. If the value of the exponent is negative (decay), the value decreases toward, but never actually reaches, zero. The rate of decrease slows over time.

Exponential growth and decay processes occur in many situations in the physical, social, and behavioral sciences. Here are a few examples. The first is truly famous.

Achilles and the Tortoise. About 2,300 years ago, Greek mathematicians posed this problem. Imagine a race between the Greek hero, Achilles, and a tortoise. Achilles generously grants the tortoise a head start. At the beginning of the race, the tortoise is at distance D_0 ahead of Achilles. At each second, Achilles halves the distance between himself and the tortoise. Clearly Achilles is going faster than the tortoise. But he never actually catches the tortoise!

The Greeks saw this as a paradox, for they were sure that if the race were run Achilles would catch the tortoise. The matter was not fully resolved until the seventeenth century when Newton and Leibniz, in parallel discoveries, developed the calculus. Phrased in modern terms, the problem is

$$\frac{dD}{dt} = -rD, \tag{4-13}$$

where $-r$ is the rate at which Achilles reduces the distance between himself and the tortoise. Applying equation (4-12) with an appropriate change of variables,

$$D_t = D_0 e^{-rt}. \tag{4-14}$$

Because D_t never actually reaches zero, Achilles never catches the tortoise! But he does come arbitrarily close, and catches up at $t = \infty$.

The next model applies to survival of a population that has no entrants, such as the veterans of World War II or the group of individuals born at the same time. Such groups are called *cohorts*.

Simple Mortality Model. Let N_0 be the number of people originally in the cohort. Individuals drop out of the cohort at rate p. This is a version of the Achilles and the tortoise problem, in which

$$\frac{dN}{dt} = -pN$$
$$N_t = N_0 e^{-pt}. \tag{4-15}$$

Equation (4-15) is not a good model for people because the probability of "leaving the population" increases as one ages. On the other hand, this is a good population model for many birds and small mammals, who are usually killed by accident or predation at a constant rate before they reach old age. It is also a good model for the failure rate of many electronic components.

Finally, we have a common business example, compound interest.

The Debt of El Cid. In the twelfth-century Spanish epic *El Cid*, the hero, Ruy Diaz (El Cid, "The Leader"), is forced to go into exile in Moorish territory. Before he leaves, he borrows money from the Jewish bankers of Burgos to support his family and followers. That they were Jewish is important to the story. Medieval Christians were not allowed to charge each other interest.

Suppose that El Cid borrowed C_0 pesetas (1 peseta $\approx$ .01 euros) at a rate of interest u. The money owed increased at the rate

$$\frac{dC}{dt} = uC, \tag{4-16}$$

and after t time periods, El Cid owed $C_t = C_0^{tu}$.

Exactly the same thing will happen to you if you don't make payments on your credit card account. A glance at the positive exponential curve in Figure 4-1 shows that unpaid loans can rapidly get out of hand. El Cid seized Valencia from the Moors in order to settle his debts. I hope you will find a simpler, more peaceful solution.

Next, we look at an example where it seems as though the exponential law should apply, but it does not. It illustrates why differences

TABLE 4-1. *Performance in Autobiographical Memory*

Retention Interval (Half Years)	Percent Recalled
1	70
2	50
3	44
4	46
5	43
6	40
7	35
8	33
9	33

Source: Data taken from Wagenaar (1986), Table 2.

between a theoretical and an observed function may themselves be of interest.

Long-Term Forgetting. The Dutch psychologist Wilhem Wagenaar conducted an experiment in which he studied his own memory over a period of six years.[1] Each evening he wrote down what had happened to him that day, omitting only what he describes as "intimate details." At the end of six years, he attempted to recall the details of randomly chosen events. Table 4-1 shows the percent of details recalled as a function of the age of the memory. Does this data conform to the exponential model of forgetting? How would you estimate the forgetting rate? Are there systematic deviations from the model? If there are, what do they imply?

Let us take the first question: Does the exponential decay model apply? The extent to which data conform to a model is called the *fit* of the model to the data. There are well-developed statistical procedures for determining what the fit is. I will allude to these techniques briefly. More detailed discussions can be found in textbooks on statistics.

Figure 4-2 shows Wagenaar's data and the best-fitting exponential model for that data. The model was obtained using a standard statistical method known as *least squares fitting*. Write $x_{observed,t}$ for the data points in Table , and write $x_{predicted,t}$ for the predicted value of the data points. By the definition of the exponential model,

$$x_{predicted,\, t} = x_{predicted,0} e^{-rt},$$ (4-17)

---

[1] Wagenaar (1986).

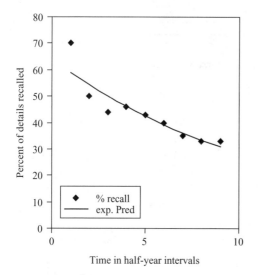

Time in half-year intervals

FIGURE 4-2. An exponential model fit to Wagenaar's retention data (Table 4-1). The symbols mark observed data points.

where r is the unknown rate of change in the amount of information retained and x_0 is the percentage of the information that Wagenaar could have reported if he had been queried immediately after an event occurred. Our goal is to estimate r and x_0.

The first step in estimation is to convert the data to a linear form, making it easier to work with. Let $y_{observed,t} = \ln(x_{observed,t})$, where ln is the natural logarithmic function. Applying this transformation to the predicted values,

$$y_{predicted,t} = \ln(x_{predicted,t})$$
$$y_{predicted,t} = \ln(x_{predicted,0}e^{-rt}) \qquad (4\text{-}18)$$
$$y_{predicted,t} = \ln(x_{predicted,0}) - rt.$$

The last line of equation (4-18) is the linear form that we seek. Standard statistical methods (covered in courses in statistics, but not here) are used to find values for r and x_0 that minimize the quantity $\Sigma_t (y_{observed,t} - y_{predicted,t})^2$. This is a reasonable definition of fit, for the sum would be zero (perfect fit) if the observed and predicted values were identical, and increases as they move apart. The degree of fit obtained is often evaluated by the squared correlation between observed and predicted values, R^2. R^2 ranges from one, for a perfect fit, to zero, which is the expected value of R^2 if there is no relation between the observed and predicted values.

Figure 4-2 shows the results of fitting Wagenaar's data to the best-fitting exponential model. The R^2 value is .87, which is fairly good for data from a memory experiment of this size, but leaves some room for improvement. More importantly, as the figure shows, the deviations from the model are systematic. Memory for more recent events is better than the model predicts, but as the age of memory increases, the initial drop in retention is faster than predicted. For the period from two years (four half years) to nine half years, the fit of the model to the data is quite good.

When faced with discrepancies like this, there are two things that a mathematical modeler can do. The first is to consider alternative but fairly minor modifications of the model in the hopes that they will improve the fit.

Turning to the literature on memory, we find that D. C. Rubin and A. E. Wenzel[2] conducted a massive review in which they evaluated 105 different mathematical models against 210 published data sets! (Wagenaar's was not included.) Among other things, they concluded that one of the best-fitting models was a variant of the exponential, in which the decay is in the square root of time,

$$x_t = x_0 e^{-r\sqrt{t}}. \tag{4-19}$$

This suggests that decay of memory occurs in a "psychological" time that is compressed relative to actual time. I applied this model and found that it fit somewhat better ($R^2 = .90$), but that the improvement is hardly marked. Furthermore, the same systematic deviations between model and data were found; forgetting was too rapid for the model at first, but it fitted the model well at later time periods.

The modeler then has to do some thinking. Unsystematic differences would be shown by data points scattered off the curve, over its entire length. That would be evidence that many variables other than the model variable (here, age of memory) influence the outcome. In this case the differences between data and the model are systematic, suggesting that rather than being a single decay process, memory may consist of two or more forgetting processes acting on different time scales. Some such models have been suggested,[3] but going into them would lead us too far into psychology. What we are concerned with is the message for mathematical modeling.

One of the most important steps in science is the detection of patterns in data. Mathematical modeling is a way of specifying, precisely, what pattern we are looking for. Systematic deviations between data and model can be extremely informative, for they tell us what we do not understand.

---

[2] Rubin and Wenzel (1996).
[3] See Bahrick and Hall (1991), for one such theory, together with supporting data.

We will now look at some more complicated models, involving more than one variable and both difference and differential equations. When possible, it is advisable to solve such models algebraically. However, that is not always possible. This is not cause for despair, for a surprising bit can be learned by graphical and numerical analyses, as will be shown in the following three-variable model.

4.4. NUMERICAL ANALYSIS: THE TRANSMISSION OF JOKES AND COLDS

From an epidemiological viewpoint, the transmission of colds and infectious diseases, such as influenza, are influenced by behavioral parameters. To begin, we analyze this process by an oversimplified model. We start with some infected people. Assume that a person with a cold meets a second person. If the second person has not already had the cold, then there is some probability, b, that the second person will catch the cold. Fortunately, though, there is also a probability, c, that a cold or flu will subside. Once a person has recovered, he or she has a temporary immunity.

Something of the same process applies to rumors and jokes. We start with people who know the story. Each time a person who knows the joke and still thinks it is interesting encounters someone who does not know the story, there is a probability, b, that the story will be passed on. There is also some probability, c, that a person who knows the story decides not to pass it on anymore.

I will use the terminology of cold transmission to illustrate the mathematics. Rather than talk about numbers of people in the population, it is convenient to talk about the fraction of population in various states of transmission.

First define

x_t = the fraction of the population who have the cold,

y_t = the fraction of people who have not had the cold, and

$z_t = 1 - x_t - y_t$ be the fraction of people who have recovered and are immune.

$b(0 < b \leq 1)$ = the probability that in any time period a cold will be transmitted by an encounter between an active carrier and a person who has not yet had the cold.

$c(0 < c \leq 1)$ = the probability that a person who has the cold will recover and be immune.

We also assume that in each time period, every person randomly encounters one other person in the population. This is called *random mixing*.

An overly simple model of cold transmission is

$$x_{t+1} = (1 - c)x_t + bx_ty_t$$
$$y_{t+1} = y_t - bx_ty_t = y(t)(1 - bx_t) \qquad (4\text{-}20)$$
$$z_{t+1} = z_t + cx_t.$$

The first line of (4-20) says

> the fraction of people who have a cold at time $t + 1 =$ the fraction of people who had the cold at time t and did not recover

plus

> the fraction of meetings during time t between a person with a cold and one without, *multiplied by* the probability that the person without the cold caught it.

I strongly suggest that the reader say, in words, what each of the other lines of equations 4-20 means.

Now for a numerical example. Suppose that initially $x_0 = .05$, $y_0 = .95$, and $z_0 = 0$. We consider a cold that lasts an average of 7 days, so that c is approximately .14, and that is fairly contagious, $b = .3$. Figure 4-3 shows what happens over a 60-day period. The fraction of people with active infections rises from .05, at the start, to a maximum of slightly more than .25 at about 20–22 days. The number of infections falls thereafter, and is near zero by the end of the period. By this time, about 70% of the people in the population have had the infection and become immune.

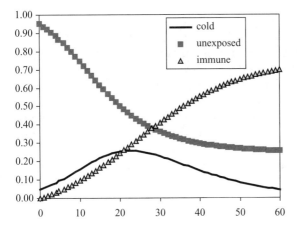

FIGURE 4-3. The predicted course of a cold, influenza, or rumor epidemic using a simplified model. $x(0) = .05$, $b = .3$, $c = .14$.

Exploring the Model

In order to show that the model portrays what is going on, we have to compare the behavior of the mathematical model to observations of the actual situation. What is done is to vary the *initial conditions* and the *parameters* in order to bring the model as close to the data as possible. We have already seen one example of this, in fitting the exponential model to Wagenaar's memory data. There we used a closed-form expression to find the best-fitting values. In other situations, the problem is harder because there is no way to find the best-fitting values analytically. Therefore, the modern practice often is to search for the best possible values using a computer. The technique will now be illustrated, with an emphasis on the logic of the search, rather than upon the algorithms that would be used in a real situation.

Here the initial condition is the assumption that .05 of the individuals in the population start with the cold. The parameters are our assumptions about the probability that a healthy person will catch a cold when he or she is exposed to one (b) and how long a cold is likely to last (c). Once the initial conditions define the starting state of the system (at $t = 0$) the parameters control the transitions from one system state to the next. Often the changes introduced by varying the initial conditions and the parameters are obvious, but, as we are about to see, variation sometimes produces surprises.

We will now go through this process, using simulated data that I generated in such a way that it was related to but did not exactly fit the model.

Figure 4-4 shows the data for absences due to colds in a (hypothetical) school system. It also shows the predicted number of cases at each time period, using the model given, and multiplying the "colds" numbers by the total number of students, 18,174.[4] The data are "lumpy," in the sense that they do not seem to fit any smooth curve. This is typical of actual data. They usually reflect the fact that the real system is subject to some influences that are not represented in the mathematical model.

Figure 4-4 shows that the model predicts many more infections than there are. The prediction is bad right from the start, before the parameters can have much influence. This is an indication that our initial conditions are not correct. Since the initial infection rate seems to be half that initially built into the model, let us drop the initial infection rate (starting condition) to .025. The result of this change is shown in Figure 4-5.

This model does a good job of predicting the initial rise in infections but predicts too many infections. Can we adjust the parameters in such a

---

[4] This number was chosen because it approximated the number of students in the Seattle school system, as of 2003.

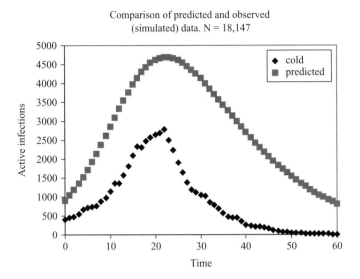

FIGURE 4-4. Simulated and predicted data for absences due to colds in a school district with a population of 18,174 students. Initial starting value = .05, $b = .3$, $c = .14$.

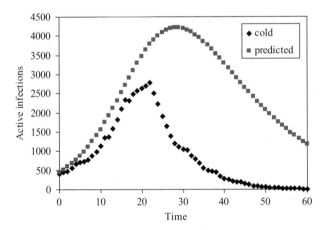

FIGURE 4-5. A second comparison of data to the cold model, with a .025 starting value.

way that the model can be brought closer to the data? This forces us to think about both the model and the process that is being modeled.

In the case of the cold model, the disease might be more contagious than we thought (so b is too low) or the length of an infection might

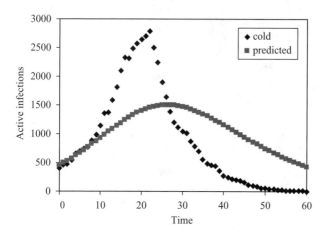

FIGURE 4-6. The model fit with starting condition $= .025$, $b = .3$, and $c = .2$.

be longer than we thought (c is too low). The fact that the model and data agree about the initial rise in infections suggests, but does not prove, that the contagion rate, b, is about right. On the other hand, the fall in infections during the later stages of the epidemic is very poorly modeled.

Suppose that we increase the "get cured" parameter, c, from .14 to .2. The result is shown in Figure 4-6.

This change lowers the peak value too much. But we still have an additional parameter to deal with! People seem to be catching the cold faster than we thought. So let us increase the predicted susceptibility by increasing the "contagion" parameter to .4. Before we discuss the results, try to answer the following question:

Clearly increasing the contagion parameter will increase the rate at which the number of infections rises. What will it do to the rate at which people become immune?

The results of raising the contagion rate are shown in Figure 4-7. Clearly we are getting closer, although things are still not quite right.

The biggest discrepancy seems to be that the fall in infections is greater in the data than in the model. This suggests a further increase in the "cure" parameter, to $c = .25$. The result is shown in Figure 4-8. We now have a pretty good estimate of the rising and falling portions of the curve, but we miss badly in predicting the peak infection rate.

As our final estimate, we change the contagion rate, b, to .45. The result is shown in Figure 4-9. This looks pretty good, and so we stop at this point to ask a few questions.

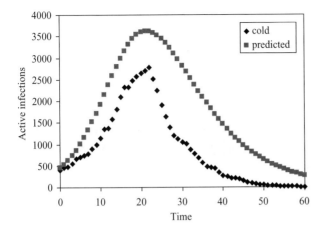

FIGURE 4-7. The model fit with start $= .025$, $b = .4$, and $c = .2$.

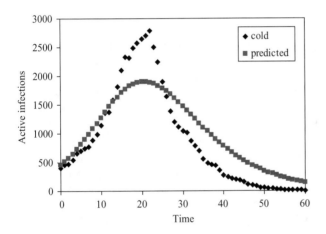

FIGURE 4-8. Model and data, with start $= .025$, $b = .4$, $c = .25$.

4.5. QUESTIONS ABOUT MODELING

1. *Is this what scientists really do?*
   Yes, with some refinements. First, the models are usually much more complicated than the model shown here. For instance, in our target model, we assumed that there was a single probability, c, of going from the infected to non-infected state, regardless of how long a person had had a cold. In a more realistic disease model, the probability of becoming non-infected increases the longer that you have been infected.

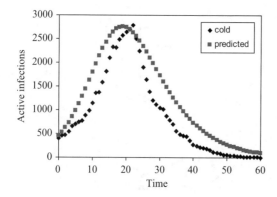

FIGURE 4-9. Comparison of "observations" to predictions with a starting state $x_0 = .025$, $b = .45$, $c = .25$.

2. *Do scientists really adjust parameters this way?*
   No, not exactly. Scientists do not adjust parameters and starting values "by eyeball." Ideally, there will be an analytic method for determining the best parameters, as was the case for the exponential decay model. In other cases, computers are used to try out different combinations of parameters. The illustration given here approximates this sort of solution.

3. *Is it always possible to get close agreement between the model and the data?*
   Alas, no, even if you have the right model! In most situations in the social sciences, the natural process being described is produced both by the effects being modeled and by other things. This is the open system–closed system problem, once again. In the population example, we assumed that the population is static; that is, people are not going in and out. In any real-world example, we would also have to deal with the effects of migrations into and out of the population. Nevertheless, for all its artificiality, the model-fitting process shown here is not that far from what happens in practice.

4. *What sort of conclusions can be drawn from modeling?*
   The equations in a model are generated from assumptions about the causes of what is being observed. If the resulting equations provide a good fit to the data, this is evidence that the causes assumed in the model may be the causes operating in the real world. It is never conclusive evidence, though, for there always might be some other process that generated an even better description, or a description of more data. The goal is not to "prove a theory"; it is to find where current theories break down so that they can be improved. The more extensive the exploration, though, the more accurate the models become. Science is always tentative, but some things are more tentative than others!

Even with these qualifications, the modeling exercise is highly worthwhile. The quest for ever more accurate models is only one reason why modeling can be valuable. Sometimes the parameter values are of interest in themselves. In the modeling exercise here, we settled on a *b* value of .45. This suggests that the infection will be passed on in roughly half the encounters between an infected and an uninfected person. A finding like this would be an argument for quarantining infected individuals, especially if the disease is serious. For example, the SARS virus, a severe disease related to influenza, is highly contagious and, in fact, SARS patients are quarantined. Tuberculosis is also a severe pulmonary disease, but it is much less infectious, and so tuberculosis patients are not severely quarantined.

A third use of modeling is to predict future values. Suppose that an epidemiologist found that the model just given did accurately describe past epidemics. If a new flu bug appeared, the epidemiologist could use the first few days' or week's reports to estimate the parameters, and then predict how severe the epidemic was likely to be. This information could (and sometimes does) guide decisions about public health expenditures. Using our example again, early indications of a highly contagious disease are valuable because, if a disease is highly contagious, health professionals can take precautions to avoid being infected when they interact with patients. This is exactly what happened on the first appearance of the SARS virus, in the summer of 2003.

Another use of models is to evaluate "what if" scenarios. In these scenarios the modeler investigates the effects of changing some of the parameters of the model, not to match the data but rather to see what would happen if some action were taken that would influence that parameter. This process is very much like what we did for the cold model, in order to fit data to the model. The only difference is that this time there are no data; the adjustment process is interesting in itself. Studies of the weather provide a good example in the physical sciences. Various models have been used to demonstrate what we think the effects might be of global warming, or (during the Cold War) of the nuclear fallout and firestorms that would have resulted from a major exchange of nuclear weapons.

Many readers will have already heard of the global warming example. Indeed, when we think about it, we realize that we are quite used to seeing mathematical models used in the physical sciences. To close this section I provide three examples of actual modeling in the social and behavioral sciences, and then present a challenge problem. First, the examples.

1. *Creutzfeldt-Jakob (CJ) disease.* This disease is a debilitating, wasting, and fortunately quite rare degenerative disease attacking the

nervous system. The disease develops slowly. Symptoms may not appear until years after a person is infected. There seem to be two sources for the infection. One is genetic susceptibility. In addition, though, a person may become infected by eating meat from an animal that had the related "mad cow" disease. In this case, a person may not show symptoms of CJ until as much as 10 years after the meat has been eaten.

In the late 1990s, an unusual number of CJ cases appeared in the United Kingdom. They are believed to have been due to meat from animals with undetected cases of mad cow disease. After heroic efforts, health authorities believe that they have eliminated mad cow disease in Britain. But how many incidences of CJ disease are now latent in the population, to appear sometime in the next 10 years?

Two models of the epidemic have been offered.[5] The models predict annual incidences of the disease in Britain that, depending on the model and parameters used, range from dozens to about a thousand cases per year. While this may seem small in a country of roughly 100 million people, the previous incidence of CJ disease was fewer than 10 cases a year.

2. *Normal aging.* Colloquially, it is well known that as people age they become slower. Several models describe age-related slowing as a result of changes in more basic processes, such as the efficiency of neural transmission. In these models a neural process is described, a mathematical model is derived from the neural processes (exactly like the steps demonstrated in the simple epidemiological model), and the model is shown to fit the data from a variety of experiments.[6]

3. *The disappearance of large mammals.* During the late Pleistocene (about 50,000 years ago), large mammals roamed North America. We had mastodons, mammoths, giant bison, and a ground sloth bigger than the present-day grizzly bear. These huge beasts disappeared around 10,000 years ago. The earliest pieces of evidence for humans in North America are the Clovis arrowheads, about 13,000 years old. Could the first human habitants of North America have hunted the giant mammals to extinction? On the one hand, it seems unlikely. The Clovis people were almost certainly aboriginal hunter-gatherers, moving on foot. The organized, well-equipped (and mounted) hunting parties of the Plains Indians did not appear until about 500 years ago. On the other hand, one of the Clovis arrowheads was found in the ribs of a giant bison.

---

[5] Huillard d'Aignaux, Cousens, and Smith (2001); Valleron et al. (2001).
[6]. Ratcliff, Spieler, and McKoon (2000).

J. Alroy developed a model that contained parameters for such things as the hunting skill of early North Americans (kills per hunter per year), the geographic dispersal of different herbivore species, the gestation period of the prey animals, and the dispersal rate of the human population. Many more parameters were used. After extensive investigation of the model with different settings, Alroy concluded: "It is hard to find a combination of parameter values that permits all species to survive."[7] His model showed that extinction could take place with surprisingly low human population densities and that the extinction probably took place over a period of about 1,500 years.

The models just described were much more complicated than the simple cold (or rumor) model developed here. Both the simple and the complex models depend upon the same logic. So now we go to the challenge problem.

In the cold example, we dealt with a homogeneous population and assumed random mixing. Here is a more realistic situation.

Challenge Problem: How Should an Influenza Vaccine Be Distributed?

In the fall of 2004, just as the influenza season was about to begin, failures in the manufacturing process left the United States with about half as much vaccine as expected. Fortunately, the ensuing influenza season was quite mild. This situation could happen again, especially if the epidemic were based on a novel virus. How should the vaccine be distributed? Here are the considerations:

1. Leaving aside key personnel, such as physicians, who must be vaccinated in order to maintain the health delivery system? There are three classes of individuals to consider: senior citizens (over 65), healthy young people and adults, 14–64, and children 13 and under.
2. In addition to the recovery parameter, c, some consideration must be given to mortality. This means that a death rate parameter, d, has to be added to the model. The death rate parameter varies markedly across the three classes of people. It is highest in senior citizens, then in children, and lowest in healthy adults.
3. Contagion rates vary both within and across the three populations. Children are the most contagious because they tend to be in closer contact with one another, especially in the lower school years. Contagion rates also vary across groups; children and adults have more contacts with each other than do children and senior citizens.

---

[7] Alroy (2001), p. 1893.

4. Various policy decisions can be made that will change the parameters. For instance, a vaccination program can be instituted. This lowers the contagion rate for those vaccinated, and also reduces the length and severity of symptoms (i.e., alters the c and d parameters) for vaccinated people. In addition, public health campaigns can be conducted that encourage people to wear masks, avoid crowds, and so on. These are generally most successful with adults and senior citizens, less so with children.

How would you model this situation to investigate the effects of various policies? Would it make any difference whether your goal was to decrease the number of people infected or the number of deaths? How would the modeling process change if your goal was to avoid premature loss of life, rather than simply minimizing deaths? To give this mathematical content, the life expectancy of a newborn in the United States (circa 2004) is 76 years. The life expectancy of a 72-year-old is 14 years; that is, the average person who is 72 today can expect to live to 86. Therefore, the loss of a newborn means a loss of 76 years of life, whereas the loss of a 72-year-old is a loss of 14 years. How could a model be developed to find policies that minimize loss of years of life, as defined earlier, instead of just minimizing deaths?

Mathematical modeling in the behavioral and social sciences deals with some very important issues.

4.6. GRAPHICAL ANALYSIS: THE EVOLUTION OF WAR AND PEACE

The exponential decay model illustrated the use of algebraic techniques to derive predictions from a model. The jokes-and-colds model illustrated the use of numerical methods to do the same thing. In this section, graphic techniques will be used to study the evolution of model systems. We then use these techniques to explore a model of interactions between two opponents ("wars") developed by Lewis F. Richardson. Richardson's personal story is worth a brief note.

Historical Note

Lewis Fry Richardson (1881–1953) was a British applied mathematician. His chief claim to fame has nothing to do with the behavioral or social sciences. During and after World War I, he developed the first mathematical models of the weather. He divided Europe into squares and considered how weather fronts would evolve as temperature and pressure stabilized across adjacent squares. This was quite a sophisticated idea for the time, but it failed because there were not as many weather observations as the models demanded, and because the numerical details could not be worked out in the pre-computer age. It would be 50 years before meteorologists would have both the data and computing power required for Richardson's daring attempt.[8]

Richardson then turned his talents toward what is arguably the greatest problem facing the social sciences, the prevention of war. Richardson, a member of the Society of Friends (Quakers), had served as an ambulance driver during World War I and, understandably, became deeply disturbed by the horrors of war. World War I had been preceded by an arms race between England and Germany. When Adolph Hitler's Nazi Party won the 1933 German elections Germany began to rearm. Richardson tried to understand the probable behavior of Germany and other European powers by developing models that he thought could be used to predict what might happen. The models predicted war, as will be described. According to legend, in 1938 he wrote to the *London Times* requesting that his equations be given front page billing. He feared that if they were not known the world might fall into war.

Well, the *Times* did not publish Richardson's work, and in 1939 World War II began. Who knows what might have happened if the equations had been published? Surely the world would have paid attention to mathematical models!

Richardson continued to worry about arms races until his death in 1953. Ironically, he died at the start of one of the greatest arms races in the world, the Cold War between the Union of Soviet Socialist Republics and the United States of America.[9]

I do not know if the legend about the *Times* is true. I do know that Richardson's equations are an elegant example of how simple principles can be used to generate complex phenomena. They also represent an interesting example of one of the great difficulties of mathematical modeling, getting the right data.

So here they are!

Richardson's Hostility Model (Expanded)

My development is based on one of Richardson's early articles, which was republished in an anthology by J. R. Newman.[10]

Two protagonists arm themselves for a fight. Let x_t be the level of arms of one protagonist at time t, and y_t be the level of arms of the other. Subsequently, the subscript t will be dropped unless it is needed to consider the system at two points in time.

The variables $\{x,y\}$ form a system because they are mutually inter-dependent. Let $S_t = (x_t, y_t)$ be the state at time t. Irreconcilable conflict

---

[8] Hayes (2001).   [9] Hayes (2002a).   [10] Newman, (1956), Richardson and Pear, 1946.

(war) is assumed to break out if the two variables move toward positive infinity, $S_t \rightarrow (\infty, \infty)$. Eternal peace and international marshmallow roasts break out if $S_t \rightarrow (-\infty, -\infty)$. More seriously, although the equations are defined for negative values of x and y, it is not clear what the definition of "negative arms" is. This is an example of a situation that is encountered fairly frequently in modeling. Models do not necessarily apply to all situations that can be defined mathematically, as some of these situations may be thought to be impossible or of little interest.

Richardson concentrated on the rate of change in arms of one combatant, as a function of the level of arms of the other:

First assumption: The rate at which combatant x arms is proportional to the level of armaments of y and vice versa.

$$\frac{dx}{dt} = ay$$
$$\frac{dy}{dt} = bx \tag{4-21}$$
$$a,b > 0.$$

Figure 4-10 shows the first of several graphs that will be used to present Richardson's model. All points in the upper right-hand quadrant of this graph represent situations in which both protagonists have some arms $(x, y > 0)$.

Consider a point $S_t = (x_t, y_t)$ in this quadrant. We are interested in the position of some subsequent point, S_{t+k}, $k > 0$. The dashed arrows in the figure represent the signs of dx/dt and dy/dt in each of the four quadrants, with an arrow pointing upward or to the right representing an increase.

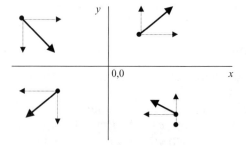

FIGURE 4-10. A diagram of the relations between successive points in Richardson's initial war model. Once the system is in the positive quadrant $(x, y > 0)$, each successive point must lie above and to the right of its predecessor. If the system is in the negative quadrant $(x, y < 0)$, there is a similar motion down and to the left. If the system is either of the other two quadrants, movement is toward the origin.

When x and y are both positive, $x_t < x_{t+k}$ and $y_t < y_{t+k}$, one arrow points to the right while the other points upward. The solid arrow shows the movement of the system as a whole. S_{t+k} is always upward and to the right of S_t. The system moves inexorably to (∞, ∞).

By an analogous argument, the system goes to $(-\infty, -\infty)$ if it ever enters the lower left quadrant (negative values of x and y). However, it is hard to interpret just what this means.

If the system ever enters the first quadrant, where both parties have a non-zero level of arms, it proceeds inevitably to the (∞, ∞) point, which Richardson interpreted as "war." At each step, the rate of movement upward or to the left will be greater than it was at the previous moment. This is shown in Figure 4-11, which illustrates movement at three successive points in the upper right-hand quadrant. The further the system goes toward positive infinity, the faster it goes.

Question: Suppose the system is started in the second or fourth quadrants. What determines whether or not it will move to (0,0)? Under what conditions will it cross into the first quadrant? The third?

A *point of equilibrium* is a point at which a system stops moving. In Richardson's simple model the origin (0,0) is a point of equilibrium. For at this point

$$\frac{dx}{dt} = a \bullet 0 = 0$$

$$\frac{dy}{dt} = b \bullet 0 = 0. \tag{4-22}$$

In Richardson's interpretation, the only way that the simple model produces peace is if both parties disarm. The equilibrium is *unstable*, because any displacement of x or y from zero will, depending upon the

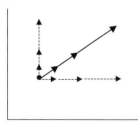

FIGURE 4-11. Under the conditions of the simple model movement toward (∞, ∞) is accelerated whenever the system is in the positive quadrant.

nature of the displacement, send the system toward (∞, ∞) or ($-\infty$, $-\infty$). Because of this instability, Richardson regarded his initial model as too prone toward predicting disaster. Therefore, he considered some more complicated cases.

Acceptable Levels of Armament

Suppose that each opponent is willing to permit the other a non-threatening level of armament for legitimate purposes, such as internal policing or protection against a third party. The United States made a variant of this argument in its nuclear disarmament talks with Russia, following the collapse of the Soviet Union. The Americans and Russians agreed that each should maintain nuclear arms sufficient to discourage any nation from attacking, but not sufficient in size and quality to allow either side to overwhelm the other's retaliatory power. The mathematical expression is

$$\frac{dx}{dt} = a(y - Y)$$
$$\frac{dy}{dt} = b(x - X),$$

(4-23)

where X and Y, are the permissible levels allowed x and y, respectively.

Figure 4-12 shows that all this does is translate the original analysis to a new point of unstable equilibrium, (X, Y) instead of $(0,0)$.

The Burden of Arms

This led Richardson to his third model, which is the last that we shall discuss. He argued that the rate at which a nation armed should be proportional to the level of its opponent's arms, but should decrease

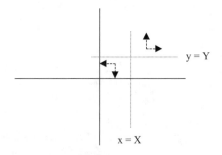

FIGURE 4-12. Richardson's arms race model with permissible levels of armament, (X, Y), allowed for each party.

proportional to the level of its own arms. His argument for this assumption was that the expense of a high level of armament exerts a slowing influence on an arms race. We have

$$\frac{dx}{dt} = ay - cx$$

$$\frac{dy}{dt} = -dy + bx \tag{4-24}$$

$$a,b,c,d > 0.$$

The conditions for an equilibrium are

$$\frac{dx}{dt} = 0 \Leftrightarrow y = \frac{c}{a} \bullet x$$

$$\frac{dy}{dt} = 0 \Leftrightarrow y = \frac{b}{d} \bullet x. \tag{4-25}$$

These are the equations for straight lines passing through the origin, as shown in 4-13. Whenever the system is on the $y = (c/a)x$ line, nation x maintains its current level of arms. The same is true for nation y whenever the system is on the $y = (b/d)x$ line.

The system as a whole is in equilibrium only at points that are on both lines. As Figure 4-13 shows, this occurs only at the origin, $S_t = (0,0)$, unless the two lines are identical,

$$\frac{c}{a} = \frac{b}{d}. \tag{4-26}$$

Another way to think of this equation is that it implies that the product of the two hostility coefficients, a and b, must be equal to the product of the two cost-of-arms coefficients, c and d. However, this condition does not imply symmetry. The condition $ab = cd$ could be met if the cost of arms was higher than the hostility coefficient for one party (say, $a < c$), while for the other party, hostility was higher than the cost of arms ($b > d$). In this case the opponents are asymmetric, in the sense that for one, the cost of arms must be higher than the hostility coefficient, while for the other, the cost of arms must be lower than the hostility coefficient. This case is shown in Figure 4-14.

The line shown in Figure 4-14 will be called the *line of joint stability*. It is the locus of all points at which both opponents cease changing their levels of arms. Hence, any point on the line of joint stability is an equilibrium point.

Unfortunately, none of the equilibrium points are stable. Suppose that the system is initially on the line of joint stability, and is then displaced by some random event that moves either y upward or x to the left. The system will move to a new equilibrium point, to the upper right of the

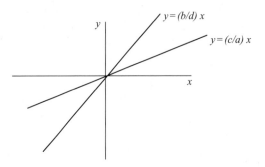

FIGURE 4-13. Richardson's model for increases in rate of arming proportional to the opponent's arms level and for decreases in rate proportional to the level of one's own arms.

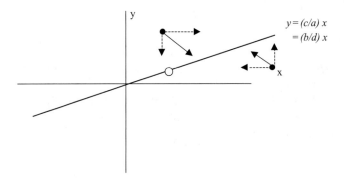

FIGURE 4-14. Suppose that the system is initially in equilibrium and the condition $c/a = b/d$ holds. This is shown by the open circle. If the system is displaced upward (increase in y) or rightward (increase in x), it will move back toward the equilibrium line but at higher values for x and y.

point at which it started. This corresponds to the two opponents stabilizing their armaments at higher levels than they were before the perturbation. Conversely, if one party decreases its own arms level, its opponent will also decrease, stabilizing the system at a point to the lower left on the line of joint stability.

It can be argued that this model approximates what happened during the Cold War between the United States and the USSR from 1945 until 1991. The Cold War was characterized by periods of equilibrium, where both sides stabilized their arms level, with the United States somewhat better armed. Then one side would make a breakthrough in weapons design, or respond to a political threat by repositioning troops in a more advantageous position. The other side would respond, and after a while there would be a new period of stability, at a higher level of armament, but once again with the United States better armed than the USSR. A breakthrough occurred when Mikhail Gorbachev, the last premier of the USSR, removed Soviet troops from what was then East Germany. This would correspond to a reduction in y. Both sides reduced their forces, reaching a new stable point with reduced arms. Richardson's simple model did predict what happened!

The problem with the stability shown in Figure 4-14 is that it relies on the special conditions of equation 4-26. Richardson believed that the hostility parameters (a,c) would always be greater than the cost parameters. This meant that the conditions of 4-26 could never be met, for

$$(a > c) \,|\cap|\, (b > d) \Rightarrow ab > cd$$
$$a > c \Rightarrow \frac{a}{c} > 1 \hspace{3cm} (4\text{-}27)$$
$$b > d \Rightarrow \frac{b}{d} > 1.$$

Richardson's argument for this pessimistic assumption was that governments reacted almost immediately to threats, while cost-cutting measures were introduced over fairly long intervals. Figure 4-15 shows this situation graphically, using arrows to indicate the direction of motion of x and y in each region of the space.

Figure 4-15 shows that the direction of movement is controlled by the position where the system is relative to the lines defining $dx/dt = 0$ and $dy/dt = 0$. If the system is ever located in a region where both x and y are positive (i.e., where both opponents have some arms), it then moves to positive infinity. War is inevitable once the arms race begins. That is why Richardson was pessimistic about Europe in the 1930s.

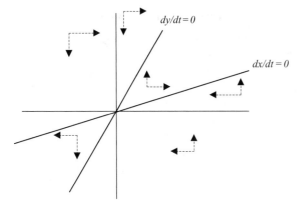

FIGURE 4-15. An analysis of Richardson's most general model. If $x > 0$ and $y > 0$, the system will move to (∞, ∞).

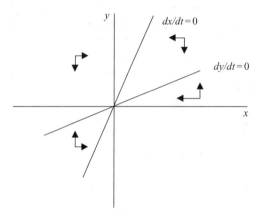

FIGURE 4-16. If the cost of arms exceeds the perceived benefits of arming ($c > a$ and $d > b$), the system will move toward a stable equilibrium at $(0,0)$.

Of course, an analogous conclusion can be reached about movement from a situation of joint negative arms ($x,y < 0$) toward the negative infinity point. While the definition of negative arms is unclear, one can conceive of situations characterized by exchanges of compliments or, more likely, engagement in trade.

Finally, suppose that we had a situation in which the cost of armaments exceeded the level of hostility for both opponents. In other words, suppose Richardson was wrong about how parliamentarians react to hostile threats or increases in the arms budget. This case, shown in Figure 4-16, is similar to Figure 4-15 except that the line that originally represented $dx/dt = 0$ now represents $dy/dt = 0$, and vice versa. The system moves toward a stable equilibrium at $0, 0$. This is a highly desirable state of affairs.

Challenge Problem: The General Conditions for System Stability

Within the framework of Richardson's model, it seems to be difficult to find conditions that will not lead to conflict. That does not mean that the model is wrong; the history of humanity suggests that war is disturbingly frequent. Suppose that Richardson's notion of acceptable levels of armament (Equation 4-23) were to be combined with an assumption that parliaments will be swifter to react to threats than to the cost of arms ($a > c$, $b > d$). Does this make any difference to the argument, and if so, how?

The cold/joke and war models are both models of systems evolving over time. The ways in which these models were analyzed is instructive. In both cases, the models were analyzed using graphics. However, the use of graphics was quite different. In the cold/joke model, graphic analysis was used to determine the effects of varying values of parameters. In a sense, graphics substituted for arithmetic. Or, to be more honest, the arithmetic was relegated to a computer and the result of the arithmetic was displayed graphically. In the case of Richardson's war model, graphics were used to find general solutions that depended upon the relative size of numbers but not their absolute size. In this case, graphical analysis substituted for algebra. Both techniques are certainly valuable. In some cases, though, we may want to proceed directly to the algebra. That is what is done in the next example.

There is another important contrast between Richardson's work and the disease transmission model. Disease transmission models are intended to be applied, and are applied, to real data. The models actually used are more complicated than the one presented here, but the principles are the same. The models are used to evaluate threats to public health and to plan possible countermeasures. Are they taken seriously?

At his retirement in December of 2004, U.S. Secretary of Health and Human Services "Tommy" Thompson identified what he considered the two most serious threats to the nation's health. One of these was the possibility of a pandemic of influenza, brought on by a virus mutating from an avian to a human-lethal form, and then jumping the species barriers from birds to humans.[11] The secretary's concern was based on two things: first, a few isolated cases of an avian virus infecting humans in Asia and second, mathematical modeling that showed that under certain, believable conditions, an avian virus could spread in a manner similar to the progress of a worldwide pandemic in 1918–19. Secretary Thompson was convinced by modeling, for at the time there was no compelling evidence that the 1918 epidemic actually was of avian origin. Research completed the following year showed that the secretary's fears were well founded, because the 1918 outbreak was caused by a mutated avian influenza virus.

Whether or not the legend about the *London Times* is true, Richardson's war models were certainly not taken seriously in his time. One of the reasons is that Richardson was not able to connect his models to data. Do you use the absolute arms budget of a country? If this is done, the large countries tend to be more warlike. Do you use the arms budget *per capita*? If this is done, small countries may appear more warlike. Do you use the arms budget as a percentage of the gross domestic product? If this is done, a country that has large natural resources and a small population (e.g., Saudi Arabia) will appear peaceful. Richardson himself used the arms budget per employed person, which seems to have been accepted.

Connecting with data is important. Richardson's models are interesting conceptually, but it is not clear how one operationalizes them. Models of the spread of disease, which can be connected to data, are used to make major policy decisions.

---

[11] The other was the possibility that terrorists would poison an important part of the nation's food supply.

4.7. MAKING LOVE, NOT WAR: THE GOTTMAN-MURRAY
MODEL OF MARITAL INTERACTIONS

Enough of diseases and wars! We next look at a model of love! Or to be more accurate, a model of the interactions between romantic partners. The modeling techniques resemble Richardson's, but are more elaborate.

Toward the end of the twentieth century, Professor John Gottman, a clinical psychologist on the faculty of the University of Washington, found a way to use a brief interview to characterize relationships between romantically involved couples. Gottman had couples come into his laboratory for a 15-minute conversation about some topic of difficulty in their relationship. The conversations were recorded on videotape. Gottman and his colleagues then coded each person's statements in a variety of ways. We will be interested in only one coding, whether or not the statement was encouraging (positive affect) or disparaging (negative affect). Gottman and his colleagues collaborated with James Murray, a professor of mathematics at Washington, to develop several mathematical models of the interactions between partners.[12] The model that I will describe, which I refer to as the Gottman-Murray model, is one of these.[13]

In the Gottman-Murray model, each person is assumed to have a characteristic level of positivity in his/her speech, and to carry forward some of the level of affect from their expressions during the previous time period. Let P_t be the positivity level of an expression at time t, with positive values indicating positive affect, and negative values negative affect. The basic equation for a person's reaction to his or her own statements is

$$P_{t+1} = r_p P_t + a, \qquad (4\text{-}28)$$

where r_p is a positive constant less than one, reflecting the extent to which a person continues the tone of conversation expressed in the previous time period, and a is the typical level of affect (which may be positive or negative) in the person's conversations. Write $\Delta_{t+1}(P)$ for the difference between the positivity level at times t and $t+1$ ($\Delta_{t+1}(P) = P_{t+1} - P_t$). (This is the analog of a differential for the case of finite intervals.) The conversation level is in equilibrium if there is no change in affect; that is, $\Delta_{t+1}(P) = 0$. The condition for this is

$$\begin{aligned}
\Delta_{t+1} &= 0 \Leftrightarrow P_{t+1} = P_t \\
P_t &= r_p P_t + a \\
P_t &= \frac{a}{1 - r_p}.
\end{aligned} \qquad (4\text{-}29)$$

---

[12] Gottman et al. (2002).   [13] See Murray (2001) for a related model.

Equation 4-29 shows that the equilibrium point for a single speaker, uninfluenced by a partner, can have either positive or negative affect, depending upon the sign of a. For brevity, and because the imputation seems to mirror the mathematics, I will refer to a person who is characterized by a positive value of a as a *Pollyanna*, and a person characterized by a negative value as a *Grinch*. These definitions do not require that a Pollyanna always produce positive communications or that a Grinch always produce negative communications. The terms are defined for the equilibrium point only.

If the speaker begins at affect level P_0 it is easy to see that $P_1 = r_p P_0 + a$, and that $P_2 = r_p(r_p\, P_0 + a) + a$, or, equivalently, $P_2 = r_p^2 P_0 + a(r_p + 1)$. At the next step,

$$P_3 = r_p P_2 + a$$
$$P_3 = r_p^3 P_0 + r_p(a(r_p + 1)) + a$$
$$P_3 = r_p^3 P_0 + a(r_p^2 + r_p) + a$$
$$P_3 = r_p^3 P_0 + a(r_p^2 + r_p + 1).$$

Extending this pattern,

$$P_t = r_p^t P_0 + a \sum_{k=0}^{t-1} r_p^k$$

$$P_t = r_p^t P_0 + \frac{a(1 - r_p^t)}{1 - r_p},$$

(4-30)

because

$$\sum_{k=0}^{t-1} r_p^k = \frac{1 - r_p^t}{1 - r_p}.$$

A proof of this statement is given in a footnote.[14]

Equation (4-30) can be thought of as a model of changes in affect over the course of a monologue. Gottman and Murray were interested in changes during a dialogue between two partners. In order to model the dialogue we need terms for the influence of the husband on the wife, and vice versa.

---

[14] The summation is of the form

$$\sum_{k=0}^{K} r^k.$$

Let $I_{hw}(t)$ be the husband's influence on his wife at time t, and $I_{wh}(t)$ be the wife's influence on the husband. Gottman and Murray consider a *bilinear* influence model, in which the degree of influence depends upon whether the speaker's statement is positive or negative, letting H_t and W_t be the husband's and wife's statements at time t. The effects of these statements are, for the husband on the wife,

$$I_{hw}(t) = b_1 H_t \Leftrightarrow H_t > 0$$
$$I_{hw}(t) = b_2 H_t \Leftrightarrow H_t < 0 \tag{4-31}$$
$$b_1 < b_2.$$

Analogous equations apply for the wife's influence on the husband, with coefficients c_1 and c_2, $c_2 > c_1$. The requirement that the coefficients for negative affect be greater than those for positive affect came from Gottman's observation that negative communications seem to have a greater influence on one's partner than do positive communications.

This is a geometric series. The sum S_K, for any value of K is given by

$$S_K = \sum_{k=0}^{K} r^k$$

$$rS_K = \sum_{k=0}^{K} rr^k$$

$$rS = \sum_{k=1}^{K+1} r^k.$$

Taking the difference of these terms,

$$S_K - rS_k = \sum_{k=0}^{K} r^k - \sum_{k=1}^{K+1} r^k$$
$$S_K - rS_k = (r^K + r^{K-1} + \dots + r^2 + r + 1)$$
$$\qquad\qquad - (r^{K+1} + r^K + r^{K-1} + \dots + r^2 + r)$$
$$S_K - rS_k = 1 - r^{K+1}$$
$$S_K(1 - r) = 1 - r^{K+1}$$
$$S_K = \frac{1 - r^{K+1}}{1 - r}.$$

Making the substitutions $K = t - 1$ and $r = r_p$ establishes the equation in the text.

When both partners communicate positively with each other,

$$W_{t+1} = b_1 H_t + [r_w W_t + a]$$
$$H_{t+1} = c_1 W_t + [r_h H_t + d],$$

(4-32)

where the first term on the right represents the partner's influence on the speaker's behavior and the second term represents the speaker's own influence on his or her behavior, due to leftover effects of speech at the previous time period. The a and d terms are constants representing the wife's and husband's typical level of affect. In the case of negative communications, b_1 and c_1 are replaced by b_2 and c_2, as appropriate. The roles of the a and d terms are identical in their respective equations. Importantly, this means that the sign of a determines whether the wife is a Pollyanna or a Grinch, while the sign of d does the same for the husband.

As in the Richardson model, we are particularly interested in equilibriums. A positive equilibrium occurs if the two exchange positive messages for the wife, $W_{t+1} = W_t = W_+$, and for the husband $H_{t+1} = H_t = H_+$. A little algebra shows that

$$W_+ = \frac{b_1}{1 - r_w} H_+ + \frac{a}{1 - r_w}.$$
$$H_+ = \frac{c_1}{1 - r_h} W_+ + \frac{d}{1 - r_h}.$$

(4-33)

A second equilibrium occurs at (H_-, W_-) with b_2 and c_2 substituted for b_1 and c_1.

In words, the points of equilibrium for the husband and wife are linear functions of the other's point of equilibrium. This begins to look like Richardson's model for a stable arms race. However, the Gottman-Murray model is more complicated because the case of a message with negative affect must be considered. Because negative affect messages have greater influences than positive affect messages, the movements in husband and wife interchanges appears as in Figure 4-17. Arrows have been added, as was done for graphs of Richardson's models, to show how the system defined by husband and wife communications will change when neither partner's communications are at a stable level of affect.

The picture painted by Figure 4-17 is a mildly rosy one. The system equilibrium points (neither husband nor wife changing affect level) are the points where the H and W functions intersect. There are two such intersections, one where both husband and wife are exchanging positively charged messages (the ideal) and one where they are both exchanging negative messages (to be avoided). Furthermore, the arrows

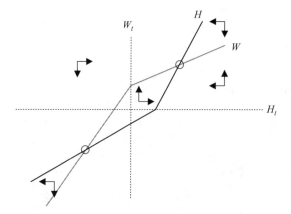

FIGURE 4-17. The bilinear equations for the affect of messages between a husband and wife, according to the Gottman and Murray model. The model is shown for the case of two Pollyannas ($a_1, d_1 > 0$).

show that over time the exchanges will go to either of these two points. And now (oh, cautious happiness) the equilibrium point for negative messages is unstable. If the system can be moved off this point by either the husband or wife being just a little less negative (system moves up or to the right, or both), the system will then move to the equilibrium point for positive messages.

But caution is called for. If insults escalate, and both partners become more negative than they are at the negative stabilization point, the couple is headed for negative infinity, which probably means the divorce court.

Marriage counselors should be encouraged. If the counselor encounters two Polyannas who seem to be stuck on exchanging insults, all the counselor has to do is to get one of the partners to be a little bit more positive.

This seems too good to be true. If it were an accurate model, almost all marriages would eventually be happy, divorces would never happen, and great stories such as *Anna Karenina* and the movie *Double Indemnity* would never have been written. Therapy would always work! But that is not the world we live in.

The Gottman-Murray model can accommodate unhappy marriages. It does so by considering the equilibrium point for each partner's speeches when not influenced by the other partner, either H_t or W_t equal to zero. Equation 4-33 becomes

$$W = \frac{a}{1 - r_w}.$$

$$H = \frac{d}{1 - r_h}.$$

(4-34)

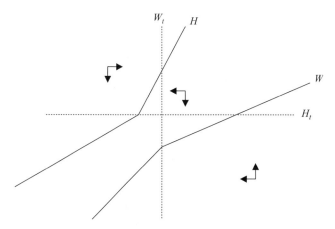

FIGURE 4-18. Movement of conversations for the case of two Grinches in the Gottman-Murray model. The system is bilinear because different linear equations apply for reactions to statements with positive or negative affect.

These are the points at which the H or the W functions in Figure 4-17 cross the W_t or H_t axes, respectively. The sign of these points depends upon the signs of a and d. As defined earlier, these are the conditions for determining whether a person is a Polyanna or a Grinch.

Figure 4-18 shows the movement of the model when a and d are both negative, two Grinches conducting a romance. This is a recipe for disaster. No matter where the system begins, it inevitably moves into a region in which it heads for $(-\infty, -\infty)$. Two negative people are not meant for each other.

Challenge Question: What Happens When Polyanna Meets the Grinch?

Explore the case in which one of the two partners is positive when uninfluenced, but the other is negative. Different cases have to be explored, for the system's behavior depends upon how positive and negative the two equilibrium points are, compared to each other.

4.8. CONCLUDING COMMENTS ON MODELING SIMPLE SYSTEMS

In social and behavioral sciences we can often observe the process of change, but cannot clearly see where the change is leading. This chapter has illustrated three techniques for using models of the process of change to show where a system might be going.

Algebraic analysis is the best technique to use when it is available, because algebraic analysis proves how a system will behave. The disadvantages of using algebra are that closed-form solutions may not be available for complicated systems and that algebraic arguments are difficult to present to people who do not have mathematical training themselves. This becomes an issue when scientists want to communicate findings to policymakers or to the general public, as I believe they should.

Graphic analysis can be every bit as rigorous as algebraic analysis, and has the additional advantage that graphic results are easy to present to non-specialists. The downside of using graphics is that this method only works when there are a small number of variables to be considered. Graphs can become "busy" and hard to interpret when as few as three variables are involved.

Numerical simulation techniques can be applied to virtually any problem. However, they do lead to problems. While there are sophisticated algorithms for fitting models to data numerically, these techniques are not perfect. Going into the details would not be appropriate here. Suffice it to say that in some cases numerical simulation can become trapped on a sub-optimal solution, thus making a model look worse than it actually is. A second problem with numerical modeling is that the output can be so complex that the analysis itself is hard to interpret. Sometimes this is inevitable, for there is no guarantee that every problem has a simple solution. Nevertheless, the purpose of modeling is to aid humans in understanding a problem, not to show that a computer can fit numbers to data.

The models presented in this chapter are simple, in two senses. The models dealt with only one or two variables. Obviously, there are real-world situations that require consideration of many more variables. In addition, all the models except the cold/joke problem dealt with situations in which the change in one variable was a linear function of the change in the other variable. All the terms in these models were of the form ax, where a is a constant and x a variable of the model. The cold/joke model was non-linear because it contained a term for mixing the sub-populations of people who had colds and people who were immune; that is, there were equations that contained the term cxy, where c is a constant and x and y are variables. Such terms can considerably complicate an analysis, and can also lead to unexpected results in the modeling process. The next chapter provides some examples.

These complications make modeling more difficult but they do not make it impossible. In fact, they probably make modeling more important than ever. Complicated systems are a fact of the world. We must deal with disease spread, conflicts, and ecological changes. The alternative to modeling is trying to develop an accurate intuitive understanding of what is going on. Such understandings are likely to be far more simplified, and far less accurate, than a well-thought-out model.

APPENDIX 4A. A PROOF OF THE EXPONENTIAL GROWTH EQUATION

The differential equation is

$$\frac{dx}{dt} = kx. \tag{4A-1}$$

Multiplying each side by dt/x produces

$$\frac{dx}{x} = kdt \tag{4A-2}$$

Integrating each side,

$$\int_{0}^{x_t} \frac{1}{x}dx = \int_{0}^{t} kdt \tag{4A-3}$$

$$Ln(x_t) = kt + C,$$

where C is the constant of integration. Exponentiating both sides of (4A-3),

$$x_t = Ce^{kt}, \tag{4A-4}$$

which is the law of exponential growth. Set $t = 0$, so that $kt = 0$, $e^0 = 1$, and

$$x_0 = C. \tag{4A-5}$$

5

Non-linear and Chaotic Systems

5.1. CONTINUOUS CHANGE AND SUDDEN JUMPS

Chapter 4 dealt with systems that followed one of two courses. They either moved smoothly toward a point of equilibrium or careened off toward infinity. They also had the nice property of being predictable. Most of the time we can develop an analytic solution in order to see where a system is going. When analytic solutions are not possible we can, thanks to modern computers, work out enough specific numerical examples so that we have a good idea of how the system behaves.

Another characteristic is less obvious, but in practical situations may be just as important. Every system has a starting state and some parameters that control the process of transition from one state to another. When we are dealing with an actual phenomenon, like the spread of rumors or exchanges of insults, we never know for sure what the starting state and the parameters are, and so we use statistical methods to approximate them. Statistical methods work because it is possible to approximate the behavior of the real-world linear system by a tractable mathematical system that has the same functions and almost, but not quite, the same starting state and parameters. In order to apply the Gottman-Murray equations to a particular pair of romantic partners you do not need to know the exact starting state of their relationship, nor do you need to know the exact values of the influence parameters. If your estimates of these values are close enough, and if the model accurately reflects the dynamics of interactions in marriage, your prediction will be reasonably close to actual behavior.

Things do not always behave this way. In a recent, generally non-mathematical book, *The Tipping Point*,[1] Malcolm Gladwell described social and behavioral phenomena that seem to change state in an abrupt, discontinuous manner. His examples include the rapid adoption of a

---

[1] Gladwell (2000).

shoe style, a dramatic drop in crime in New York City in the 1990s, and an explosion and then receding of a virulent pneumonia epidemic in the Netherlands. Gladwell writes about the power of a few well-placed initial cases, the ability of a new idea (or virus) to spread, and the importance of the context in which an event occurs. What I will do in this chapter is show how some of these behaviors can be treated mathematically.

A key point in the mathematics is the distinction between *linear* and *non-linear* systems. The conventional linear equation $y = ax + b$ (a and b constants) applies to a one-variable linear equation. For the two-variable x,y, a function $f(x,y)$ is linear if $f(ax + by) = af_1(x) + bf_2(y)$. The idea generalizes to three or more variables. The key point is that the effect on the system caused by changes in x are additive to effects caused by changes in y, and so on.

Systems in which rates of change are non-linear functions of system variables may neither settle down to an equilibrium point nor fly off toward positive or negative infinity. In some situations, the resulting system has no single equilibrium point, but still is quite predictable because the system settles down into a cycle, where specific states appear in a regular sequence. Such systems will be called *cyclic* systems. The point about the system settling down is important. A non-linear system may start in a state that is outside of the set of states involved in its stable cycle, but once in the cycle it stays there. Just as different starting points could lead to different equilibrium points in a linear system, different starting points in a non-linear system may lead to different cycles.

The term "cycle" tends to make us think of easily detected cycles, such as the days of the week. This is not necessarily the case; some cycles can be extremely long and complicated. What is actually cyclic behavior can appear to be erratic and even random to an observer who sees only part of the cycle.[2]

This brings us to another important point about non-linear systems. Sometimes small differences in starting states or parameters lead to large differences in system performance. Therefore, if we use statistical approximations that are just a little bit off from the true values, the mathematical model may behave very differently from the real-world system. Systems like this are called *chaotic functions*.

We will begin by looking at a cyclic function that is not chaotic, and then examine some behavioral science applications of chaotic systems.

---

[2] The algorithms used to generate random numbers in computers provide a good example. They are cyclic functions with an extremely long cycle length.

5.2. THE LOTKA-VOLTERRA MODEL OF PREDATOR AND PREY INTERACTIONS

I own a cabin in a forest on the Olympic Peninsula, on the Pacific Coast near the U.S.-Canadian border. A few years ago I noticed that I was seeing an increasing number of deer in the woods. Then I began to notice signs of cougar (mountain lion) habitation, and actually saw two of these large, elusive predators. Deer sightings dropped precipitously. Lately I have seen few cougar signs. I may be seeing an arc on the full circle of life. This summer I saw more deer.

My vignette illustrates a situation in which predator and prey populations maintain a dynamic balance. In the mid-1920s, A. Lotka and, independently, V. Volterra proposed a mathematical model of population fluctuations produced by predator-prey interactions. This model has proven to be extremely popular as a rhetorical and teaching device. As of December, 2004, there were at least 45,000 World Wide Web sites discussing the Lotka-Volterra equations, generally in the context of notes for a university course.[3] The Lotka-Volterra model is a good place to begin, for it is an example of a non-linear system that is cyclic but not chaotic.

Let N represent the number of prey and P the number of predators in a system consisting of just these two species. The Lotka-Volterra model assumes two rules for rate of change in each population over time. For the prey,

$$\frac{dN}{dt} = aN - bNP$$
$$\frac{dN}{dt} = N(a - bP) \tag{5-1}$$
$$a, b > 0.$$

This is a non-linear system because of the term NP. The first line of (5-1) states the concept. It says that the prey population increases exponentially (as defined in Chapter 4) in the absence of predators ($P = 0$). If there are predators the prey population increases as before, but also decreases at a rate proportional to the number of possible encounters between one predator and one prey. The second line is an algebraic simplification that is useful in analyzing system behavior.

---

[3] The search was in December, 2004. Lotka and Volterra also produced models for situations in which two species compete for food. Some of the Web sites referred to these models. However, the predator-prey model seems to have been much more popular.

For the predator population, the rate of change over time is

$$\frac{dP}{dt} = -cP + dNP$$

$$\frac{dP}{dt} = P(dN - c) \tag{5-2}$$

$$c, d > 0.$$

Again the top line best represents the conceptual situation, and the bottom line the algebraic simplification. The top line says that in the absence of prey the predator population will decrease exponentially (think of cougars either starving or moving to a new forest after the deer have gone) and that the rate of increase in the predator population is proportional to the number of possible predator-prey encounters.

The predator-prey model is clearly non-linear, for the rates of change in each population are proportional to, among other things, the product of the sizes of the predator and prey population (the NP term).

Following the procedure that was successful in understanding the Richardson and Gottman-Murray models, we first consider the points at which the populations are neither increasing nor decreasing. For the prey population there are two possibilities:

$$\frac{dN}{dt} = 0 \Leftrightarrow (N = 0) \vee \left(P = \frac{a}{b}\right). \tag{5-3}$$

The first case, $N = 0$, is not interesting. Once the population is gone it's gone, and no manipulation within the system will bring it back. The importance of the second condition can be seen by looking at a graph of changes in the predator-prey system, as depicted in Figure 5-1. Only the positive quadrant of the space is shown, as negative population values would make no sense. As the figure shows, the rate of growth of the prey population goes to zero when the predator population equals a/b, the ratio of the natural growth constant for the prey population to the proportion of potential predator-prey encounters that result in the death of a prey. It is worth noting that in any realistic situation, a must be greater than one, or the prey population would decline exponentially in the absence of predators. The b parameter will always be less than one, and is likely to be very small, because the number of actual predator-prey encounters will be much less than the number of possible encounters and because many predator-prey encounters result in the prey escaping. Therefore, a/b will be greater than one and might be substantial.

In the case of the predator population,

$$\frac{dP}{dt} = 0 \Leftrightarrow (P = 0) \vee \left(N = \frac{c}{d}\right). \tag{5-4}$$

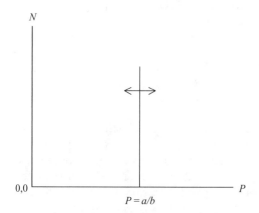

FIGURE 5-1. An initial depiction of the phase space for the Lotka-Volterra model of predator and prey. Whenever P has the value a/b, the derivative dN/dt is zero, regardless of the value of N. This is shown by the double-headed horizontal arrow. The double heads indicate that the direction of motion of the system is unknown.

The $P = 0$ case, no predators, is of little interest. The rate of change in the predator population is zero (i.e., the system is moving vertically in the phase space) if $N = c/d$. The two conditions are combined in Figure 5-2. At this point, we know that there is an equilibrium point at the intersection of the two conditions, $(P, N) = (a/b, c/d)$. We can also state conditions for zero growth of P and N separately.

We can say more. If the system is not in equilibrium at either $(0, 0)$ (a lifeless desert) or at $(a/b, c/d)$, it will cycle about the $(a/b, c/d)$ point, with alternating rises in the predator or prey population. The argument for this assertion is illustrated graphically in Figure 5-3, which can be consulted as an aid in following the algebraic discussion.

Suppose the system begins at any point at which there are fewer than $P = a/b$ predators. Let this point be $(a/b - \alpha, N)$, where $0 < \alpha < a/b$. At this point:

$$\frac{dN}{dt} = N\left(a - b\left(\frac{a}{b} - \alpha\right)\right)$$
$$\frac{dN}{dt} = Nb\alpha \tag{5-5}$$
$$\frac{dN}{dt} > 0.$$

In terms of Figure 5-3, the system will move upward (increasing N) at any point to the left of the vertical line $P = a/b$. This represents situations in which there are not enough predators to offset the exponential increase in the prey population. The rate at which the system moves is

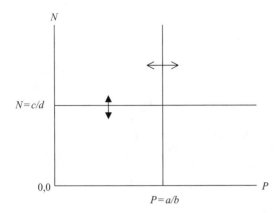

FIGURE 5-2. A second view of the phase space of the Lotka-Volterra model. The rate of change of the prey population is zero (i.e., the system point is moving horizontally) if $P = a/b$. The system moves vertically if $N = c/d$. P, $N = a/b$, and c/d is an equilibrium point.

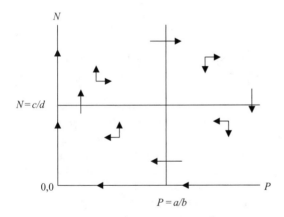

FIGURE 5-3. A complete picture of movement in the Lotka-Volterra predator-prey system. The system cycles around the point $P = a/b$, unless it touches either of the axes $P = 0$ or $N = 0$. In the former case, the prey population will grow exponentially and unchecked; in the latter case, the predator population declines exponentially to zero.

proportional to α, and so the rate of upward motion decreases if, for any reason, the system is moved toward the right, that is, toward the a/b vertical line.

A similar argument shows that if the system is started at any point to the right of the $P = a/b$ line in Figure 5-3 it will move downward, reflecting the fact that the large number of predators is decreasing the prey population.

The combined effect of these relations is shown by the upward and downward pointing arrows in Figure 5-3. They indicate how the system moves to reflect different balances of predator and prey populations.

The points exactly on the $P = a/b$ line represent those points at which the number of predators is exactly equal to the number required so that their kills exactly balance the exponential increase in the prey population. Therefore, the size of the prey population has stabilized. But the number of predators may be changing!

The horizontal $N = c/d$ line represents the points where there are exactly enough prey to keep the predators from decreasing. Below this line the predator population has to decrease to accommodate to scarcity in prey:

$$\frac{dP}{dt} = P\left(d\left(\frac{c}{d} - \delta\right) - c\right)$$

$$\frac{dP}{dt} = -Pd\delta \qquad\qquad (5\text{-}6)$$

$$\frac{dP}{dt} < 0,$$

where $0 < \delta < c/d$. Similarly, if the sytem is above the $N = c/d$ line, at some point $(P, N) = (c/d + \varepsilon, N)$, $\varepsilon < 0$, the numbers of predators increases, $dP/dt > 0$.

Figure 5-3 shows how these equations produce motion in phase space. If the system is started at any point other than the equilibrium point (a/b, c/d) it will cycle around that point. (The cycling is not necessarily circular.) Because the system does not return to the equilibrium point after displacement, the equilibrium is unstable. In addition, the displacement must not be large enough to cause the cycle to touch on the lines $P = 0$ or $N = 0$, for at that point one of the two populations disappears.

The Lotka-Volterra equations predict cycling of prey and predator populations, with rises and falls in the prey population preceding rises and falls in the predator population. Such cycles are observed in a few natural settings. The predator-prey relation between snowy owls and snowshoe rabbits in Northern Canada is often cited, although this cycle only approximates the Lotka-Volterra situation. In general, though, the Lotka-Volterra equations are best regarded as an idealization. What is interesting is how, and why, natural populations deviate from the Lotka-Volterra model.

The Lotka-Volterra equations oversimplify natural predator-prey cycles in two ways. They do not consider any limits on the prey population other than the presence of predators. In practice, the prey would be limited by limits on their own space and food supply. In addition, predators may be limited by other things than the availability of prey, and predators may have to deal with their own predators.

The deer-cougar example at the beginning of the chapter has all of these characteristics. Deer populations are limited by the available food supply. Cougars will defend a territory against other cougars, even if there is enough food for both animals. This limits the number of cougars in a forest. Although deer are their main source of food, cougars will prey on smaller mammals, including domestic cats and dogs. Both deer and cougars are subject to human predation. It is interesting to note that under some circumstances, human predation can actually stabilize the cycle. When deer are scarce, cougars are more likely to encroach upon human domains. People react by hunting ("controlling") cougars. This aids in the recovery of the deer population.

While a system defined by the Lotka-Volterra equations is cyclic, it is not chaotic. The cycle is determined by the starting point and the four parameters. Small changes in the starting value and the parameters produce relatively small, regular changes in the cycle, providing that the resulting cycle does not touch either axis, and thus eliminate either the predator or the prey population.

In the next sections we examine models that do produce chaotic behavior.

Challenge Questions

1. Explore a variation of the Lotka-Volterra model in which the prey and/or the predator population size is limited by a fixed constraint other than the size of the other population. I recommend at least some numerical simulations.

2. Cats, which prey on small mammals, will have litters of from six to eight kittens. Cougars typically have two cubs. What does the effect of predator fecundity (the c parameter) have on the model? Does this suggest anything about how evolutionary pressures might have changed the reproductive rate of these two different hunters, who have evolved to deal with different niches? What requirement is placed on the reproductive rate of the prey in order to have a niche that supports a predator who has a particular rate of reproductivity?

5.3. THE LOGISTIC EQUATION: INTRODUCTION AND BEHAVIOR WHEN $k < 1$

In *Tipping Point*, Gladwell describes an outbreak of syphilis that occurred in Baltimore in the mid-1990s. After having been fairly constant from year to year, the number of cases of children born with the disease increased an astonishing 500% from 1995 to 1996. What could have caused such a dramatic change? Gladwell discusses three possibilities: intensification of sexual activity associated with the use of crack cocaine, reduction in the availability of treatment facilities, and a housing relocation project that had the unexpected side effect of widening the social network for commercial sex. He points out that none of these effects was dramatic. Crack cocaine had been around a long time, so a new brand would have only increased activity slightly. The treatment facilities were reduced but not eliminated, and the commercial sex network was expanded but not remotely magnified by 500%. Why would these small causes have such a large effect?[4]

This section introduces a surprisingly simple model of how an explosive epidemic like the one in Baltimore could occur. There will be no attempt to model actual data. Phenomena such as those that Gladwell described can be partially understood by exploring an innocent-appearing, but ultimately chaotic, function.

Consider an arbitrarily large population, and let x_t, $0 \leq x_t \leq 1$, be the fraction of people in the population who are infected at time t. We treat time as discrete and assume, as in the random mixing model for colds (Chapter 4), that people encounter each other randomly. We also assume that a person who is infected at time t will move to a non-infectious state at time $t+1$.[5] The rate of change in the number of infected individuals is proportional to the probability that an infected person will encounter an uninfected one. Under these conditions,

$$x_{t+1} = kx_t(1 - x_t)$$
$$k > 0. \tag{5-7}$$

This equation has been applied to a number of epidemiological situations other than disease transmission. For instance, in ecology, equation (5-7) has been applied to situations in which a population of organisms (from moths and beetles to deer) is limited only by the available food supply. In this case, x_t is the size of the population at time t, expressed as a proportion of the maximum sustainable population, and k is a growth parameter. It can also be applied to situations involving behavioral mimicking, such as yawning. Here, x_t is the proportion of people yawning at a given instant, and the product $x_t(1 - x_t)$ reflects the probability that a person who is not yawning is looking at a person who is.

---

[4] Gladwell (2000), Chapter 1.

[5] Whether or not this is reasonable depends upon the situation. In the case of a variety of brief gastrointestinal infections ("stomach flu"), it is. In the case of syphilis, it is reasonable for situations in which t refers to the time interval after which virtually every person infected at the beginning of the period has been treated. Other interpretations are possible, e.g., letting infection refer to repeating a rumor.

Now let's consider a curious fact about the natural world, where these equations are supposed to apply. The sudden explosion of syphilis in Baltimore has already been mentioned. In ecological examples, populations of insects may suddenly expand or apparently disappear for no clear reason. In the Pacific Northwest, for instance, the fir forests may have a dark green hue for years and years, and then one year the trees will host a plague of tiny beetles, producing the rust brown of dead fir needles. In other cases, infestations are cyclic. An example is the "seven year locust" plagues that break out in the Midwest and South of the United States. Lice infections sporadically break out, even in the neatest and cleanest day-care units, kindergartens, and pre-schools. In less well-scrubbed societies than ours, louse infestations wax and wane. Meningitis is a more serious case, which can also produce sudden outbursts. Why?

These phenomena may be linked to some unusual properties of equation (5-7) which we now explore.

Equation (5-7) contains the function

$$y = x(1 - x) \tag{5-8}$$

where $0 \le x \le 1$.

This is called the *logistic* equation. It is graphed in Figure 5-4. The value of y rises from 0 (at $x = 0$) to a maximum of .25 at $x = .5$, and falls again to 0 at $x = 1$.

The behavior of the logistic equation places limits on the k parameter in Equation (5-7). If x_t is a proportion of a maximum value, the value of x_t

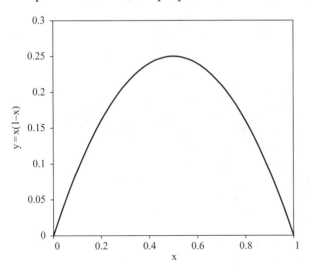

FIGURE 5-4. The logistic equation. The function begins at zero, rises to a maximum of .25 at $x = .5$, and then subsides to zero again.

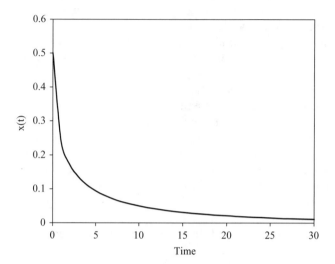

FIGURE 5-5. Course of x_t over time, an example of the decay situation, $k < 1$.

must be restricted to the 0-1 interval. Therefore, we only consider situations in which k falls in the interval $0 < k \leq 4$.

If k is less than 1, and x_t is the current infected state, the proportion of the population in the infected state falls in each successive time period, declining exponentially toward zero. This is illustrated in Figure 5-5. Figure 5-6 illustrates why the decay occurs. This figure combines the logistic function with the identity function, $y = x$. This combination turns out to be the key to understanding why logistic functions behave the way they do, and so the graph's use should be examined carefully.

This is best done by going through an example. Suppose that we start with $x_0 = .5$ and $k = .95$, as in Figure 5-5. To get the next point, extend an arrow upward from $x = .5$ to the $y = k \, (1 - x)$ curve. This provides the value of x_1. Repeat the procedure starting at $x_1 = .2375$, producing $x_2 = .1720$. The system is "moving down the hump" to the left of the model function, heading toward zero. However, it will never actually get there; zero is approached in the asymptote.

What would happen if we were to make a small change in parameters? The answer is "nothing much," providing that we keep the k parameter below 1. Figure 5-7 illustrates this, by comparing two logistic functions with slightly different parameters. Changing x_0 changes where the logistic function begins. Nevertheless, whenever k is between zero and one, the logistic function decays smoothly and approaches zero in the asymptote.

Figure 5-7 illustrates an important point about *non-chaotic* functions. Suppose that we mis-estimated parameters and thought that the phenomenon we were observing was following the dark line, when it was

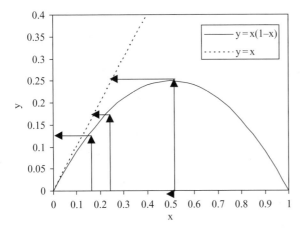

FIGURE 5-6. An explanation of the behavior of the logistic curve with $k = < 1$. Suppose the system begins at $x_0 = .5$ and $k = .95$. The value of x_1 is .2375, illustrated by the rightmost vertical and horizontal arrow. A value of $x_1 = .2375$ produces a value of $x_2 = .1720$, as shown by the middle vertical and horizontal arrow. The same principle is repeated to find x_3, and then onward (values beyond x_3 are not shown). The value of x_t declines exponentially toward zero.

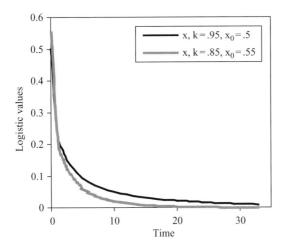

FIGURE 5-7. When k is less than one, the decay functions are not too different for small differences in parameters. The function is not chaotic.

actually following the gray line. The error in prediction due to using one equation to estimate the other would be small at first but would become increasingly larger as t increased. In the informal literature on chaos theory this is sometimes called a "linear" characteristic, and it is certainly true that linear equations would exhibit this property. However, we just illustrated the property for two non-linear equations. Therefore, I will call it the *gradual degradation* principle. A system exhibits gradual degradation if (a) slight changes in the parameters cause only slight changes in the system's position in phase space at low values of *t*, and (b) the discrepancy between the predicted and actual position of the system increases regularly as *t* increases.

Statistical estimation rests on the assumption that the function to be estimated degrades gradually. For that reason a statistical estimate of a parameter need not be absolutely accurate. Even if there is a small amount of error in estimation predicted values will be only slightly off from actual values. Systems (and system-generating functions) that do *not* have this property are called *chaotic systems* or *chaotic functions*.

5-4. NON-ZERO ASYMPTOTES AND CYCLES AS *k* INCREASES

What happens when *k* is greater than one? This is an important question, for a per-unit increase in observations is often a realistic assumption. To illustrate, in Gladwell's example of syphilis infections one of the effects of reducing medical services would be to increase the average time between infection and treatment. This would increase the number of sexual contacts per infected person and, in the model, increase the value of *k*.

We begin by looking at values of *k* that are just above one, and for small differences in x_0. Figure 5-8 compares the $k = .95$ case with the $k = 1.05$ case. For $k = 1.05$, the asymptotic value is no longer zero. Figure 5-9 illustrates this more dramatically, by comparing the $k = 1.05$

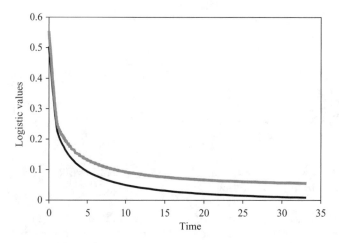

FIGURE 5-8. For $k = .95$, slightly less than one (dark line), the system declines asymptotically toward zero. For $k = 1.05$, slightly greater than 1 (gray line), the system has a non-zero asymptote.

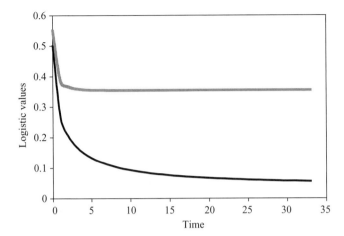

FIGURE 5-9. Further increases in k from 1.05 (dark line) to 1.55 (gray line) raise the asymptote.

and the $k = 1.55$ case. The discrepancies between the functions are now quite large. Nevertheless, the value of k determines the asymptotic value and the system degrades gradually.

In infectious disease examples this represents a change between a disease's dying out and the disease's assuming a steady, albeit moderately low, level of continuous infection. Analogous interpretations apply to such situations as outbreaks of beetle infections (ecology) and the prevalence of rumors or beliefs (social psychology, sociology).

Figure 5-10 shows why this happens. Figure 5-10 is analogous to Figure 5-6, but with $k = 1.55$. Now consider the following argument, which is a verbal statement of the "arrows" approach illustrated in Figure 5-6, applied to Figure 5-10:

1. Whatever the current value, on the abscissa, the next value of the function will be given by determining the value, on the ordinate, of the logistic function at the point indicated by the current value.
2. If the value on the abscissa is at the point where the logistic function intersects the identity function, then the next value is equal to the current value, and so the asymptotic value has been reached.

What is more, we can find that point analytically. It will be the point at which x maps onto itself, so that $x_{t+1} = x_t$. Designate this (asymptotic) value by x^*. It has to satisfy the equation

$$x^* = kx^*(1 - x^*)$$
$$x^* = \frac{k - 1}{k}$$

(5-9)

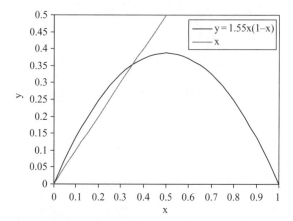

FIGURE 5-10. Why the asymptote changes. For $k > 1$, the logistic function intersects the identity function. If the point of intersection is reached there will be no further changes in the value of x.

subject to the restriction that k is greater than one. For instance, in the case of $k = 1.05$, the asymptotic value should be $.05/1.05 \sim .0476$, while for $k = 1.55$ the asymptote should be $\sim .3548$. These values are in agreement with the graphic solutions in Figure 5-9.

Equation (5-9) also shows that the asymptote is a function of k, not x_0. Two systems that start at different places but have the same value of k have identical asymptotic values. In the case of infections and rumors, the steady state does not depend upon the number of initial infections (or believers). It depends upon the infection rate.

The examples so far have all shown a regular decline toward an asymptote. Things change as k is increased. Figure 5-11 shows the first complication. The figure compares the $k = 1.55$ function with a $k = 2.5$ function. At $k = 2.5$ the system initially oscillates about the asymptotic value, and then settles down to a steady decay toward its asymptote. Oscillation is a qualitatively different behavior, one that we have not seen before. In addition, this pair of functions does not exhibit gradual degradation because the discrepancy between the two functions at first increases, then decreases, then increases again, decreases, and finally settles down to (nearly) a constant as the two systems move toward their asymptotic values.

To understand what has happened, examine Figure 5-12, which is an analog of Figures 5-6 and 5-10, with $k = 2.5$. Once again the arrows trace out how the value of x changes over time. The value initially moves across, rather than closer to, the point at which $kx(1 - x)$ intersects the identity line. Each time it moves across the intersection point represents one of the oscillations shown in Figure 5-11. Eventually the system "settles down" to a decay toward its steady state.

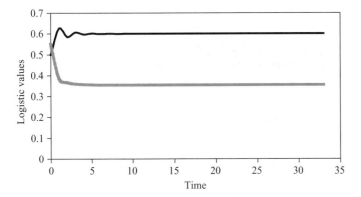

FIGURE 5-11. A comparison of system values as the k parameter is increased from $k = 1.55$ to $k = 2.5$. Instead of a steady movement to the asymptote, the system first oscillates and then settles down to an asymptotic value.

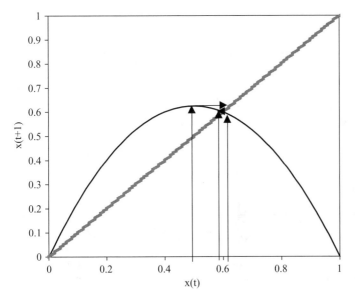

FIGURE 5-12. The cyclic behavior occurs as the logistic function "seeks" to intersect with the identity function.

Figure 5-13 shows another change in system behavior, as k is increased from 2.5 to 3.3. The system no longer approaches an asymptotic value. (In the jargon of chaos theory, it no longer approaches a point attractor.) Instead, the system cycles back and forth between two values, .823 and .479.

Figure 5-14 shows why cyclic behavior occurs. The system becomes trapped at two different points that map into each other. Algebraically

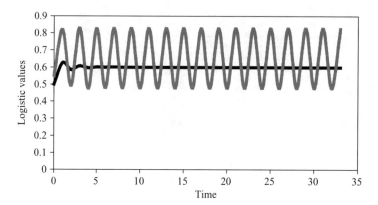

FIGURE 5-13. For some values of k the system cycles. The figure compares $k = 2.5$ (dark line) to $k = 3.3$ (gray line).

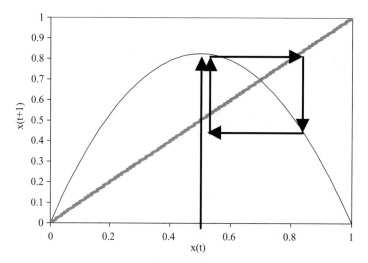

FIGURE 5-14. The explanation of why cyclic behavior occurs. The $k = 3.3$ case is shown. The system starts at $x_0 = .5$ and is quickly trapped in a cycle.

there are two points, x and x', such that

$$x = kx'(1 - x')$$
$$x' = kx(1 - x). \tag{5-10}$$

Although the starting state does not influence the frequency and amplitude of the cycle, it does determine the phase of the cycle. This is shown in Figure 5-15.

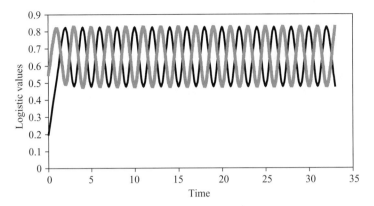

FIGURE 5-15. Changes in initial value can now produce a phase shift, $k = 3.3$ for both functions.

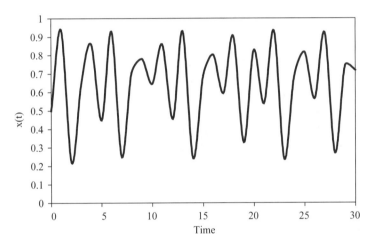

FIGURE 5-16. Strange behavior begins to occur as k is increased still further. The case of $k = 3.75$ is shown.

5.5. CHAOS

As k is increased further ever-more irregular, behavior is observed. This is illustrated in Figure 5-16, where $k = 3.75$. The path is irregular, to say the least. There seems to be some repetition, but it is certainly not the simple cyclic behavior observed earlier. In fact, if we extend the period of observation, as is done in Figure 5-17, even more irregularities appear. Figures 5-16 and 5-17 make it clear why such behavior is referred to as chaotic.

The gradual degradation property has been lost, and in a most irregular way. This is shown in Figure 5-18, which compares two chaotic functions that start at the same place and that differ only slightly in the

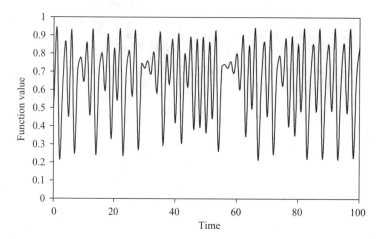

FIGURE 5-17. Extended observations of the $k = 3.75$ case show that the cycle is even more irregular than was apparent in the first 30 observations.

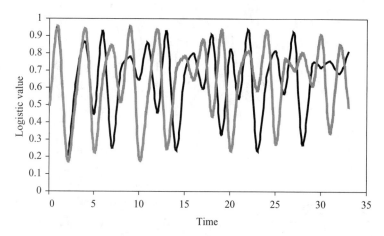

FIGURE 5-18. The case of $k = 3.75$ (dark line) and $k = 3.80$ (gray line). A slight shift in parameters causes even more confusion!

value of k. At first ($t = 1$ to 5), the two functions are almost identical. They then go back and forth, sometimes resembling each other and sometimes differing drastically.

What happens if the starting conditions are varied slightly, while k is held constant? An example is shown in Figure 5-19 for $k = 3.75$, $x(0) = .5$ and .55. The functions are almost identical at the start, then grow apart as before. However, they come close together again at intervals. At $t = 18$ the difference is .903 compared to .912. Then they split apart. At $t = 26$ it is .585 versus .844. If you were observing the data over time, it would be

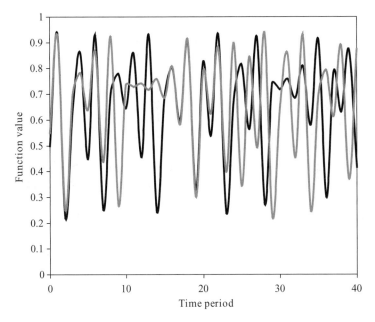

FIGURE 5-19. If the value of *k* is in the chaotic range (here 3.75), slight differences in starting values can break down the gradual degradation property. The starting value is .5 for the dark line and .55 for the gray one.

easy to mistake one function for another at the start. Therefore, long-term predictions of the system's state might break down. Or they might not, depending upon the exact time for which the prediction was made!

5.6. CHAOS AND NETWORK MODELS

The logistic function is useful as a way of demonstrating the properties of chaotic systems. It has also proven to be a useful tool in some ecological applications, especially for modeling fluctuations in populations that expand and contract within fixed boundaries, such as the fish in an isolated lake.

To what extent is the logistic function a model for human activity? I have drawn a loose analogy between logistic functions and situations involving the spread of disease and rumor, but there was no serious effort to show that logistic functions actually approximate data on the course of an epidemic of either the biological or gossip type. As a case in point, when discussing the Baltimore outbreak of syphilis, all I did was show that a logistic model could mimic the way that a small increase in infectivity might lead to a major change in the asymptotic rate of infection. No attempt was made to go beyond a qualitative statement about similarities in the behavior of the model and the outbreak. And in fact, when you think about it, the explanation offered to map the logistic equation onto the mechanics of the spread of disease and rumor is a bit forced.

There are two ways to go beyond such analogies. One would be to compare the data from epidemics, courses of rumors, and so forth to the behavior expected from a chaotic model. This could be a very difficult task, even if the chaotic model was right, because in a truly chaotic system, any error in estimating starting conditions and parameters could generate large discrepancies between observed and predicted behavior. Anyone who wants to use chaotic models to study human behavior will have to wrestle with this issue.

Another approach is to investigate the (possibly chaotic) behavior of non-linear models that are more complicated than the logistic model, but easier to justify to those who have experience with the phenomena at hand. In this section I will go a little ways beyond the logistic equation, by looking at network models of how neural activity, news, or medical infections might be passed around. It turns out that models of social and neural networks have some characteristics that appear to be related to chaotic functions.

To begin, I will offer three examples of applications of network modeling:

1. Timing by *neural networks*. Humans and other animals have some sense of brief periods of time. This sense can be disrupted by certain interventions, such as the use of marijuana. This suggests that we have a clocking mechanism in our brains. How might you make a functional clock out of neurons?

2. *Discussions of wild rumors.* Some rumors keep recurring within a restricted population. Rumors of extraterrestrial (ET) landings are a good example. There is evidently a group of believers who talk among themselves about the latest news of ETs. Some of these rumors seem to go in cycles, others maintain a continuous level, and still others show bursts of activity and inactivity in a seemingly random fashion.

    One of the reasons that a rumor dies out is that people simply get tired of transmitting it. Suppose that there is a population of N individuals, and that each individual either just heard of the rumor or has tired of talking of it. For brevity, define these people as being active and passive believers. At each time period an active person passes on the rumor to everyone he or she meets, and then becomes inactive. Suppose further that at each time period every person meets k ($k < N - 1$) randomly chosen individuals, and receives the rumor if one or more of these individuals is in the active state. The receiver then becomes active if he or she was previously inactive.

3. *Infestations of head lice.* Head lice are the bane of primary school teachers. Even in the best-scrubbed of societies, very young

children do become infested, and do pass these pests on to their playmates. The infested child then returns home, is thoroughly scrubbed by parents, and after a brief period is returned to school ... possibly to be reinfected.

Assume that in a class containing N students each child plays with k randomly chosen playmates ($k < N - 1$). If the child is unaffected and any one or more of the playmates is infected, the child becomes infected but will not be immediately noticed, and can spread lice the following day. On the other hand, any child who is currently infected to the point of being able to spread lice will be disinfected that evening.

Although these three situations are quite different on the surface, they can all be modeled by a network of N nodes, where each node is designated as either being active or inactive. Each node receives input from k ($k < N-1$) randomly chosen nodes. Let N_t be the number of nodes in active state at time t. If a node is active at time t it becomes inactive at time $t+1$. On the other hand, if a node is inactive at time t and receives input from at least one active node, then the receiving node becomes active at time $t+1$.

A graphic example of this process is shown in Figure 5-20 for the case $N = 5$, $k = 2$. I suggest that the reader examine the figure carefully, to develop an intuitive feeling for the process.

Space (and human comprehension!) only permits the display of small networks, such as that shown in Figure 5-20. The five-node network in the figure has only $2^5 = 32$ possible states (combinations of nodes that are active and inactive). Not all states can be reached. In fact, the network shown in the figure will cycle back and forth between the states shown on the left- and right-hand sides. If this, or any, network ever reaches a state in which all nodes are active, then all nodes will be inactive at the next and all subsequent time periods.

This sort of network is called a *reentrant* network because the nodes in the network connect to each other. What we will consider is the expected output of the network, which is defined as the number of active nodes. In the neural circuit example, one could regard this as a signal of total activity, sent to some center that is external to the network. In the case of the rumor and head lice examples, this would be either the extent to which a rumor was being passed about or the number of infected children, quantities whose variation over time might be of considerable interest. Let us look at an algebraic analysis of how the network would function.

Define the following quantities

N = number of nodes in a network
N_t = number of nodes active at time t
k = number of randomly chosen connections into each node.
x_t = the fraction of nodes active at time t, $x_t = N_t/N$.

Time =   *t*   *t* + 1

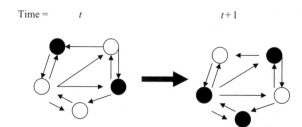

FIGURE 5-20. An example of a network in which activation is passed from node to node. The active nodes, shown in black, pass activation to the inactive nodes, shown in white, and then become inactive. An example is shown for the case $N = 5$, $k = 2$, which is a small network compared to those usually studied. The state of activation at time t is shown on the left, at time $t + 1$ on the right.

We want to know the probability that a node that is inactive at time t will be active at time $t + 1$. However, it turns out to be easier to find, first, the probability that the node in question will remain inactive at time $t + 1$. This can happen only if all the nodes that pass input into the target node are also inactive.

The probability that an inactive node remains inactive is equal to the probability that the k nodes providing input to the target node are also inactive.

The probability that any one randomly chosen input node is active is, obviously, N_t/N. Therefore, the probability that any node is inactive is the complement, $(1 - \frac{N_t}{N})$. The probability that all k randomly chosen input nodes are inactive is $(1 - \frac{N_t}{N})^k$.

Substituting x_t for N_t/N, the probability that at least one node provides input to the target node is $1 - (1 - x_t)^k$.

In addition to having at least one active input node, the node of interest must also have been inactive at time t. Because x_t is the probability that a randomly chosen node would be active at time t, $1 - x_t$ is the probability that the node was inactive. Combining the two lines of reasoning, the probability that a randomly chosen node will be active at time $t + 1$ is

$$x_{t+1} = (1 - x_t)(1 - (1 - x_t)^k). \tag{5-11}$$

Equation 5-11 does not contain any expression for N, the number of nodes in the network. This is paradoxical, for we have already seen that the possible values of x_t are finite and influenced by N. For instance, the only possible values of x_t for the network shown in Figure 5-20 are .4 and .6. Furthermore, these values would be impossible to reach in a network of either 4 or 6 elements!

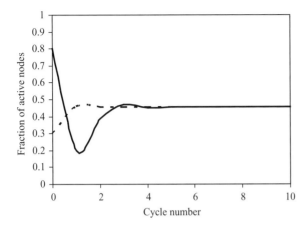

FIGURE 5-21. Changes in the fraction of active nodes in a network with low values of the control parameter (sparse connectivity). The case shown is for $k = 3$ and starting values of .8 (solid line) or .3 (dashed line). After brief oscillation about the asymptotic value, both starting values lead to the same asymptotic level of activity.

The reason for the paradox is that equation (5-11) applies to the expected value of the fraction of activated nodes, where the expectation is computed across all possible networks with control parameter k. As was defined in Chapter 2, the expectation can be interpreted as the average value obtained in an infinite number of samples of possible situations. It need not be equal to a value that would be obtained in any one situation.

The next step is to investigate how the behavior of reentrant networks varies as the values of the starting state and the control parameter (x_0 and k) vary. The term *sparsely connected* will be used to refer to a network with a small number of connections per node; as k is increased, the network is said to be *richly connected*.

The first case to be considered is a minimally connected network, in which each node receives input from only one other node. Applied to the rumor case, a minimal network would be created if each person only talked to one other, randomly chosen person in the network. If $k = 1$, equation (5-11) is identical to the logistic equation, and so the fraction of active nodes would decline monotonically to zero. Rumors or infections die out naturally in a minimally connected network.

Many social networks are sparsely connected, with k values in the range 2–5. These values would be reasonable for such things as the number of children a child plays with in a day, or the number of conversations a person has with others interested in the topic of a rumor. Figure 5-21 shows changes in activity in networks of this sort. The level of activity will first oscillate for a bit, and then move toward a non-zero asymptote, that is, a steady level of neural activity, rumor mongering, or,

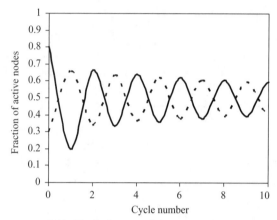

FIGURE 5-22. The behavior of the network model with the control parameter $k = 8$. As before, the starting values are .8 (solid line) and .3 (dotted line). The asymptotic value has been changed to be close to .5 (compare to the asymptote of about .46 in Figure 5-18). The approach to the asymptote is oscillatory and slower than the approach observed with lower values of k.

to the despair of primary school teachers, a steady level of head lice infection. The asymptote depends upon the value of the control parameter; all the starting value determines is the course to the asymptote. While there may be some oscillation at first, the oscillations are damped as x_t moves toward its asymptotic value.

In moderately connected networks, with k in the range 8–15, the oscillatory period is lengthened, but the damped oscillation toward the starting value is still apparent. This is shown in Figure 5-22, which is a duplicate of Figure 5-21, except that the control parameter has been changed to 8. Although the starting values do not exert any effect on the asymptote they do determine the phase of the oscillation.

The nature of the oscillation can be seen by extending our observations from 10 to 100 cycles. This is shown in Figure 5-23 for $k = 8$ and a starting value of .8.

You may have noticed that the asymptotic value appears to be just a little below .5. The model predicts that once a rumor (or lice infection) starts in a sparse or moderate, but not minimally connected, society, behavior settles down to a steady state in which about half the individuals are rumor spreaders (or are infected). How long the system takes to reach this state, and how wildly levels of rumor spreading (or lice infection) vary before the steady state is reached depends on the degree of connectivity. Swings in level are wider, and the asymptote is approached more slowly, as the degree of connectivity increases.

Restricting our attention to sparsely or moderately connected networks makes sense if a connection refers to an encounter between people, within

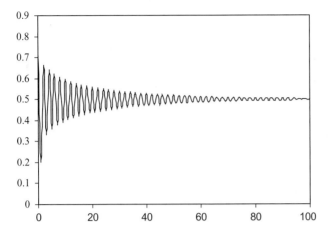

FIGURE 5-23. The fraction of nodes active (ordinate) as a function of the number of cycles of the network model (abscissa). If the control parameter is increased to $k = 8$, the fraction of active nodes oscillates about an asymptotic value, but the oscillation is markedly damped after about 50 cycles.

the space of a day or less. The restriction definitely does not apply to the neural network example. A neuron may receive input from hundreds or even thousands of other neurons.[6] Such networks can be modeled by a network with a control parameter on the order of 100 or more. The behavior of such tightly connected networks has an interesting characteristic.

Figure 5-24 illustrates the behavior of a network with a control parameter $k = 100$. The figure makes it appear that the fraction of active nodes in the network oscillates back and forth between the starting value, $x(0)$, and its complement, $(1 - x(0))$. The reason for this, and the slight deception in the figure, is apparent when the algebra of equation 5-11 is examined. As k is increased without limit, we have

$$\lim_{k \to \infty} ((1 - x)(1 - (1 - (1 - x)^k))) = (1 - x). \tag{5-12}$$

so that in a hypothetical "infinitely connected network," there would be undamped oscillation,

$$
\begin{aligned}
x_1 &= 1 - x_0 \\
x_2 &= (1 - x_1) = x_0 \\
x_3 &= 1 - x_0 \\
etc.
\end{aligned}
\tag{5-13}
$$

[6] Thompson (1993).

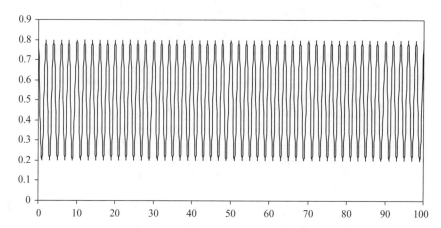

FIGURE 5-24. The fraction of nodes active on the first 100 cycles in a tightly connected network ($k = 100$, $x_0 = .8$). Compared to the early examples, there is a high amplitude oscillation, and very slow damping toward an asymptote. It can be proven, though, that the network will eventually oscillate toward an asymptote a very little bit below .5.

If k is finite, as it would have to be in any real network, the oscillation would be very slowly damped.

Consider what this means for the neural net application. Networks consisting of thousands of individual neurons, with a control parameter in the 100–1,000 range, are realistic. Such a network would act like a clock. It could also serve as a pacing mechanism, providing signals to control rhythmic activity of muscles or other organs. If the network was perturbed by outside increases or decreases in its total activity, it would recover and return to clocklike action, though perhaps with changed amplitude.

Of course, this mathematical excursion does not prove that an actual biological timer is controlled by a randomly connected neural network; modeling can never do this alone. What the excursion does show is that a clocklike mechanism can be built out of a simple reentrant neural network.

5.7. CLOSING COMMENTS ON CHAOS

This chapter is at best an introduction to the mathematical concept of chaos. There are many other chaotic functions besides the two illustrated here. In fact, one of the things that surprised me, when I first looked into the field, was how common chaotic functions are. I have not discussed the phenomenon called period-doubling, nor given any consideration to the relation between chaos theory and fractals. I leave these topics for mathematicians. The text by G. P. Williams is a good starting point.[7]

Chaotic functions are sometimes confused with "random effects," that is, errors in observation that make prediction difficult. The two are separate concepts. As an example, weather prediction is difficult both because of chaotic relationships between physical variables and because of inaccuracies in the initial conditions. The latter are statistical errors. Using the Scholastic Assessment Test to predict how well high school students will succeed in college is difficult because of, among other things, errors in measurement when grades are used as an estimate of what students have learned. There is no indication that the system is chaotic; it is just that the measurements are somewhat inaccurate.[8]

Chaotic systems are fun to play with, which may partially account for the number of discussions of chaos in various scientific applications. They also present an interesting challenge for data analysis. If a chaotic model accurately describes the phenomena we are looking at, then prediction is extremely difficult without fantastically accurate data. As a result, there have been many enthusiastic speculations suggesting either that something we do not clearly understand, such as the onset of schizophrenia, may be generated by a chaotic system or that the dominant scientific model, which assumes that we are dealing with non-chaotic phenomenon, is fundamentally flawed. There is at least one popular science book that is full of such speculations.[9] It has lots of pictures, anecdotes, and speculations, but I do not believe it has a single equation.

I think that this is overdoing things. Chaos theory has a place in science. It will sometimes be an important place. If I were dealing with some data that did not conform to my current non-chaotic model, my first step would be to try to develop another non-chaotic model. I would not immediately assume that I had encountered chaos. But I would keep in mind the fact that chaos does exist.

---

[7] Williams (1997).

[8] So that I do not spread misunderstanding, let me be clear that the tests used to predict college performance are far more accurate than chance. College admission officers would be foolish to stop using the SAT. They do not, and never have, claimed that it is a perfect predictor.

[9] Gleick (1987).

6

Defining Rationality

Personal and Group Decision Making

6.1. AXIOMATIC REASONING

One of my favorite plays is Christopher Fry's 1948 London hit *The Lady's Not for Burning*. The play takes place in medieval times. A young woman, Jenny Jourdemain, has been accused of being a witch. She then observes some very unusual behavior, including the request of a soldier who wants to be executed because he is weary of life. Jenny, who prides herself on her own logical approach to life, says that she cannot believe that rational people are behaving the way that the people around her are behaving. She is particularly concerned about the magistrates' certainty that she should be burned at the stake. Jenny regards this as illogical, for if she were a witch, she would simply fly away.

People raised in the Western European–North American tradition, and particularly those raised in the more secular branches of that tradition, generally see rational behavior as good and irrational behavior as bad. But who defines rationality? How do we connect rationality to behavior? This chapter will explore these questions, with respect to individual and group decisions.

The approach that will be taken was established by one of the greatest mathematicians of all time, the legendary geometer Euclid of Alexandria (325?–265? B.C.E.), whose work has been studied for more than 2,300 years! Euclid did not invent geometery. Pythagoras preceded Euclid by about 200 years. Before that, the Babylonians solved geometric problems, and the Egyptians must have had some rough and ready knowledge of geometry, for they built the pyramids centuries before Euclid. What Euclid did do was to introduce a method of analysis, *axiomatic reasoning*, to systematize knowledge about geometry. In addition to laying the basis for problem solving in geometry, Euclid presented a technique for argumentation that is basic to mathematics.

Euclid stated five rules for drawing conclusions in mathematics (e.g., *If equal things are added to equals, the wholes are equal*) and five axioms about what we today call Euclidean space (e.g., *A straight line can be drawn between any two points*). He then applied the rules to the axioms in order to derive the basic theorems of plane geometry. This was a monumental contribution. But important as it is, plane geometry was Euclid's second most important contribution. The most important contribution was the idea of axiomatic reasoning.

This chapter deals with two attempts to define rational behavior using Euclid's techniques. The first, the Von Neumann-Morgenstern approach to decision making, takes an axiomatic approach to economic decision making by individual decision makers. The second, Arrow's discussion of voting procedures, examines how groups might choose between alternatives. This is usually cast as the problem of defining rational voting systems in an election, but the argument applies to any group choice of alternatives, not just the choice of candidates for a political office.

We shall meet Jenny again. But first, we look at the reasoning of a real historical character.

6.2. DECISION MAKING UNDER RISK

In 49 B.C.E., the Roman general Julius Caesar marched homeward after seizing Gaul (modern France, Switzerland, and Belgium) for the Republic of Rome. In order to maintain the republican character of the city, Roman law required a returning general to disband his army before crossing the Rubicon, a river to the north of the city. When Caesar learned that his enemies planned to attack him after he disarmed, he took his army across the Rubicon, used it to seize power, and became the first Roman emperor. The Republic was dead forever.

When Caesar crossed the Rubicon he said, "The die is cast," likening his action to those of a gambler who stakes his fortune on a roll of a die, without knowing, for sure, what is going to happen. The analogy is apt for very many things, ranging from a prosaic decision to have or decline an omelet at a restaurant brunch (it might be contaminated), to decisions about stock purchases, to choices of medical treatments, and finally, to the decision to go to war.

In all of these examples there is no guarantee of certainty. One action is selected from several alternatives, based on the decision maker's estimates of the probabilities that the action will result in certain outcomes. This is called *decision making under risk*. In a decision under risk the decision maker knows what alternative actions are available, and knows the probabilities of the consequences associated with each action. The following prosaic example illustrates the idea.

TABLE 6-1. *Payoffs for Purchasing or Not Purchasing a Computer Warranty for $300, to Ensure a Computer That Costs $700*

Your Action	Computer Works (p = .7)	Machine Requires Fixing (p = .2)	Machine Collapses (p = .1)
Buy warranty	−300	−200	+400
Do not buy warranty	0	−100	−700

Note: Payoffs are indicated for different states of nature (i.e., status of the computer) with associated probabilities. The cost of the warranty must be considered in establishing the payoffs.

Purchasing Warranties. You purchase a computer for $700. The salesperson offers you a warranty guaranteeing free repair of the computer for one year, at a cost of $300. Should you buy the warranty?

Whether or not you should purchase the warranty depends upon your estimate of the probabilities and costs of the potential outcomes. Suppose that you estimate that there is a .7 chance that the computer will continue to work throughout the warranty period, a .2 chance that it will require fixing at a cost of $100, and a .1 chance that the device will collapse and have to be replaced. Table 6-1 summarizes the situation.

A widely accepted decision rule is to calculate the *expected value*, which is the value for each outcome given each choice, weighted by the probability of the outcome. This is the value that the decision maker would receive, on the average, if the choice in question was taken over a large number of decisions. In the warranty problem, let W represent purchasing the warranty and $\sim W$ not purchasing it, and let $E(X)$ be the expected value of taking option X. The expected values for the two actions are

$$E(W) = .7(-300) + .2(-200) + .1(400)$$
$$E(W) = -210$$
$$E(\sim W) = 0 + .2(-100) + .1(-700) \tag{6-1}$$
$$E(\sim W) = -90.$$

Because $E(\sim W) > E(W)$, you should not purchase the warranty. However, you should be prepared to pay about $100 for repairs.

More generally, the decision maker should choose the alternative that maximizes expected value. The argument for doing so is that expected value can be interpreted as the average return to the decision maker, over a long series of repeated choices. Therefore, maximizing expected value is an appropriate policy decision because, on the average, that is the best thing to do.

This argument is the basis for insurance. The expected value of the warranty (or insurance policy) is always negative from the viewpoint of the purchaser and positive from the viewpoint of the insurer. Because the insurance company issues many policies, its return will be close to the expected value. By the same token, Las Vegas casinos can exist only because the expected value of the average gamble is negative to the gambler and positive to the house. An occasional gambler makes a fortune, but in the long run, the house (and the insurance company) win. Why, then, does anyone gamble or buy insurance?

6.3. THE CONCEPT OF UTILITY

There must be a problem with this analysis. Buying insurance is usually considered rational. Millions of people gamble, and I, for one, would hesitate to say that the mere fact of gambling is a form of irrationality. Why is this the case?

The decision-theory argument is that people do not try to maximize monetary returns. Instead, they try to maximize the value of those returns. In the case of insurance companies and gambling casinos, the two are the same; these institutions are in the business of making money. Individual decision makers may not feel that way at all. They are in the business of seeking fortunes and avoiding disasters. Consider a homeowner who is offered a chance to buy a fire insurance policy on a $500,000 home at a cost of $2,000. The homeowner might be rational to purchase the policy, because to the homeowner, the personal cost of a loss of $500,000 might be more than two hundred and fifty times the personal cost of a loss of $2,000 in insurance fees. People do not necessarily maximize objective economic rewards; they maximize the subjective value of those rewards.

This observation is not new. In the eighteenth century, Daniel Bernoulli, a mathematician in the court of Catherine the Great of Russia, proposed the following thought experiment, called *the St. Petersburg paradox*.

Suppose that a gambling house offers the following game. The house tosses a fair coin. If it lands heads, the house pays the gambler $2 and the game ends. If the coin lands tails, the house tosses the coin again. This time if it lands heads, the house pays the gambler $4 and the game ends. If it lands tails, the coin is tossed for a third time. If the coin lands heads, the house pays out $8, otherwise . . . the game is continued until the coin lands heads. In the general case, if the coin lands heads for the first time on trial t, the house pays the gambler the sum of $\$2^t$.

Here is the catch. The gambler has to pay to enter the game. How much would you pay? $5? $10? $100? I have asked this question of my students in several classes, carefully not offering to act as the house. The typical answer is somewhere around $2 to $3.

My students were very cautious. Bernoulli showed that if a gambler is trying to maximize expected value, in terms of dollars, he or she should be willing to pay far more. In fact, the gambler should be willing to pay any price that the house asks! Here is why.

The probability of Bernoulli's game ending on the first coin toss is (1/2), that it ends on the second (1/4), that it ends on the third (1/8), and so forth. The winnings increase, from 2 to 4, 4 to 8, and so forth. Applying (6–1) to calculate expected value we have

$$E(St.Petersburg) = \frac{2}{2} + \frac{4}{4} + \frac{8}{8} + \cdots\cdots$$

$$E(St.Petersburg) = \sum_{t=1}^{\infty} \frac{2^t}{2^t} = \sum_{t=1}^{\infty} 1 \tag{6-2}$$

$$E(St.Petersburg) = \infty.$$

A gambler should be willing to pay any amount to enter the game! Bernoulli did not think any gamblers would do so. But why?

Bernoulli argued that people do not respond to the expected value of a payoff in currency. Instead, he argued (putting a modern term in his mouth) that they are sensitive to the expected *utility* of a reward, where utility means, roughly, "what it is worth to you." Bernoulli further argued that a transformation from money value to utility value, $U(x)$, should obey two axioms:

Axiom A1. *People will always prefer more money to less. Therefore, for any two amounts of money, x and y, $x > y \Leftrightarrow U(x) > U(y)$.*

Axiom A2. *As the amount of money increases, the value of a fixed increment in money decreases.*

The first assumption certainly seems reasonable enough. The second assumption is called *decreasing marginal utility of money*. Examples abound. A hospital nursing aide earning, say, $30,000 a year might be quite interested in doing extra work in order to make $35,000 a year. A major league baseball player earning $2,000,000 a year has little incentive to raise his pay to $2,005,000.

So far, this is a pure example of axiomatic reasoning. However, Bernoulli then took an arbitrary step. He selected the well-known logarithmic transformation for $U(x)$ on the grounds that it satisfies both axioms. Formally, he argued that

$$U(\$x) = K \cdot ln(\$x), \tag{6-3}$$

where K, a constant greater than zero, is the constant of proportionality. Therefore, the utility of $\$2^t$ would be Kt. The expected utility of the gamble becomes

$$U(St.\,Petersburg) = K \sum_{t=1}^{\infty} \frac{t}{2^t},$$ (6-4)

which has a finite value, because the terms of the series approach zero as t increases without limit. Therefore, there should be some finite amount that a gambler would pay to enter the game. If the house charges more the gambler should decline.

In addition to resolving the paradox, Bernoulli's transformation can also be used to explain why people buy warranties and insurance polices. The following example uses unrealistic numbers, to make the arithmetic easy.

Suppose that you purchase an appliance for \$1,024 (\$2^{10}\$). You are offered a full-replacement warranty for \$512 (\$2^9\$). You estimate that there is one chance in two that the appliance will break down during the warranty period, and that if it does, it will have a junk value of \$1. As before, let W be the action of buying the warranty, and $\sim W$ be the action of declining the warranty.

From an expected value viewpoint,

$$E(W) = 1024 - 512 = 512.$$
$$E(\sim W) = \frac{1}{2}1024 + \frac{1}{2}1 = 512.5.$$ (6-5)

So you should lean toward not buying the warranty. However, in terms of Bernoulli's logarithmic utility function,

$$U(W) = K[\ln_2(512)] = K9$$
$$U(\sim W) = K\left[\frac{1}{2}\ln_2(1024) + \frac{1}{2}\ln_2(1)\right] = K5,$$ (6-6)

where K is the unknown constant of proportionality. You definitely should buy the warranty.

On the other hand, Bernoulli's reasoning makes it difficult to justify entering a fair lottery. To see this, suppose that we turn the example around. Suppose that you have a chance to purchase a \$512 lottery ticket for a lottery where there is one chance in two that you will receive \$1,024; otherwise you receive \$1. Write G for the action of gambling (buying the ticket) and $\sim G$ for the action of declining the ticket. If Bernoulli's logarithmic function applies, then

$$U(\sim G) = K9$$
$$U(G) = K\left[\frac{1}{2}\ln_2(1024) + \frac{1}{2}\ln_2(1)\right] = K5.$$ (6-7)

So you should not purchase the lottery ticket.

TABLE 6-2. *A Decision under Risk Not Involving Money*

Alternative actions	Rain (p = .7)	No rain (p = .3)
Carry umbrella	Dry, look reasonable	Dry, look silly
Do not carry umbrella	Wet, look silly	Dry, look reasonable

These examples represent a good deal of generosity on the part of either the insurance company or the gambling house, for neither the warranty nor the lottery allows for a percentage "off the top" for the company or the house. The insurance company could (and would!) have charged a considerable premium, for there is a substantial difference in utility units between $U(W)$ and $U(\sim W)$. On the other hand, the gambling house could not add on any fee, because the lottery would be rejected even if it was fair in terms of expected values.

Clearly this poses a problem, for people do accept lotteries and quite often make risky investments. To make things even more confusing, many people will both buy insurance policies and purchase lottery tickets. And to top it all off, all Bernoulli tried to do was explain the utility of money. I live in the Pacific Northwest where the skies are gray day after day but drenching rain is unusual. How can Bernoulli's analysis deal with the decision problem presented in Table 6-2?

Bernoulli's axiomatic approach to decision making was laudable, but his particular solution fell down on three counts. While money usually has decreasing marginal value, there can be circumstances in which it does not. There are decision situations where monetary value is not reasonable, but the concept of utility as the general worth of an outcome is reasonable. Finally, Bernoulli's choice of the logarithmic function was arbitrary. The logarithmic function is compatible with his axioms, but so are infinitely many other functions.

Instead of trying to define a specific, all-purpose utility function, we need to have a justifiable procedure for defining a class of permissible utility functions, and then for determining the appropriate function in a particular situation. This task was accomplished in the 1940s by John Von Neumann (the same man for whom Von Neumann machines are named) and Oscar Morgenstern. Their analysis[1] established the foundation for much of the modern study of decision making in economics and psychology. It is interesting both for its own sake and because of the style of argument that they used.

----

[1] Von Neumann and Morgenstern (1947).

6.4. VON NEUMANN AND MORGENSTERN'S AXIOMATIC APPROACH TO DECISION MAKING

Von Neumann and Morgenstern's approach to rational decision making parallels Euclid's approach to geometry. First they defined the primitive concept of a decision under risk. Then they presented axioms defining the behavior of a *rational decision maker* facing such a situation. The definitions and axioms were used to show that the decision maker could be thought of as maximizing his or her expected utility. They then provided a procedure for inferring what the utility function was from observations of the decision maker's behavior.

According to Von Neumann and Morgenstern, a decision under risk is a choice between lotteries. Let $X = \{x, y, z\}$ be a set of possible outcomes of a decision. The set contains all possible objective rewards, which could be money, possible dinner companions, places to go on a vacation, or what-have-you. Intuitively, these are the things that could be won in a decision situation. There is no requirement that X be finite. This means that X can be defined as a conceptual set, for example, the set of all possible money rewards.

Von Neumann and Morgenstern defined a lottery to be a triple, (x, p, y), where x and y are members of X, and p is a probability. (More generally, the letters w, x, y, z will be used to denote outcomes and p, q, r will be used to denote probabilities.) In the lottery, (x, p, y), you get x with probability p and y with probability $1 - p$.

Let $A = \{(x, p, y)\}$ be the set of all possible lotteries involving elements of X. The decision maker's task is to choose between pairs of elements of A, that is, to choose between pairs of lotteries. This includes simple presentations of a prize, for the event "the decision maker receives x" is equivalent to the lottery $(x, 1, y)$ or, for simplicity, just $(x, 1)$.

The "rainy weather" example of Table 6-2 can be put into the Von Neumann and Morgenstern notation:

$$A = \{\text{take umbrella} = (\text{dry reasonable}, p, \text{dry silly}) \\ \text{no umbrella} = (\text{wet silly}, p, \text{dry reasonable})\}, \tag{6-8}$$

where p is the probability of rain. The decision maker expresses a preference by taking (or not taking) an umbrella. More generally, write

$$xpy \supset wqz \tag{6-9}$$

to indicate that the decision maker either prefers lottery (x, p, y) to lottery (w,q,z) or is indifferent between them.[2] This is called a *weak preference* for

---

[2] Note that the symbol $\supset$ is not being used to indicate set containment, as it normally is. Unfortunately, this choice was required by the set of symbols available to me on a word processor, even using special mathematical symbols.

(x,p,y) over (w,q,z). To save space, the symbol $\approx$ will be used to indicate the "indifference" situation in which $(xpy) \supseteq (wqz)$ and $(wqz) \supseteq (xpy)$.

Von Neumann and Morgenstern proposed six axioms to define a rational decision maker. They can be presented in several ways. The presentation here is modeled after one developed by R. D. Luce and H. Raiffa.[3]

Axiom A1.   All lotteries of the form $(x\ p\ y)$ are in **A**.

The decision maker must be ready to choose between any of the infinite number of pairs lotteries that could be formed by combining a pair of potential rewards and a probability of obtaining one reward p. The set is infinite because p is defined on the real interval from 0 to 1.

Axiom A2.   The relation $\supseteq$ weakly orders all members of **X**.

The decision maker has a weak preference ordering, say, $x \supseteq y \supseteq z \supseteq w$, for the possible outcomes.

This axiom implies three things. The first, *reflexivity*, is that a reward is equivalent to itself. A rational decision maker should be indifferent between $(x\ p\ x)$ and $(x\ q\ x)$, regardless of the values of p and q. The second, *comparability*, is that the values of any two outcomes in **X** can be compared. The third is transitivity; if x is weakly preferred to y, and y is weakly preferred to z, then x is weakly preferred to z. In symbols,

$$(x \supseteq y) \bullet (y \supseteq z) \Rightarrow (x \supseteq z), \tag{6-10}$$

where the dot indicates conjunction and the arrow indicates implication. As an example of (6-10), using strong preference, if you prefer chocolate to strawberry and strawberry to vanilla, you should prefer chocolate to vanilla.

With a bit of thought one can come up with examples in which people do not appear to be able to compare all possible rewards, and situations in which preferences do not appear to be transitive. However these are descriptive statements. Von Neumann and Morgenstern were defining rationality, rather than trying to describe what people might do.

Axiom A3. $((x,\ p,\ y),\ q,\ y) \approx (x,\ pq,\ y)$.

A decision maker should be indifferent between a one-stage and a two-stage lottery that produce the same probabilities of prizes. Imagine that x is "all expenses paid vacation trip to Hawaii" and y is "all expenses paid vacation trip to Aspen." Lottery one is a choice between (a lottery ticket for "Hawaii, .5, Aspen") and (Aspen, 1), with a probability of .5 that you receive the lottery ticket. Lottery two is a choice between Hawaii and

[3] Luce & Raiffa, 1956.

Aspen, with a probability of .25 (= .5 × .5) of receiving the ticket to Hawaii. According to Von Neumann and Morgenstern, a rational decision maker should not discriminate between these lotteries.

Axiom A4. $(x \approx y) \Rightarrow (x, p, z) \approx (y, p, z)$.

This axiom asserts (as do many real lotteries) that one equivalently valued prize may always be substituted for another. The axiom does not say that such a prize always exists; it merely says that if there are equivalent prizes substitution is permitted.

Axiom A5. $(x \supseteq y) \Rightarrow (x \supseteq (x, p, y) \supseteq y)$.

A rational decision maker should always have a weak preference for a sure thing involving x than a lottery involving x and some other prize y that does not have greater value $(x \supseteq y)$. If Mrs. Field's chocolate chip cookies are at least as good as Famous Amos's chocolate chip cookies, then you should weakly prefer a Mrs. Field's cookie to a lottery ticket giving you a choice between Mrs. Field's and Famous Amos's, and weakly prefer the lottery ticket to one of Famous Amos's cookies.

Axiom A6.   If $x \supseteq y \supseteq z$, then for some p, the relation $y \approx (x, p, z)$ holds.

If possible rewards are weakly ordered there is a lottery such that the decision maker is indifferent between the middle reward and a lottery involving the higher and lower reward. If you weakly prefer chocolate to strawberry and strawberry to vanilla, then there is some gamble (value of p) such that you would be indifferent between a gift of strawberry ice cream or a lottery ticket involving chocolate and vanilla.

When axioms A1–A6 hold it is possible to assign numbers, $u(x_i)$, to all possible outcomes (elements of **X**), called the *utility* of the x_i's, $u(x)$ in such a way that the decision maker's behavior is equivalent to maximizing expected utility.

Let x_{max} and x_{min} be the most preferred and least preferred elements of **X**. Such elements exist by Axiom 2. Therefore, by Axiom 5 for any other element, x_i, there is some value of p, p_i such that $x_i \approx (x_{max} \, p_i \, x_{min})$. Arbitarily assign the upper and lower bounds of the utility scale to $u(x_{max})$ and $u(x_{min})$. For every other reward x_i in **X**, determine the probability value p_i for which A6 holds, and assign $u_i(x_i)$ by the rule

$$u(x_i) = p_i u(x_{max}) + (1 - p_i)u(x_{min})$$
$$u(x_i) = p_i(u(x_{max}) - u(x_{min})) + u(x_{min}).$$

(6-11)

Suppose that we were to ask a decision maker to choose between these ice cream flavors: {chocolate, strawberry, vanilla, and peppermint}. By experimentation, we find that the decision maker's preferences are

   chocolate $\supseteq$ vanilla $\supseteq$ strawberry $\supseteq$ peppermint.

By asking the decision maker to choose between lotteries, we further observe that

   (vanilla) $\approx$ (chocolate, .5, peppermint) and
   (strawberry) $\approx$ (chocolate, .25, peppermint).

Abrbitrarily assign a utility of 100 to the most preferred reward, chocolate, and a value of 0 to the least preferred reward, peppermint. Applying equation (6-11), vanilla will be assigned a utility of 50 and strawberry a utility of 25.

   Further applications of the other axioms allow us to evaluate the utility of any lottery. For example, the lottery (chocolate, .5, vanilla) has a utility of .5 (100) + .5 (50) = 75, and the lottery (strawberry, .5, peppermint) has a utility of .5 (25) + .5 (0) = 12.5.

   The utility values assigned by this procedure are not unique because they depend upon the arbitrary assignments of utility values to x_{max} and x_{min}. However, all permissible scales are linear transformations of each other. The reasoning behind this statement is as follows.

   For any two outcomes x_i and x_j to which equation (6-11) has been applied,

$$u(x_i) > u(x_j) \Leftrightarrow p_i > p_j. \tag{6-12}$$

The difference between the two utility values will be

$$u(x_i) - u(x_j) = (p_i - p_j)(u(x_{max}) - u(x_{min})). \tag{6-13}$$

The same relationships would apply to any other assignment $u^*(x)$ of utilities to rewards, achieved by assigning different values to $u(x_{max})$ and $u(x_{min})$. For any two different utility functions, u and u^*,

$$\frac{u(x_i) - u(x_j)}{u^*(x_i) - u^*(x_j)} = \frac{u(x_{max}) - u(x_{min})}{u^*(x_{max}) - u^*(x_{min})}$$
$$\frac{u(x_i) - u(x_j)}{u^*(x_i) - u^*(x_j)} = K(u,u^*). \tag{6-14}$$

In words, for any pair of outcomes, x_i and x_j, the difference in utilities measured in scale u will be a constant ratio of the difference between utilities measured in the u^* scale. This is a necessary and sufficient condition to ensure that any utility function is a linear function of any other utility function. For any two expressions of utility, u and u^*, it is always true that

$$u^*(x) = K(u,u^*)u(x) + c(u,u^*),$$ (6-15)

where $K(u,u^*)$ and $C(u,u^*)$ are constants characteristic of the pair of scales under consideration.

Von Neumann and Morgenstern's utility theorem is very important. It says that if a person behaves like a rational decision maker, as defined by A1–A6, then that person is behaving as if he or she assigned utility functions to each reward and then chose the lottery with the highest expected utility. The theorem further states that if a utility function is found that can be made to mimic the decision maker's choices, then that function is unique up to a linear transformation. This will never change the decision maker's choices, because if lottery (x, p, y) has a higher expected utility than lottery (z, q, w) in one utility scale, then it will have a higher expected utility in all linear transformations of that scale.

Von Neumann and Morgenstern did *not* say that utility is a linear function of objective value, for example, that the utility of money is linearly related to money. (If they had, they would have immediately run afoul of the St. Petersburg paradox.) Indeed, it is generally agreed that the utility function for objective value is a non-linear function.

There is an analogy to this result in physics, the measurement of temperature. Imagine that we have a set of beakers of water, heated to varying temperatures. We then fill glasses with mixtures of waters drawn from pairs of beakers, and ask a temperature judge to compare the temperature of mixtures, one pair at a time. All the judge tells us is which mixture is hotter. Now suppose that the judge does this using a thermometer, rather than making a psychological judgment. We could infer the readings on the thermometer up to a linear scale. This means that we could assert that the judge was using, say, the Fahrenheit scale or some linear transformation of it (including the Celsius scale). We could not tell which linear scale was being used. The same logic applies to choices based on economic preference.

Von Neumann and Morgenstern's approach goes beyond Bernoulli's. Instead of assuming an arbitrary transformation from monetary value to utility, the Von Neumann and Morgenstern conceptualization of choice applies to any set of comparable outcomes and provides a constructive procedure for computing utilities for any lottery between outcomes.

6.5. THE UTILITY OF MONEY

The case of the utility of money is of special interest because, after all, money is an extremely useful commodity! The problem is also of interest because in the case of money, the set of outcomes **X** is conceptually infinite, and in practice far too large for us to apply the constructive procedure described earlier. No one could conduct an experiment that explicitly determined the value of every sum of money, from $0 to $100,000,000 or more. We need some regular function, $u(\$x) = f(\$x)$ for calculating a decision maker's utility for money. And remember, this function will be a characteristic of a decision maker, rather than a characteristic of money itself. It is quite reasonable to expect different decision makers to have different functions for the utility of money. Indeed, as will now be shown, the insurance and gambling industries would not work if the industries and their customers had the same utility functions for money.

The trick is to observe how a rational decision maker deals with decisions under risk involving money (or rewards with agreed-upon monetary values). We then infer key mathematical properties of the utility function for money from the decision maker's behavior. We first look at this for the case of insurance, which is considered a rational purchase in many situations. What sort of utility function for money leads a person to buy an insurance policy?

Suppose that the utility function $u(x)$ has the following properties:

$$\frac{du}{dx} > 0$$

$$\frac{d^2u}{dx^2} < 0. \tag{6-16}$$

This is a *negatively accelerated* function. It is a mathematical restatement of Bernoulli's axioms.

Figure 6-1 illustrates the form of a function obeying conditions (6-16). The following example, based on Figure 6-1, shows why a certain amount of insurance can be a good buy.

Suppose that you own some commodity (e.g., a house, car, or crop) that has value 8 in arbitrary monetary units, for example, $800,000. This is shown at point A on the ordinate in Figure 6-1. Suppose further that you anticipate a hazardous situation (e.g., a hurricane) that will occur with probability .5 and that, if it does occur, will reduce the value of the commodity to 2 monetary units. According to Von Neumann and Morgenstern, this situation is equivalent to the lottery (2, .5, 8). If you lose, the utility of your wealth will be the utility of 2, at point B. The expected wealth, if you accept this gamble, is 5. The expected utility of the gamble is halfway between these two utilities, at point C on the ordinate.

Suppose you are offered an insurance program at a cost of 3 units of wealth. If you accept, your remaining wealth will be 5 units. The utility of the remaining wealth is at point D. Because $D > C$, the insurance is worth its cost in utility units. This is true even though the expected value in

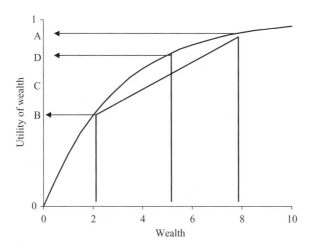

FIGURE 6-1. An illustration of a utility function that justifies buying insurance, but forbids the purchase of lottery tickets. (See the text for an explanation.)

monetary units of the lottery, that is, not buying insurance, is equal to the cost of the insurance.

More generally, consider any lottery of the form (x, p, y), where x and y are in monetary units. Let $(z, 1)$ be the "lottery" of receiving z monetary units for certain. A decision maker is said to be *risk aversive* if z can be found that satisfies the following conditions:

$$z \leq px + (1 - p)y$$
$$(z, 1) \supset (x, p, y). \tag{6-17}$$

In words, a decision maker is risk aversive if he or she prefers receiving a "sure thing" that is less than or equal to the expected value of a gamble to participating in a gamble.

Insurance companies and risk-aversive clients get along, for utility is a function of the decision maker, not the commodity under consideration. The insurance company's utility for money is very nearly identical to money. Therefore, when insurers are dealing with a moderately risk-aversive client, they can make money by charging somewhat more for insurance than they expect to have to pay out in claims. To see this, reexamine Figure 6-1 and imagine that the insurance company sells the policy for 4 units. This moves the utility of insured property downward but, as inspection of the figure shows, the utility would still be well above point C. The offer is a good deal for both the risk-aversive decision maker and the insurance company.

Now what about the case of gambling casinos? To be concrete, suppose that you have a current wealth of 5 units, which corresponds to the

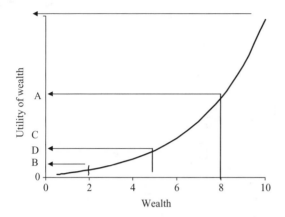

FIGURE 6-2. A decision maker whose utility function is positively accelerated in wealth should be willing to purchase a lottery ticket whose cost, in units of wealth, is greater than the expected value, in wealth, of the lottery.

utility value marked at point D in Figure 6-2. A casino offers a lottery ticket, at a cost of 3 monetary units, that pays 6 units with probability .5, otherwise nothing. In Von Neumann and Morgenstern's terms, you are being offered a choice between two lotteries, the residual "lottery" of 5 units for sure (you do not buy the ticket), (5,1) or the lottery (2, .5, 8). We have already seen that a risk-aversive decision maker prefers the sure thing, (5,1). The moral of this story is that a risk-aversive decision maker never buys a lottery ticket unless the odds are in the decision maker's favor. And, of course, the lottery company cannot afford to make this offer.

If the conditions in equation 6-16 are replaced by

$$\frac{du}{dx} > 0$$

$$\frac{d^2u}{dx^2} > 0,$$

(6-18)

the utility function will be *positively accelerated*, as shown in Figure 6-2. This changes things around.

As in Figure 6-1, A represents the utility of the decision maker's wealth if the lottery is won, B represents the utility of wealth if the lottery is lost, C, halfway between A and B, represents the utility of the expected value of the lottery, and D represents the utility of wealth if the decision maker does not participate in the lottery. As C > D, it is now rational to participate in the lottery. The expected utility of the lottery may exceed the expected utility of not participating, even though the expected value of the lottery is less than the expected value of non-participation.

More generally, a decision maker is said to be *risk seeking* when the inequality and preference in equation 6-17 are both reversed,

$$z \geq px + (1 - py)$$
$$(x, p, y) \supset (z, 1).$$
(6-19)

A gambling casino can do business with a risk-seeking decision maker, for such a decision maker is willing to pay more for a lottery ticket than its expected value in monetary terms. However, an insurance company cannot do so, for the risk seeker will prefer to take his or her chances, rather than take precautions against a disaster.

To complete the argument, a decision maker is said to be *risk neutral* if the inequality and preferences in equations 6-17 and 6-19 are replaced by equality and indifference:

$$z = px + (1 - py)$$
$$(x, p, y) \approx (z, 1).$$
(6-20)

The insurance company and the gambling casino do not have to be absolutely risk neutral, that is, interested only in money. The only requirement is that the insurance company be less risk averse than the decision maker, and that the gambling casino be less risk seeking. The analysis here is further complicated by the fact that the decision maker, as has been presented here, considers a single transaction. The insurance company and the gambling casino establish policies, to be applied over many cases. Therefore, they can reasonably assume that their earnings, as a whole, will be very close to the expected values, even though an occasional person may present a large claim (insurance) or win the jackpot (gambling). What are gambles for the policy holder and gambler are very nearly sure things for the insurance company and the casino.

Von Neumann-Morgenstern's utility theory can account for the observation that people will buy insurance and that people will purchase lottery tickets. But what about people who do both? One approach is simply to write off such behavior as irrational. However, this is not necessary. The Von Neumann and Morgenstern approach does not require that a decision maker have some relatively simple utility function. Rather, the utility function is something to be discovered by observation of the decision maker's choices. The explanation offered for a person who both has insurance and buys lottery tickets shows how flexible the theory can be.

In most state and national lotteries, the probability of winning is very low, but the winning payoffs are well beyond the total wealth of a typical player. Insurance, by definition, involves payoffs that protect current wealth. In addition, we take out insurance against anticipatable risks, such as the danger of having an automobile accident. The probability of

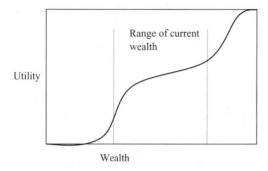

FIGURE 6-3. This utility curve would lead a decision maker to purchase insurance to protect wealth and simultaneously participate in a low probability–high payoff lottery. (See text for an explanation.)

such an event is far higher than the probability that a player will win a state or national lottery.

Several authors have suggested that what this means is that the act of winning a lottery would have a huge payoff, in utility units, because it would permit a winner to change his or her lifestyle in some major way. Insurance, on the other hand, provides a payoff that restores one's current lifestyle. Translating this to mathematical terms, the suggestion is that within the range of "everyday" transactions, most people have diminishing marginal utility for money; the conditions of equation 6–16 hold. On the other hand, when wealth moves toward the range in which lifestyle changes are possible, the utility curve is positively accelerated. Then, when wealth reaches a plateau characteristic of a new lifestyle, the utility curve again becomes negatively accelerated, until increased wealth permits a jump to a second, even more opulent, lifestyle.

The same thing can occur on the downside. At a certain point, losses may mount to the point at which further losses hardly matter at all.

Figure 6-3 shows the form of the utility curve that would be derived from this sort of reasoning. This curve does permit a decision maker to buy both insurance policies and lottery tickets.

6.6. A SUMMARY OF THE ARGUMENT

Von Neumann and Morgenstern's analysis has been enormously influential in economics and in the psychological study of decision making. Therefore, it is important to realize what the approach is, and what it is not.

Von Neumann and Morgenstern described a *normative* model of how decision makers ought to behave. First, they asserted that decision making could be reduced to a choice between lotteries. Next, they presented six axioms defining rational behavior. Most people regard these rules as eminently reasonable. Von Neumann and Morgenstern then showed that a decision maker who follows these rules can be thought of as agglomerating all the characteristics of different choices into a single index, the utility function, and then choosing between lotteries on the basis of their expected utility. In addition, they showed how a rational decision maker's utility function can be inferred from an observation of choices. The construction procedure only works if the decision maker's choices satisfy the six axioms.

Von Neumann and Morgenstern did not claim that any actual decision maker follows these procedures. Their theory is not, in itself, a psychological theory of decision making. What it provides for psychology is a reference point. By contrasting the behavior recommended by the Von Neumann and Morgenstern model to actual behavior we have a way of describing how far human decision making is from the ideal.

The term "ideal" or "rational" decision maker is sometimes misunderstood. The concept of ideal or rational carries a connation of "one best solution" for a decision problem. Rationality in the Von Neumann and Morgenstern sense refers to rationality, given the way that the decision maker construes the problem. Decisions under risk involve two subjective elements, the utility function and the assignment of probabilities. Decision makers who have different utility functions, or who make different assignments of probabilities to outcomes, may rationally make different decisions when faced with what an outside observer might regard as identical decision situations.

We have already seen how this works in the case of utility functions. A decision maker with a negatively accelerated utility function (Figure 6-1) will buy insurance and decline to purchase lottery tickets; a decision maker with a positively accelerated utility function (Figure 6-2) will decline insurance and purchase lottery tickets; while a decision maker with the convoluted utility function shown in Figure 6-3 will buy both insurance policies and lottery tickets. To complete the possibilities, a decision maker whose utility function is linear in wealth will decline both actual insurance policies and actual lottery tickets. Do you see why?[4]

---

[4] Neither insurance companies nor gambling casinos offer their customers a fair lottery, in the sense that the expected value of the payoff, in monetary terms, is equal to the premium or the "charge for playing" levied by the house's percentage in a casino. If they did, then in the long run, both the insurance company and the casino would break even, and they are in the business to make money. A decision maker whose utility function is a linear function of wealth will reject both actual insurance policies and actual lotteries, for such a decision maker does not wish to pay either the premium or the house percentage. There are certain cases in which decision makers appear to behave in exactly this manner. Large universities may regard money as equivalent to utility over a very large range. These institutions often "self insure," a euphemism for saying that they pay for insurable losses out of their own pocket, but do not pay premiums. Universities are also prone to invest their endowments conservatively. They do not invest in low probability–high payoff ventures.

The same argument applies to choices between things that are not obviously monetary. Returning to fiction, at one point in *The Lady's Not for Burning*, Jenny's jailor offers her a choice between being burned as a witch or suffering what Victorian era writers referred to as "the fate worse than death." On learning of this the soldier, who is also being held captive, says, "Of course you refused." Jenny replies that she is thinking about it. Neither the soldier nor Jenny was irrational, but their utilities may have differed.

The view that decision making is a choice between lotteries carries with it the assumption that the decision maker can assign probabilities to the outcomes involved in each lottery. Note the phrase "can assign," rather than "knows." The distinction is important. A decision maker can only be asked to make rational choices based upon what the decision maker believes to be the case. Therefore, when a rational person casts a decision problem as a lottery, that rational person has to use his or her subjective estimates of probabilities. These estimates may turn out to be wrong, but that is a separate issue.

The insurance industry's reaction to the terrorist attack on New York City on September 11, 2001, provides an interesting illustration of the use of subjective probabilities. In 2002, the U.S. Department of Homeland Security estimated the relative probabilities of future attacks on various U.S. cities. Large, prominent cities, such as New York, Washington, DC, Chicago, and Los Angeles, were estimated to be 100 times more likely to be attacked than relatively small regional centers, such as Des Moines, Iowa. Cities of middling size and prominence, such as Seattle, were deemed to be 20 times as likely to be attacked as was Des Moines. Insurance agencies adjusted their rates for damage due to terrorism; a million dollars worth of insurance cost 100 times more in Los Angeles than it did in Des Moines.

There are many situations in which insurance companies assess different risks, and charge different premiums, for insurance against the same type of loss. Insurance rates for automobile theft, for instance, do vary from place to place. These variations are based upon statistical analyses of the relative frequencies of thefts in different cities. These can be considered objective estimates of the probability of theft. The estimate of the probability of a terrorist attack was entirely a subjective process. Nevertheless, if the insurance companies believed these estimates, whether or not they were true in some objective sense, the companies were rational to set their rates accordingly.

On the other hand, decision makers are not free to use any set of estimates. Von Neumann and Morgenstern's analysis depends very strongly on the assumption that the decision maker's probabilities follow the restrictions for a probability calculus, as defined in Chapter 2. There is ample evidence that people do not always do this. The 2003–4 presidential primary campaign provided a nice example. On August 23, 2003, a commentator[5] placed on his website his estimate of the odds on each candidate's winning the election. Odds can easily be converted to probabilities; for example, if the odds are 3:1 that a particular candidate will win, it follows that the probability is $3/(3+1) = .75$. The columnist's list covered all announced candidates plus Senator Hillary Clinton, who had repeatedly stated that she was not running.[6] The individual probability estimates totaled .52. This violates the definition of a probability function.

Errors in the other direction also occur. In 2004, a London turf accountant ("bookie," to Americans) posted the odds on various cities hosting the Olympics in 2012. When converted to probabilities, his estimates added up to more than one.

I find it hard to think of any definition of rationality that permits the sum of mutually exclusive, exhaustive probabilities to be anything other than one. But, as will be discussed in section 6.7, that does not mean that real people, as opposed to rational decision makers, do not do just this.

There are decision situations that cannot be recast as decisions under risk. One is a *game*, in which the decision maker is playing against an informed, rational opponent. In this case, each choice of action by a decision-maker will be observed and countered by the opponent. Von Neumann and Morgenstern also presented an analysis of games, but we will not pursue it here.

The other case is *decision making under ignorance*. In this case, the decision maker knows what outcomes might occur, but does not know their probabilities. Put another way, the decision maker knows what could happen, but does not have any way of estimating the likelihood of each possibility. Opinions differ about what the appropriate decision-making strategy should be. I do not know of any convincing mathematical argument for dealing with decisions to be made under ignorance. However, such situations do occur. As of 2005, several million dollars had been spent taking astronomical observations in the search for extraterrestrial intelligence (SETI). What is the probability that such life exists? We have no idea.

6.7. PSYCHOLOGICAL RESEARCH ON DECISION MAKING

Psychologists are concerned with descriptive theories of what people actually do, rather than normative theories of what they should do. Psychologists had little trouble showing that actual decision making does not always fit Von Neumann and Morgenstern's normative

---

[5] "The Kudzu Files," self-described as the ravings of a southern liberal.
[6] And, in fact, she did not run for president in 2004.

prescriptions. Developing an adequate descriptive theory has proven to be much harder.

Most psychological theories of decision making can be thought of as modifications of the Von Neumann and Morgenstern approach, even though they sometimes are presented as completely new formulations. Psychologists who approach decision making this way ask how one has to modify the notions of utility and probability to fit actual problems into the lottery framework. A second, rather smaller, group of researchers have raised questions about the use of the lottery model itself. I will concentrate on the proposals of the first group, because the second group rejects the mathematical framework.

The Allais Paradox

Shortly after Von Neumann and Morgenstern published their work, a French economist, Maurice Allais, posed a problem that presents a challenge to their approach almost as compelling as the challenge the St. Petersburg paradox posed to theories that emphasized maximization of expected monetary rewards. There are several versions of the Allais paradox.

The paradox is based on expected behavior in two situations:

Situation 1. Choose between (a) receiving $1 million for sure or (b) a lottery in which there is a probability of .1 that you will receive $5 million, .89 that you will receive $1 million, and .01 that you will receive nothing.

Situation 2. Choose between (c) the lottery ($5 million, .1, 0) or (d) the lottery ($1 million, .11, 0).

Allais claimed that most people would prefer to receive alternative (a) in situation 1 and alternative (c) in situation 2. Subsequent experiments, in which people are asked to imagine themselves in varying versions of the Allais paradox, have confirmed this preference.[7]

The paradox becomes apparent when the utilities are worked out. Suppressing the "$" and writing M for "million," the choice of (a) in situation 1 implies that

$$1 \cdot u(1M) + 0 \cdot u(0M) \; > \; .1 \cdot u(5M) + .89 \cdot u(1M) + .01 \cdot u(0)$$
$$.11 \cdot u(1M) - .01 \cdot u(0) \; > \; .1 \cdot u(5M).$$

Choice of (c) in situation 2 implies that $.1 \cdot u(5M) > .11 \cdot (1M)$. Clearly we have a contradiction. And why has this occurred? Suppose that the rewards were placed in three boxes, red, green, and blue, and that the

---

[7] See, for instance, Kahneman and Tversky (1979).

choices were between boxes, with probabilities associated with each box and, in some cases, probabilities not adding up to 1, to allow for the possibility that no box will be chosen.

In situation 1:
Choice a: Red ($1M) with probability .11, Green ($1M) with probability .89.
Choice b: Blue ($5M) with probability .10, Green ($1M) with probability .89.
In situation 2:
Choice c: Blue ($5M) with probability .10
Choice d: Red ($1M) with probability .11.

If a person makes choice (a) in situation 1 and (c) in situation 2, the relative utilities of the red and blue boxes must have changed as a function of the lottery in which they appear. This violates the substitutability axiom. Yet it seems clear, from the empirical data, that most people do indeed choose (a) and then (c). What has gone wrong?

Two arguments have been made. One is that this is a sort of "mind game" that hides the nature of the choice, because we would not normally think of "$ 1M for sure" as the lottery (*$1M, .11, $1M*). The analysis using the red, green, and blue boxes makes this much clearer and I, for one, think that people would be much more rational if presented with the boxes than if presented with the choices in their usual form. If you accept this argument, you should merely, and regretfully, note that otherwise rational decision makers can be bamboozled. Perhaps that is one function of advertising. There is another approach.

Prospect Theory

One can argue that Von Neumann and Morgenstern's approach is not challenged by the Allais paradox, for they were concerned with a normative rather than a descriptive theory of decision making. An obvious question, then, is "What would a descriptive theory look like, and how can the Allais (and other) paradoxes be explained within it?" This is the tack taken by Daniel Kahneman, Amos Tversky, and their colleagues. Kahneman and Tversky's work was motivated by the Allais paradox and several other observations of behaviors that violate the predictions of utility theory but that do not, on their face, seem to be what one would call irrational. Kahneman[8] has written a brief and highly readable discussion of their general approach. There is room here for only two of Kahneman and Tversky's many examples of cases where behavior departs from the rational view of utility theory.

---

[8] Kahneman (2003).

The first example deals with reactions to certainty and to a distinction between gains and losses. According to the utility theory approach, the utility of an outcome is a monotonically non-decreasing function of its objective value, that more money is always preferred to less money. Kahneman and Tversky report on a number of observations of the following sort, in which the numbers refer to units of money (for the studies were conducted in several countries):

> *Situation 3.* Choose between the lottery (4000, .8, 0) or receive 3,000 units for sure.
> *Situation 4.* Choose between the lottery (− 4000, .8, 0) or pay 3,000 units for sure.

When university students were asked what they would do in situation 3, they chose to receive the certain reward, by a considerable majority. However, when students were asked what they would do in situation 4, they chose the lottery. That is, they choose a certain outcome when dealing with gains, and choose a gamble when faced with losses. In terms of the gambling and insurance decisions discussed earlier, the students decline to gamble but refuse insurance. This violates the concept that a sum of money has the same utility whether it is to be won or lost.[9]

The next example, which is very widely cited, deals with the concept of *framing*. People are given the following cover story (which I abbreviate from the original).[10]

A public health official is concerned about a potential outbreak of a disease that is expected to kill 600 people. Two alternative plans have been prepared.

> *Situation 5.*
> Program A1. If this program is adopted, 200 people can be saved.
> Program A2. If this program is adopted, there is a 1 / 3 chance that 600 people will be saved, and a 2 / 3 chance that 400 will die.
> *Situation 6.*
> Program B1. If this program is adopted, 400 people will die.
> Program B2. If this program is adopted, there is a 1/3 probability that nobody will die, and a 2 / 3 probability that 600 people will die.

In situation 5, college students (and physicians in an analogous study) choose program A1, preferring a certain saving of 200 lives to a gamble with the same expected value. In situation 6, students and physicians choose program B2, preferring a lottery rather than accepting an absolute loss of equal expected value. But these situations are identical except for wording. The only difference is that one situation uses wording that stresses gain and another uses wording that stresses loss.

---

[9] Kahneman and Tversky (1979).   [10] Tversky and Kahneman (1981).

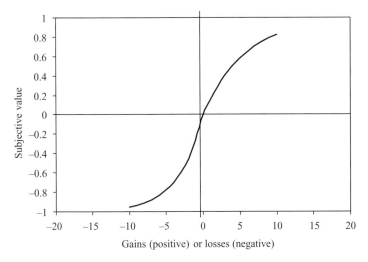

FIGURE 6-4. The prospect theory function for subjective value as a function of gains or losses. The rate of change in subjective value is greater for a loss than for a gain of an equal amount.

Kahneman, Tversky, and their associates used these examples, and many others, to show that preferences between lotteries change, depending upon whether or not the focus is on gains or losses. They concluded that there were two reasons that utility theory failed to describe behavior. One was that the utility of a reward depends upon whether it was seen as a gain or a loss. This effectively moves the zero point of utility to present wealth, which is not, in itself, inconsistent with utility theory. Their second reason was more serious. Utility theory assumes that the decision maker does deal with probabilities as if they were probability measures (Chapter 2). Kahneman and Tversky argued that they do not.

As a substitute they offered *prospect theory*.[11] In prospect theory, subjective value (utility) is determined by gains and losses around a zero point of present wealth, rather than a zero point of zero objective value. A further assumption is that the rate of change in subjective value is greater for losses than for gains. A hypothetical function with these properties is shown in Figure 6-4. Given these assumptions, a rational person should prefer a certain gain over a gamble with equivalent expected value, but should prefer to gamble with losses than to accept a certain loss.

In dealing with probabilities Kahneman and Tversky pointed out that the Allais paradox is only a paradox because subjective probabilities are

---

[11] Kahneman and Tversky (1979).

assumed to satisfy the definition of a probability measure. The paradox disappears if we assume two things. The first is that certainties are overvalued. Thus, an alternative that reduces the probability of a loss from .01 to 0 is considered more valuable than an alternative that reduces the probability of a loss from .02 to .01. The second assumption is that probabilities are underadditive. Instead, when calculating expected values, probabilities are replaced by a weighting function, $\pi(p)$, where $\pi(p) + \pi(1 - p) < 1$. This assumption requires non-linear transformation of probabilities, and is incompatible with utility theory.

Kahneman and Tversky argued further that the way in which people deal with probabilities ensures that subjective probability estimates will not conform to other requirements of a probability measure. As evidence, they constructed a number of cases in which subjective estimates of probability violate the laws of probability. One of the best known of these examples is the *conjunction paradox*, exemplified by the *Linda problem*.[12]

Linda is described to college students as being in her thirties, bright, college educated, and strongly interested in social causes. The students are then asked which is the most likely outcome, that Linda is a bank teller, that she is a feminist, or that she is a bank teller and active in the feminist movement.

A substantial number of people say that Linda is more likely to be a bank teller and a feminist than she is to be a bank teller. This violates the law of conditional probability, which requires that for any two events, A and B, $P(A \cdot B) \leq P(A)$. This is only one of several other cases in which subjective estimates of probability appear to violate the rules of the probability calculus.[13]

Tversky and Kahneman (1983) explained the conjunction paradox by saying that instead of applying the probability calculus to the problem, people consulted their memory and asked how representative Linda's description was, compared to the description they could construct, given what they knew about bank tellers and feminists.

In theory, utility theory could be replaced by prospect theory, if we knew the nature of the mapping between objective probabilities, p, and Kahneman and Tversky's weight function, $\pi(p)$. While this issue has been explored, psychologists have yet to come up with a compelling, empirically accurate model of this transformation. Examples such as the Linda problem make one wonder whether or not this issue can be treated axiomatically. This raises a larger issue. Do people make decisions by weighing the odds in the current situation or do they rely on analogies to previous experiences?

[12] Tversky and Kahneman (1983).
[13] Hammond (1996) and Hunt (2002) provide more detailed discussions.

Some Disturbing Observations from the Field

Research intended to move the Von Neumann-Morgenstern approach toward a descriptive theory has generally been conducted within a university setting. Students participate in experiments where they are asked to imagine what they would do if they were confronted with this or that situation. The resulting data have been used to develop descriptive theories that are still within the general Von Neumann-Morgenstern approach, although they differ in details. Prospect theory is a good example. This research has been conducted with a good deal of rigor, using appropriate experimental controls. Nevertheless, it does rely on observations of what people say they would do, rather than observations of what people actually do.

People who have studied the behavior of decision makers outside the laboratory have questioned the Von Neumann-Morgenstern lottery model. They argue that, first of all, people do not calculate probabilities and utilities. Instead, they rely on their experience to develop imaginary scenarios of what is likely to happen if they take this or that action, and then choose the best scenario. Therefore, if you want to know what a decision maker will do, you want to know about his or her experience, rather than how the decision maker calculates utilities and probabilities.[14] A second criticism that students of "real-life" decision making make is that the lottery model itself is often inapplicable. The lottery model assumes that the decision maker knows what alternatives are available and then commits to an irrevocable decision. Actual decision makers are keenly aware that often they will not discover what the alternatives are until they begin to take action.[15]

We look again at fiction to sum up this argument. How did Jenny Jourdemaine handle the choice between being burned at the stake or accepting the jailor's indecent proposal? She discovered a third alternative not in the lottery. She and the soldier escaped.

Whatever the best approach to descriptive theory, there can be no question about the powerful influence that the Von Neumann and Morgenstern approach and its derivatives have had on economics, psychology, and related disciplines. Von Neumann and Morgenstern's book is considered a classic analysis of decision making. Herbert Simon, who first called attention to the discrepancy between the laboratory model and the behavior of business executives, received the Nobel Prize in Economics in 1976. Daniel Kahneman received the Nobel Prize in Economics in 2002. (His colleague, Amos Tversky, had died a few years earlier.) The debate over utility theory has been conducted by intellectual heavyweights.

---

[14] Beach (1990); Klein (1998).   [15] Wagner (1991).

6.8. THE PROBLEM OF VOTING

Von Neumann and Morgenstern were concerned with the rationality of an individual decision maker. Many decisions are made by groups, and groups are composed of individuals. Different people may, rationally, have different preferences either because they have different utility functions or because they have different beliefs about subjective probabilities. But often the group has to make a choice. How is the choice to be made?

In the political arena, the modern answer seems to be democracy, a form of government that Winston Churchill described as "the worst system devised by the wit of man, except for all the others."[16] An analogous argument, the principle of "one dollar, one vote," is applied in corporate decision making, when shareholders have voting rights proportional to their investment in the company. These are all expressions of a more general issue: How are group decisions to be made so that the decision reflects the will of the people?

Quite a few voting systems have been explored. In addition to the simple "one person, one vote, majority rules" characteristic of a pure democracy and the weighted-voting-scheme characteristic of corporate decisions, we have "supermajority" systems, in which the winning candidate must have some fixed percentage of the vote, where that percentage is greater than 50%. Both voting systems are common. In the United States and most other developed democracies, mayors, parliamentary representatives, and (in the United States) governors, congressional representatives, and senators are chosen by majority vote. Supermajorities may be required on particular issues. In the United States, many municipalities require supermajorities to approve increases in taxes (e.g., in deciding upon a levy on property to support schools), and in the U.S. Congress a presidential veto can only be overridden by a 2/3 majority in both the Senate and the House of Representatives. In some elections the winner can be declared by a plurality (the candidate with the most votes wins), even though that candidate may not have received a majority of the votes.

This hardly exhausts the number of systems in use. Many democratic choices are made using a two- or even three-tiered system. In a parliamentary system voters within a district choose representatives, who then vote for a national leader. The United States chooses its national leader in a convoluted variety of this system. In the first step voters within each state vote for national candidates. The candidate with the most votes (a plurality system) within a state is declared the winner of that state. The winner of a state is awarded that state's electoral votes, with one electoral vote for each of the congresspersons from that state plus an extra two

---

[16] Peter (1977).

votes, representing the state's senators). In order to be declared president, a candidate must win a majority of the electoral votes. If no candidate has a majority in the electoral college the choice is made by an election within the House of Representatives, where the representatives from each state meet separately and determine their state's vote by majority choice.

On several historic occasions this system has produced results that differ from the results that would be produced by a direct one-citizen, one-vote method. As of this writing (2005), three, and possibly four, presidents were elected although they had lost the popular vote.[17]

Another popular system is the Hare balloting system, sometimes referred to as "first past the post" balloting. Hare ballots have been used to choose parliamentarians in Australia and Ireland.[18] Voters rank-order their individual preferences for candidates or actions. The decision then takes place in one or more rounds. In round one, only first-place votes are considered. If one of the candidates receives a majority that candidate is declared winner. Otherwise, the candidate with the fewest first-place votes is dropped from consideration. Voters who placed that candidate first have their preferences moved up, so that their second-place votes are treated as first-place votes, third place as second place, and so on. This is called redistribution. A second round of counting is conducted. Once again, if one of the candidates receives a majority of first-place votes, that candidate is selected. Otherwise, the votes of the candidate with the fewest votes in the second round are redistributed. The process continues until a winner is declared.

Finally, in a weighted voting scheme, each voter is given two or more votes, which the voter can then redistribute among the candidates.

Voting systems can be thought of as *social welfare functions* (SWFs). A social welfare function takes as its input the rank orders of individual preferences and produces, as output, a rank ordering of the alternatives for the entire society. As you might imagine, different SWFs can return different results for the same set of individual preferences. This is seen in the following example of a nine-person society, with voters $a, b, c, d, e, f, g, h, i$ and alternatives x, y, z. Let $a: x, y, z$ represent the fact that voter a

---

[17] John Quincy Adams in 1824, Rutherford B. Hayes in 1876, and George W. Bush in 2000 all lost in the popular vote. Hayes and Bush were elected to the presidency by the Electoral College, after heated debates over the legitimacy of the vote in certain states. Adams lost to Andrew Jackson by a large margin in the popular vote, 41% to 31%, but was selected by the House after the Electoral College vote was split among Adams, Andrew Jackson, and two other candidates. In 1800, Thomas Jefferson was elected by the House after he tied with Aaron Burr in the Electoral College. The nationwide popular vote was not recorded until 1824, and so we do not know whether Jefferson or Burr received the most popular votes.

[18] The system is also used in some professional societies, including the American Psychological Association.

prefers the alternatives in the order x,y,z, and so on. Suppose that the preferences are as follows:

a: x,z,y
b: x,z,y
c: x,z,y
d: x,z,y
e: y,z,x
f: y,z,x
g: y,z,x
h: z,y,x
i: z,y,x

Who should be elected? There is no majority winner, so any majority and supermajority voting systems cannot produce a decision. A plurality system will choose x first, followed by y, then z. Write this $x>y>z$. Under the Hare system, z is thrown out on the first round of balloting, and z's votes redistributed to y, who then wins the election. If we then remove y from the ballot, z defeats x, 5 votes to 4. This produces the ordering $y>z>x$. Finally, as is sometimes done, we might use a weighted-preference voting scheme in which 2 points are awarded for a first-place choice, 1 for second, and 0 for three. Candidates are then ordered by their point count. Using this method, x has 8 votes, y has 8, and z has 11, producing the order $z>x=y$. Depending on the voting system used, the results are

Majority or supermajority: No ordering.
Plurality: $x>y>z$.
First-past-the-post: $y>z>x$.
Weighted-preference voting: $z>x=y$.

Would something like this be likely to happen in a real election? The answer is emphatically "Yes!" The most famous recent example is the United States presidential election of 2000.

There were three serious candidates: George W. Bush, Al Gore, and Ralph Nader. Nader had much less support than either Bush or Gore. Politically, they were clearly ordered on a conservative to liberal dimension, with Bush the most conservative and Nader the most liberal. Gore received the most popular votes but Bush won in the Electoral College. If the Hare system had been used in the 2000 election, within each state, Nader would have gone out on the first round in every state, but a redistribution of the Nader votes to Gore would very probably have weighted the Electoral College to Gore.

Political thinkers have spent quite a bit of time trying to find the fairest possible voting system. Alas! We now know that none ever will be found.

The economist Kenneth Arrow has proven that it is impossible to develop a voting system (i.e., an SWF) that simultaneously satisfies all the requirements that a social welfare function ought to meet.[19] Arrow's work represents a breakthrough in our understanding of the ways in which social choices can be derived from individual choices.[20]

6.9. DEFINITION AND NOTATION

Consider a society of N individuals, $\{a, b, c, \ldots n\}$. When N is large enough so that enumeration of individual choices is clumsy, we will refer to the ith individual, where i ranges from 1 to N. As a notational convenience, n will always refer to the "highest numbered" member of the society. Choices are to be made between at least three alternatives, $\{x, y, z\}$. These could be interpreted either as candidates or choices of a course of action.

The notation $x >_a y$ indicates that individual a prefers alternative x to alternative y. Only strict preferences will be considered at the individual level. If some subset A of the individuals prefer x to y, we write $x >_A y$. The notation $x >_S y$ indicates that the SWF determines that x is to be preferred to y by the society as a whole.

If a point is to be made about preferences in general, without regard to the identity of the person or group holding the relation, the subscript on the ">" will be dropped. On occasion it will be useful to reverse the relationship, for example, writing $x < y$ instead of $y > x$.

We will consider the possibility that the SWF does not discriminate between x and y, written $x \sim_S y$, but will show that this cannot happen.

On occasion it will be necessary to refer to a pairwise comparison without indicating what its value is. This will be written $x : y$.

Preferences are *transitive* if the following relation holds:

$$(x > y) \bullet (y > z) \Rightarrow (x > z). \tag{6-21}$$

Transitivity is equivalent to saying that there is a strict linear ordering of alternatives, that is, for some individual, a, or for the SWF, $x >_a y >_a z$ (or some other ordering).

A *preference profile* is a collection of preferences for all possible pairs of alternatives. In the case of the 2000 election, two of the six possible preference profiles were (Bush > Gore, Gore > Nader, Nader < Bush) and (Gore > Bush, Bush > Nader, Nader > Gore). More generally, preference profiles will always be written in the order $(x : y, y : z, z : x)$.

A preference profile is said to be *rational* if the preferences are transitive. Otherwise they are intransitive and, hence, irrational. If relations are irrational, the three relations will always be either $(>, >, >)$ or $(<, <, <)$.

---

[19] Arrow (1963).
[20] In 1972, Arrow received the Nobel Prize in Economics for his contributions to this field.

In the 2000 presidential election example just given, the first profile is rational and the second is irrational.

A preference profile for more than three alternatives is rational if and only if all subsets of three alternatives contained within the profile are transitive. The intuition here is that when a preference profile is rational, the alternatives can be ordered $w > x > y > z$ for the case of four alternatives. This is only possible if all subsets of three alternatives can also be ordered. This fairly obvious point permits us to restrict our attention to the three alternative case. If it can be shown that rationality of the SWF profiles cannot be guaranteed for three alternatives, we know, immediately, that rationality cannot be guaranteed for more than three alternatives.

A *social welfare function* (SWF) is a function that takes as input a set of preference profiles, one for each member of a society, and produces as output a preference profile for the society as a whole.

A *rational unrestricted domain social welfare function* (RUDSWF) is a function that takes as its input any combination of individual rational preference profiles and produces, as output, a rational preference profile for society as a whole.

This definition restricts our attention to a situation in which each individual within a society has a rational preference profile, which amounts to saying that each individual can produce a linear ordering of the alternatives.

6.10. ARROW'S AXIOMS: THE RESTRICTIONS ON SOCIAL WELFARE FUNCTIONS

Arrow argued that any RUDSWF should satisfy the following axioms:

Unanimity (U). *If all individuals in a society have the same preference on a given pairwise comparison, then the social welfare function should have the same preference on that comparison.*

To go back to the 2000 U.S. election example, if every voter in the United States preferred Gore to Nader, then the SWF should also prefer Gore to Nader. More generally, for a society of N individuals,

$$(\forall i(x >_i y)) \supset (x >_s y). \tag{6-22}$$

This certainly seems reasonable. Intuitively, it is a very weak restriction to place on the SWF.

No Dictatorship (ND). *Suppose that the value of the SWF is identical to the preference for a particular individual (arbitrarily, the nth) on every comparison across all possible combinations of rational individual (voter) profiles. Such an individual will be called a dictator (D). There should be no dictator.*

Why is this reasonable? If individual n is a dictator, the SWF will agree with n on every pairwise comparison of alternatives, including those in which every individual in the society has the opposite preference. Note that the *ND* condition rules out an extreme version of dictatorship in which no one agrees with the leader's choices.

Independence of Irrelevant Alternatives (IIR). *The direction of preference of the SWF in a pairwise comparison involving one pair of alternatives must be invariant across all values of comparisons involving a third alternative.*

Looking once again at the 2000 election, suppose that some SWF produced Gore $>_s$ Bush. This preference should be maintained regardless of where the SWF placed Nader.

This is a case where the abstract version may actually be easier to see than a concrete example. Suppose that the SWF produces the preference $x >_s y$. A preference can be represented geometrically as a line running from left (preferred) to right (not preferred). We know that x_____y on this line. Rational comparisons involving z restrict z to one of the following three places:

a. If z is the most preferred alternative, to the left of x:
   z_____x_____y.
b. If z is the intermediate alternative, between x and y:
   x_____z_____y.
c. If z is the least preferred alternative, to the right of y:
   x_____y_____z.

The IIR condition seems reasonable.

Transitivity (T). *The social welfare function must produce a rational ordering for all combinations of rational preferences of individual voters. In other words, if all individual preferences are transitive the SWF must be transitive.*

Arrow's theorem is

There is no rational universal domain social welfare function that simultaneously satisfies restrictions U, ND, IIR, and T.

Another way to say this is that if a voting scheme has to satisfy U, ND, IIR, and T, no voting scheme can be guaranteed to produce a rational preference profile for society, even though each individual voter within the electorate has a rational preference profile.

This is discouraging, for it amounts to saying that an individually rational electorate cannot be guaranteed a rational social outcome, regardless of what scheme is used to aggregate votes.

On the other hand, the theorem does not say that the SWF never produces a rational outcome. What the theorem says is that, given any

SWF, there will always be some combination of rational voter profiles for which the social preference profile is irrational.

6.11. ILLUSTRATION OF THE DEFINITIONS AND CONCEPTS FOR THE THREE-PERSON SOCIETY

A "society" of three individuals, $\{a, b, c\}$, will be used to illustrate the argument. In the next section the general case of an N-person society will be considered.

In the three-person society[21] there are 8 possible combinations of preferences for each of the $x:y$, $y:z$, and $z:x$ comparisons. These are enumerated in Table 6-3. Rows 1–8 show all possible combinations of $x:y$ preferences, rows 9-16 all possible combinations of $y:z$ preferences, and rows 17-24 all possible combinations of $z:x$ comparisons. Columns labeled a, b, c and SWF show the preferences for each individual and for the SWF, where it is known.

A *voter profile* is a collection of the preferences of all individual voters in a population. Any possible voter profile for the three-person society can be determined from Table 6-3. Select one row from rows 1–8, to determine the $x:y$ preferences. Then select an entry from rows 9–16 to determine $y:z$ preferences, and from rows 17–24 to determine the $z:x$ preferences. An individual profile is rational (transitive) if it contains at least one ">" and one "<" comparison. A profile for person a that contains entries from rows 2, 11, and 22 specifies preferences $x>_a y$, $y>_a z$, $z<_a x$. This corresponds to the ordering $x - y - z$, which is a transitive relation, and therefore rational. However, the combination of rows 2, 11, 17 produces the ordering $x>_a y$, $y>_a z$, $z>_a x$, which is not transitive, and thus not rational.

Selection of rows implies the individual profiles for all voters. When dealing with the three-person society, it is convenient to define profiles by the rows involved. As an example, profile (2, 13, 20) contains the individual profiles $(x>_a y, y<_a z, z>_a x)$, $(x>_b y, y>_b z, z<_b x)$, $(x<_c y, y>_c z, z<_c x)$. These correspond to the linear orderings $(z\ x\ y)$ for a, $(x\ y\ z)$ for b, and $(y\ x\ z)$ for c. Each of these is rational, and so the collection of voting profiles as a whole is rational. Therefore, the SWF has to produce a rational social preference profile for the society as a whole. The reader is invited to consider what social welfare function might do so.

The last column of Table 6-3 is the value of the SWF for the three pairwise comparisons. Six of the entries in this column have already been filled in, because they are constant no matter what the SWF is. They correspond to cases in which all individuals express the same preference, either > or <, for the relevant pairwise comparison. By the unanimity (U)

---

[21] The three-person society illustration and the following proof of Arrow's theorem are modifications of illustrations and proofs presented by V. Dardanoni (2001).

TABLE 6-3. *Combinations of Individual Preferences and the Preference of the SWF in the Three-Person Society*

	a	b	c	SWF
x:y comparisons				
1	>	>	>	> (U)
2	>	>	<	
3	>	<	>	
4	>	<	<	
5	<	>	>	
6	<	>	<	
7	<	<	>	
8	<	<	<	< (U)
y:z comparisons				
9	>	>	>	> (U)
10	>	>	<	
11	>	<	>	
12	>	<	<	
13	<	>	>	
14	<	>	<	
15	<	<	>	
16	<	<	<	< (U)
z:x comparisons				
17	>	>	>	> (U)
18	>	>	<	
19	>	<	>	
20	>	<	<	
21	<	>	>	
22	<	>	<	
23	<	<	>	
24	<	<	<	< (U)

axiom, the social welfare function must have the same preference. This is indicated by the notation $>$ (U).

Table 6-3 contains only one place in which to enter the value of the social welfare function for each collection of pairwise comparisons. This reflects the independence of irrelevant alternatives (IIR) axiom. The value of the SWF for a given set of preferences for one comparison must be the same regardless of the value of the SWF for any collection of comparisons involving alternatives not in the first comparison. As an example, in the three-person society, the value of the SWF for row 2 in the profile

(2, 13, 20) must be the same as the value of the SWF for row 2 in all other profiles in which row 2 appears.

6.12. A PROOF OF ARROW'S THEOREM

Arrow's theorem will now be proven. The proof will take place in several steps. While the proof to be presented is general, it may be helpful to the reader to follow it through for the case of the three-person society.

The first step is to establish a lemma:

The Non-Indifference Lemma.   *The social welfare function can never be indifferent between alternatives.*

Proof:

Construct two collections of profiles, I and II, consisting of the same x:y and z:x comparisons, each of which contains at least one disagreement between individuals and a y:z comparison that contains no disagreements because, in the first profile, all individual comparisons are $>_i$'s, and in the second profile they are all $<_i$'s. Profiles (2, 9, 23) and (2, 16, 23) are examples for the three-person society.

By the U axiom, the values of the SWF for the y:z comparison in collection I must be $>_s$ while it must be $<_s$ in collection II. At this point we have

SWF, collection $I = (\_, >_s, \_)$; SWF collection $II = (\_, <_s, \_)$, where $\_$ indicates that we do not know the value of the comparison.

Assume, by hypothesis, that the SWF for the z:x comparison, which, by IIR, must be the same in both collections, takes on the indifference value $\sim_s$. Therefore,

SWF, profile $I = (\_, >_s, \sim_s)$; SWF profile $II = (\_, <_s, \sim_s)$.

The SWF must produce transitive profiles. Therefore, in collection I,

$$(y >_s z \sim_s x) \Rightarrow y >_s x, \tag{6-23a}$$

but in collection II,

$$(y <_s z \sim_s x) \Rightarrow y <_s x. \tag{6-23b}$$

Therefore, profile I must be $(<_s, >_s, \sim_s)$ and profile II must be $(<_s, <_s, \sim_s)$. By the IIR axiom, an admissible social welfare function must provide the same value for a given comparison (here the x:y comparison) across all values for comparisons involving a third alternative. But, as equations (6-23) show, if the social welfare function is indifferent between x and z, then changes in the y:z comparison can change the value of the x:y comparison.

Accordingly, a permissible social welfare function must never produce an indifference relationship ($\sim_s$), because to do so would lead to a contradiction.

This completes the proof of the non-indifference lemma. ■

Strictly speaking, this point has been proven for the $z:x$ comparison. However, it is easy to prove the point for all comparisons, by simply permuting the roles played by the $x:y$, $y:z$, and $z:x$ comparisons in the proof.

The non-indifference lemma alone is sufficient to rule out a plurality system as a SWF.[22]

A second lemma establishes a limit on arbitrary power that is wider than the ND condition.

No Local Dictatorship (NLD): *If all the voters except one have one preference, and the single voter has the opposite preference, the social welfare function must agree with the majority preference.*

The ND axiom says that an individual cannot overrule the other voters in all preferences. The NLD lemma says that an individual cannot overrule all other voters in any preference. If there is such a case, the individual will be referred to as a *local dictator*. The U, IIR, and ND axioms imply that a local dictator cannot exist.

Proof:

The lemma will be proven by showing that allowing a local dictator leads to a contradiction.

Suppose that in the $x:y$ comparison, one individual, say, person n, has preference $x >_n y$, and the other n-1 voters have preference $x < y$. (Row 7 in Table 6-3 is an example). Let person n be a local dictator for the $x:y$ comparison, and thus dictate the social preference,

$$(x >_s y) \Leftrightarrow (x >_n y) \tag{6-24}$$

by hypothesis (H).

Construct a profile for the SWF, profile III, that contains the $x:y$ comparison and add to it a $y:z$ comparison in which every voter, including person n, has preference $y > z$. At this point there are three incomplete profiles, for the SWF, the local dictator, and everyone else:

Profile III-SWF $(>_s (H), >_s (U), \_s)$,
Profile III-local dictator $(>_n (H), >_n (U), \_n)$,
Profile III-SWF (everyone else) $(<_i (H), >_i (U), \_n)$.

By axiom T, the local dictator and the SWF must both choose $z < x$. Everyone else will be free to choose either $z > x$ or $z < x$. However,

---

[22] Major elections have ended in a tie, as in the case of the U.S. Electoral College tie in 1800. Some interesting rules have been introduced as tiebreakers. These include flipping a coin, and in one jurisdiction in the state of Arizona, the candidates may agree to play a hand of poker.

their choice does not matter because the SWF has already been determined.

This shows that under one set of circumstances, unanimity in the $y:z$ comparison, the SWF must agree with the local dictator. But what if there is no unanimity over the $y:z$ comparison? This does not matter. According to the independence of irrelevant alternatives axiom, once the relation $z < x$ (or $z > x$) has been asserted, it cannot be changed by changing the value of some other choice. If you decide that you prefer chocolate to vanilla, vanilla to strawberry, and chocolate to strawberry, that is rational. Changing your mind to prefer strawberry to vanilla should not affect your assertion that chocolate is preferred to strawberry.

By IIR, once the SWF for $z:x$ has been established in one profile, it must be maintained in all other permissible profiles. Therefore, if the SWF allows for local dictatorship in the $x:y$ condition, it must require agreement between the SWF and the local dictator in the $z:x$ condition. Trivially, we could switch this argument to consider those social profiles in which unanimity in the $z:x$ comparison forces the SWF to comply with the local dictator in the $y:z$ comparison. Unanimity in $y:z$ could be used to force agreement with the dictator in $x:y$. Therefore, allowing a local dictator violates the ND axiom. Accordingly, any SWF that permits a local dictator cannot be allowed.

This proves the no local dictator (NLD) lemma. ■

To set the stage for the proof of the theorem itself, let us consider what the NLD lemma implies for the three-person society. Because of the NLD lemma, the SWF must always agree with the majority, with whatever choice has been taken by two out of three members of the society. Therefore, we now have a requirement for the SWF for all possible collections of profiles. The resulting choices are shown in Table 6-4. Examination of this table shows that there are situations in which the individual profiles are transitive but the SWF is not. An example is the collection (2, 11, 21). This produces

Profile IVa	$(x >_a y,\ y >_a z,\ z <_a x)$
Profile IVb	$(x >_b y,\ y <_b z,\ z >_b x)$
Profile IVc	$(x <_c y,\ y >_c z,\ z >_c x)$
Profile IV(SWF)	$(x >_s y,\ y >_s z,\ z >_s x)$.

Each of the individual profiles is transitive but the profile for the SWF is not. This proves that there is no RUDSWF for the three-person society.

The final step is to show that similar conflicts arise in a society of arbitrary size, N.

Final step. *The NLD lemma, transitivity, and IIR imply that there will be some collection of voter preference profiles in which every individual profile is rational but the SWF profile is irrational.*

TABLE 6-4. *The Combination of the U Axiom and the NLD Lemma Dictate the Value of Any SWF for All Possible Collections of Profiles in the Three-Person Society*

	a	b	c	SWF
x:y comparisons				
1	>	>	>	> (U)
2	>	>	<	>
3	>	<	>	>
4	>	<	<	<
5	<	>	>	>
6	<	>	<	<
7	<	<	>	<
8	<	<	<	< (U)
y:z comparisons				
9	>	>	>	> (U)
10	>	>	<	>
11	>	<	>	>
12	>	<	<	<
13	<	>	>	>
14	<	>	<	<
15	<	<	>	<
16	<	<	<	< (U)
z:x comparisons				
17	>	>	>	> (U)
18	>	>	<	>
19	>	<	>	>
20	>	<	<	<
21	<	>	>	>
22	<	>	<	<
23	<	<	>	<
24	<	<	<	< (U)

Note: This combination can produce an irrational SWF for a collection even though the individual profiles in each collection are rational. The collection (2, 11, 21) is an example.

Proof:

Step 1 in the proof is to construct the collection of voter profiles shown in Table 6-5. In the $x : y$ comparison the first $N - 1$ voters express preferences $x > y$, and the Nth voter has preference $x < y$. By the NLD lemma, the SWF takes the value $x >_s y$. In the $y : z$ preference voter $N-1$ has preference $y < z$.

TABLE 6-5. *The First Step in Constructing a Case That Illustrates the Incompatability of Arrow's Axioms*

	$x:y$	$y:z$	$z:x$
1	>	>	<
2	>	>	<
3	>	>	<
	//	//	//
	//	//	//
	//	//	//
$N-3$	>	>	<
$N-2$	>	>	<
$N-1$	>	<	>
N	< key	>	>
SWF	> NLD	> NLD	< T

Note: The preferences of the SWF in columns $x:y$ and $y:z$ are established by the NLD lemma. The direction of preference of the SWF in the $z:x$ column is required because the SWF must be transitive.

TABLE 6-6. *The Second Step in the construction*

	$x:y$	$y:z$	$z:x$
1	<	>	<
2	<	>	<
3	<	>	<
	//	//	//
	//	//	//
	//	//	//
$N-3$	<	>	<
$N-2$	> key	<	<
$N-1$	<	<	>
N	<	<	>
SWF	< NLD	> T	< Table 6–5, IIR

Note: The value of the SWF in the $x:y$ comparison has been established by the NLD rule. The $z:x$ column is unchanged from Table 6-5; therefore, the SWF must express preference $z <_s x$ by the IIR axiom. The last three voters (N, $N-1$, $N-2$) in the $y:z$ column express the preference $y<z$, while voters $1 \ldots n-3$ have the preference $y>z$. The value of the SWF must be $y >_s z$ in order to maintain transitivity.

The other $N-1$ voters have preference $y > z$. In the $z : x$ comparison the first $N-2$ voters have preference $z < x$; the last 2 have preference $z > x$. The SWF must be $z <_s x$ in order to maintain transivity (T).

Step 2 is to construct the collection of profiles shown in Table 6-6. This table is constructed from Table 6-5 by (a) switching all $x : y$ preferences, and then moving the key voter up two steps, from voter N to voter $N-2$. The Nth voter assumes the preference of the first $N=3$ voters, which is now $x > y$. By the NLD lemma, the SWF preference must be $x <_s y$. The $z : x$ preferences are copied from the $z : x$ preferences in Table 6-5. By the IIR axiom, the value of the SWF is unchanged, $z <_s x$. The $y : z$ preferences are established by leaving the first $N-3$ preferences unchanged from their values in Table 6-5, $y > z$, and switching the last three voters to $y < z$. By the T axiom, the SWF for the $y : z$ comparison must be $y >_s z$.

Step 3 is shown in Table 6-7. The $x : y$ column in Table 6-7 is constructed from Table 6-6 by switching all $x : y$ preferences, and then moving the key voter up another row, from voter $N-2$ to $N-3$. By the NLD lemma, the SWF must be $x >_s y$. The $y : z$ preferences are copied from Table 6-6. By IIR, the SWF preference is $y >_s z$. Finally, the $z : x$ preferences are established by letting the first $N-4$ retain their original $z < x$ preference and switching the last 4 voters to the preferences $x > z$. In order to maintain transitivity the SWF must have value $z <_s x$.

Further tables can be constructed by applying the procedure used in step 2 to Table 6-7, the procedure used in step 3 to create the resulting table, then applying the procedure of step 2, and so forth. Consider any step, k, where $2 \leq k < N-1$. The table produced by step k can be described as follows:

The $x : y$ preferences for all voters except voter $N-k$ will be $x < y$ if k is even or $x > y$ if k is odd. Voter $N-k$ will have the opposite preference. By the NLD lemma, the SWF will have value $x <_s y$ if k is even or value $x >_s y$ if k is odd.

The $y : z$ preferences of the first $N-(k+1)$ voters will be $y > z$. The preferences of the last $k-1$ voters will be $y < z$. If k is even voter $N-k$ will have preference $y < z$; if k is odd voter $N-k$ will have preference $y > z$. The SWF will always have preference $y >_s z$. If k is even this value will have been established by the transitivity (T) axiom. If k is odd the value of the SWF will have been established at step k-1, and carried forward by the IIR axiom.

A similar relation holds for the $z : x$ comparisons. The $z : x$ preferences of the first $N-(k+1)$ voters will be $z < x$. The preferences of the last $k-1$ voters will be $z > x$. If k is even voter $N-k$ will have preference $z < x$; if k is odd voter $N-k$ will have preference $z > x$. The SWF will always have preference $y <_s z$. If k is even the value of the SWF will have been established at step $k-1$, and carried forward by the IIR axiom. If k is odd this value will have been established by the transitivity (T) axiom.

TABLE 6-7. *The Third Step in the Construction*

	$x:y$	$y:z$	$z:x$
1	>	>	<
2	>	>	<
3	>	>	<
	//	//	//
	//	//	//
$N-4$	>	>	<
$N-3$	< key	>	>
$N-2$	>	<	>
$N-1$	>	<	>
N	>	<	>
SWF	> NLD	> Table 6-6, IIR	< T

Note: The key voter is moved up to voter $N-3$ and the $y:z$ comparisons copied from the previous table. The first $N-4$ $z:x$ preferences are set to $z < x$, and the last 4 set to $z > x$. The SWF preference for the $z:x$ comparison must be $z <_s x$ to main transitivity.

The reader can easily verify the conditions by carrying the argument forward two or three steps beyond Table 6-7.

Now consider the situation when $k = N-1$. Suppose that N is even, and hence k is odd. The situation is shown in Table 6–8. The $x:y$ preference for the SWF is $x >_s y$, as required by the NLD lemma. The $y:z$ function is $y >_s z$, established on step $k - 1$, and carried forward by the IIR. Therefore the SWF preference for the $z:x$ comparison must be $z <_s x$ by the T axiom. However the only voter who has the preference $z < x$ is voter 1. Therefore if the SWF is $z >_s x$ voter 1 would be a local dictator, which is prohibited by the NLD lemma.

To finish the proof, suppose that N was odd, and $k = N-1$ even. This would produce a table analogous to Table 6-8, where the $x:y$ preferences and SWF were switched, the $z:x$ preferences and SWF were determined by IIR, and the conflict between T and NLD occurred in the $y:z$ preferences.

This completes the proof.■

It has been shown that U, T, IIR, and ND can be used to derive NLD, and that T, IIR, and NLD lead to a contradiction. Therefore the simultaneous assertion of U, T, IIR, and NLD leads to a contradiction. It is impossible to develop an SWF that satisfies the definition of a RUDSWF. No perfect voting system exists.

TABLE 6-8. *The Last Step in the Proof*

	$x:y$	$y:z$	$z:x$
1	$>$	$>$	$<$
2	$< key$	$>$	$>$
3	$>$	$<$	$>$
	$''$	$''$	$>$
	$''$	$''$	$''$
$N-4$	$>$	$<$	$>$
$N-3$	$>$	$<$	$>$
$N-2$	$>$	$<$	$>$
$N-1$	$>$	$<$	$>$
N	$>$	$<$	$>$
SWF	$\geq NLD$	$> IIR$ *from previous* step	$< T ; > NLD$

Note: At step $N-1$ the construction produces a contradiction between the NLD lemma and the T axiom.

6.13. COMMENTARY ON THE IMPLICATIONS OF ARROW'S THEOREM

Arrow's theorem is an elegant example of the power of axiomatic reasoning. An expression of the collective will of a society ought to be a function of the will of the individuals in it. In practice, though, every voting system seems to have problems. So the search for a better voting system is certainly a worthy endeavor. But what would a "perfect voting system" be? Arrow put forward four requirements on a voting system: transitivity of preferences, the requirement that the voting system agree with a unanimous choice by the voters, the requirement that no individual voter be able to dictate society's choices, regardless of how many people disagree with this individual, and the requirement that the choice between two alternatives not be affected by the presence of a third alternative. Who would argue with these rules? But they are inconsistent.

On the other hand, all is not quite lost. What saves us is the word "universal." Arrow was interested in social welfare functions that would render an appropriate decision for any combination of voter preferences. This includes the N possible combinations involving "one against the rest." Such combinations are probably not very likely in large elections, such as the U.S. presidential election or even a municipal election. The possibilities of this happening in a small election, such as a club or a university department faculty, cannot be disregarded. The problem becomes more acute if we define a "voter" as a bloc of voters, and require that the outcome of the election depend upon the preferences of the blocs. To take a timely example, as I write this (2005), the assembly of the country of Iraq is trying to develop a voting system for that country. Iraq itself is said to be split between ethnic Kurds and ethnic Arabs who follow either the Shia or Sunni branch of Islam. One of the problems the Iraqi assembly will have to deal with is how to reconcile the preferences of these three (often hostile) blocs. We are getting perilously close to the three-person society, which does not have a rational universal domain social welfare function.

6.14. SUMMARY COMMENTS AND QUESTIONS ABOUT AXIOMATIC REASONING

Euclid showed that numerous theorems about measurements on a plane follow from an axiomatic definition of the primitive terms "point" and "line." The result, Euclidean geometry, was a monumental achievement in itself, for both its practical applications and its contribution to pure mathematics. The method by which Euclid developed geometry, axiomatic reasoning, may have been even more important.

For more than two thousand years after Euclid it was believed that the physical world conformed to his geometry. Then Einstein showed that we do not actually live in a Euclidean world, even though the Euclidean approximation is sufficient for all of us except astronomers and astrophysicists.

There are parallels between Euclid's approach, and Einstein's modification of Euclid's results, and the studies of decision making described in this chapter. Von Neumann and Morgenstern applied axiomatic reasoning to economic decision making. They showed that eminently reasonable restrictions on what a rational choice is implied the existence of a utility function. They then showed, from the axioms, that any permissible utility function must be linearly related to all other such functions. Next, Kahneman and Tversky and their followers constructed experiments showing that people often do not behave in the way that they should, if the Von Neumann and Morgenstern axioms are true. This parallels some of the observations of the behavior of light that demonstrated that Einstein's theory better represented the nature of space than Euclid's did. How should we change the definition of rationality? Which of the Von Neumann and Morgenstern axioms are questionable?

Arrow used deduction from axioms to prove that something could not happen, that no rational universal domain social welfare function could ever exist. Are his axioms sacrosanct? Which ones are questionable? Is there some other axiomatization that could be defended and that could lead to a RUDSWF? These questions are still under debate.

The questions raised lie at the intersection between economics, psychology, and political science. Mathematical analysis is not likely to dictate answers to practical problems concerning economic choice, the estimation of worth, or the construction of voting schemes. Mathematical analysis can spotlight the key issues.

7

How to Evaluate Evidence

7.1. THE LEGACY OF REVEREND BAYES

Is it going to snow today? The radio says it is snowing to the north, but where I live the weather generally comes from the southwest. The sky is gray, but the temperature is a bit above freezing. There is no wind, but the air is heavy with moisture. Evidence is accumulating! But what does it mean?

In Chapter 6, we looked at situations in which the rewards for an action could only be known up to a probability distribution. In that chapter the probabilities were assumed to be known. Here we look at how they might be established. This is the process of *evidence evaluation*. It is part and parcel of medicine, economics, legal proceedings, weather prediction, military planning, and just about every other area of human endeavor. We first examine a general model for evidence evaluation, known as *Bayesian reasoning*. We then look at a very important special case, the *signal detection problem*. This problem first came to the attention of applied psychologists and engineers during World War II, when they were asked to determine rules for interpreting radar and sonar signals. The issues are more general. A bank manager acts like a signal detector whenever he or she has to decide whether or not an applicant is a good enough risk to be granted a loan.

Our modern ideas about evidence evaluation stem from a remarkably simple theorem developed in the eighteenth century by the Reverend Thomas Bayes, a non-conformist (i.e., not Church of England) Protestant minister in Kent, England. Remarkably little is known about Bayes, even though he was a Fellow of the Royal Society. Only two of his papers have survived, both published after his death in 1761. His reasoning survived for posterity because of his instructions to an heir.

In his will Bayes directed that one of his mathematical papers, along with a 100 pound inheritance, be sent to Richard Price, also a minister and also a member of the Royal Society. Price, who was a much more active scholar than Bayes, published Bayes's paper in the *Proceedings of the Royal Society*. At first it did not make an immediate stir, but 20 years after the death of Bayes, people began to realize its importance. Today, Bayes' theorem is central to much of modern statistical inference, and some of its ramifications are still under exploration. The theorem is of interest here, not for its statistical applications but because it tells us how a rational decision maker should revise his or her ideas in the face of evidence.[1]

Bayes introduced the problem with what seems a silly example. Suppose that you want to estimate how likely a billiard player is to make a shot. Before play begins your estimate will be based on your knowledge of the player and the game. The player takes the first shot and it either succeeds or fails. How should you estimate the probability that the player will make a second shot?

Bayes's talk about billiards was only by way of introduction. To see what he was really up to we need to look at the reasoning of a somewhat later, and to be honest, non-existent, Englishman: the great fictional detective Sherlock Holmes. This vignette both illustrates Bayesian reasoning and demonstrates the difference between deductive reasoning and probabilistic inference.

Holmes stressed that reasoning from evidence is a process of elimination. Any theory must account for the evidence; otherwise it is just plain wrong. In *The Sign of the Four*, Holmes advises Watson that once the evidence has contradicted all but one theory, then that one, however improbable to begin with, must be the truth. Note the implicit idea here. One begins with several theories of what might have happened, each with some initial believability. Evidence does not prove that one theory is right; it winnows out the incorrect ones, until only one is left.

Holmes's abstract argument is made concrete in another story, *Silver Blaze*. A valuable racehorse has been stolen from a stable, occupied only by the horse and a fierce watchdog. The Lord of the Manor suspects that strangers seen lingering in the area may have broken in and taken the horse. But Holmes says,

"Then there is the curious business of the dog in the night."
The Lord replies, "But the dog did nothing in the night."
Holmes's aide and chronicler, Dr. Watson, says, "That is what is curious."

Holmes has realized that the theory "A stranger did it" implied that the dog would have barked. But the dog did nothing. Ergo, a stranger did not do it. (And, in fact, one of the grooms did.)

Holmes was not above a logical blunder. In *A Study in Scarlet*, the very first Sherlock Holmes story, the great detective concludes that Dr. Watson, whom he has just met, is an army surgeon recently invalided back to England because of wounds received in Afghanistan. How did Holmes deduce this? He observed that Dr. Watson had the air of a

[1] Bernstein (1996).

military man, had pallor under a tan, was holding his arm stiffly, and was a physician. The facts could all be explained by assuming that Watson had been with the British Army in Afghanistan.

Two modern students of logic have pointed out that Watson could have replied: "I am an army doctor, but I have not been in Afghanistan. I have been in a Swiss sanitarium recovering from TB. The sun is responsible for my tan, and I injured my arm in a climbing accident."[2] Holmes had observed that Watson's appearance was compatible with his having been in Afghanistan, but failed to consider that there were other explanations for the appearance. In logical terms, Holmes knew that A implied B, he observed B, and then he erroneously concluded A. This contrasts to his reasoning in *Silver Blaze*, where he knew that A implied B, observed NOT B, and correctly concluded NOT A.

The authors of books that advise people "how to think"[3] applaud the reasoning in *Silver Blaze* and deplore the reasoning in *A Study in Scarlet*.

One of my students in a class on critical thinking was not so sure. She took issue with both Holmes examples. Holmes, and logicians in general, analyze a problem as if (a) evidence either is or is not compatible with a particular theory, and (b) as if theories are to be treated equivalently regardless of their believability. My student pointed out that in life outside of logic the links between theory and data are probabilistic.

The dog did nothing on the night the horse was stolen. The student wanted to know how often the watchdog barked at strangers. Only after she had checked out the dog's behavior would she be willing to acknowledge the strength of Holmes's reasoning. She had similar reservations about Holmes's conclusion that Watson had been in Afghanistan, and about Johnson-Laird and Byrne's criticism of that conclusion. She was willing to acknowledge that Watson might have gotten his tan and his injury in Switzerland, rather than Afghanistan, and for that matter in many other places as well. But, she wanted to know, were wounded veterans of the British Afghan campaign common in London? Was it common for Englishmen to go to Swiss sanitariums in the late nineteenth century, the time when *A Study in Scarlet* was supposed to have taken place?

What my student did, quite correctly, was to convert the absolutes of the fictional story into the probabilistic links that are characteristic of real life. As I wrote a "4.0" grade in my notebook I had the feeling that the ghost of Reverend Bayes was in the room, smiling.

7.2. BAYES' THEOREM

Imagine that a decision maker has in mind a finite set, $\mathbf{H} = \{H_j\}, j = 1 \ldots J$, of J mutually exclusive hypotheses, and that these hypotheses exhaust

---

[2] Johnson-Laird and Byrne (1991), pp. 1–2.   [3] See Halpern (2002).

the set of possible hypotheses. In the detectives' case, this would be the set of theories about how a crime might have been committed. In a medical case, it would be the diagnoses under consideration. Each hypothesis is assigned an a priori probability of being correct, prior to the observation of any evidence. Let $P_0(H_j)$ stand for the probability that hypothesis H_j is true at "time zero," prior to the observation of any evidence. From the definition of a probability measure (Chapter 2),

$$0 \le P_0(H_j) \le 1$$
$$\sum_{j=1,J} P_0(H_j) = 1. \tag{7-1}$$

At time 1 the decision maker acquires a piece of evidence E_1. Each hypothesis assigns a probability to the evidence, $P(E_1|H_j)$. Read this as "The probability that E_1 will be observed, under the assumption that hypothesis H_j is true." Bayes asked, "Under these circumstances, what is the probability that each of the hypotheses is true, *after* the evidence has been observed?" In our notation, what is $P_1(H_j|E_1)$, which is read as "The probability that hypothesis j is true, after observing evidence E_1?" The process is iterative over consecutive pieces of evidence,

$$P_1(H_j) = P(H_j \mid E_1)$$
$$P_2(H_j) = P(H_j \mid E_2) \tag{7-2}$$
etc.

To take a less fanciful case than Sherlock Holmes, think of a radiologist examining an image for evidence of cancer. Let H_c be the hypothesis "patient has cancer." $P_0(H_c)$ would be the radiologist's a priori estimate of the probability that the patient had cancer. Next, let E_L be the event that a "lump" appears on the radio image. $P(E_L|H_c)$ would be the probability that the lump would be there, assuming that the patient did have cancer. Since the lump is there, the physician wants to know $P_1(H_c) = P(H_c|E_L)$, the probability that patient has cancer given that the evidence of a lump has been observed. This is called the *posterior probability* of the event.

Bayes began with the definition of the joint probability of any two events, A and B:

$$P(A \bullet B) = P(A)P(B|A)$$
$$P(A \bullet B) = P(B)P(A|B), \tag{7-3}$$

where the dot indicates conjunction. This is the definition of joint probability established in Chapter 2. The first line says that the probability of A and B's both happening is equal to the probability that A happens times the probability that B happens if A happens. The second line reflects the fact that A and B play symmetric roles.

Suppose, for simplicity, that we are considering only two hypotheses, H and $\sim H$. Applying equation 7-3 to the righthand side of equation 7-2,

$$P_0(E)P(H|E) = P(E|H)P_0(H)$$

$$P_0(H|E) = \frac{P(E|H)P_0(H)}{P_0(E)}, \qquad (7\text{-}4)$$

The next step is to calculate the denominator, $P_0(E)$. In the medical example, this is the a priori probability that the image would show a lump whether or not the patient had cancer. Because H and $\sim H$ are mutually exclusive,

$$P_0(E) = P(E|H)P_0(H) + P(E|\sim H)P_0(\sim H). \qquad (7\text{-}5)$$

Substituting equation 7-5 into equation 7-4 produces the desired term:

$$P_1(H) = P(H|E) = \frac{P_0(H) \cdot P(E|H)}{P_0(H) \cdot P(E|H) + P_0(\sim H) \cdot P(E|\sim H)}. \qquad (7\text{-}6)$$

This is Bayes' theorem, applied to the special case in which there are only two possible hypotheses. The next step is to generalize the theorem to the case of several hypotheses. Because, by definition, the hypotheses are mutually exclusive and exhaustive, it follows that the a priori probability of observing E is the sum of the probabilities that E will be observed under any one of the hypotheses, weighted for the a priori probability of that hypothesis. Therefore, and using the notation of equations (7-1) and (7-2), the probability that the kth hypothesis is true is

$$P_1(H_k|E) = \frac{P_0(H_k) \cdot P(E_1|H_k)}{\sum\limits_{j=1..K} P_0(H_j) \cdot P(E_1|H_j)}. \qquad (7\text{-}7)$$

In equation (7-7), the numerator is, as before, the product of the probability that the evidence would be observed if hypothesis H_k were true and the probability that the hypothesis H_k is true. The denominator is the sum of such terms over all possible hypotheses, and therefore is the a priori likelihood of the evidence being observed. The expression as a whole is called the (Bayesian) likelihood of hypothesis H_k, after observing evidence E.

7.3. SOME NUMERICAL EXAMPLES

The following numerical examples illustrate the use of Bayes's theorem. They also illustrate certain conceptual and practical distinctions that affect how we might interpret a Bayesian analysis.

Further Reasoning about Silver Blaze

When Holmes and Watson were first called in to find Silver Blaze they were told that vagrants had been in the area, and that the landowner suspected that the vagrants had stolen the horse. The landowner's suspicions were reasonable, but there were other explanations. For instance, the landowner might have stolen the horse himself, to cash in on the insurance. (This has happened!) Another possibility was that one of the stable hands had stolen the horse, perhaps for resale. After investigating a bit further, Holmes found that the dog was quite familiar with the stable hands, was very protective around strangers, and had some but not a lot of acquaintance with the landowner.

If Reverend Bayes, instead of Holmes, had been called in, he would have reasoned as follows. (I take the liberty of making up the numbers, but Bayes made up the reasoning.)

Hypotheses:
  V = Vagrants stole the horse. $P_0(V) = .7$
  L = Landowner stole the horse. $P_0(L) = .1$
  S = Stable hand stole the horse. $P_0(S) = .2$.

Relation of dog (evidence) to hypotheses: (B = Barking, $\sim B$ = No Barking).
  The dog would almost certainly bark at strangers. $P(B|V) = .9$, $P(\sim B|V) = .1$
  The dog sometimes barked at the landowner. $P(B|L) = .5$, $P(\sim B|L) = .5$
  The dog hardly ever barked at stable hands. $P(B|S) = .1$, $P(\sim B|S) = .9$.

The dog did not bark, $E = \sim B$. A priori, this could have happened in three ways; the dog could have failed to bark at a vagrant, or at the landlord, or at a stable hand. So we have

$$P_0(\sim B) = P(\sim B|V)P_0(V) + P(\sim B|L)P_0(L) + P(\sim B|S)P_0(S)$$
$$P_0(\sim B) = (.1)(.7) + (.5)(.1) + (.9)(.2) \tag{7-8}$$
$$P_0(\sim B) = .30$$

Next, calculating the a posteriori probability that a vagrant took the horse,

$$P_1(V) = \frac{P(\sim B|V)P_0(V)}{P_0(\sim B)}$$
$$P_1(V) = \frac{(.1)(.7)}{.30} \tag{7-9}$$
$$P_1(V) = .233.$$

Because the dog did nothing in the night, the probability of the horse having been stolen by a vagrant drops from .7 to just a little more than .23.

Going through similar calculations, the probabilities of the various hypotheses have shifted to

$$P_1(V) = .233$$
$$P_1(L) = .167$$
$$P_1(S) = .600,$$

rounded to three decimal points. It is beginning to look like an inside job. Holmes concluded that it *was* an inside job. The Rev. Bayes would have probably advised him to look for a little more evidence![4]

An important point in this, admittedly made-up, example is that the selection is to be made between conceptual hypotheses. Therefore, we are dealing with subjective rather than frequentist probabilities. Often a fair bit of agreement can be obtained on the relation between the hypotheses and the evidence (the $P(E|H)$ terms). It may be very difficult to obtain agreement on the a priori probabilities (the $P_0(H)$ terms), as these are necessarily subjective.

Medical Diagnosis

This example has been chosen to contrast the use of Bayes' theorem for making conceptual choices, as in the Sherlock Holmes example, to a diagnostic situation where the choice is between objectively definable states of the world. It also demonstrates an interesting way to improve human reasoning.

The example is based on an investigation of medical decision making that extended laboratory demonstrations to a practical situation.[5] The investigators asked practicing physicians to consider the following scenario, which I paraphrase from the original.

> *The probability that a randomly chosen woman age 40–50 has breast cancer is .01. If a woman has breast cancer, the probability that she will have a positive mammogram is .80.*
>
> *However, if a woman does not have breast cancer, the probability that she will have a positive mammogram is .10.*

---

[4] The evidence was forthcoming. Later in the novella Silver Blaze is found running free, with a cut on his leg. Then the groom (head stable hand) is found dead, with his skull bashed in. Vagrants are again suspected. But Holmes deduces, because of what the dog did not do and other bits of evidence, that the groom stole Silver Blaze, intending to injure him so that he could not run well in a coming race. When the groom began to cut Silver Blaze's leg the horse reared up, kicking him in the head. The murderer in *Silver Blaze* was Silver Blaze. He pled self-defense.

[5] The example is taken from Hoffrage and Gigerenzer (1996).

> *Imagine that you are consulted by a woman, age 40–50, who has a positive mammogram but no other symptoms. What is the probability that she actually has breast cancer?*

Twenty-four physicians were asked to respond. The median probability estimate was .70.

Let M indicate a positive mammogram reading and C be the state of having cancer. The Bayesian calculations are

$$P_1(C) = \frac{P_0(C)P(M|C)}{P_0(C)P(M|C) + P_0(\sim C)P(M|\sim C)}$$

$$P_1(C) = \frac{.01 \times .80}{01 \times .80 + .99 \times .10} \tag{7-10}$$

$$P_1(C) = \frac{.008}{.008 + .099}$$

$$P_1(C) = .075.$$

The physicians' median answer overestimated the probability of cancer by almost a factor of ten! However the .70 estimate is just a little below the .80 value given for $P(M|C)$. Evidently the physicians confused the probability that a woman who had cancer would have a positive mammogram ($P(M|C)$) with the probability that a person who had a positive mammogram would also have cancer ($P(C|M)$).

This is by no means an isolated finding. The error apparently arises because people who are not trained in statistics fail to realize the importance of the a priori probabilities, here the initial probability of cancer, $P_0(C)$. In cases of choices between conceptual analyses, such as the *Silver Blaze* example, the a priori probabilities are a matter of personal opinion. In diagnostic situations such as the cancer example, it is reasonable to interpret probabilities as relative frequencies, which can be determined objectively. When this is done, the a priori probabilities are referred to as *base rates*. The error of ignoring base rates has been demonstrated so often that psychologists have a name for it, the *base rate fallacy*.

Discussions of the base rate fallacy are usually presented from the mathematician's viewpoint: What can be done with people who just won't compute? The German psychologist Gerd Gigerenzer has argued that this is inappropriate. It is not reasonable to expect ordinary people to be mathematicians; it is reasonable to expect physicians and applied mathematicians to work hard at presenting their finding in a comprehensible way. And in this case, that turns out to be surprisingly easy to do. Use frequencies instead of probabilities.

This was done in the cancer study. The investigators presented the same problem to a different set of 24 physicians, but this time they stated the problem in terms of frequencies. Instead of saying "The probability that a randomly chosen woman has cancer is .01," they said, "Ten out of every 1,000 women have breast cancer." Instead of saying "If a woman has cancer the probability of a positive mammogram is .8," they said, "Eight out of ten women with cancer will have a positive mammogram." The other probability statements in the problem were altered to frequency statements in a similar manner. Of the 24 physicians who were asked the question using the frequency format, 11 responded with a close approximation to the Bayesian answer. There are a number of replications of this finding.[6]

Gigerenzer advised that a physician should not think "How likely is this symptom, given the disease?" but, rather, "When I see this symptom, how often does it turn out that the patient has this or that disease?" Something similar would be good advice for all decision makers.

7.4. CALCULATING THE ODDS

One of the uses of Bayesian reasoning is to determine "the odds" on a particular hypothesis, after observing some evidence for or against that hypothesis. The odds are defined as the ratio of the probability that a hypothesis is true to the probability that it is not true:

$$\text{"Odds on H"} = \frac{P(H)}{P(\sim H)}. \tag{7-11}$$

Suppose a piece of evidence is observed. The resulting odds can be calculated by substituting Bayesian definitions into (7-11) and simplifying,

$$\frac{P_1(H)}{P_1(\sim H)} = \left[\frac{P(E|H)}{P(E|\sim H)}\right] \cdot \left[\frac{P_0(H)}{P_0(\sim H)}\right]. \tag{7-12}$$

The separation of terms into square brackets highlights an importance conceptual distinction. The first factor, $[P(E|H)/P(E|N\sim H)]$ can be thought of as a "strength of evidence" factor; it evaluates how probable the evidence is given that H is the case compared to how probable the evidence is if H is not the case. The second factor, $[P_0(H)/P_0(\sim H)]$, is the a priori odds ratio. The a posteriori odds go up as (a) the evidence for H is discriminating, $P(E|H) > P(E|\sim H)$, and (b) the prior odds for H are high. This seems reasonable.

The following example illustrates the fact that the two factors refer to very different things.

Suppose I learn that (a) one in ten law-abiding Americans in my hometown owns a handgun, (b) one in one thousand of the residents in

---

[6] Gigerenzer (2000).

my town is a dangerous criminal, and (c) nine of ten dangerous criminals own handguns. I discover that my tennis opponent owns a handgun. What is my estimate that my opponent is a dangerous criminal?

At first thought, my discovery might be a bit disturbing. It appears that owning a gun is characteristic of criminals, and not at all characteristic of non-criminals. My opponent seems to be exhibiting behavior typical of dangerous criminals.

Computing the Bayesian odds proves to be reassuring.

$$\text{Odds on criminality} = [.9/.1][1/1000]$$
$$= 9/1000 \tag{7-13}$$
$$= .009.$$

This is up from my earlier estimate of one a in thousand, but not high enough to warrant calling the cops! And it is certainly far below the nine-to-one odds suggested by looking at the strength of evidence alone!

The moral of the story? You cannot just look at how well the hypothesis fits the evidence; you also have to look at the a priori odds on the hypothesis.

We meet this issue in the following section, in the discussion of the signal detection problem.

7.5. SOME EXAMPLES OF SIGNAL DETECTION

In a *signal detection* situation an observer receives a signal that varies in strength. The signal may have come from a target or may be irrelevant background variation in signal strength ("noise"). The observer's task is to decide whether or not a target was present. To get a flavor of the topic, consider the following examples.

Military Alarms. The mathematical theory of signal detection was originally developed during World War II to handle military applications. During that war surface ships and submarines played a deadly cat and mouse game, in which each stalked the other. Surface ships used sonar ranging to locate enemy submarines. The sonar device sent a sound pulse into the water. If it hit a submarine an echo would bounce off the submarine's metal hull, producing a characteristic sound. However, echoes could also bounce off rocks, whales, and schools of fish. The characteristics of the echo changed depending upon the temperature and density of the water. Sometimes the echo that returned was obviously from a submarine, sometimes it obviously did not come from a submarine, and sometimes "it might have been" either.

Radar target detection posed the same problem. How certain should a ship's captain be before he fires on an intruding aircraft? Two dramatic examples of the problem occurred in the 1980s. In the first incident, a U.S. destroyer escorting a tanker in the Persian Gulf detected a "suspicious" radar signal. The ship's captain decided that it was not suspicious enough to take defensive action. In fact, the signal came from an Iraqi aircraft that attacked and nearly sank the U.S. ship. About a year later, the cruiser *USS Vincennes* detected a radar signal in a somewhat similar situation. The *Vincennes* fired, shooting down an Iranian commercial airliner that was carrying over a hundred pilgrims on their way to Mecca.

These two captains were mistaken. In the meantime, though, hundreds, if not thousands, of innocent signals were correctly detected as harmless, and in a number of cases, hostile intruders were properly attacked. At the time the *Vincennes* fired on the Iranian transport it was involved in a night engagement with several torpedo boats, unseen but providing radar signals that had correctly been identified as hostile. During the investigation into the *Vincennes* incident the captain testified that one of the reasons he decided that the radar signal was from a hostile aircraft was that it was reasonable to believe that the *Vincennes* was the target of a combined surface and air attack.

Medical Screening. Every year hundreds of thousands of people are screened for the presence of a variety of diseases. The tests are never perfect. How certain does a physician have to be that a person has a problem before the physician recommends treatment?

Airport Security Screening. How suspicious do airport security screeners have to be before they decide to single out a passenger for a thorough search? Equally relevant, how does an airport manager decide whether or not the screeners at a particular station are making good or bad decisions?

Criminal Justice. Warren Burger, once the Chief Justice of the United States, said in several public speeches that the only way that you could be sure of convicting every criminal would be to lock everyone up, and that the only way that you could be sure of never imprisoning an innocent person would be to let everyone go. In 2004, the state of Virginia took Chief Justice Burger's advice to heart.

Like many states, Virginia was spending a great deal of money holding minor drug offenders in jail. In order to reduce this expense the state instituted a system of background checks to determine sentencing. The background check included age, gender, marital status, and a number of other demographic factors. On the basis of this check, a first-time offender was assigned a score supposed to reflect the likelihood that he or she would violate a law again. Virginia's official guidelines for sentencing recommended jail for offenders scoring 38 or higher. Some form of community-based punishment was recommended for offenders who scored below 38.[7]

Justice Burger's remarks address only the likelihood of making a mistake. The state of Virginia policy was clearly motivated both by the likelihood of making a mistake and the cost of the mistake.

A second criminal case illustrates the interaction between costs and probabilities in a different way.

In U.S. criminal law a person is presumed innocent unless the evidence shows "beyond a reasonable doubt" that he or she committed the crime. But what does "reasonable doubt" mean? In civil trials, the criterion is that the defendant is innocent unless "the preponderance of the evidence" is for the plaintiff. The contradiction between these criteria was shown dramatically in the trials of O. J. Simpson, in his younger days a famous professional football player. Simpson was accused of murdering his wife. He was found innocent in a criminal trial, and then found liable for millions of dollars in damages for wrongful death in a suit brought by the dead woman's family. The evidence was the same in both cases. How can these findings be reconciled? Was one jury irrational and the other not? According to the theory of signal detection, both juries may well have behaved appropriately.

We will revisit the military and medical problems, the Virginia policy, and the O. J. Simpson trials after having dealt with the mathematics of signal detection.

7.6. A MATHEMATICAL FORMULATION OF THE SIGNAL DETECTION PROBLEM

There are three perspectives that you can take on signal detection: the perspective of an *observer*, who decides whether or not a target is present; the perspective of a *decision analyst*, who tries to understand the observer's performance; and the perspective of a *policymaker*, who specifies how the observer is supposed to behave.

This section provides an analytic discussion of the basic signal detection problem from the observer's point of view. Certain restrictive assumptions will be made in order to simplify the mathematics. At various times I will indicate where these assumptions can be relaxed, but will not go into details. The more general problems are treated in any of several books on signal detection.[8]

An observer receives signals that are chosen randomly from either a target (*T*) or a noise (*N*) distribution. For example, a sonar operator receives a signal that may have come from a submarine or may have come from some other object in the sea. Signals may be of varying

---

[7] Barzelon (2005).   [8] E.g., MacMillan and Creelman (2004).

strength. Each time a signal is presented the observer has to decide whether it came from the target or noise distributions.

Definitions and Assumptions

A1.   The signal strength, x, is indicated by a real number x in the range $-\infty \ldots +\infty$.

A2.   The distributions of signal strengths from the target distribution has probability density function $f_t(x) = f(x|M_t, S_t)$ where M_t and S_t are the mean and standard deviation of the target distribution. Signals from the noise distribution are chosen from a distribution with probability density function $f_n(x) = f(x|M_n, S_n)$. The distributions of the target and noise populations are identical except for changes in the mean and standard deviation.

The standard scores for the target and noise distributions are

$$z_t(x) = \frac{x - M_t}{S_t}$$
$$z_n(x) = \frac{x - M_n}{S_n}.$$
(7-14)

Then $f_t(x) = f(z_t(x)|0,1)$ and similarly for f_n. For simplicity of notation, I will refer to $f(z(x))$ (or $z_t(x)$ or $z_n(x)$), with the mean of 0 and standard deviation of 1 understood.

Recall, from Chapter 2, that for any particular value z, and probability density function $f(z)$, the cumulative probability function F is

$$F(z) = \int_{-\infty}^{z} f(z)$$
$$F(z) = P(Z < z),$$
(7-15)

where $P(W)$ is the probability of any statement W. Cumulative probability functions are defined for the target and noise distributions, F_t and F_n, in this manner.

A3.   The probability density function $f(z)$ is known, defined for any real number z, symmetric, and monotonically declining in the absolute value of z, written $|z|$. That is, $f(z) = f(-z)$ and $|z_1| > |z_2|$ implies that $f(z_1) < f(z_2)$. The further the value of x is from $M(x)$ (and hence z from 0), the smaller the probability density function.

If z is known, the probability statement $P(Z < z)$ is determined. Conversely, if $P(Z < z)$ is known, z is determined:

$$P(Z < z) = F(z)$$
$$z = F^{-1}(P(Z < z)).$$
(7-16)

For any value of signal strength, x, we want to know $P(X < x)$ for the target and noise distribution, or *vice versa*. The following relations are important:

$$z_t = F_t^{-1}(P(Z < z \mid T))$$
$$z_n = F_n^{-1}(P(Z < z \mid N)), \tag{7-17}$$

where T stands for "target present" and N stands for "target not present."

The following property of $f(z)$ is a consequence of its symmetry:

$$\int_z^\infty f(y) = \int_{-\infty}^{-z} f(y) \tag{7-18}$$
$$1 - F(z) = F(-z).$$

What this means is shown in Figure 7-1. The area under the curve to the left of $-z$ is equal to the area under the curve to the right of z.

In introductory discussions of signal detection f and F are assumed to be the standard normal (Gaussian) distribution. The normal distribution is one of the class of symmetric distributions, $f(z) = f(-z)$. The model to be developed does not depend upon the assumption of normality, but the assumptions that the distribution is known and symmetric are central to the argument.

A4. The expected value of signal strength when a target is present is equal to or greater than the expected value of the signal strength when the target is absent,

$$M_t \geq M_n. \tag{7-19}$$

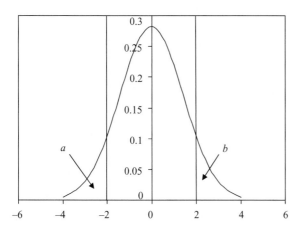

FIGURE 7-1. An illustration of equation 7-18. The illustration is for the case $z = 2$, but the principle applies for any value of z. Area a is equal to area b.

The Basic Signal Detection Situation

Figure 7-2 is a graph of the signal detection situation for the special case in which both the target and noise distributions are normally distributed with identical standard deviations. Signals are drawn from either the target or the noise population, centered on means M_t and M_n, respectively. An observer sets some criterion value, c, and classifies a signal of strength x as "target present" if the signal strength exceeds c ($x > c$). Otherwise, the observer decides "target absent." What sort of performance can we expect in this situation?

Define the following terms: $P(H) =$ Probability that a signal from the target distribution will be correctly identified (a *hit*).

$P(M) =$ Probability that a signal from the target distribution will not be identified (a *miss*).

$P(FA) =$ Probability that a signal from the noise distribution will be misclassified as a target (a *false alarm*).

$P(CR) =$ Probability that a signal from the noise distribution is correctly identified as such (a *correct rejection*).

Obviously,

$$P(H) = 1 - P(M)$$
$$P(FA) = 1 - P(CR). \qquad\qquad (7\text{-}20)$$

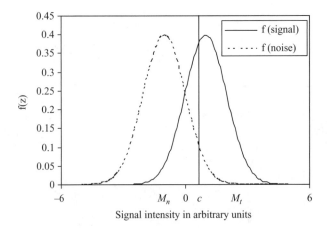

FIGURE 7-2. The basic signal detection situation. A signal is drawn from either the signal or noise distributions, centered on M_t and M_n, respectively. These distributions are identical, except for their means. The observer sets a *criterion level* at c. Any signal that has strength greater than c (to the right of the vertical line) will be classified as a target. Otherwise it is classified as noise.

A perfect observer would, of course, make no errors. All target signals would be identified as such and there would never be a false alarm. Figure 7-2 shows why this is impossible. Both the target and noise distributions are defined over the range $\pm \infty$. Therefore, there will be some portion, however small, of the area under the target and noise distributions on either side of the point $x = c$. $P(M)$ and $P(FA)$ will always have values greater than zero.

The extent to which this is a problem depends upon the extent to which the means of the distributions differ. The extent of this difference provides a measure of the observer's accuracy,

$$d' = \frac{M_t - M_n}{S_t},$$
(7-21)

where S_t is the standard deviation of the target distribution. (Recall that in the basic situation, it is assumed that the distributions have the same standard deviations, $S_t = S_n = S$.) Large values of d' indicate that the target and noise distributions lie far apart on the underlying scale of signal strength. Therefore, the observer can discriminate target from noise with a high degree of accuracy. Low values of d' arise when the target and noise distributions overlap a great deal, making target detection difficult. Therefore, it is appropriate to regard d' as a measure of the observer's skill. However, "skill" should not be interpreted as solely a measure of personal competence. The d' measure reflects both the quality of evidence available to an observer and the observer's competence in processing that evidence.

Given a fixed value of d', the observer can control the type of error that occurs. Lowering c will increase the hit rate, at the cost of an increased false alarm rate. Raising c will lower the false alarm rate, while decreasing the hit rate. This is a mathematical way of stating Chief Justice Burger's warning that a verdict is always a compromise between the chance of jailing the innocent or releasing the guilty. We can be a bit more analytical.

7.7. THE DECISION ANALYST'S PROBLEM

Step 1 – Identifying the Criterion

What has been shown is that an observer's behavior, in terms of the probability of hits and false alarms, can be determined if f, d', S, and c are known. Now consider the situation from the point of a *decision analyst*, a person who wants to understand how an observer is behaving. The decision analyst is willing to assume f, but does not know the values of d' and c. However, the analyst can observe $P(H)$ and $P(FA)$. These observations can be used to determine d' and c.

Decision analysis has important practical applications. For example, in medicine, "tissue committees" review pathology specimens obtained during an operation in order to determine whether the decision to operate was correct or not. In the ideal case, the committee will also review patient records to determine whether cancers or similar problems developed in patients who were not operated on. In the military case, special exercises are conducted in order to determine the characteristics of radar and sonar lookouts. In the State of Virginia case, the decision to set the cutoff for releasing a minor felon from jail at 38 was made after an examination of background records of offenders who did or did not commit subsequent offenses within a fixed period of years after being released. A felon who had a screening score of 38 and did commit an offense after release would be regarded as a hit (identified as probably going to commit a crime and did so), while a felon with a score higher than 38, but who did not commit a subsequent crime, would be considered a false alarm.

Assume that the decision analyst can examine records of cases in which the analyst knows both the observer's decision and the true origin of the signal. Therefore, the analyst knows the observer's hit rates and false alarm rates, $P(H)$ and $P(FA)$. The way in which d' and c can be determined will now be explained.

Figure 7-3 expands on Figure 7-2 to provide a depiction of the decision situation and the two probabilities. As both of the distributions are probability distributions, the area under each of the curves is one. The area under the solid line, f_t, and to the right of the criterion point, c, is equal to the probability of a hit. The area under the dashed line, f_n, and to the right of c is equal to the probability of a false alarm.

The hit and false alarm rates determine the standard scores for the criterion, in terms of the target and noise distributions. From equation (7-14),

$$P(H) = 1 - F_t(z_t(c))$$
$$P(FA) = 1 - F_n(z_n(c)). \tag{7-22}$$

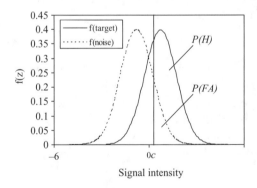

FIGURE 7-3. The relation between two signal strength distributions, c, and the probability of a hit or a false alarm.

$P(H)$ and $P(FA)$ are observables. Therefore, $z_t(c)$ and $z_n(c)$ are determined by the data, through the application of equation (7-17).

To get a clear picture of what this means, consider the situation solely with respect to the target distribution. Figure 7-4 shows the relation of the criterion to the target distribution. The probability of a hit is given by the area under the curve from $z_t(c)$ to ∞ on the z_t scale. Applying equation (7-18) produces

$$P(H) = \int_{z_t(c)}^{\infty} f(z_t(x))$$

$$(7\text{-}23)$$

$$P(H) = F(-z_t(c)).$$

Because $P(H)$ is an observable and F is known (by hypothesis), the inverse relation can be applied

$$-z_t(c) = F^{-1}(P(H)).$$

$$(7\text{-}24)$$

The condition with respect to false alarms is depicted by duplicating Figure 7-4, but this time using the $z_n(x)$ scale. This is shown in Figure 7-5. In this figure, the probability of a false alarm is given by the area under the curve and to the right of the $z_n(c)$ point. By an argument identical to the argument that lead to equation 7-24,

$$-z_n(c) = F^{-1}(P(FA)).$$

$$(7\text{-}25)$$

At this point three things have been done. First, the basic signal detection situation has been defined. Second, two key parameters of this

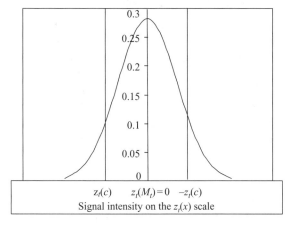

FIGURE 7-4. The relation between the threshold, c, and the target distribution plotted on the $z_t(x)$ scale. Only the signal distribution is shown.

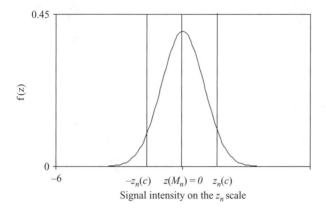

FIGURE 7-5. The relation between the threshold, c, and the noise distribution plotted on the $z_n(x)$ scale.

situation, d' and c, have been defined and their meaning explained. Third, it has been shown that observations of hits and false alarm rates, $P(H)$ and $P(FA)$, provides enough information to locate c relative to the means of the target and signal distributions, using the standardized scales for each distribution. What is needed is some way to relate these scales to each other and to the underlying signal intensity scale, x. If this can be done, the decision analyst can use observations of $P(H)$ and $P(FA)$ to determine the observer's skill parameter, d', and criterion, c, on a scale of signal intensity. The next section shows how.

Step 2 – Analyzing the Receiver Operating Characteristic

The *receiver operating characteristic* (ROC) is a plot of hit rates as a function of false alarm rates, across all possible values of c. In addition to providing a way to identify d' and c, the ROC offers a way to check on the assumptions made about the probability density functions, f_t and f_t.

Figure 7-6 illustrates what ROC curves look like, for the special case in which $S_t = S_n$ and f is the normal distribution. Each of the curves displayed is for a different value of d'. The diagonal line corresponds to the case $d' = 0$, which would be the case if the target and noise distributions had identical means, thus giving the observer no way of distinguishing between target and noise signals. In this circumstance, the observer would be equally likely to produce a hit or a false alarm.

The ROC curve is useful in itself, as a graphic way of displaying an observer's performance. It also provides a way of solving the scaling problem. The key to doing this is to realize that the $z_t(c)$ and $z_n(c)$ refer to the same point, c, on the signal intensity scale.

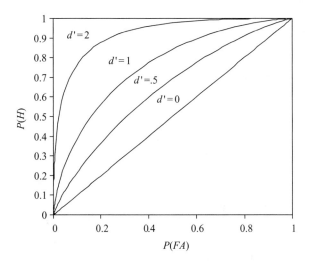

FIGURE 7-6. An example of a Receiver Operating Characteristic plot, assuming that f_t and f_n are normal distributions differing in their means, but with identical standard deviations. Perfect performance would be given by $P(H) = 1$, $P(FA) = 0$, the upper left-hand corner. This point is approximated as d' increases, but is only reached, in the limit, for $d' = \infty$. With the value of d' fixed, performance is determined by varying c. Decreasing c moves an observer's performance up and to the right on the appropriate d' curve. This corresponds to an increase in both the hit and false alarm rate.

$$z_t(c) = \frac{c - M_t}{S_t}$$

$$c = S_t z_t(c) + M_t$$

$$z_n(c) = \frac{c - M_n}{S}$$

$$c = S_n z_n(c) + M_n$$

$$S_t z_t(c) + M_t = S_n z_n(c) + M_n \qquad (7\text{-}26)$$

$$S_t z_t(c) = S_n z_n(c) + M_n - M_t$$

$$z_t(c) = \frac{S_n}{S_t} z_n(c) + \frac{M_n - M_t}{S_t}$$

$$z_t(c) = \frac{S_n}{S_t} z_n(c) - \frac{M_t - M_n}{S_t}$$

$$z_t(c) = \frac{S_n}{S_t} z_n(c) - d',$$

where the last line follows from the definition of d'.

From equations (7-24) and (7-25), $-z_t(c) = F^{-1}(P(H))$ and $-z_n(c) = F^{-1}(P(FA))$. Taking the negative of the last line of equation (7-26) and substituting produces

$$-z_t(c) = \frac{S_n}{S_t}(-z_n(c)) + d'$$

$$F^{-1}(P(H)) = \frac{S_n}{S_t}F^{-1}(P(FA)) + d'. \tag{7-27}$$

If the target and noise distributions have equal standard deviations, equation (7-27) simplifies to

$$F^{-1}(P(H)) = F^{-1}(P(FA)) + d'. \tag{7-28}$$

Equations (7-27) and (7-28) provide expressions for the theoretical quantities S_n/S_t and d' in terms of the observables $P(H)$ and $P(FA)$. Equation (7-27) says that if the ROC is converted to a plot in standard scores, the resulting function will be linear with a slope equal to the ratio of the standard deviations of the noise and target distributions. Equation (7-28) states that if the target and noise distributions are equally variable

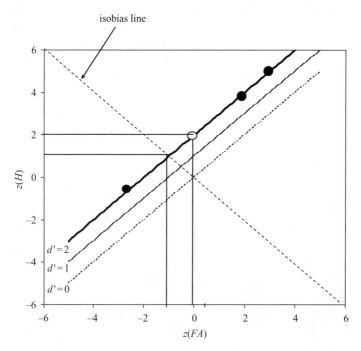

FIGURE 7-7. ROCs transformed from a plot of $(P(H), P(FA))$ pairs into $(z(H) = F^{-1}(P(H)), z(FA) = F^{-1}(P(FA)))$ pairs. Three ROCs are shown, for $s_n/s_t = 1$ and various values of d'. See the text for the significance of the other markings on the figure.

$(S_t = S_n)$, the slope of the function will be one. The argument is illustrated in Figure 7-7.

We now turn to the concept of signal strength, x. This is assumed to be an internal reaction of the observer. Nevertheless we can characterize it.

M_t and M_n are points on the signal strength scale, and so $d' = (M_t - M_n)/S_t$ is an interval on the same scale, divided by S_t, which is also defined in signal strength units. In order to establish a scale unit, let $S_t = 1$. Accordingly, equation (7-27) becomes

$$F^{-1}(P(H)) = S_n F^{-1}(P(FA)) + d'$$
$$d' = F^{-1}(P(H)) - S_n F^{-1}(P(FA)).$$
$$(7\text{-}29)$$

If the target and noise distributions are equally variable ($S_n = S_t$), equation (7-29) has the simpler form $d' = F^{-1}(P(H)) - F^{-1}(P(FA))$.

The analysis depends upon the assumptions that the forms of the distributions are known, identical, and symmetric functions. These assumptions can be checked against the data.

Suppose that the observer can be induced to set (at least) three different criterion levels, c_1, c_2, and c_3, under otherwise identical observation conditions. In an experimental situation, this can be done by asking the observer to decide "target present": whenever the observer thinks there was a reasonable chance of the signal coming from the target distraction (condition 1), when he or she is "pretty sure" that the signal was from a target (condition 2), or when the observer is virtually certain that the signal was from the target distribution (condition 3). In other words, the observer is asked to emphasize making hits and avoiding false alarms to different degrees in each condition. A rational observer would adjust his / her criterion so that $c_1 < c_2 < c_3$. The transformed ROC should be linear, as in Figure 7-7, with an intercept equal to d', the skill parameter, and a slope equal to S_n, the variability of the noise ratio compared to the variability of the target distribution.

If the transformed ROC is not linear one of the assumptions of the basic detection situation must have been violated. Fortunately, there are ways to analyze signal detection behavior without these assumptions.[9]

The analyst's next task is to determine the observer's criterion value, c. In order to assign a number to c, we have to identify a zero point on the signal strength scale. Conceptually, two definitions of "zero signal strength" have been proposed. One is to define zero as the midpoint of the noise distribution, $M_n = 0$. The argument for doing so is that this is the expected value of the signal intensity when no target is present. Under this definition, the location of the criterion on the signal intensity scale is

$$c = S_n z_n(c),$$
$$(7\text{-}30)$$

---

[9] E.g., Egan (1975); MacMillan and Creelman (2004).

and the location of the target mean is

$$M_t = d', \tag{7-31}$$

as this is the difference between the two means, in signal strength scale units.

An alternative approach is to define $x = 0$ as the criterion level at which the probabilities of the different types of correct decisions, hits and correct rejections, are equal. This will be referred to as the *isobias point*. At the isobias point the probabilities of the different types of errors, misses and false alarms, are also equal. I find this definition of a zero point more compelling conceptually. Unfortunately, the problem of establishing the means and the criterion point becomes a bit more involved.

At the isobias point the probability density functions for the two distributions will be equal:

$$z_t(0) = -z_n(0). \tag{7-32}$$

This condition is shown graphically in Figure 7-8, for the case in which the target and noise distributions have equal variance. As the two distributions draw apart (d' increases), the absolute values of $z_t(0)$ and $z_n(0)$, which depend upon the distances of the means from the intersection point, will increase. The points that satisfy equation (7-32) fall on the negative diagonal of Figure 7-7, which is called the *isobias line*. The values of $z_t(0)$ and $z_n(0)$ for a particular value of d' are determined by the point at which the isobias line intersects the $-z_t(x) = -s_n z_n(x) + d'$ line for a given value of d'. (The case for $d' = 2$, $S_t = S_n$ is shown in Figure 7-7).

We will first position the mean of the target distribution relative to the origin at the isobias point, and then position the criterion point relative to the origin.

From the definition of isobias, $f_t(z_t(0)) = f_n(z_n(0))$. Because $M_t \geq M_n$, $z_t(0)$ must be equal to or less than zero, while $z_n(0)$ must be non-negative. By symmetry, $f_n(z_n(0)) = f_n(-z_n(0))$ and by the assumption of monotonicity f_n only takes this value at $z_n(0)$ and $-z_n(0)$. Therefore $z_t(0) = -z_n(0)$. Applying equation (7-26), with $c = 0$, and recalling that $S_t = 1$ by definition,

$$z_t(0) = \frac{S_n}{S_t}(z_n(0)) - d'$$

$$z_t(0) = \frac{S_n}{S_t}(-z_t(0)) - d' \tag{7-33}$$

$$z_t(0)(1 + S_n) = -d'$$

$$z_t(0) = -\frac{d'}{1 + S_n}.$$

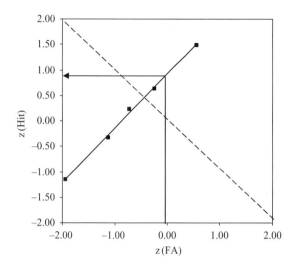

FIGURE 7-8. The ROC derived from the data in Table 7.1. The solid line is the line of best fit to the data. It has a slope of 1.05. The intercept (z(Hit) at z(FA) = 0) is .8, establishing d'. The broken line is the isobias line.

Therefore M_t must lie $d'/(1 + S_n)$ units above the isobias point. For any value of the criterion, c,

$$z_t(c) = -F^{-1}(H)$$
$$z_t(c) = c - M_t$$
$$c = z_t(c) + M_t \tag{7-34}$$
$$c = z_t(c) + \frac{d'}{1 + S_n}.$$

This completes the analysis. Under assumptions that can be checked, and that in fact often do seem to fit many situations, the decision analyst can determine the observer's skill parameter, d', criterion for decision making, c, and the relative variability of the noise and signal distributions, S_n, from observation of the hit and false alarm rates.

Why would you want to do this? The utility of signal detection theory will be illustrated in a worked analysis, followed by some remarks concerning actual applications.

7.8. A NUMERICAL EXAMPLE OF ROC ANALYSIS

Here is a worked example, together with a "cover story" that refers to a problem in airline security.

Suppose that we want to test airline baggage screeners' ability to detect illegal material in suitcases, by looking at the X-ray image as a bag passes through a detection machine. The Transportation Safety Authority (TSA) could conduct an experiment in which inspectors plant bags that sometimes contain illegal material on the baggage security line. Screeners could then look at the images and classify each bag as falling into one of six possible categories:

-3:   Absolutely does not contain illegal material
-2:   Very unlikely to contain illegal material
-1:   Probably does not contain illegal material

1:   Might possibly contain illegal material
2:   Probably contains illegal material
3:   Certain to contain illegal material.

Screeners are supposed to set one of these criteria for opening bags for a more extensive check, depending upon how suspicious the X-ray image is. All bags should be at least as suspicious-appearing to satisfy category -3. Slightly more suspicious-looking bags would justify a category -2, and so forth, until very suspicious bags justified a category 3 rating.

Table 7-1 shows hypothetical data from such an experiment, along with the related z values. Hits and false alarms were classified by assuming that the screener always used the highest judgment category that was seen as appropriate. For example, consider an item that the screener judged to be a 2 on the "suspicion" scale. It can be assumed that the same screener would have considered the item to be "more than 1," "more than -1," and so forth.

Figure 7-8 shows the ROC produced by plotting the z values in Table 7-1. The slope is 1.05, which is sufficiently close to 1 to make us willing to accept that target and noise distributions have equal variability. The following computations are based on the $S_n = S_t$ case. Because all cases would receive at least a -3 rating (first row of table), there are a total of 381 noise and 370 target cases (first row, third and fourth columns).

Now consider the number of cases that received at least a 2 rating. The 40 cases from the noise distribution that received a 2 rating are added to the 10 cases that received a 3 rating (second column, last and next to last rows), showing that 50 cases from the noise distribution received at least a 2 rating. By the same token, 138 cases from the target distribution received at least a 2 rating. The probability that a signal from the noise distribution would meet this criterion is $P(FA) = 50/381 = .131$, as shown by the next to last row, column labeled $P(FA)$. The $F^{-1}(P(FA))$ value is -1.12058 (column labeled $z(FA)$). By similar reasoning, the values for $P(H)$ and $F^{-1}(P(H))$ are .372 and -.32339.

Having checked the assumption that $S_n = 1$, d' can be determined. It is $z(H) - z(FA) = .797$. The value of c for a rating of 2 is .722.

TABLE 7-1. *Hypothetical Data for Frequency with Which Different Categories Are Given in a Rating Experiment*

Category	Freq|Noise	Freq|Target	CumFreq (No Target)	CumFreq (Target)	P(FA)	P(H)	z(FA)	z(H)
−3	110	25	381	370	1	1		
−2	116	72	271	345	0.711	0.932	0.557145	1.494154
−1	65	55	155	273	0.406	0.737	−0.23572	0.636694
1	40	80	90	218	0.236	0.589	−0.71851	0.225459
2	40	91	50	138	0.131	0.372	−1.12058	−0.32399
3	10	47	10	47	0.026	0.127	−1.93906	−1.14056

Note: 6 rating levels correspond to 5 boundaries between categories. (More generally, k rating levels produce $k-1$ category boundaries, and hence $k-1$ different values for c).

If you repeat these computations for every rating value except −3 (which, by definition, would include all cases), you will find some variation. The d' values range from 1.02 to to .797. This is due to random variation in the data, which in fact was produced by a computer simulation that permitted random variation. Such variation is typical of actual data from experiments.

The data pose a problem for a policymaker. The hit rate $P(H)$ for the "certain to contain" category is only .127, which means that the miss rate is .873. Letting almost nine of every ten contraband bags through would be unacceptable in a transportation security situation, and so at the least, the inspector would tell the screener that he or she did not have to be absolutely certain in order to decide to inspect the bag further.

Further analysis reveals another problem. Consider the most extreme example, setting the criterion to "very unlikely." Here the hit rate is .932, which implies a miss rate of .078; about 1 in 13 illegal items get through. This sounds scary. What would you do?

Missing illegal material is only part of the problem. A .932 hit rate produces a false alarm rate of .771. People without contraband in their bags vastly outnumber people who are carrying contraband, so if the screeners operate at the .932 rate, three out of every four airline passengers would be singled out for further inspection. Imagine the chaos.

The problem is that the d' value, about .8, is too low. Exhorting the screeners to be more careful would not help; the problem is one of inadequate screening skill. The screeners have to be better trained, or their work situation has to be changed to allow them to concentrate more, or better screening machinery has to be provided, or perhaps all of the above.

I stress that these data were made up to illustrate signal detection theory, and do not represent actual data! Although the TSA does conduct inspections that can produce the data for a signal detection analysis, I do not know if they actually use the theory. In some cases the theory may be used without observers being aware of it. See the radiology example in Section 7.10.

The TSA example illustrates two important aspects of decision analysis. The analyst wants to know what the performance level is and, equally important, whether performance is limited by an inappropriate criterion or by lack of detection skill. The example illustrates a situation in which the problem is lack of skill. The remedy would be to increase training or obtain better scanning equipment, or both.

Sometimes all that is needed is a change in the criterion. Recall the World War II example, in which signal detection theory was used to analyze the performance of naval lookouts. Naval lookouts serve for four-hour periods, called *watches*. The navy found that the longer a sailor had been on watch, the more likely he was to fail to spot a submarine. At first, this was thought to be because the sailors' observing skills dropped as they became tired or bored. Signal detection analyses showed that this was not the case. The d' parameter was constant across the watch, but the criterion level, c, rose. This was good news for the navy, because the problem could be solved just by telling lookouts to guard against this error late in the watch.

How vigilant should an observer be? Target detection is always good, and false alarms are always bad, but one comes with the other. The next section discusses how c should be set. This discussion will connect signal detection theory to Bayesian reasoning.

7.9. ESTABLISHING A CRITERION

We now shift to the perspective of a decision policymaker. The policymaker's job is to decide how the observer should behave, which in essence means deciding where the observer should set c. In the case of human observers, there is also the practical question of communicating the policymaker's decision to the observer in a way that the observer can understand. The policymaker cannot simply tell the observer "Set your criterion at $c = 1.5$" (or any other number) because c is a point on the observer's internal scale of signal intensity, and therefore is not available to the policymaker. Even if the policymaker were to know c, it is not clear that an observer would be able to translate between the policymaker's command and his / her own internal feelings. Suppose the Transportation Safety Administration authority instructed its screeners to stop any airline passenger who registered over 1.5 on the screener's internal feeling of suspicion. Would the screeners know what to do?

Fortunately there is an easy solution. To understand it, though, it is important to distinguish between the evidence available to the observer and the policymaker. To the observer, the evidence is the signal strength, x. From the policymaker's view, though, the evidence is the observer's report, not the signal itself. In the medical example given at the start of this chapter, a radiologist, acting as an observer, examines an X-ray or similar image and "computes" an internal feeling, x, representing the extent to which the radiologist believes the image displays a tumor. A surgeon, acting as a policymaker, uses the radiologist's report to decide whether or not to operate.

Translating this to the jargon of signal detection theory, the observer knows that the signal strength was x. The policymaker, acting on the observer's report, knows only that either $x > c$ or $x \leq c$.

The policymaker's task is a decision under risk, as described in Chapter 6. The strength of a signal, x, is evidence available to the observer. Associated with this evidence there is some probability, $P(T|x)$, that a target is present, and some probability, $P(N|x)$, that the signal was from the noise distribution. The question the policymaker wants to answer is *how strong does x have to be in order to justify the decision "target present"?* In order to answer this question, we have to know the consequences of the decision. Let

$U(H)$ = Utility of a hit
$U(FA)$ = Utility of a false alarm
$U(M)$ = Utility of a miss
$U(CR)$ = Utility of a correct rejection ,

where utility is the subjective value of an outcome, as defined in Chapter 6. Typically, $U(M)$ and $U(FA)$ will be zero or negative, because these are errors. The policymaker wants the observer to decide "target" whenever the expected value of acting as if a target was present exceeds the expected value of acting as if no target was present. This condition is stated as

$$P(T\,|\,x) \cdot U(H) + P(N\,|\,x) \cdot U(FA) > P(N\,|\,x) \cdot U(CR) + P(T\,|\,x) \cdot U(M)$$
$$P(T\,|\,x) \cdot (U(H) - U(M)) > P(N\,|\,x) \cdot (U(CR) - U(FA)).$$
$$\frac{P(T\,|\,x)}{P(N\,|\,x)} > \frac{U(CR) - U(FA)}{U(H) - U(M)}. \tag{7-35}$$

The term on the left-hand side of the last line is the *odds* on the target's being present, given that a signal with strength x has been observed. The term on the right-hand side is defined by the reward structure, that is, by the payoffs for the various things that may happen. Assuming that the odds increase as the signal strength increases, the criterion point should be set at the lowest value, c, that satisfies equation (7-35).

The problem is that the observer does not know $P(T\,|\,x)$; the observer only knows x. If x took on discrete values, we could regard this as a Bayesian problem, and apply

$$P(T\,|\,x) = P(T)P(x\,|\,T)$$
$$P(N\,|\,x) = P(N)P(x\,|\,N). \tag{7-36}$$

Substituting into the last line in equation (7-36),

$$\frac{P(T) \cdot P(x\,|\,T)}{P(N) \cdot P(x\,|\,N)} > \frac{U(CR) - U(FA)}{U(H) - U(M)}$$
$$\frac{P(x\,|\,T)}{P(x\,|\,N)} > \left[\frac{P(N)}{P(T)}\right] \cdot \left[\frac{U(CR) - U(FA)}{U(H) - U(M)}\right]. \tag{7-37}$$

Because x is a continuous signal, the left-hand side of (7-37) is replaced by

$$\frac{f_t(x)}{f_n(x)} > \left[\frac{P(N)}{P(T)}\right] \cdot \left[\frac{U(CR) - U(FA)}{U(H) - U(M)}\right]. \tag{7-38}$$

The left-hand side of equation (7-38) is determined by functions of x, values defined within the signal detection situation and thus, in principle, available to the observer. The right-hand side is defined by two classes of parameters that are outside of the signal detection situation itself, but available to the policymaker. The leftmost square brackets contain a term that is defined by the probabilities of target and noise signals, without regard to signal strength. The rightmost square brackets contain a term that is defined by the relative payoffs for hits, misses, correct rejections, and false alarms.

This analysis shows that a signal detection problem has been connected to the decision problem within which the signals are to be analyzed. Providing that the ratio $f_t(x) / f_n(x)$ never decreases as x increases continuously (which seems to be the case for most decision situations), all that one needs to do is to find $x = c$ such that the ">" sign in equation (7-38) can be replaced by an equality. Writing r for the right-hand side of equation (7-38),

$$\frac{f_t(c)}{f_n(c)} = r. \tag{7-39}$$

This can be thought of as the lowest odds that the policymaker will accept.

Determining c is straightforward for the basic case of normally distributed signals. The ratio reduces to

$$\frac{f_t(c)}{f_n(c)} = \frac{\frac{1}{\sqrt{2\pi}s}e^{-\frac{1}{2}\left(\frac{c-M_t}{s}\right)^2}}{\frac{1}{\sqrt{2\pi}s}e^{-\frac{1}{2}\left(\frac{c-M_n}{s}\right)^2}} \tag{7-40}$$

$$\frac{f_t(c)}{f_n(c)} = e^{-\frac{1}{2s^2}\left((c-M_t)^2 - (c-M_n)^2\right)}$$

Using r to express the desired odds, and converting to logarithms,

$$\text{Ln}(r) = -\frac{1}{2}\frac{1}{S^2}\left((c - M_t)^2 - (c - M_n)^2\right). \tag{7-41}$$

By definition, $S = 1$. If $x = 0$ is placed at the isobias point, $M_t = d'/2$ and $M_n = -d'/2$. This simplifies the right-hand side of equation (7-41),

$$-\frac{1}{2}\left(\left(c - \frac{d'}{2}\right)^2 - \left(c - \left(-\frac{d'}{2}\right)\right)^2\right) = -\frac{1}{2}\left(\left(c^2 - cd' + \frac{d'^2}{4}\right) - \left(c^2 + cd' + \frac{d'^2}{4}\right)\right)$$

$$-\frac{1}{2}\left(\left(\frac{c^2 - cd' + d'^2}{4}\right) - \left(\frac{c^2 + cd' + d'^2}{4}\right)\right) = -\frac{1}{2}\left(2cd'\right) = cd'$$

producing

$$\text{Ln}(r) = cd'$$
$$c = \text{Ln}(r)/d'. \tag{7-42}$$

This is an important conclusion. In the basic signal detection situation, a policymaker can specify c by specifying r, the lowest odds that the policymaker is willing to accept in any individual case. Equation (7-42) also shows that c is inversely proportional to d'. In words, observers who have large d' can afford to set lower criteria, thus reducing the number of misses, and still satisfy the policymaker's requirement.

This conclusion shows that there is a solution to the criterion-setting problem. However, it begs the issue of how one might communicate this conclusion to an observer, in order to tell the observer how to act. Here there are two situations in which different procedures are used:

Situation 1. In situation S1, the policymaker can manipulate the observer's sensitivity directly. This is the case if the "observer" is a machine. To illustrate, consider the case of smoke detectors, which are widely used for the automatic detection of fires in buildings. How sensitive should they be? You want a smoke detector to go off when there is an uncontrolled fire, but you do not (normally) want it to go off whenever someone lights a cigarette. The sensitivity of a smoke detector can be set to reflect the prevalence of serious fires and the consequences of hits, misses, and so on. The detectors in a gasoline storage depot ought to be more sensitive than the detectors in the typical home. In signal detection terminology, setting detector sensitivity is equivalent to setting c and, as just shown, given knowledge of the situation, the optimal value of c can be determined.

Situation 2. The observer is a human being, so c cannot be set directly. There is an excellent example here, the problem of using polygraphs ("lie detectors") to detect falsehood. The polygraph records physiological responses made by an examinee during an interview. The records are then interpreted by an operator (observer), who decides, with varying degrees of confidence, whether or not the examinee is telling the truth. Suppose a policymaker were to instruct the polygraph operator: "Report that the examinee is lying if your subjective feeling that you are dealing with a liar results in (probability of this feeling|liar)/(probability of this feeling|honest person) is greater than r." This instruction would be impossible to follow. Fortunately, there is a way out. In practice, this is the technique used to train human observers.

The trick is to look at the situation from the policy maker's point of view. The policy maker does not know x; all he/she knows is what the observer recommends. If the observer says "target present" ("liar" in the polygraph case), the policymaker only knows that $x > c$, where c is whatever criterion the polygraph user is using. In other words, from the viewpoint of the policymaker, the evidence is $(x > c)$ or $(x < c)$, not x. Furthermore, for any fixed c, we know that $P(x > c|T) = P(H)$ and $P(x > c|N) = P(FA)$. That, and knowledge of the relative frequencies and the reward structure of the environment, are all that the policymaker needs to know. Equation (7-37) applies:

$$\frac{P(H)}{P(FA)} > \left[\frac{P(N)}{P(T)}\right] \cdot \left[\frac{U(CR) - U(FA)}{U(H) - U(M)}\right]. \tag{7-43}$$

Write R for the right-hand side of equation (7-43), so that the *overall* ratio of hit and false alarm rates takes over some set of test cases of known origin, approachs but does not quite reach R. The observer's hit/false alarm rate should be as low as possible, while satisfying the relation

$$\frac{P(H)}{P(FA)} \geq R. \tag{7-44}$$

This is a behavioral benchmark that a rational observer can meet.

7.10 EXAMPLES

This section presents examples to illustrate the combination of decision making, Bayesian reasoning, and signal detection. The first example is made up to illustrate the procedure. It also shows an area in which signal detection probably is not used, although it might be. The second is based on an actual case. The third is based on common medical practice.

Example: The Attorney's Problem

Consider the case of a Department of Justice anti-fraud attorney who is deciding whether or not to bring a lawsuit against a firm that the attorney suspects is guilty of making fraudulent claims about the effect of its product. Suppose that the attorney knows the following facts in advance of considering the evidence:

A consumer organization has estimated that one out of eight firms in the industry engages in fraudulent advertising. Therefore, the odds on a randomly chosen firm being a fraudulent advertiser are 7:1.

The average settlement in such cases is three million dollars plus expenses.

The expense of bringing a suit is usually about half a million dollars. Assuming that in this case utility and dollars are equivalent, $U(H) = \$3,000,000$, $U(FA) = -500,000$.

The cost of not bringing suit against a firm that is not engaging in fraudulent advertising is zero.

Firms that engage in fraudulent advertising typically cheat the public
of about two million dollars.
Therefore, $U(CR) = 0$, $U(M) = -\$2,000,000$.

The attorney then asks an investigator if the claims made in the
advertisements are likely to be true. The investigator says that the claims
are twice as likely to be false as to be true. Is this high enough to warrant
initiating a suit?

From the right-hand side of equation (7-43),

$$R = \left[\frac{P(N)}{P(T)}\right] \cdot \left[\frac{U(CR) - U(FA)}{U(H) - U(M)}\right] = \left[\frac{7}{1}\right] \cdot \left[\frac{0 - (-500,000)}{3,000,000 - (-2,000,000)}\right]$$

$$\left[\frac{7}{1}\right] \cdot \left[\frac{0 - (-500,000)}{3,000,000 - (-2,000,000)}\right] = 7 \cdot \left(\frac{500,000}{5,000,000}\right)$$

$$R = .7.$$

The investigator's conclusion about the claims can be interpreted as
$P(H)/P(FA) = 2/1$. Because 2 is greater than .7, an indictment is called for.

Example: Detecting Potential Spies

Between 2000 and 2005, the United States government was embarrassed
by two serious breaches of national security. In one, the Robert Hansen
case, it was discovered that an FBI employee had passed vital information to the Soviet government during the Cold War period. In the other,
the Wen Ho Lee case, the Department of Justice accused Wen Ho Lee, a
scientist at the Los Alamos atomic energy laboratories of passing classified information to the government of the People's Republic of China.
The government was unable to prove its major accusation, although
Dr. Lee did plead guilty to a lesser charge of mishandling classified
information. In signal detection terms, the department was widely criticized for a miss in the Hansen case and a false alarm in the Lee case.

Polygraph tests played a role in both investigations. As a result of
these and other incidents Congress asked the National Academy of
Science (NAS) to examine the scientific status of polygraph investigations. This example is based on the NAS report.[10]

Advocates of polygraph testing told the NAS committee that the
conclusions of a properly trained examiner were 90% accurate. By this,
they meant that the examiner gave a correct decision 90% of the time.
Although the committee report contains some skeptical remarks about
the lack of evidence for this statement, eventually the claim was accepted. The committee then addressed a policy question: Should the Atomic
Energy Commission (AEC) and other government agencies give

[10] Committee to Review Scientific Evidence on the Polygraph (2003).

polygraph tests to all their employees? They concluded that this practice would be doubtful, based on the following reasoning:

The AEC employs approximately 10,000 people. Assume, for the sake of argument, that 10 of them are spies. (This is probably a high figure.) A polygraph screening that would catch 9 of the 10 spies would falsely implicate 999 innocent people. At the least, this would pose a substantial administrative burden.

The committee's reasoning was based on a straightforward Bayesian argument. Let E be the event "examiner concludes that the examinee is a liar." Spies are the targets, T, and in this case, innocent people are noise, N. According to the experts' testimony $P(E|T) = .9$ and $P(E|N) = .1$. What is desired is $P(T|E)$, the probability that the examinee is a spy, given that the examiner believes he or she is lying. From Bayes' theorem:

$$P(T \mid E) = \frac{(.9)(.001)}{(.9)(.001) + (.1)(.999)}$$

$$P(T \mid E) = .0089.$$

We can go a little bit further. The fact that the experts claimed that the accuracy rate was identical for both identification of spies and identification of innocence implies that $P(H) = P(FA)$. Therefore, the expert examiner must be operating at the isobias point, $c = 0$. If we assume that the basic model applies, we can calculate d' by applying equation (7-29):

$$d' = F^{-1}(P(H)) - F^{-1}(P(FA))$$

$$d' = F^{-1}(.90) - F^{-1}(.10)$$

$$d' = 2.563,$$

where F is the cumulative standard normal distribution function. Given d', we can calculate R, the hit / false alarm rate for different values of c. Figure 7-9 shows this calculation for the c increasing from 0 to 5. Examining this figure is instructive.

It is difficult, if not impossible, to calculate the reward structure for capturing spies versus harassing innocent individuals. However, we can make a statement about frequencies. Suppose that we wanted to set the polygraph criterion at a value such that if the polygraph was positive, there was a 50:50 chance that the individual was a spy. This means that the polygraph criterion would have to be set so that

$$\frac{P(H)P(Spy)}{P(FA)P(innocent)} = 1$$

$$\frac{P(H)}{P(FA)} = \frac{9990}{10}.$$

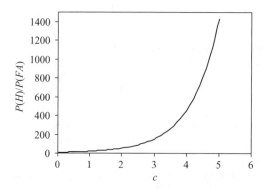

FIGURE 7-9. The hit/false alarm ratio for various values of the criterion, c, in the NAS analysis of the feasibility of screening personnel using polygraphs.

R has to be 999. Figure (7-9) shows that this value can be obtained, at a value of about $c = 4.9$. At this value, though, $P(H)$ is only .12, so approximately six out of every seven spies would be let go.

Using calculations similar to this,[11] the NAS committee concluded that polygraph screening of all AEC personnel was not a good idea. The committee pointed out though, that the polygraph was being used to locate a rare event, the presence of a spy. In Bayesian terms, the base rate of target cases was only one in a thousand, and the costs of a false alarm were considerable. Suppose, instead, that a security breach had occurred and that only 10 people could have committed it. Assuming only one spy, this reduces the base rate to 1 in 10. Under these situations, in order to have a 50:50 chance of detecting the spy, R has to be 9. This is achievable, at $c = 0$, the point at which the experts said that the polygraph was "90% accurate." However, the 90% statement is misleading because it confuses $P(E|T)$, which is what the experts reported, with $P(T|E)$, which is what the investigating officer would want to know. Even though the number of suspects has been reduced by a factor of a thousand, the polygraph examiner would be equally likely to accuse an innocent or a guilty person.

Example: Diagnostic Radiology

Physicians are not usually trained in signal detection theory per se. Indeed, the ones I have talked to almost uniformly say "What's that?" Nevertheless, medical diagnostic procedures are directly related to signal detection theory. The following example is based on radiological screening for breast cancer.[12] In this procedure, a mammogram

---

[11] The NAS committee used a form of signal detection theory that does not require the assumptions of the basic model.

[12] I thank Karen May Hunt, M.D., for the figures in this example.

(radiological image) is made of the patient's breasts. The radiologist then scans the image to see if it shows a cancerous tumor. If the physician thinks that a cancerous tumor is present, tissue is taken from the breast, an obviously invasive procedure, and the tissue is examined by a pathologist (*biopsy*). Regular mammograms are recommended for women of middle age and above, as breast cancer is a leading cause of death.

From the radiologist's perspective there can be four outcomes. A *true positive* (TP) is a case in which the biopsy shows that the tumor is cancerous. A *false positive* (FP) occurs if the tumor is not cancerous. A *true negative* (TN) is a case in which the radiologist does not think that a cancer is present and the patient does not develop other signs of breast cancer within a year following the examination. A *false negative* (FN) occurs when the radiologist does not think that a cancer is present but signs of cancer do develop within the year.

The terms *TP, FP, TN*, and *FN* usually refer to the number of cases in each category. However, they can be thought of as rates by simply dividing the number of cases per category by the number of mammograms examined by the radiologist. This could be of the order of 10,000 or more a year. We will assume that this has been done, and that the rates can be treated as probabilities. This is in agreement with the frequentist definition of probability (Chapter 2).

Radiologists are evaluated using two measures of performance, the *positive predictive value (PPV)* and the *sensitivity (S)*. The *PPV* is

$$PPV = \frac{TP}{FP + TP}. \tag{7-45}$$

In words, the *PPV* is the ratio (cancers detected) / (cancers diagnosed). If a patient is told that a radiologist has diagnosed her mammogram as positive, and that the radiologist has a *PPV* of 33%, the patient knows that the odds are one to two ($\sim .33 / (1-.33)$) that she actually has cancer. Since untreated breast cancers are often fatal, a biopsy would certainly be in order.

As in the polygraph screening case, a signal is being used to detect a rare event. In this case, though, the costs of a false alarm, while not negligible, are not nearly as large as in the case of falsely accusing a person of a major felony.

The equation for sensitivity is

$$S = \frac{TP}{FN + TP}. \tag{7-46}$$

This is the ratio (cancers detected)/(cancers present). In words, it is the probability that the radiologist will detect a cancer if one is present.

Typical values for a good radiologist might be $S = 90\%$ and $PPV = 35\%$. The discrepancy between the two numbers is produced because of the incidence rate. The base rate of breast cancer is about .005 in an otherwise unscreened population of women. (While this is low in absolute terms, it still makes breast cancer a discouragingly common disease.)

Although PPV and S are not signal detection measures, they map directly onto signal detection, as the following analysis shows.

We begin with sensitivity. The TP rate can be thought of as the probability that two things occur: that a cancer is present and that the radiologist diagnoses cancer. Similar interpretations follow for the other rates. Therefore,

$$S = \frac{TP}{FN + TP}$$

$$S = \frac{P(x > c \mid T) \cdot P(T)}{P(x \le c \mid T) \cdot P(T) + P(x > c) \mid T) \cdot P(T)} \tag{7-47}$$

$$S = P(x > c \mid T)$$

$$S = P(H).$$

The medical sensitivity index is the hit rate.

The PPV is a bit more complicated:

$$PPV = \frac{TP}{FP + TP}$$

$$PPV = \frac{P(x > c \mid T) \cdot P(T)}{P(x > c \mid N) \cdot (1 - P(T)) + P(x > c \mid T) \cdot P(T)}$$

$$PPV \cdot [P(x > c \mid N) \cdot (1 - P(T)) + P(x > c \mid T) \cdot P(T)] = P(x > c \mid T) \cdot P(T)$$

$$PPV \cdot [P(x > c \mid N) \cdot (1 - P(T))] = P(x > c \mid T) \cdot P(T) - PPV \cdot (P(x > c \mid T)P(T))$$

$$PPV(P(x > c \mid N)) \cdot (1 - P(T)) = P(x > c \mid T) \cdot P(T) \cdot (1 - PPV)$$

$$P(x > c \mid N) = \left[\frac{P(T)}{1 - P(T)}\right] \cdot \left[\frac{1 - PPV}{PPV}\right] \cdot P(x > c \mid T)$$

$$P(FA) = \left[\frac{P(T)}{1 - P(T)}\right] \cdot \left[\frac{1 - PPV}{PPV}\right] \cdot P(H). \tag{7-48}$$

In the last line of equation (7-48), the first term in square brackets on the right is the ratio (base rate) / (1−base rate). The second term in square brackets is the inverse of the odds that a positive diagnosis is correct. Finally, by equation (7-47), $P(H) = S$. Using the numbers given for a good radiologist, we would have

$$P(H) = S = .90$$

$$P(FA) = \left[\frac{.005}{1 - .005}\right]\left[\frac{.65}{.35}\right].90$$

$$P(FA) \approx .008.$$

If we are willing to assume the basic model, then from Equation (7-29),

$$d' = F^{-1}(.90) - F^{-1}(.008)$$
$$d' = 3.69.$$

In the basic model, by equation (7-34), $M_t = d'/2$, and $c = M_t - F^{-1}(H)$. Therefore, in this case, $c = 1.845 - F^{-1}(.90) = .563$.

This example illustrates an important point in communication. The S and PPV parameters map directly onto the parameters in signal detection theory, and so clearly, radiologists are being treated as observers. Why not use the d' and c statistics? Because the S and PPV statistics are easy to understand without first taking a course in signal detection. Considerations like this are important whenever the results of mathematical modeling are to be communicated to real-life decision makers.

7.11 FOUR CHALLENGE PROBLEMS

This chapter has presented the mathematical theory of signal detection and discussed several of its applications outside of the laboratory. There are also many situations in which signal detection methods might be used, but are not. Instead of summarizing the arguments already given, I will close with four challenge problems. Three are based upon social problems that were very much in the news as this book was being written, and will probably stay there for the foreseeable future. The challenge to the reader is to decide whether or not Bayesian reasoning and/or signal detection theory can be applied. If neither method can be applied, explain to yourself why not. If one or both methods can be applied, consider the likely effects of the application.

The fourth challenge problem is purely mathematical. It should serve as a good check of your understanding of the basic concepts involved the theory of signal detection.

Challenge Problem 1: Racial Profiling

Consider this case, which I was once asked to comment on.

A police force had been accused of "racial profiling," that is, harassing African Americans by consistently stopping them for suspicious behavior. The American Civil Liberties Union maintained that profiling was obvious because police stopped roughly twice as many African Americans, proportional to their numbers in the population, than they did whites.

One's first thought is that signal detection analysis and Bayesian reasoning could be used to determine whether or not the police (a) set lower thresholds for stopping African Americans than for stopping whites, and if so (b) whether they were justified in doing so. Could this analysis be carried out? If not, why not?

Challenge Problem 2: Profiling in Homeland Security Issues

Here is a problem that at first seems to be identical to the police profiling issue, but I believe raises somewhat different issues.

It has been claimed that Transportation Security Agency personnel are more likely to conduct aggressive searches of people who appear to be of Middle Eastern origin than they will of other passengers. The intellectual case for doing so was stated nicely in an op-ed piece in the *New York Times* (Feb. 6, 2002) by Fedwa Meta-Douglas, an Indiana University professor who is herself a Lebanese American and who described herself as having a "classic Mediterranean appearance." She noted that she is frequently and sometimes very thoroughly examined. (She said her worst experience was in Cairo!) However, she does not resent this. In Meta-Douglas's own words, "it is a fact that the particular terrorist group sworn to our destruction, Al Qaeda, is made up largely of Middle-Easterners. It is not unreasonable to direct increased attention to passengers with some connection to the Middle East."

Meta-Douglas's argument was not couched in mathematical terms, perhaps because the *New York Times* motto, "All the news that's fit to print," would rule out mathematics on the op-ed page. We can recast her argument into decision-theoretical terms.

I understand her as saying that the cost factors are essentially the same for all travelers; everyone is equally inconvenienced by an extensive search, regardless of their origin. The cost to a traveler of a miss – the cost of actually being on a plane with a terrorist – is horrendous. However, the prior odds are different for different ethnic groups; the odds for the risk, $P_0(T) / P_0(N)$ are greater for travelers of apparent Middle Eastern origin than they are for the rest of us. Therefore, a lower strength of evidence is required to justify the decision to search a Middle Eastern traveler than to search somebody who does not have the "classic Mediterranean appearance."

The American Civil Liberties Union (ACLU) has argued heatedly against profiling, on the grounds that every American, regardless of race, religion, and ethnic origin, is entitled to equal protection under the law. ACLU spokespersons have repeatedly, and correctly, said that the vast majority of Middle Easterners are not terrorists. To what extent is this relevant from a decision-theoretic viewpoint?

A second argument that the ACLU has made is that the act of singling out and examining an innocent individual of a particular ethnic background is more costly than examining a non-ethnic person (if such a person exists), either because the search is consistently more intrusive or because the person is more likely to feel humiliated because of feelings of being singled out on the basis of ethnicity. Advocates associated with particular ethnic groups have also used this argument. What do you think of it? How does it translate into decision-theoretic terminology?

The third argument that the ACLU has used, and the one that I think it most believes in, is that we have simply framed the decision procedure the wrong way. According to this argument, no matter what the outcome of a signal detection or Bayesian analysis, profiling is unconstitutional because it amounts to using an ethnic-based cue to guide official behavior. Proponents of this argument agree that so long as the issue is framed as one of preventing hijacking, profiling may be rational. If we look at the issue more broadly, as one of maintaining the basic principles of civil rights and liberties, then the costs of any form of discrimination have to be considered. What do you think of this argument?

Challenge Problem 3: A Last Look at Homeland Security

Newspaper articles attacking homeland security procedures often point out that baggage screening is not perfect. Suppose that a baggage-screening system detects explosives that are in bags 9 out of 10 times, that is, $P(H) = .9$. Suppose further that the screening system gives false alarms about 1 in 10 times, $P(FA) = .1$. Therefore, 10% of the bags that are screened are erroneously screened. As something on the order of 100 million bags are screened annually, this means that if this system is deployed, there will be 10 *million* errors in baggage checking. Should the system be deployed or should we go to a more expensive method of checking baggage? What does Bayesian analysis and signal detection tell us? Does this analysis make you want to take the train? Would publicizing error rates like these embolden terrorists to attack? What considerations should go into the reasoning of both the passenger and the terrorist?

Challenge Problem 4: A Return to Mathematics

Suppose that the standard model applies but that there is a marked difference in the variability of signals from target and noise distribution. For argument, assume that S_n is very much greater than S_t. Does this pose any problem for the procedure of setting some criterion c and classifying a signal as "target present" if x exceeds c?

8

Multidimensional Scaling

Surveying the Geography of the Mind

8.1. THE BASIC IDEA

Aristotle observed that when we thought of one thing we were led to think of similar things. He was certainly right. It seems natural to say that ice cream is like sherbet, and that ice cream is more like sherbet than it is like pizza! Most of the time judgments of similarity are made almost without thought.

Categorical thinking is an equally natural thing to do (and Aristotle noted this, too). We speak of how to deal with DOGS, without necessarily referring to a particular dog. A good meal is supposed to have an entrée, green vegetables, and a starch. A politician may be categorized as a typical Republican, Democrat, or Socialist. We use such categorizations in our reasoning, by imputing characteristics of a class to characteristics of an individual. In 2002, my representative to Congress was a woman and a Republican (The Hon. Jennifer Dunn). You could immediately impute characteristics of the class to Rep. Dunn: guessing (correctly) that she was a fiscal and social conservative but, because she is a woman, being less sure that she espoused the anti-birth-control rhetoric of some members of the Republican Party at that time. (She did not.) As Aristotle noticed once again, objects are grouped together into classes because they are similar to each other in some way, although wide variation may be permitted in other ways. Continuing with my example, knowing that Rep. Dunn is a woman and a Republican helps you guess her policy positions but does not help you guess the color of her eyes or whether or not she likes to ski.

Similarity can be indicated in many ways. One is to use adjectives. Would you say that a zebra was identical to, very much like, somewhat like, rather different from, or totally dissimilar from a horse? From an elephant? I could also ask you to rank horse and zebra on a scale of similarity, from 0 (totally dissimilar) to 5 (identical). It is not clear, though, whether or not it would be a good idea to regard these numbers as more than rankings. If the zebra–horse contrast received a 4 and the zebra–elephant contrast a 2, it seems clear that you see the zebra as being more like a horse than an elephant, but it is not clear that you see the horse as twice as similar (4/2) to a zebra as the elephant is.

Questions about relative similarity can be presented to (some) animals. Primates and some species of dolphins can be taught to do a procedure known as *delayed match to sample*. The animal is first shown a target stimulus, denoted by A. Stimulus A is then removed and the animal is shown a pair of stimuli, the original target A and a distractor, B. The animal is rewarded if it approaches or points to the original stimulus, A. (As a control, other animals can be taught to point away from the original stimulus.) No matter what the actual stimuli are, the task is always to approach (or avoid) the original stimulus.

Now suppose that instead of presenting A, followed by the pair (A,B), we presented A followed by (B,C). If the animal approaches B we infer that the animal sees B as being more like A than C is like A. The logic of the procedure is identical to asking a person if a zebra is more like a horse or an elephant.

Similar questions can be asked about classes. It has been shown, many times, that people can reliably rate objects as "good" or "bad" members of a class. To me, and I suspect to most of my readers, a robin is a highly typical bird, and an ostrich is highly atypical. I grant that a biologist can argue that "being a bird" is actually a binary property; robins and ostriches are birds, and bats are not. That is not the point. We are dealing here with everyday conceptualizations, rather than scientific ones. To psychologists, the object of the game is not to see whether a person agrees with a biologist; the object is to determine how a person represents objects and classes in the mind.

Psychologists have approached this issue in several ways. The method to be described here is called *multidimensional scaling* (MDS). It is a way of constructing a mathematical model representing how a person thinks about similarity between objects. The method is also used to investigate how people think about physical spaces. For instance, to what extent does your representation of geographic distances between European cities correspond to reality?

Multidimensional scaling rests on two ideas. The first is that we can assume that a person's mental representation of objects has the properties of a metric space. (Let us postpone just what that means for a moment.) The second assumption is that people can provide reliable judgments of relative similarities and distances. For instance, you may not know exactly how far Seattle, Washington, is from either Vancouver in British Columbia or from Portland, Oregon. You could still be fairly certain that Seattle is closer to Vancouver than to Portland. It turns out

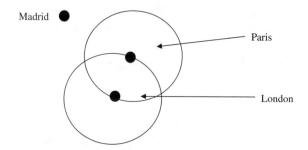

FIGURE 8-1. If Paris and London are closer to each other than Madrid is to either, Madrid must lie outside of two identical circles, one centered on London and the other on Madrid.

that relative judgments alone are often sufficient to recover the way in which a person thinks about geographic information.

The logic will be illustrated by judgments of distances between European cities. Write X-Y for the distance between X and Y. Suppose that a person makes the following judgments, all of which are correct statements of geographic relations:

Paris – London < Paris – Madrid
London – Paris < London – Madrid.

These judgments constrain the possible locations of points within a two-dimensional space. Madrid must lie somewhere outside of a circle centered on Paris, with London on the circumference, and outside a circle centered on London, with Paris on the periphery. The two circles must have radii of identical lengths (see Figure 8-1).

If we add the further belief that

Paris – London > Paris – Brussels
London – Brussels < Paris – Brussels

then Brussels must lie somewhere on a circle inside the London-Paris and Paris-London circles, but closer to London than to Paris. Now suppose we are also told that Brussels is farther from Madrid than either London or Paris. This means that Brussels must be on the side of the London-Paris circle farthest from Madrid. The situation is shown in Figure 8-2.

By progressively increasing the number of known relations, we progressively decrease the range of possible locations for each city. To see this, the reader may want to look at a map of Europe, and ask what restrictions exist if Barcelona is added to the example.

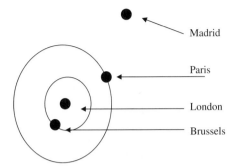

FIGURE 8-2. Given the further restrictions that Brussels is closer to London than it is to Paris, but that Brussels is not as far from Paris as London is, Brussels must lie someplace within the Paris-London circle, within a circle of less than half the radius of the Paris-London circle. If we are given the further restriction that the distance from Brussels to Madrid is farther than the distance from London to Madrid or Paris to Madrid, Brussels must be moved to some point on the Paris-London circle on the opposite side from Madrid.

8.2. STEPS AND TECHNIQUE

This argument just given, and the illustration in Figures 8-1 and 8-2, are intended solely to demonstrate that the information in comparative judgments is sufficient to locate objects in a Euclidean space. In practice, MDS does not proceed by "drawing circles." MDS is a computer-intensive technique that proceeds in the following steps:

1. Suppose that there are N objects to be compared. The initial data consist of rankings of each of the distances that an individual reports. These are used to develop an $N \times N$ matrix $D = [d_{ij}]$, i, $j = 1 \ldots N$, where the d_{ij} entry represents the ordinal ranking of the distance (smallest to largest) between object i and object j. Since these are, strictly speaking, estimates rather than distances, this is called the *disparity matrix*, where d_{ij} is the relative disparity between objects i and j.
2. An initial choice of the number of dimensions is made. Let the first guess be K_0. This is usually fairly low.
3. An estimate is made of possible locations, by calculating an initial data matrix

$$X = [x_{ik}] i = 1 \ldots N, k = 1 \ldots K_0, \tag{8-1}$$

    where x_{ik} is the co-ordinate assigned to the ith object on the jth dimension.

    The distances between each pair of points are then computed. If we are dealing with a Euclidean space, as we would be in the geographic example, the distance between locations would given by the generalized Pythagorean theorem:

$$s_{ij} = \left(\sum_k |x_{ik} - x_{jk}|^2 \right)^{1/2} \tag{8-2}$$

where s_{ij} stands for distance and $|z|$ is the absolute value of quantity z.

These are then converted into rank orders of distances. Thus, $r_{ij} = 1$ if s_{ij} is the greatest distance calculated from the $\{x_{ij}\}$ estimated locations, 2 if it is the second greatest, and so on.

4. The rank order distances are then compared to the relative distances observed in the data, by calculating a measure called "stress." A popular stress measure is

$$Stress = \frac{\displaystyle\sum_{i=1}^{N-1} \sum_{j=i+1}^{N} (d_{ij} - r_{ij})^2}{\displaystyle\sum_{i=1}^{N-1} \sum_{j=i+1}^{N} d_{ij}^2}, \tag{8-3}$$

where d_{ij} is the relative distance measure assigned by the person making the judgments, and r_{ij} is the rank order of the distance estimated from the coordinate assignments made by the computer. The numerator will be zero if the two rank orders agree. Otherwise, stress will have some positive value. The denominator is a scaling term that standardizes the stress measure to reflect the number of distances being compared.

Computer programs have been written to do this. The programs work by making successive changes to the locations of the objects (the rows of matrix X) until a minimum level of stress is attained. The details of these programs are not important. What is important is the principle involved.

Suppose that the person's estimates of distances, D, were in fact based on the location of points in a Euclidean space of K_0 dimensions. In this case a solution with zero stress can always be found, although you may spend a bit of computing time doing so. The solution is usually not unique. Therefore, in some cases, the algorithm computes stress several times, using different initial starting locations, to determine whether or not the solution depends upon the arbitrary initial starting points. In most interesting cases it does not.

Suppose that the stress cannot be reduced to zero. The user must decide either to accept a "low enough" level of stress or to search for a more accurate solution. If a lower stress solution is desired the number of dimensions is set to $K_1 = K_0 + 1$ and the process is repeated. Providing

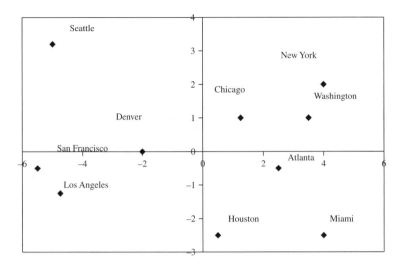

FIGURE 8-3. A multidimensional scaling solution used to place nine U.S. cities, using flying distances as distances between them. Picture based on Figure 1.2 of S.S. Schiffman, M. L. Reynolds, and F. W. Young (1981), *Introduction to Multidimensional Scaling: Theory, Methods and Application*, Academic Press.

that the original estimates actually did refer to objects located in a Euclidean space, a solution can always be found for N objects and $K = N - 1$ dimensions. In practice, a solution of much smaller dimensionality can usually be found.

What does it mean to accept a non-zero level of stress? We can visualize this by continuing with the geographic example. The cities of Europe are located in a three-dimensional space, because they are on the surface of the Earth. Therefore, given enough inter-city judgments, it is impossible to get a two-dimensional solution with zero stress. However, you can drive the stress quite low, for two-dimensional maps of large regions, such as Europe, are pretty accurate. If your estimates included cities as far west as London, as far east as Moscow, as far north as Stockholm, and as far south as Granada or Naples, you would probably have to move to three dimensions in order to get an acceptable solution. That would certainly be the case if you included cities in the opposite hemisphere. A solution for the set of cities {London, Paris, New York, Stockholm, Granada, Johannesburg, Cairo, Singapore, Rio de Janeiro, Buenos Aires, Miami, Honolulu, San Francisco, New Delhi, Kabul, Dubai, and Moscow} requires three dimensions.

An alternative way to conduct MDS is to start with (one hopes accurate) estimates of disparities, instead of rank orders. This is shown by Figure 8-3, which displays an MDS program solution for nine cities, based on actual flying distances, rather than on rankings of the distances. In this case, only two iterations were made, and the relative locations are almost exact.

8.3. EXTENSIONS TO NON-GEOMETRIC DATA

Geographic examples were offered to convince the reader that MDS works. MDS is often used with conceptual objects, things that we can think about but that are either so complex or so vaguely defined that we think about them holistically, rather than as a collection of properties. The idea on which this is based is that a similarity judgment can be treated in the same way, mathematically, as a closeness judgment. Saying that "a zebra is more like a horse than an elephant" is analogous to saying "Paris is closer to London than it is to Madrid." The objects being rated for similarity may have properties, just as cities have geographic coordinates, but these play no direct role in the MDS algorithm. As we shall see, they are important in interpreting the results.

When MDS is used in this way the resulting model is called a *semantic space*. Suppose that we were interested in developing a semantic space to represent how a person thinks about animals. A respondent could be asked to make similarity judgments between pairs of animals. If we let 100 stand for perfect similarity and 0 for no similarity at all, the rating for LION-LION should be 100 (a lion is perfectly like itself), while LION-TIGER might be rated 95, LION-WOLF 80, and LION-RABBIT only 2. Inverting the similarity ratings, this would allow us to say that TIGERS are more like LIONS than WOLVES are like LIONS, and so forth. The MDS technique would then be applied to the ratings, to uncover the respondent's semantic space for animals.

One of the first applications of MDS, by the psychologist Mary Henley,[1] did exactly this. College students rated the similarity of 30 different animals, using a variety of procedures. (One of the strengths of this study was that it showed that consistent results could be obtained across different behavioral indices of similarity.) Multidimensional scaling showed that the data could be modeled quite well by a three-dimensional Euclidean space. Two of the three dimensions are shown in Figure 8-4, using 10 of the original 30 animals.

This space clearly has dimensions (because we assumed that it was Euclidean), but what do the dimensions mean? This requires something of an inspired guess.

The horizontal dimension of Figure 8-4 seems to order animals in terms of size: mice to the left, elephants to the right. The vertical

---

[1] Henley (1969).

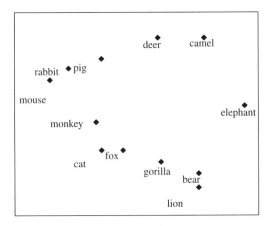

FIGURE 8-4. A semantic space for animal names. The positions are selected from Henley (1969), Figure 2. The original plot was based on similarity relations for 30 different animals.

dimension seems to order animals in terms of fierceness: herbivores to the top, predators to the bottom. Intermediate cases, such as the monkey and the fox, occupy intermediate positions on the ferocity scale. Henley interpreted a third dimension (not shown) as a "resemblance to people" dimension, for its effect is to separate the gorilla, chimpanzee, and monkey from the other 27 animal names that she used. Whatever your choice of names in this particular example, the general point remains. When the only starting point is a set of similarity judgments, without any objective measurement for item variation, naming dimensions relies on a knowledge of the objects being rated, rather than on mathematical analysis.

8.4. EXTENDING THE IDEA TO CONCEPTUAL CLASSES

Logically, a class is a set of objects. *Bears, trees,* and *members of the English royal family* are all names for sets of individual class members. Extrapolating to semantic space models, if an individual is to be represented by a point in a semantic space, then a class should be represented by a region. An example is shown in Figure 8-5. This figure was based on my own rating of the similarity of nine animals found in the Pacific Northwest forest. The example shows both the advantages and limitations of MDS.

The Henley dimensions come out strongly. Dimension 1 appears to be a predacity dimension, running from the harmless deer toward the formidable cougar, wolf, and bear. Dimension 2 is clearly a size dimension, from the mouse at the top (in MDS, the positive and negative ends of a dimension are arbitrary) to the elk, bear, and cougar at the bottom. The

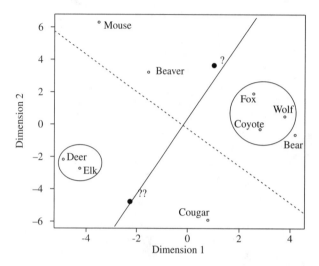

FIGURE 8-5. A multidimensional scaling solution for animals of the Pacific Northwest of North America, based on the author's intuitions about similarities between each pair of animals. Different classification rules are indicated by the lines and circles (see text).

cougar is something of an anomaly, for this animal is about the size of a wolf and more predacious than the bear. The positioning is because I rated the cougar as dissimilar to the other carnivores on the grounds that the it is a feline, whereas the wolf, fox, and coyote are canids. If a three-dimensional solution is used, the cougar rises to a "plane of its own," above the two-dimensional surface shown here.[2]

Classes of animals are clear. The diagonal line separates the predators from the herbivores. Canine predators are indicated by the circle encompassing the fox, wolf, and coyote, with the bear just outside the line. The two members of the deer family also form a tight group.

Now suppose that you encountered an animal with a description that placed it at the "?" position. Is it a predator or a herbivore? Is it a member of the dog family? And what about an animal at the position marked by the double question mark? Is it a carnivorous cat or an aggressive elk?

More abstractly, if semantic scaling can serve as a psychological model of what goes on in the mind, some classification rule, based on semantic

---

[2] The three-dimensional solution does not perfectly accord with my intuitions. I had hoped that the solution would elevate the cougar and place the cougar roughly over the wolf. However, the solution elevated the cougar and placed the cougar equidistant between the elk and the wolf.

space, should predict how people will classify new items. This is a very active field of research, and it would hardly be appropriate here to go over all the evidence. What we can do is explain the three sorts of classification rules that have been investigated.

One classification rule that has been widely studied is the linear classification rule. This is illustrated graphically by the line in Figure 8-5. Algebraically, this amounts to basing classifications on a "goodness of class" rule defined by a linear combination of cues. The idea is to classify an unknown case by determining its projection on a line perpendicular to the line separating the classes, as shown on the dotted line in Figure 8-5. If a linear classifier (LC) wanted to identify the unknown animal as a carnivore or predator, the LC would measure the "extent the animal appears to be a carnivore" by

$$c = w_1 p_1(?) + w p_2(?) + D, \tag{8-4}$$

where c is the extent to which the unknown case appears to be a carnivore, w_1 and w_2 are the weights of dimensions 1 and 2 in the discrimination, and $p_1(?)$ and $p_2(?)$ are the positions of the unknown case on the two dimensions. The weights establish the orientation of the classification line, while D provides a value for the case of an object positioned at the origin. The rule obviously generalizes to the case of k dimensions. This sort of classification is closely related to signal detection, as described in Chapter 6.

An alternative rule is to associate each class with a prototypical case, somewhere in the center of the class. An object's classification is then determined by the extent to which it resembles the prototype. This idea can be traced back to Plato, who argued that an object is a member of a class to the extent that it represents a prototypical class member.

Plato's notion of prototypical reasoning can be represented by an MDS solution in which a central point (usually the centroid) of the positions of a set of class members represents the prototype for that class. An example is shown in Figure 8-6, for the class BIRDS. The prototype theory of classification accounts for an interesting observation. People will rate class members by their degree of goodness. For instance, a ROBIN is considered by most people to be a "good" BIRD, while an OSTRICH is not, even though to a biologist, they are both equally birds. According to the prototype model of classification, a ROBIN is a good BIRD, and an OSTRICH is not, because of their relative distances from the prototype BIRD.

Both the linear and prototype models of categories are called *early computation models* of conceptual categories. Early computation models assume that as a person accumulates experience he/she makes calculations

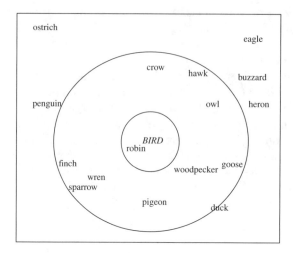

FIGURE 8-6. A hypothetical semantic space for various types of birds. The prototypical BIRD would be located at the center of the occupied points, as shown. The circles represent iso-similarity contours around the prototype point. From Hunt (2002).

that divide the mental space up into regions, or that update a prototype point.

An alternative model is the *exemplar model*. According to this model, people learn about categories by encountering objects of known classification and storing them in a semantic space determined by object characteristics. When an object of unknown classification is encountered its position in the semantic space is determined, based on its characteristics. The space is then searched to locate the closest object of known classification, the *nearest neighbor*. The new object is assumed to belong to the same class as the nearest neighbor. Because the procedure for defining a class is not activated until there is an item to be classified the exemplar model is a *late computation* model.

To gain an appreciation of the exemplar model, look back to Figure 8-5, and consider the "??" point. This point is right on the line separating the carnivores from the herbivores, which means that an LC would find it an ambiguous case. However, the ?? point is closer to ELK than to COUGAR, and so according to an exemplar model, the animal in question must be a herbivore.

Crude as it is, the exemplar model has an interesting mathematical property. Imagine that there is an M dimensional Euclidean space, X, and K classes of objects $\{C_k\}$, $k = 1 \ldots K$, to be located in that space. Therefore, every point in the space can be represented as an M dimensional vector, x.

Each point is associated with a probability density $f_k(x)$, for each class, and each class has a characteristic probability, P_k, associated with it.

A *nearest neighbor classifier* (NNC) operates in the following manner:

1. During the training phase, the NNC observes N cases, each drawn randomly from one of the K classes, with class k chosen with probability P_k. The location of an item from class C_k is chosen in accordance with its probability density function. Therefore, the probability that an item from class k is placed at exactly point x is $f_k(x)$. The NNC records the point's location and its class.

2. During the test phase, the NNC is shown a new item and asked to assign it to a class. The NNC does this by following the nearest neighbor rule. Let the new point be located at point x^*. The NNC locates the closest point, x, to x^* that is occupied by a member of the training set. Assign the new object to the same class as the member of the training set.

The NNC can be shown to be moving toward the *maximum likelihood solution* to the classification problem as N increases. The maximum likelihood solution is a special case of Bayesian reasoning, as described in Chapter 6. The rapidity with which the NNC moves toward the Bayesian solution is surprising. Maximum likelihood classification can also be considered an analog of signal detection, but in this case, the signal strength for each target class is associated with a point in multidimensional space, instead of being associated with a point on a line.[3]

Variants of this model include considering the k nearest neighbors, weighted by distance, or perhaps giving less credence to examples encountered in the distant past.

8.5. GENERALIZATIONS OF SEMANTIC SPACE MODELS

Semantic space models are elegant. The technique first arose in psychology, but since then has been used in a variety of fields. Many of the uses are associated with marketing. For instance, the technique has been used to study consumer perception of different cola drinks. It has also been useful in political science, where similarity ratings can be obtained for political issues or candidates.

For simplicity, I have assumed that similarity can be related to the Euclidean distance between objects. This is a strong assumption in two ways. The first is that Euclidean distance assumes that it makes sense to

---

[3] Ashby and Perrin (1988).

average resemblances across different dimensions. This is often reasonable. For instance, on encountering a strange animal in the woods, it makes sense for us to treat it with a degree of caution that depends both upon its size and predacity. I would not be bothered upon encountering a weasel (fierce, but small), while I would be careful around an elk (mild mannered but big as a horse). On the other hand, there are exceptions. To illustrate, I will again use a political example.

I previously described my congresswoman, Rep. Dunn, as a woman and a Republican. She could also be described as having been divorced, a mother, a member of the House of Representatives, and a resident of Washington State. Representative Dunn's term overlapped with that of Hillary Rodham Clinton, a senator from New York. Senator Clinton could be described as a woman, a Democrat, married, a mother, a senator, and a resident of New York State. To what extent were Dunn and Clinton similar? It simply does not make sense to amalgamate their similarities as women and their differences in political allegiance to come up with some sort of average. Yet that is what a Euclidean metric would do.

Multidimensional scaling can handle this sort of situation. The MDS algorithm can be applied to all metric or *Minikowski* spaces. A Miniskowski space is an N dimensional space $X = [x_{ij..N}]$ in which points are specified by N dimensional vectors, and the distance between any two points, $x_i = (x_{i1} \ldots x_{iN})$ and $x_j = (x_{j1} \ldots x_{jN})$, is given by

$$d_{ij} = \left(\sum_{n=1}^{N} |x_{in} - x_{jn}|^{\tau} \right)^{1/\tau}, \tag{8-5}$$

where τ is the Minikowski parameter. A Euclidean space is a Minikowski space with $\tau = 2$. The case $\tau = 1$ is called a city block space, by analogy to the effective distance between locations in a city, where travel is restricted to the streets. In a city block space, similarity in one dimension cannot be traded off against similarity in another dimension. My contrast between political figures is an example. The resemblance between objects that vary in shape and color is another.

The extent to which two objects are seen as similar to each other often depends upon the context. Okinawa, the Hawaiian Islands, and Jamaica are like one another in the sense that they are all tropical islands, but quite unalike in their cultures. Representative Dunn and Senator Clinton appear to differ substantially in their positions on some issues but to be in substantial agreement on others.[4] This can be handled in

---

[4] Representative Dunn advocated the position that Americans have a virtually unrestricted right to gun ownership, while Senator Clinton supported restrictions on gun ownership. Both supported a woman's right to obtain an abortion.

multidimensional scaling by using a distance function in which different dimensions receive different weights, with the weighting depending upon the context. This produces

$$d_{ij} = \left(\sum_{n=1}^{N} w_n \left| x_{in} - x_{jn} \right|^{\tau} \right)^{1/\tau} \tag{8-6}$$

with a restriction on the weights to produce an appropriate scaling. Weighting schemes can also be used to represent differences between individuals, on the grounds that two people may categorize objects using the same semantic space, but assign different degrees of importance to various dimensions of the space.

It has also been argued that a judgment of similarity does not depend upon the perceived distance between objects in a semantic space but upon some non-linear transformation of that distance. For example, the similarity between two objects might be a negative exponential function of their perceived distance. Writing s_{ij} for the similarity between objects i and j, we have

$$s_{ij} = e^{-kd_{ij}}. \tag{8-7}$$

This captures the intuition that the marginal decrease in perceived similarity grows smaller as distance grows greater. From the viewpoint of a mouse, there may be quite a difference between a rabbit and a beaver, but elk and deer are just simply big.

8.6. QUALIFICATIONS ON THE SEMANTIC SPACE MODEL

Semantic space models based on multidimensional scaling are based on the assumption that similarity judgments are consistent with the metric (Minikowski) representation. Therefore, all distance (or similarity) judgments must satisfy the axioms for a metric space. These include the symmetry axiom:

$$d_{ij} = d_{ji}, \tag{8-8}$$

which amounts to saying that the distance from here to there has to be the same as the distance from there to here. This certainly applies to geographic distances, Paris–London = London–Paris. We might be willing to say that a person who maintained that this equality did not hold was being irrational. The case for symmetry in similarities is harder to make on intuitive grounds. Is a zebra as much like a horse as a horse is like a zebra? In fact, there is a much-cited example to the contrary. College students rate North Korea as being quite similar to China but do not think that China is similar to North Korea.

This is only one of the metric axioms that might be contradicted by similarity judgments. Going further would lead us into the topic of alternative mathematical representations for mental spaces, which is further than we should go here.[5] In many cases, though, the data do satisfy the metric axioms. MDS scaling then provides a useful way of thinking about similarities and categorical reasoning.

Challenge Problem

Try to think of an example of a situation in which it would be appropriate to use the MDS technique to develop a Euclidean semantic space with at least three dimensions. Then try to think of an example in which a city block space would be more appropriate. Finally, try to think of an example of similarities that violate the symmetry axiom, and hence cannot be analyzed using MDS.

[5] See Hunt (2002), Chapters 8 and 9, for a discussion.

9

The Mathematical Models Behind Psychological Testing

9.1. INTRODUCTION

Psychological tests have become part of our life. If you decide to enlist in the Army, you will be given the Armed Services Vocational Aptitude Battery (ASVAB). This is a general measure of your cognitive skills, with some emphasis on skills that are likely to be useful to the Army. If instead you decide to go to college, you will probably have to take the Scholastic Assessment Test (SAT), which measures cognitive skills relevant to academic pursuits. Standardized interviews are part of the initial stage of employment for many jobs, ranging literally from a policeman to a computer programmer. Often these include a personality test to see if you are the right person for the job. What has mathematics got to do with the development of these tests?

The answer turns out to be "quite a bit." The reason has to do with the way that cognitive and personality traits have been defined.

In an idealized scientific investigation concepts are defined first, and measures to evaluate them are defined second. For instance, we have a concept of weight, the gravitational attraction between a body's mass and the Earth. The typical bathroom scale measures weight by the distortion of a spring when someone steps on the platform. The idea of building this sort of scale came from the definition of weight. Weight itself is not defined by distortion of the spring.

In many cases, theorists interested in intelligence and personality have done things in the opposite way. Psychologists have begun with an almost intuitive notion of what the dimensions of intelligence and personality are, constructed test situations in which these traits are (hopefully) revealed, and then used mathematical procedures to summarize the results. The original concepts are then revised on the basis of the summaries, new testing situations are developed, and the operation begun anew.

The success of such an enterprise depends upon two things: the test maker's ability to construct good tests and the mathematical techniques used to summarize the results obtained from testing. Mathematics does not help in the first step. Generating tests that evaluate the desired concept requires a good deal of creative thought. The next step is to check to see if these situations have indeed produced reasonable data. Mathematics can help here, for bad tests will lead to disorderly results. In a more positive vein, good mathematical summaries can point the way to further test development. Therefore, the mathematics behind the tests are certainly important, even if knowing the mathematics, alone, does not tell us how to make a good test.

To take a concrete example, let us look at ASVAB. It contains several sub-sections, containing questions on the following topics:

General science	Paragraph comprehension
Arithmetic reasoning	Numerical operations
Coding speed	Word knowledge
Auto shop information	Mathematical knowledge
Electronics information	

The questions are at the level of difficulty appropriate for a typical high school graduate. The SAT is similar, but has a more academic emphasis. Some of the skills evaluated are

Word meaning	Writing
Sentence completion	Paragraph comprehension
Numerical operations	Understanding mathematical relations

The SAT questions are somewhat more difficult than the ASVAB questions, but the principle behind the two tests is the same. Overall cognitive ability is assessed from performance on a variety of tests that require somewhat different cognitive skills.

The ASVAB and SAT are officially described as predictive measures. The word *intelligence* is never used by either the Armed Services or the Educational Testing Service, which developed the SAT.[1] However, the

---

[1] The reason *intelligence* is not used in non-technical journals is probably that the term has acquired a great deal of emotional content. Most of this is due to assertions that intelligence is (a) inherited genetically and (b) differentially distributed across races and ethnic groups. We will not enter into this controversy! The term will be used here solely as a shorthand for the clumsier term "individual differences in cognitive ability."

situation is not much different if you examine many tests that are avowedly tests of intelligence. The Wechsler Adult Intelligence Scale (WAIS), which is widely used in clinical psychology and special education, evaluates, among other things, vocabulary, paragraph comprehension, and the ability to see patterns in sequences of abstract geometric shapes.

If we move from intelligence to personality, a similar picture emerges. Psychologists have developed literally hundreds of situations that are believed to evaluate people's personality. There was even one test in which people were asked to sit in a chair, awaiting a person who never seemed to come. The chair was wired to determine how much the person fidgeted while waiting. This was taken as an indication of patience.[2] Far more commonly, though, people are simply asked questions about themselves or about how they view life in general. For example:

Which of these statements is most correct?

(a) Many of the unhappy things that happen in people's lives are simply due to bad luck.
(b) People's misfortunes result from the mistakes they make.

Such choices are supposed to measure "locus of control," which is a shorthand for the extent to which a person views the world as one in which you or outside forces are in control. Another example:

Check whether the answer is "yes," "no," or "uncertain" to the following statements:

I am happy most of the time.
I am certainly lacking in self-confidence.

These items are considered to measure "social introversion."

In both cases, a total score, for "locus of control" or "social introversion," is derived from the sum of scores on a number of items like these. A typical personality test will contain several different scales, each generating different scores.

In both intelligence and personality testing a person's scores can be represented as a vector of numbers, derived from scales that are supposed to measure fairly narrow abilities. The intuition behind this procedure is that the narrowly defined scales are all different reflections of the same underlying, more general, ability. For instance, many cognitive tests include a sub-test that evaluates the examinee's vocabulary. We would not want to define a person's cognitive ability solely in terms of his or her vocabulary, but we would be willing to say that

[2] M. M. Hunt (1993).

vocabulary had something to do with intelligence. We want some way to summarize the various scores and indicate how each score relates to the underlying dimensions of mental competence. In the case of personality evaluation, there are hundreds of scales that might be (and probably have) been developed. We suspect that these all represent different manifestations of a small number of underlying personality traits. What are these traits?

Let us state this as a mathematical problem. Define the matrix $X = [x_{ij}]$, where x_{ij} is the score of the ith individual on the jth *observable* variable. We suspect that these scores are derived from a smaller set of values on *unobserved* latent traits, $F = [f_{ik}]$, where f_{ik} is the score of individual i on the kth latent trait. We wish to know four things:

How many latent traits there are;
The score of each person on each latent trait;
The relations between the observable variables and the latent traits; and
How the latent traits relate to one another.

In this chapter, these issues will be stated as mathematical problems. In order to do so, though, the presentation has to be a bit convoluted. Although this is not a book on statistics, certain statistical concepts are necessary for developing the topic. These are presented in the following section. Once they have been developed, they will be utilized to attack the measurement problem.

The measurement problem itself can be stated in two ways. One is to use conventional "high school" algebra. This works, but it leads to a complicated set of equations. The second way of stating the problem is to use the notation of matrix algebra. This leads directly to an easily understood set of equations – so long as the reader knows matrix algebra! I have taken both methods, providing two parallel sections, so that the reader can choose the presentation he or she prefers.

Finally, the presentation will be carried up to the point at which the various parameters to be identified have been described. The numerical techniques used to estimate these parameters are covered in advanced courses in statistics. I will simply assert that the techniques exist and give a few examples of their use.

9.2. A BRIEF REVIEW OF CORRELATION AND COVARIANCE

Test construction, interpretation, and analysis all depend on the statistical concept of *correlation*, which in turn depends upon the ideas of *variance* and *covariance*. I will introduce them briefly. Readers who are familiar with these concepts may wish to skip directly to Section 9-3.

Readers who are not familiar with these concepts but are familiar with matrix algebra may prefer to read the discussion in Appendix 9A, rather than going through the more cumbersome, standard algebraic presentation in Sections 9-2 and 9-3. However, all readers should be sure that they understand the diagram presented in Figure 9-2 at the end of Section 9.3, as it presents graphic conventions that will be used later, to depict algebraic relationships.

Testing is based on two simple ideas. The first is that the thing we are measuring should show appreciable variety. By definition, if there is no variety then there are no individual differences. The second is that if we have two measures that purport to be measuring the same thing (e.g., two tests of intelligence), then these tests should order the examinees in exactly the same way, except possibly for scoring conventions and some sort of error in measurement. If the error of measurement is low, then we only need use one of the measures, for we should get the same result no matter which measure we chose (except for scoring conventions). For instance, if students' heights were measured in inches and centimeters we would certainly use only one of the scores. However, if we think there is some error of measurement, it makes sense to combine test scores in the hope that any error will wash out over several measurements. Judgments of figure skating, gymnastics, and diving illustrate this principle. Judges' ratings of a performance are added together on the assumption that each rating is an imperfect measure of performance quality. Therefore, the combined judgment should be closer to a conceptual perfect measure of the underlying trait than any one observable measure is.

Suppose that we have two measures, both of which show variation but that are (on their surface at least) measures of two different underlying traits. If one of the measures can be used to predict the other, there is probably some sort of association between the underlying quantities.

Take an example from education and psychology. High school students' scores on the SAT measure one thing, a student's grade point average (GPA) in college measures another, but it turns out that there is a moderately positive relation between the two. While it is not always true that people with high SAT scores have reasonably high GPAs, it is true more often than not. Reasonable scientists have argued that this is because the SAT score and the GPA both reflect a student's underlying mental ability ("general intelligence").[3] I do not want to take sides in this debate. (At least, not here!) My point is that it is impossible to investigate this issue seriously without some understanding of the mathematical model behind test construction and interpretation.

Suppose that two different measures are taken in each of N equivalent conditions. The obvious case is the one of two different tests, each given to

---

[3] Gottfredson (1997); Jensen (1998).

the same individuals. Let $\{X_i\}$ and $\{Y_i\}$ be the set of measurements on tests X and Y, where $i = 1 \ldots N$. The *variance* of a set of scores is the expected squared distance of a score from the mean of all the scores:

$$Var(X) = \frac{1}{N}\sum_{i=1}^{N}(X_i - M(X))^2, \tag{9-1}$$

where *Var* refers to the variance, and $M(X)$ is the mean of the X scores. $Var(Y)$ and $M(Y)$ are defined similarly.

The following example shows why variance is a reasonable measure of variability. Suppose that the two sets of scores are

$$X = \{2,4,6,8\} \qquad Y = \{1,3,7,9\}.$$

The means are the same, $M(X) = M(Y) = 5$. There is clearly more variability in the Y scores than in the X scores, for the two X scores closest to the mean are only 1 unit away from it, and the most extreme scores are only 3 units from the mean (e.g., $|4 - 5| = 1$ and $|2 - 5| = 3$), while in the Y set, the scores closest to the mean are two units away ($|3 - 5| = 2$) and the extremes are four units away ($|1 - 5| = 4$). This is reflected in the variances:

$$\begin{aligned} Var(X) &= \frac{1}{4}\sum\left((-3)^2 + (-1)^2 + 1^2 + 3^2\right) = 5 \\ Var(Y) &= \frac{1}{4}\sum\left((-4)^2 + (-2)^2 + 2^2 + 4^2\right) = 10. \end{aligned} \tag{9-2}$$

To simplify the notation, it helps to write equations in terms of the deviation of each score from the appropriate mean,

$$\begin{aligned} x_i &= X_i - M(X) \\ y_i &= Y_i - M(Y). \end{aligned} \tag{9-3}$$

These are called *deviation scores*. Throughout this chapter, I will follow the convention of denoting deviation scores by lowercase letters.

In this notation, the variance is

$$\begin{aligned} Var(X) &= \frac{1}{N}\sum_i x^2 \\ Var(Y) &= \frac{1}{N}\sum_i y^2. \end{aligned} \tag{9-4}$$

The standard deviation is the square root of the variance.

$$SD(X) = Var(X)^{\frac{1}{2}}, \tag{9-5}$$

and similarly for Y. The standard deviation is useful in statistics, for it often has an interpretation in terms of the percentage of scores within a certain range of the mean. For instance, in Appendix 2B, it was pointed out that if scores are distributed normally, one-third of the scores will lie between the mean and one standard deviation below the mean, and one-third of the scores will lie between the mean and one standard deviation above the mean.

In the case of test scores, we are particularly interested in associations, that is, the extent to which a score on one measure conveys information about a score on another. Does a high score on the SAT provide a useful prediction of a student's GPA on graduation from college?

The measurement of association is based on the idea of covariation, which is the tendency for high scores on one test to be associated with high scores on another. Negative covariation is also possible. High scores on one test might be associated with low scores on another. For example, high scores on intelligence tests are associated with low scores on records of criminal behavior, although the relationship is not a very strong one.[4] A measure of the extent of covariation will now be presented.

The *covariance* is the expected value of the product of the deviation scores of X and Y,

$$Cov(X,Y) = \frac{1}{N} \sum_{i=1}^{N} (X_i - M(X))(Y_i - M(Y))$$

$$Cov(X,Y) = \frac{1}{N} \sum_{i=1}^{N} x_i y_i.$$

(9-6)

Comparison of equations (9-6) and (9-4) shows that the variance is the covariance of a score with itself.

The covariance will be large and positive if two tests order observations in the same way, and large and negative if the tests order the observations in opposite ways. To see this, consider the following ordered data sets:

$$W = \{1, 2, 3, 4\} \quad X = \{1, 2, 4, 3\} \quad Y = \{4, 3, 2, 1\} \quad Z = \{1, 4, 3, 2\}.$$

Each set has the same variance because they are the same numbers. Applying equation (9-4), this is 1.25. In W and X, the rank order of the corresponding values is identical except that the highest and the next highest values are interchanged. By contrast, in W and Y, the order of magnitudes is reversed. If we compare W to Z, the order of magnitudes is jumbled; the extreme values that are in the first and fourth position in W have been moved to the middle positions in Z. The covariances of

---

[4] Herrnstein and Murray, 1994.

W with X,Y, and Z data sets are

$$Cov(WX) = 1;$$
$$Cov(WY) = -1.25$$
$$Cov(WZ) = .25$$

Variances and covariances are influenced by changes in the scale, that is, the unit of measurement. To see this, suppose we transform the X scores to $X' => aX$ and Y to $Y' => bY$, with a and b both greater than zero. An example would be a change in measurement from pounds and inches to kilograms and centimeters. The deviation scores will be changed similarly, so that $x' => ax$ and $y' => by$. The variances of the transformed scores are

$$Var(x') = \frac{1}{N} \sum_i (ax_i)^2$$

$$Var(x') = \frac{a^2}{N} \sum_i x_i^2 \tag{9-7}$$

$$Var(x') = a^2 Var(x),$$

and by similar reasoning, the variance of y' is $b^2 Var(y)$. The covariance of the two transformed scores is

$$Cov(x',y') = \frac{1}{N} \sum_i ax_i by_i$$

$$Cov(x',y') = \frac{ab}{N} \sum_i x_i y_i \tag{9-8}$$

$$Cov(x',y') = abCov(xy).$$

In most situations, we want measures of association that are independent of scale units and the number of cases being compared. For instance, the association between height and weight should remain the same whether or not we measure in metric units or in feet and pounds.

Scale effects can be avoided by making the variance itself the unit of measure, by dividing each deviation score by the standard deviation of the measure. (There are cases where this conversion is not innocuous, but these cases do not arise too often in the social and behavioral sciences.) The result is called a score in *standard deviation units* or, more succinctly, a *standard score*. These scores were discussed in Appendix 2B, in a different context. By tradition, the lowercase z is used to indicate standard scores. The transformation from an observed variable, X, to that variable in standard scores is

$$z_{ix} = \frac{(X_i - M(X))}{Var(X)^{\frac{1}{2}}}. \tag{9-9}$$

The first subscript on the z term identifies the case (usually a person in intelligence and personality applications), and the second indicates that the standard score was derived from the original variable X. Where an indication of the case is not needed, the i subscript will be dropped.

Because of the way that the standard deviation scale is constructed, $Var(z) = 1$. To convince yourself of this, observe that equation (9-9) is a special case of equation (9-7) with $a = 1/Var(X).^{1/2}$ Substitute into (9-7) and $Var(x')$ becomes 1.

The *correlation coefficient* is a widely used measure of association. It is the ratio of the covariance of two scores to the product of their standard deviations:

$$r_{xy} = \frac{Cov(X,Y)}{Var(X)^{\frac{1}{2}}Var(X)^{\frac{1}{2}}}$$

$$r_{xy} = \frac{\sum_i x_i y_i}{\left(\sum_i x_i^2 \sum_i y_i^2\right)^{\frac{1}{2}}}. \tag{9-10}$$

The correlation coefficient is unaffected by scale. If the x and y terms are rescaled to ax_i and by_i, equation (9-10) becomes

$$r_{ax,by} = \frac{\sum_i ax_i by_i}{\left(\sum_i (ax_i)^2 \sum_i (by_i)^2\right)^{\frac{1}{2}}}$$

$$r_{ax,by} = \frac{ab\sum_i x_i y_i}{ab\left(\sum_i x_i^2 \sum_i y_i^2\right)^{\frac{1}{2}}} \tag{9-11}$$

$$r_{ax,by} = r_{xy}.$$

As an important special case, for standard scores,

$$r_{z_x z_y} = r_{xy}$$

$$r_{z_x z_y} = \frac{Cov(z_x z_y)}{(Var(z_x)Var(z_y))^{\frac{1}{2}}} \tag{9-12}$$

$$r_{z_x z_y} = Cov(z_x z_y),$$

because the variance of a standard score is identically one. This leads to an important interpretation of the correlation coefficient:

The correlation coefficient between two measures is identical to the covariance of the two measures, when each is scored in standard deviation units.

The correlation coefficient will range from 1, which represents perfect agreement in the ordering of scores, including the interval between them (e.g., the correlation between a variable and itself, in which case the covariance would be equal to the variance, and therefore be 1) to -1, which indicates complete disagreement, that is, $z_{ix} = -z_{iy}$.

The next concept to be discussed is *statistical independence*. Intuitively, two measures are statistically independent if knowledge of one score does not improve your ability to predict the other. More precisely:

Two sets of numerical observations, X,Y, are statistically independent of each other if the covariance between them is zero.

If the covariance is zero, the correlation coefficient must be zero, and *vice versa*. Therefore, the definition of statistical independence can also be stated as

Two variables, X and Y, are statistically independent if and only if r_{xy} is zero.

9.3. PREDICTING ONE VARIABLE FROM ANOTHER: LINEAR REGRESSION

As was the case for Section 9.2, this section introduces some widely taught statistical concepts, linear regression and prediction. Therefore, readers with a background in statistics may wish to proceed directly to Section 9.4. I remind these readers to make sure that they understand Figure 9-2, at the end of this section, because it introduces some conventions for drawing graphs that will be used throughout the rest of the chapter.

Scores on variable Y are predictable from variable X if there is some function f such that $Y_i = f(X_i)$. In the vast majority of cases, "prediction" means linear prediction; $f(X) = aX + B$, where A is not equal to zero. Returning to the example of the GPA and SAT scores, college admission officers want to predict GPA from the SAT score. In mathematical terminology, we want to know if we can find an equation of the form of (9-12), with non-zero B, such that

$$Y_i = BX_i + A. \tag{9-13}$$

B is the regression coefficient, that is, the slope of the line that plots Y as a function of X. A is the intercept term, the value of Y when X is zero.

It is often useful to deal with deviation scores, in which case equation (9-13) becomes

$$y_i = \beta x_i, \tag{9-14}$$

where $\beta = B \frac{SD(y)}{SD(x)}$,

Equation (9-14) requires that y_i be predicted exactly. It is likely that there will be some, hopefully small, difference between the predicted and the observed value. Call this the *residual value* e_i.[5] The prediction equation becomes

$$y_i = \beta x_i + e_i, \tag{9-15}$$

where e_i is the unknown residual term that would have to be added to correct for an error in prediction. Note that the residual term is a value in deviation units of the Y variable. β is the regression coefficient relating x and y, when scored in deviation units. The situation is shown in Figure 9-1, which you want to be sure you understand.

Although we cannot know the value of each e_i, we can make some assumptions about the distribution of the set of residual values. It can be assumed that the residual has a mean of zero (otherwise we would simply add a bias term into the equation) and that the residual is statistically independent of the value of x_i or y_i. Therefore, by assumption, $r_{ex} = r_{ey} = 0$. It is usually assumed that prediction is equally accurate for high and low values of x_i and y_i. There are situations in which this is not the case.[6]

The variance of y consists of two additive parts, one part predictable from x and one part, the residual variance, that is not predictable from X. *No causation is implied; we are talking only about mathematical relationships between scores.* The variance of y becomes

$$Var(y) = \frac{1}{N} \sum_i (\beta x_i + e_i)^2, \tag{9-16}$$

which can be expanded:

$$Var(y) = \frac{1}{N} \sum_i (\beta^2 x_i^2 + 2\beta x_i e_i + e_i^2)$$

$$Var(y) = \frac{1}{N} \left[\beta^2 \sum_i x_i^2 + 2\beta \sum_i x_i e_i + \sum_i e_i^2 \right]. \tag{9-17}$$

The middle term of the expansion, $2\beta \sum x_i e_i$, is 2β times the covariance of the x term and the residual. This is zero because, by definition, residual terms are statistically independent of other terms.

---

[5] In some applications, especially in psychology, the e_i term is referred to as an "error." This implies that there is something wrong with our measurement. I prefer the more neutral term "residual," which is generally in use in statistics, because it reflects the fact that e_i refers to that part of y_i that was not related to x_i, leaving open the question of whether additional knowledge of other test scores on individual i might not improve the prediction.

[6] See Chapter 3 (psychophysics) for an example of a situation where the residual term is proportional to the value of the variable of interest.

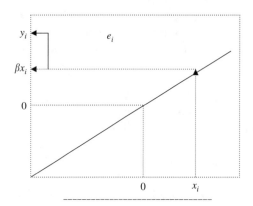

FIGURE 9-1. A graphical depiction of regression between scores in standard deviation units. The regression "line" is the equation $y_i = \beta x_i$. If x_i has the value shown, then the predicted value of y_i is βx_i. The actual value is y_i, with a residual term $e_i = y_i - \beta x_i$. The regression line (the heavy black line) has a slope of β. If the value of x_i is zero, the value of βx_i is zero. Therefore, whenever the mean x_i (predictor) score is observed, the predicted score is always its mean.

Define $y_i^* = \beta x_i$. This is the value of y_i that would be predicted from knowledge of x_i.

Equation (9-17) becomes

$$Var(y) = \frac{1}{N}\beta^2 \sum_i x_i^2 + \frac{1}{N}\sum_i e_i^2$$

(9-18)

$$Var(y) = Var(y^*) + Var(e).$$

The variance in the predicted variable will be the sum of the variances in the predicted values plus the variance of the residuals. The latter term is called the *mean squared error* (or *residual*) term. Going back to equation (9-13), clearly once the variables A and B are determined for the equation $Y = BX + A$, the β parameter follows. The A and B parameters are chosen to minimize the mean squared error term, subject to the restriction that the mean of the residuals, Σe^2, be zero. How this is done is a well-worked-out problem in statistics, and will not concern us here.

This is a good time to draw a deep breath, step back, and consider what the algebra means in terms of the example, using SAT scores to predict GPAs. Here, X stands for the SAT score and Y for the GPA. According to equation (9-18), the variance in GPA scores, which is a measure of the extent to which different people have different GPAs, can be divided into two parts: the proportion of the variance that can be statistically associated with variance in SAT scores, and the residual variance that is not associated with the SAT.

The statements about proportions refer to proportions in the population. We can never say that some percentage of an individual's GPA was predictable from the SAT and some percentage was due to other factors. We can say that the individual's GPA was above or below what would have been predicted from the person's SAT score, which is a different statement. And we always want to remember the caution expressed earlier, *correlation is not causation*. A positive correlation between the SAT score and the GPA does not mean that the SAT itself causes the GPA. In this particular case, the usual explanation is that unknown causal variables (intelligence? scholastic background? study habits?) influence both scores.

Returning to the mathematics, the next step is to examine the covariances. Substituting (9-15), the regression equation, for y into (9-6), the definition of covariances,

$$Cov(x,y) = \frac{1}{N} \sum_i x_i(\beta x_i + e_i)$$
$$Cov(x,y) = \frac{1}{N} \beta \sum_i x_i^2 + \frac{1}{N} \sum_i x_i e_i. \tag{9-19}$$

Because the residuals are statistically independent of the predictor, the second term on the right reduces to zero, leaving

$$Cov(x,y) = \frac{1}{N} \beta \sum_i x_i^2$$
$$Cov(x,y) = \beta Var(x). \tag{9-20}$$

When we deal with standard scores, $Var(z_x)$ is one, and from equation (9-13), $Cov(z_x z_y)$ is equal to the correlation coefficient. Therefore,

$$\beta = r, \tag{9-21}$$

and so the prediction equation, in standard deviation units, is

$$z_{yi} = r z_{xi} + \varepsilon_i, \tag{9-22}$$

where $\varepsilon_i = e_i / SD(y)$.

Applying equation (9-18), and recalling that the variance of a standard score is 1,

$$1 = r^2 + Var(\varepsilon) \tag{9-23}$$

holds. This shows that r^2 can be interpreted as the percentage of variance in the predicted variable that is associated with variation in the predictor variable.

Figure 9-2 presents a graphic summary of equation (9-22), showing the relationship between the predicted, predictor, and residual scores. While

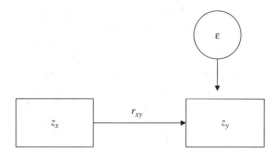

FIGURE 9-2. A graphical depiction of the regression equation for variables expressed in standard scores. Observable variables (z_x and z_y) are shown in rectangles; assumed variables (the residual, ε) are shown in circles.

a graph is hardly needed for the simple case of one score predicting another, the argument in the next section will make considerable use of graphs like this, in order to avoid involved mathematical derivations. To aid in reading this and future graphs, note that observables (here the x and y scores) are represented by rectangles, and that unobservable, conceptual entities are represented by ellipses. The relation between two variables is shown by a line, with the value of the relationship shown next to the line.

9.4. THE SINGLE FACTOR MODEL: THE CASE OF GENERAL INTELLIGENCE

We now return to the main issue: How do we decide how many latent traits, or *factors*, underlie a collection of tests that, intuitively, we believe to be measuring different aspects of personality or cognition? In the simplest case, how could we tell when several variables are all different manifestations of the same underlying trait? This question was first investigated in the early twentieth century by the British psychologist Charles Spearman, as part of his seminal work on human intelligence.[7]

Spearman believed that cognitive performance is determined largely by a person's *general intelligence*, which he thought was manifested in virtually every field of endeavor. He acknowledged, though, that in addition to general intelligence people had specific abilities. Therefore, performance on a mathematics test would be determined by general intelligence plus specific mathematical skills, while the score on a writing test would be determined by general intelligence plus specific writing skills. This theory, with some modifications, is alive and well today.[8] Its

---

[7] Spearman (1904, 1927).   [8] Johnson et al. (2004).

best-known modern proponent is a University of California (Berkeley) professor, A. R. Jensen,[9] although there are many others.

Spearman formulated his ideas mathematically. He assumed that a person's score on an observable test is a linear combination of his/her "general intelligence" (g), to the extent that general intelligence is required of the test, and a specific skill that is unique to the test alone. The specific skill term is, by definition, a residual term, such as the e_i's in Section 9.3, and is statistically independent of all other terms. The deviation scores for two tests, X and Y, would then be

$$x_i = a_{xg}g_i + s_{ix}$$
$$y_i = a_{yg}g_i + s_{iy}, \tag{9-24}$$

where a_{xg} and a_{yg} are coefficients representing the importance of general intelligence on tests X and Y, g_i is the general intelligence of person i, and s_{ix} and s_{iy} are the test-specific skills of person i.

At first, equations (9-24) appear identical to the regression equation, equation (9-15), with a renaming of variables. There is a conceptual difference. The regression equation refers to a relationship between observable variables, a score on test X and a score on test Y. Equations (9-24) relate observable scores (x_i and y_i) to the hypothetical, unobservable latent traits of general intelligence (g_i) and test-specific ability (s_{ix} and s_{iyi}). What we want to do is to estimate the extent to which individual variation in these conceptual properties, the factors, contributes to individual variation in observable test scores. Since we cannot measure the factors directly some mathematical manipulations are required.

By definition, the covariance of the specific (s) terms with any other term is zero. Therefore, the correlation between two observable tests, x and y, depends only on the extent to which each test requires general intelligence. Algebraically,

$$\frac{1}{N}\sum_i x_i y_i = \frac{1}{N}\sum_i (a_{xg}x_i + s_{ix})(a_{yg}y_i + s_{iy})$$
$$Cov(xy) = \frac{1}{N}a_{xg}a_{yg}\sum_i g_i^2, \tag{9-25}$$

and if we write this in standard score units,

$$r = a_{xg}a_{yg}Var(g), \tag{9-26}$$

where $Var(g)$ is the (unknown) variance of general intelligence in the population. Because g is a hypothetical variable, we can, without loss of

---

[9] Jensen (1998).

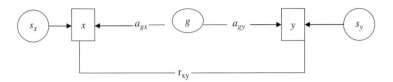

FIGURE 9-3. The relation between two tests and a hypothesized general intelligence variable. The single-headed arrows indicate causality, while the line without arrows indicates correlation without implication of causation.

generality, assume that it is measured in standard deviation units, so that $Var(g) = 1$. Equation 9-26 simplifies to

$$r = a_{xg}a_{yg}. \tag{9-27}$$

Remembering that the variance of a test is simply the covariance of a test with itself, the argument can be extended to produce

$$Var(x) = a_{xg}^2 Var(g) + Var(s_x)$$
$$Var(y) = a_{yg}^2 Var(g) + Var(s_y). \tag{9-28}$$

Converting to standard scores,

$$1 = a_{xg}^2 + Var(s_x)$$
$$1 = a_{yg}^2 + Var(s_y) \tag{9-29}$$

The terms a_{xg}^2 and a_{yg}^2 are referred to as the *loadings* of the general intelligence factor on tests X and Y, respectively. They can be interpreted as the fraction of the variance in the observable (X or Y) tests that can be accounted for by individual variations (variance) in general intelligence. The loadings can also be interpreted as correlations; a_{xg} and a_{yg} are the correlations between the X (or Y) scores and scores on a hypothetical perfect test of general intelligence.

Figure 9-3 shows these relations graphically. This figure shows that the correlation between X and Y is interpreted as being due to the influence of a common factor on both X and Y. The extent of the influence is measured by the loadings.

These observations are a step forward. But unfortunately, they also show a step backward. One observable, r_{xy}, is being expressed in terms of two unobservable parameters, a_{xg} and a_{yg}. Therefore, as equation (9-27) shows, there is no way to estimate the values of the a terms from knowledge of the r term alone. What are we to do?

The trick is to add tests. Figure 9-4 shows the relationship between g and four different tests, W, X, Y, Z. The s terms have been omitted because they can be calculated using equation (9-29), as soon as the a terms are known. The correlations have also been omitted, simply to

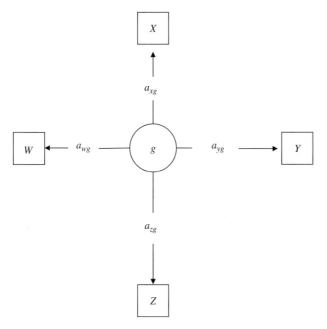

FIGURE 9-4. The relation between four tests and a hypothesized general intelligence. From this data we may construct six equations in four unknowns, thus permitting a test of the model.

make the graph more readable. Nevertheless, there are six correlations, each with a defining equation of the form of (9-27). This means that there are only four unknowns, appearing in six equations relating the unknowns to observable correlations:

$$r_{xy} = a_{xg}a_{yg}$$
$$r_{xw} = a_{xg}a_{wg}$$
$$r_{xz} = a_{xg}a_{zg}$$
$$r_{yw} = a_{yg}a_{wg}$$
$$r_{yz} = a_{yg}a_{zg}$$
$$r_{wz} = a_{wg}a_{zg}.$$

(9-30)

If the underlying model were exactly true, it would be possible to find values for the four a terms that would exactly predict the six r terms. In fact, this is virtually never the case. Instead, what psychometricians (psychologists who are interested in the mathematical modeling of test scores) do is to find those a values that produce predicted r values that are as close as possible to the observed values. Two techniques are used. One is to minimize the mean residual terms, as described. The other is to choose values that maximize the likelihood of the observation, using

TABLE 9-1. *Spearman's Data on English Public School Children's Grades*

	French	English	Math	Music	Pitch
Classics	.83	.78	.70	.66	.63
French		.67	.67	.65	.57
English			.64	.54	.51
Math				.45	.51
Music					.40

Source: Carroll (1993), p. 38.

techniques derived from Bayes' theorem (Chapter 7). The estimation problem was a formidable one in Spearman's time, a century ago, but today virtually every statistical package for computers includes routines for simple factor analysis.

One of Spearman's own studies demonstrates the sort of results that can be obtained. Table 9-1 shows the correlations between grades obtained by students in their classes in English public schools, circa 1900.

Spearman noticed the high correlations between tests, applied the general intelligence model, and obtained what he thought was a good match between predictions and observations. He lived in an age before computers, and so he was limited by his ability to calculate correlations. In 1993, John Carroll, one of the twentieth century's most distinguished psychometricians, used modern computing methods to reanalyze Spearman's data. Figure 9-5 shows the factor loadings that Carroll calculated for each of Spearman's original tests. Given these loadings, it is easy to calculate the predicted correlations. For instance, according to Figure 9-5 the correlation between English and math grades should be $.75 \times .80 = .60$. The observed figure (Table 9-1) was .64, which is quite close. Similar comparisons can be made for all other correlations.

Exactly a century after Spearman's report Ian Deary, a Scottish psychologist, applied Spearman's model to contemporary data, the English school leaving examination. Deary, of course, had a much larger data set and used computers and modern statistical techniques. Nevertheless, his results looked very much like Spearman's.[10]

An important thing to remember is that nothing that has been said mathematically is tied to intelligence. The analytic technique works with any data set. An interesting thing to do would be to apply Spearman's methods to scores on, say, a decathlon. Would we produce evidence for a generalized talent for athletics? Or would there be separate factors for arm and leg strength, endurance, and so on?

---

[10] I. Deary, Address to the 2004 meeting of the International Society for Intelligence Research, New Orleans, December, 2004.

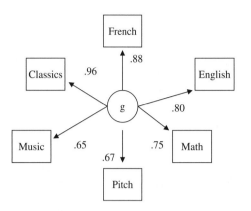

FIGURE 9-5. Carroll's (1993) reanalysis of Spearman's data on school grades.

More to the point, the same sort of reasoning can be applied to theories of personality. You could ask people to fill out questionnaires indicating all sorts of adjustment: Do you worry a lot? Are you generally happy? Do you like to go to parties? Would Spearman's model produce a single general dimension, "the adjusted personality"? It turns out that it would not. There is more than one dimension to personality. For that matter, there is more than one dimension of intelligence. This leads us to the modern expansion of Spearman's model.

9.5. MULTIFACTOR THEORIES OF INTELLIGENCE AND PERSONALITY

Although Spearman's theory of general intelligence has many proponents, it has never been universally accepted. The alternative is, obviously enough, a multifactor theory, which assumes that observable cognitive performance is determined by individual differences on several latent traits or factors of intelligence. This position was originally put forward by L. L. Thurstone,[11] whom we met earlier in discussing psychophysics (Chapter 3). Like the *g* theory, the multifactor theory has had many proponents over the years. The nature of the computations will now be illustrated, using modern data.

Lazar Stankov[12] reported a study in which Australian college students were given nine tests that were supposed to measure different aspects of cognition. Table 9-2 presents a brief description of each test.[13] A glance at

[11] Thurstone (1938). [12] Stankov (1999).

[13] The descriptions were kindly provided by Stankov. He was not the first to discover relations between tests of this sort, nor did he claim to be. (His study involved some additional measures that will not be discussed here.) What Stankov's data do for us, here,

TABLE 9-2. *The Mental Tests Used in Stankov's Experiment*

1. *Raven's Progressive Matrices*. For each item, the subject was presented with a two-dimensional 3×3 array of figures with lower right-hand figure missing. The figures formed an orderly progression by both rows and columns. The examinee had to select, from eight alternatives, a figure that could be used to complete the series in such a way that both the row and column progressions were maintained. (This sort of test is widely used in research on intelligence because it typically has a high loading on the general factor.)

2. *Letter Series*. For each of the 38 items, a list of letters was presented. The examinee was instructed to type the letter that continued the pattern in the series. For example, the sequence A B C __ would be continued with D.

3. *Animals*. Examinees saw the words "cat," "dog," and "horse" appear one at a time on a computer screen in a random order. They had to keep track of the number of times each word appeared.

4. *Vocabulary*. This was a 35-item typical multiple-choice vocabulary test.

5. *Esoteric Analogies*. Three words were presented on the screen, followed by a set of four more words. Examinees chose the word that bore the same relationship to the third word as the second did to the first. The analogies used rare words or unusual meanings.

6. *Proverbs*. A "proverb" or "saying" was displayed, followed by four alternative meanings. Examinees had to choose the appropriate meaning.

7. *Forward Digit Span*. Digits appeared randomly on a computer screen. After the series was completed, the examinee had to type it back in, in the same order. The score was the most digits an examinee could recall.

8. *Backward Digit Span*. This test was identical to the previous one except that digits had to be typed in reverse order.

9. *Line Length*. Six short vertical lines, each about one centimeter in length, were displayed in a non-aligned manner on a computer screen. The examinee had to identify, as quickly as possible, a line that was longer than the others.

Note: These tests are typical of the tests used in many studies of individual differences in cognition.

the table shows that the tasks are quite varied, but that each of the tasks appears to measure something that might be called a cognitive ability. One of the questions asked in studies like this is "Can the individual differences on these very different tasks be captured using only a small number of underlying factors?"

Stankov represented the nine tests by just three factors. That is, he represented each of the nine tests by an equation of the form

$$x_{ij} = a_{j1}f_{i1} + a_{j2}f_{i2} + a_{j3}f_{i3} + s_{ij}, \tag{9-31}$$

is to provide a particularly clear example of a pattern of results that have been found many times in the study of human intelligence.

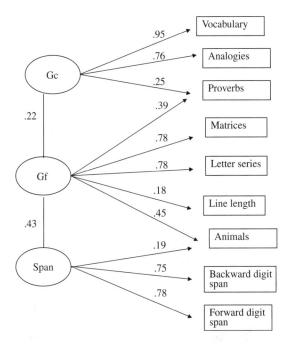

FIGURE 9-6. The factor structure extracted in Stankov's study. Three factors were extracted: Fluid intelligence (Gf), Crystallized intelligence (Gc), and (recent memory) Span. The numbers above the arrows indicate the loading of the test (rectangles) on the relevant factor (oval). Note that some tests have loadings on more than one factor. The numbers to the left of the vertical lines indicate correlations between the factors. The absence of a line between the Gc and Span factors indicates that these two factors had a correlation of less than .15, which was the threshold value for depicting a link. These results are typical of results obtained in many other studies of intelligence. The figure is based on Table 14.1 of Stankov's report.

where x_{ij} is the score of the ith individual on the jth test ($i = 1 \ldots N$, $j = 1 \ldots 9$), a_{jk} indicates the loading of test j on factor k ($k = 1 \ldots 3$), f_{ik} is the (hypothetical) value that individual i has on factor k, and s_{ij} is the residual term for the ith individual and the jth test. This is a straightforward generalization of equation (9-24) to the case of three factors, rather than a single general factor (g).

Figure 9-6 displays a three-factor solution. It is analogous to Figure 9-5, except that all loadings less than .15 have been suppressed to enhance readability.

Just what do these factors mean? The only way this can be answered is by looking at the loadings and trying to induce a pattern in the data. Here is a paraphrase of the pattern that Stankov saw.

One factor, labeled "Gf" for *fluid intelligence,* has substantial loadings on the matrix test and the letter series test. Both of these tests require that the examinee detect a pattern in a sequence of items. This is generally interpreted as an ability to detect patterns in, and hence solve, unusual situations. Spearman himself had argued that the ability to detect patterns is the essence of general intelligence.[14]

Another factor, labeled "Gc" for *crystallized intelligence,* shows substantial loadings on the vocabulary test and the verbal analogies test. This is often interpreted as the ability to apply previously acquired knowledge to the current problem. It is generally associated with tests that require skill with language.

The third factor, "Span," refers to the ability to keep in mind several pieces of information at once. This is also thought to be an important part of general intelligence.[15]

Most of the tests have loadings on just one factor, indicating that the things that determine performance on that test are the factor and the specific skill, that is, a version of Spearman's model. However, this is not universally true. The "proverbs" and "animals" tests have loadings on two factors, suggesting that solving these tasks calls on two different underlying abilities, but to somewhat different degrees.

The factors are themselves correlated. On its face, this is an indication that (a) people who are good at solving unusual problems also tend to have a good deal of acquired knowledge, and (b) that people who are good at solving unusual problems tend to be able to keep several things in mind at once.

What we are interested in is the mathematics behind statements like "Stankov found three factors." For ease of understanding, we start with a two-factor model, and then generalize it. (Readers who are familiar with matrix algebra may wish to skip to the more succinct explanation offered in Appendix 9A, and then skip to Section 9.7.)

The two-factor model for scores on tests x and y is

$$x_i = a_{x1}f_{i1} + a_{x2}f_{i2} + s_{ix}$$
$$y_i = a_{y1}f_{i1} + a_{y2}f_{i2} + s_{iy}. \tag{9-32}$$

---

[14] Spearman (1927).

[15] Stankov's interpretation is consistent with many other interpretations of similar data. However, other interpretations are possible. For instance, the tests that Stankov assigned to Gf require interpretation of visual patterns, while the tests he assigned to Gc require verbal skills. Therefore, one could argue that he measured visual and verbal abilities. The varying interpretations of factor analytic data have been hotly debated. It should be pointed out, though, that the argument is not entirely rhetorical. Modern factor analytic techniques that go well beyond those presented in this book can be used to evaluate how well different proposed factor structures fit a given data set.

The cross product term for case i is

$$x_iy_i = a_{x1}a_{y1}f_{i1}^2 + a_{x1}a_{y2}f_{i1}f_{i2} + a_{x2}a_{y1}f_{i1}f_{i2} + a_{x2}a_{y2}f_{i2}^2 + s_{ix}y_i + s_{iy}x_i$$
$$x_iy_i = a_{x1}a_{y1}f_{i1}^2 + a_{x2}a_{y2}f_{i2}^2 + (a_{x1}a_{y2} + a_{x2}a_{y1})f_{i1}f_{i2} + s_{ix}y_i + s_{iy}x_i.$$

(9-33)

Summing across cases, to produce sums of product and cross product terms (N times the variances and covariances),

$$\sum_i x_iy_i = a_{x1}a_{y1}\sum_i f_{i1}^2 + a_{x2}a_{y2}\sum_i f_{i2}^2 + (a_{x1}a_{y2} + a_{x2}a_{y1})\sum_i f_{i1}f_{i2}$$
$$+ \sum_i s_{iy}x_i + \sum_i s_{ix}y_i.$$

(9-34a)

By the definition of test specificity, all sums of cross products involving the s terms vanish, producing

$$\sum_i x_iy_i = a_{x1}a_{y1}\sum_i f_{i1}^2 + a_{x2}a_{y2}\sum_i f_{i2}^2 + (a_{x1}a_{y2} + a_{x2}a_{y1})\sum_i f_{i1}f_{i2}.$$ (9-34b)

Dividing by N produces the variance and covariance terms. Taking standard scores, and thus converting variances to 1, produces

$$r_{xy} = a_{x1}a_{y1} + a_{x2}a_{y2} + (a_{x1}a_{y2} + a_{x2}a_{y1})r_{f_1f_2},$$ (9-35)

where $r_{f_1f_2}$ is the correlation between hypothetical factors f_1 and f_2. It is, of course, an unobservable.

Compared to (9-27), equation (9-35) is another step backward. Instead of expressing one observable in terms of two unobservables, the observable has been expressed in terms of five unobservables!

As before, the way to solve the problem is to increase the number of tests. If there are $j = 1 \ldots J$ tests, then the jth test adds two terms to be estimated, a_{j1} and a_{j2}. This means that for J tests there will be $2J + 1$ terms to be estimated, the two a terms for each test and the correlation between the factors, $r_{f_1}r_{f_2}$. The number of terms to be estimated increases linearly with the number of tests to be analyzed. However, for J tests there will be $J(J-1)/2$ correlations. This means that the number of observable correlations increases quadratically with J. In the case of two factors and five tests, there will be 11 terms to be estimated and 10 correlations that can be observed, not quite enough. However, if six tests are used, there are 13 terms to be estimated and 15 observables.

We now generalize to an arbitrary number of tests, J, and factors, M, where $M < J$. Instead of x's and y's, consider tests x_j and $x_{j'}$, where j, $j' = 1 \ldots J$ and $j \neq j'$. The general form of equation 9-34 is

$$\sum_{i=1}^N x_{ij}x_{ij'} = \sum_{m=1}^N a_{jm}a_{j'm}\sum_{i=1}^N f_{im}^2 + \sum_{m=1}^{M-1}\sum_{m'=m+1}^M (a_{jm}a_{j'm'} + a_{jm'}a_{j'm})\sum_{i=1}^N f_{im}f_{im'}.$$ (9-36)

As before, dividing by N allows us to express the equation in terms of correlations. Equation (9-36) becomes

$$r_{jj'} = \sum_{m=1}^{M} a_{jm}a_{j'm} + \sum_{m=1}^{M-1}\sum_{m'=m+1}^{M} (a_{jm}a_{j'm'} + a_{jm'}a_{j'm})r_{f_m f_{m'}}. \tag{9-37}$$

There will be $J(J-1)/2$ observable. The parameters to be estimated are the JM factor loading terms, the a_{jm}'s, and $M(M-1)/2$ correlations between factors.[16] There are more observables than terms to be estimated if

$$J^2 - J > 2MJ + M^2 - M. \tag{9-38}$$

M, the number of factors, is usually considerably less than J for, after all, the point of the exercise to explain the relations between a large number of tests with a small number of factors. As a rule of thumb, in most studies $J \geq 7M$. For a fixed value of M, the left-hand side of in equality (9-38) increases quadratically with J, while the right-hand side increases linearly. Therefore, given a sufficient number of tests, the problem is solvable, in principle.

In practice, there are several problems that have not been discussed. Most of these revolve around statistical issues concerning sampling, for the observed correlations are usually considered to have been based on a sample of N observations from a much larger population. Accordingly, there may not be any set of parameter values that will exactly satisfy equation (9-35). There are several other technical issues. Going into them would lead us much further into statistics than we wish to go here! Many of these problems have been solved, and so given the existence of high-speed computers, factor analysis is a viable technique today.

9.6. GEOMETRIC AND GRAPHIC INTERPRETATIONS

There is an interesting geometric interpretation of a factor analytic study.

The normal way to plot test scores is to represent each case by the coordinates of a point in the K dimensional test space that defines a person's score on each of the K tests. That is, we plot people's scores in a space defined by tests. However, we can reverse this procedure and let each of the N persons be a dimension, and the N scores on test x (or y, or z) be the coordinates defined by the scores that each of the N people

---

[16] When Thurstone first developed multifactor theory, he assumed that the factors were independent of each other. This simplifies the mathematics but, from a psychological point of view, there is no reason that factors should not be correlated. Pragmatically, Thurstone had to assume uncorrelated factors because he could not analyze a model with correlated factors using the hand calculations and mechanical calculators available in the 1930s.

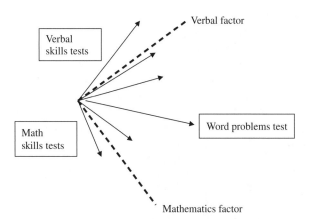

FIGURE 9-7. A geometric interpretation of a multiple factor study of intelligence. Hypothetical relationships are shown. All vectors are assumed to be embedded in an N-dimensional "people space," as defined in the text.

achieved on the test. In this approach tests are plotted in a space defined by people.

In the "people space" representation each test can be thought of as a vector in an N-dimensional space. It can be proven that the correlation coefficient between two tests is equal to the cosine of the angle between the two tests (at the origin) in "people space." Factors are defined by finding clusters of tests that point generally in the same direction in people space, and drawing a line through each cluster. A hypothetical example is shown in Figure 9-7, for tests involving verbal skills (paragraph comprehension, word knowledge, spelling, etc.) and tests involving math skills (arithmetic, algebra, geometry, etc.) One test ("word problems") is shown that loads on both a math skill and verbal skill factor.

9.7. WHAT SORT OF RESULTS ARE OBTAINED?

Having shown the mathematics behind testing, it is worth saying what has been learned.

Stankov's results closely resemble the factor structures found in many tests of intelligence. The fluid intelligence and crystallized intelligence factors are pervasive. Additionally, and as in Stankov's study, the two factors are correlated. Proponents of g theories argue that the correlation occurs because each factor is a different manifestation of general intelligence. Stankov's finding that fluid intelligence is correlated with the ability to keep track of several things at once is also fairly typical of other factor analytic studies in the field. Larger studies, involving more tests, also often find additional memory factors and a separate factor for reasoning about visual patterns.

Some investigators have pointed out that tests of Gf are largely visual and that tests of Gc are largely verbal. These investigators are also bothered by the fact that the Gf-Gc distinction does not clearly map onto neuropsychological findings concerning brain structure. These investigators argue that the correct division of underlying abilities is (a) general ability, augmented by (b) modality-specific abilities for manipulating linguistic and visual information.[17]

In the personality field factor, analytic studies have consistently identified five different dimensions of personality:

Extraversion–Introversion: The tendency to enjoy social, interpersonal activities compared to a preference for more individual, reflective activities.

Neuroticism: A measure of social stability compared to a tendency to worry a great deal about things.

Openness to experience: A tendency to like (or not like) to deal with new points of view and unfamiliar situations.

Agreeableness: The extent to which a person is trusting and sociable.

Conscientiousness: A measure of the extent to which a person attempts to discharge his or her obligations, even when not forced to do so.

Factor analysis has also been applied to measures of interests. People are asked how much they would enjoy various activities. The ratings are then factor-analyzed to isolate traits for enjoying physical activities, intellectual activities (in the sense of mathematics or science), and artistic-humanistic activities.[18]

Specialists in all of these fields – intelligence, personality, and interests – continue to debate what the best model is for their field. Thanks to modern factor analytic methods, these are debates over the analyses of data, not arguments based on anecdotes.

APPENDIX 9A. A MATRIX ALGEBRA PRESENTATION OF FACTOR ANALYSIS

This appendix has been provided as a substitute to Section 9-5 for readers who are familiar with matrix algebra. I suggest that the reader examine the example given ("Stankov's data") to motivate the analysis.

Let z_{ij} be the standard score of the ith individual, $i = 1 \ldots N$ on the jth test, $j = 1 \ldots J$. The *data matrix* is the N rows by J columns matrix

$$Z = \lfloor z_{ij} \rfloor. \tag{9A-1}$$

---

[17] Johnson and Bouchard, (2005).   [18] Ackerman and Beier (2001).

Write $x_{i\bullet}$ for the ith row of X and $x_{\bullet j}$ for the jth column. This notation will be used whenever it is necessary to refer to a particular row or column of a matrix.

The sum of cross products terms, $\sum z_{ij} z_{ij'}$, determines the association between tests j and j'. These terms are the elements of the J by J matrix

$$Z^T Z = \left[\sum_i z_{ij} z_{ij'} \right],$$

(9A-2)

where the superscript ^{T} indicates the transpose of a matrix. Because standard scoring is being used,

$$R = \frac{1}{N} Z^T Z$$

(9A-3)

is a matrix whose elements are the correlations $r_{jj'}$ between pairs of tests.

From equation (9-31), the assumption of factor analysis is that each observable score is composed of a weighted sum of an individual's scores on underlying factors, plus a test-specific score for that individual. That is,

$$z_{ij} = \sum_m a_{jm} f_{im} + s_{ij}$$

$$z_{ij} = \sum_m f_{im} a_{jm} + s_{ij},$$

(9A-4)

where the summation is over M ($M < J$) unobservable latent traits ("factors") and the f terms are in standard scores. The a_{jm} terms are the loadings of the jth factor on the mth test.

Let A be a $J \times M$ matrix, $A = \lfloor a_{jm} \rfloor$, where the entry a_{jm} is the loading of the jth test on factor m, and let $F = [f_{im}]$ be the $N \times M$ matrix whose entry f_{im} is ith case's score on the mth factor. Similarly, let $S = \lfloor s_{ij} \rfloor$ be the $N \times J$ matrix of residuals for the ith case on the j th test.

This allows us to write the data matrix in matrix notation as

$$Z = FA^T + S.$$

(9A-5)

The cross product matrix of the standardized scores is

$$Z^T Z = (FA^T + S)^T (FA^T + S)$$
$$Z^T Z = (AF^T + S^T)(FA^T + S)$$
$$Z^T Z = AF^T FA^T + S^T S,$$

(9A-6)

because, by definition, all cross product terms involving the residuals vanish. This includes all but the on-diagonal terms of SS^T, as residuals are themselves uncorrelated.

The observable, symmetrical correlation matrix is $\frac{1}{N}(Z^T Z)$, containing $\frac{1}{2}(J(J-1))$ terms determined by the data, the off-diagonal entries of $Z^T Z$. The A matrix contains $J \times M$ terms to be estimated, and the F matrix contains $\frac{1}{2}(M(M-1))$. The S matrix is a residual matrix. One way to evaluate the fit of a model to the data is to determine values of F and A that minimize the elements of S. The problem is solvable "in theory," providing that there are fewer parameters to be estimated than data points, that is,

$$\frac{1}{2}(J \cdot (J-1)) < J \cdot M + \frac{1}{2}(M \cdot (M-1)). \tag{9A-7}$$

In practice, there are a number of other conditions that must be met. These are topics for an advanced statistics course. The point to be made here is just that the general factor analytic problem is solvable, given modern computing techniques. In fact, much more complex models can be specified, in which the factors themselves have factors! But this is as far as we should go.

The reader should now return to Section 9-6.

10

How to Know You Asked a Good Question

10.1. THE PROBLEM

Chapter 9 described how psychometricians can uncover the dimensions of ability underlying performance on test batteries, such as the Scholastic Assessment Test, the Armed Services Vocational Battery, and numerous personality tests and employment assessment batteries. In this chapter, we turn our attention to the insides of individual tests within a battery. How is a test to be scored? How do we decide if a question is a good question? To take a concrete example, let us look at the problem of designing a vocabulary test.

Why would we give someone a vocabulary test at all? There are two reasons for doing so.

One is that the person may be applying for a position requiring the use of specialized vocabulary, so knowing the vocabulary is a requirement of the job. For example, in international commercial aviation all radio transmissions between controllers and aircraft are in English, albeit a very reduced version of English. Commercial pilots and air traffic controllers must display an understanding of the vocabulary and rudimentary English syntax of air control messages before receiving their licenses. Physicians and nurses have to know several hundred terms referring to parts of the body. Both these examples refer to situations in which there is an absolute standard of competence. It is easy to design a vocabulary test for this sort of situation; just identify the necessary vocabulary and see if the applicant knows it.

Suppose that instead we want to determine how broad a person's English vocabulary is. There are somewhere between five hundred thousand and a million words in English,[1] and so exhaustive testing is

---

[1] The reason that estimates are so wide is because it is not clear just what counts as a word, or whether specialized scientific terms and slang terms should be included (Crystal [1995], pp. 119, 123).

out of the question. What we need is some way of selecting a sample of words that will discriminate between those who do, or don't, have a wide knowledge of the language. How do we do that?

Another problem comes up in pre-employment testing, and to some extent in educational applications. Test makers would like testing sessions to be as short as possible, in order to reduce the cost of testing and, in the case of pre-employment testing, to reduce the chance that a good applicant will simply get tired of being tested and walk off. This is particularly a problem when the pre-employment battery is administered by computer. Industrial-organizational psychologists responsible for designing computer-delivered tests try to make them about 30 minutes long. How can this goal be achieved?

It turns out that both goals can be met by using a technique called *item response theory*. In the case of vocabulary, the idea behind the technique is obvious once you think about it. Knowing whether or not a person got question A correct is often a strong indicator of whether or not the same person will get question B correct. Suppose that an examinee correctly defines the word *feline*. There is little sense in asking whether or not that examinee knows what *cat* means. Conversely, if a person doesn't know what a *cat* is, the chances are pretty slim that he or she will know what a *feline* is.

The same logic can be applied to other fields. Take mathematical reasoning. A person who can tell you the what the value of *antiln* $(Ln(17) + Ln(3))$ is can tell you what 17×3 is.

There is a strong analogy between psychological and educational evaluations and the evaluation of a physical capability. Suppose that you wanted to know how high a person could jump. You would not ask an athlete who had just jumped over a two-meter bar to jump over a one-meter bar, nor would you ask a person who had failed to clear one meter to try to clear two meters!

10.2. AN ILLUSTRATIVE CASE: VOCABULARY TESTING

Vocabulary testing offers a good illustration of the concepts involved. In order to avoid confusion, the term *vocabulary* will be used to refer to those English language words a person understands. *Lexicon* will refer to all words in the English language. No one understands all the words of English, so the vocabulary is always a subset of the lexicon. The question to be answered is "How close is the vocabulary to the lexicon?"

The task is made easier by an obvious property of the lexicon. The frequencies with which different words are used vary greatly. Words like *cat* and *eat* are ubiquitous. A person who does not understand the sentence *Cats eat meat* has at best a rudimentary knowledge of English. Words like *feline* and *metabolize* are less common. A person who could get along quite well with English, as it is generally used, might not understand *Felines metabolize protein*. So, as a first approximation to testing a person's English vocabulary we could construct a test containing words of varying frequency, and determine the lowest-frequency (rarest) words that the examinee understands. The argument is that a person who knows rare words will also know words of high and intermediate frequency.

Note the analogy to evaluating how high a person can jump. Word frequency, a measurable property of words, is being used as a way to evaluate the difficulty people have defining words, just as the height of a bar from the ground is used to evaluate how high a person can jump. This is not a bad approximation, but it runs into problems when we deal with certain classes of words that are seldom used by most speakers of English (and hence are low-frequency, rare words) but are high-frequency terms among a subset of speakers.

To illustrate, consider the words *niggardly* (not generous, stingy) and *leptokurtic* (a statistical term describing frequency distributions that are more concentrated about the mean than the normal distribution).[2] Both are rarely used, and *leptokurtic* is probably even rarer than *niggardly*. *Niggardly* is a word that could be used widely, even though it is not, for the concept it names applies in a wide variety of situations. *Leptokurtic* is readily understood by statisticians, but the concept it identifies has little use to people outside the field. I have no trouble imagining a statistician who could define leptokurtic but could not define niggardly.

This illustration shows that if we want to order words by difficulty of definition, word frequencies provide a start, but there has to be some way of identifying words like leptokurtic that really belong in specialized dictionaries.

More generally, the difficulty of defining a word is ultimately determined by behavior, rather than by frequency of appearance.[3] Two questions must be answered. Within a population of users, what is the probability that a randomly chosen user can define the word in question? The answer determines the word's difficulty. What is the probability that a certain person, P, can define a randomly chosen word with difficulty level D? This answer determines P's vocabulary level.

There has been a subtle change of emphasis here. The definition of a person's vocabulary skill has shifted from "Can the person define a word of a certain level of difficulty?" to "What is the probability

---

[2] *The New Oxford American Dictionary* (2001).

[3] The problem arises from the way in which word frequencies are defined. Word frequencies are usually estimated by counting word appearances in written text, especially public texts such as newspapers. The estimates are not weighted by the number of readers, and so do not reflect the extent to which words may differ in terms of the frequency of people who can comprehend them.

that the person can define a word at that level of difficulty?" This is reasonable.

The next section describes how an elegant mathematical model can be used to create accurate and time-efficient evaluation. The model is certainly not restricted to vocabulary testing. It can be used in any situation in which there exists a universe of potential questions (word definitions, in the vocabulary case), each question has a level of difficulty, and ability is conceptualized as the probability that a person will correctly answer a question at a given level of difficulty.

10.3. THE BASICS OF ITEM RESPONSE THEORY

Item response theory (IRT)[4] is a mathematical technique designed to handle the evaluation of traits such as the vocabulary, mathematical reasoning, and many other cognitive abilities. Designers of educational tests make extensive use of IRT to construct tests to assess student achievement, such as those used to evaluate students and to evaluate educational programs. IRT is an especially useful tool for the construction of widely used tests because it is closely related to an efficient method of administering examinations, called *adaptive testing*. IRT itself will be explained first, then the idea of adaptive testing will be explained, and finally the relation between IRT and factor analysis will be discussed.

In IRT, the term *item* is used to refer to what is more commonly thought of as a question on a test. We begin with a data matrix, $X = [x_{ij}]$ with N rows and J columns, in which the entry x_{ij} is 1 if individual i can answer item j correctly, 0 otherwise. The *item characteristic curve* (ICC) is a function that relates the probability of a correct answer to the difficulty of the item and the level of ability ("skill" for short) of the person. In its simplest form, the ICC is

$$\Pr(x_{ij} = 1) = \frac{e^{\theta_i - \beta_j}}{1 + e^{\theta_i - \beta_j}}$$
$$\Pr(x_{ij} = 1) = \frac{1}{1 + e^{-(\theta_i - \beta_j)}},$$

(10-1)

where the second line is derived from the first by multiplying the right-hand side of the first line by $\frac{e^{-(\theta_i - \beta_j)}}{e^{-(\theta_i - \beta_j)}}$. The quantity θ_i is a measure of the ability of individual i, and β_j is a measure of the difficulty of item j. The term $\theta_i - \beta_j$ is the *ability-difficulty discrepancy*. It is positive if ability is greater than difficulty, negative if difficulty is greater than skill, and zero otherwise. Equation 10-1 is sometimes called the "one parameter model," as each item is characterized by a single difficulty parameter, β_j.

---

[4] See Embretson and Reise (2000) for an extended discussion of the theory.

The term $e^{-(\theta_i - \beta_j)}$ approaches zero if the ability-difficulty discrepancy is large and positive, approaches infinity as the ability-difficulty discrepancy takes on large negative values, and is one if ability equals difficulty (and hence the discrepancy is zero).

Three pivotal cases illustrate what such values imply for the ICC. Suppose that individual i is actually much smarter than the item is difficult. (Think of a professional writer being asked to define *cat*.) The ability-difficulty discrepancy is large and positive. Therefore,

$$\frac{Lim}{(\theta_j - \beta_j) \to \infty} \Pr(x_{ij} = 1) = 1. \tag{10-2}$$

If you test a person on an item much below that person's skill level, the probability that the item will be answered correctly approaches 1. This is as it should be.

Conversely, suppose that the individual's skill level is much below the difficulty level of the item, that is, that the question is just too hard for the person. (Think of a person who has just completed his or her first day of a course in English as a Foreign Language, and then asked to define *niggardly*.) The ability-skill level is large and negative, so $e^{-(\theta_i - \beta_j)}$ approaches positive infinity. It follows from the second line of (10-1) that

$$\frac{Lim}{(\theta_j - \beta_j) \to -\infty} \Pr(x_{ij} = 1) = 0. \tag{10-3}$$

If the skill level is far below the difficulty level, the probability that the item will be answered correctly tends toward zero.

If the skill level exactly measures the difficulty level $\theta_i - \beta_j = 0$. Since $e^0 = 1$, equation (10-1) is identically 1/2. This may seem trivial, but it highlights an important conceptual point:

In item response theory, difficulty and skill are measured on the same scale. Operationally, a person's skill level is defined by determining the difficulty level at which he or she provides a correct answer for half of the items.

Item response theory is a reasonable analysis for the cases in which a person's skill far exceeds a test item's difficulty, or where the item's difficulty exceeds the person's skill, or when difficulty and skill match. What about the in-between cases, where skill and difficulty are not identical but are not "too far" apart?

Figure 10-1 shows the ICC for ability-skill discrepancies ranging from −4 (difficulty considerably exceeds skill) to 4 (skill considerably exceeds difficulty). There are two ways to look at this chart. One is to assume that difficulty is fixed and that skill is increased gradually. Think of an individual learning English as a Second Language. What would the chances be that this person would correctly define a mildly rare

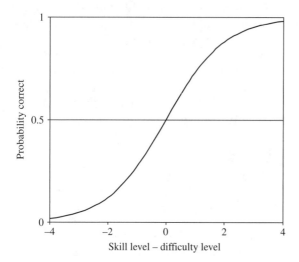

FIGURE 10-1. The item characteristic curve defined by equation 10-1, the one-parameter IRT model. The ICC defines the relation between the probability of correctly answering an item and the discrepancy between the ability of the examinee and the difficulty of the item.

word, such as *matures*? Early in instruction (left side of the figure, negative skill-difficulty discrepancy) the chances of a correct definition would be low. As skill progressed the chances of a correct definition would increase, slowly at first, and then rapidly as a larger vocabulary was acquired. When skill matched difficulty, the discrepancy would be zero and the probability of a correct definition would be .5. After further learning skill will exceed difficulty. The probability that the person will give a correct definition increases, rapidly at first, and then more slowly as it tends toward the limit of 1.

The second way to read the chart is to assume that skill is fixed and difficulty is varied. Think this time of your idea of a "typical" speaker of English. If this person is asked to define very easy words, like *cat*, the skill-difficulty discrepancy will be large and positive (right-hand side of the figure) and the probability of a correct definition will be high. As the words get harder (first defining *matures*, then *niggardly*, and so forth), the probability of a correct definition drops. The change corresponds to a move from the right-to the left-hand side of the figure.

This is all very well, providing that we know the skill levels of individuals and the difficulty levels of items. But where do they come from?

10.4. STANDARDIZATION: ESTIMATING ITEM AND PERSON PARAMETERS SIMULTANEOUSLY

IRT was intended to cover a situation in which tests are first developed by estimating item and person parameters on a reference population, and then used to measure the ability of a new group of examinees, usually for the purpose of educational or job selection. These two phases will be called the *development* and *application* phases.

In the development phase, N people take a test with J items, each of which can be scored as correct (1) or incorrect (0). The record for individual i ($i = 1 \ldots N$) will be a binary vector, $x_i = (x_{i1}, x_{i2} \ldots x_{ij})$, where the jth entry is zero or one, depending upon whether or not person i correctly answered item j. This will be called the *response vector*. The response vectors for everyone in the reference population can be collected to define the *response matrix*, $\mathbf{X} = [x_{ij}]$. Applying the results of the previous section, the a priori probability of observing the response that actually happened is

$$P(x_{ij} = 1) = \frac{e^{\theta_i - \beta_j}}{1 + e^{\theta_i - \beta_j}}$$
$$P(x_{ij} = 0) = 1 - \frac{e^{\theta_i - \beta_j}}{1 + e^{\theta_i - \beta_j}}. \tag{10-4}$$

Because x_{ij} must be either zero or one, we can assume values of θ_i and β_j and define the probability of the response:

$$L(x_{ij}|\theta_i, \beta_j) = P(x_{ij}|\theta_i, \beta_j). \tag{10-5}$$

This is called the *likelihood* function. It is the probability of the observation given the assumptions about the parameters.

The likelihood function for a response vector follows immediately. Let Π be the replicated multiplication operator, $\prod_{i=1}^{n} y_i = y_1 \cdot y_2 \cdot y_3 \ldots y_{n-1} \cdot y_n$. The response vector for individual i is

$$x_{i\bullet} = (x_{i1}, x_{i2}, \ldots x_{ij}, \ldots x_{iJ}), \ j = 1 \ldots J, \tag{10-6}$$

where each x_{ij} is either 1 (the person got the answer right) or 0 (got it wrong). Assume an ability parameter θ_i for that individual and a vector of assumed difficulty levels for the J items, $\beta_\bullet = (\beta_1, \beta_2, \ldots \beta_j \ldots \beta_J)$. Assume further that the items are conditionally independent, which means that the probability of getting an item right is determined solely by the person's ability and the level of difficulty of the item, and not on whether the other items were answered correctly or not. The probability of observing the response vector as a whole is

$$L(x_{i\bullet}|\theta_i, \beta_\bullet) = \prod_{j=1}^{J} P(x_{ij}|\theta_i, \beta_j). \tag{10-7}$$

Item and person parameters are expressed in standard score units. Therefore $\theta_i = 0$ would indicate that the ith person's skill level was at the mean of all skill levels in the population. $\theta_i = 1$ would indicate that this person had a skill level one standard deviation above the mean skill level, and so on. A similar argument applies for the β_j's that define difficulty levels of items.

A numerical example is in order. Suppose that a person with a skill level of 1 was tested on three items: a relatively easy item with a difficulty level of -1, an item of mean difficulty, 0, and an item that had a difficulty level of 1, right at the person's skill level. The discrepancies between skill and difficulty would be, in order, 2, 1, and 0.

Further suppose that this person gets the first two items correct and misses the third item. The response vector will be $x_{i\bullet} = (1,1,0)$. Applying equation (10-5), or perhaps by reading Figure 10-1, the corresponding probabilities of events under these assumptions about parameters are .90, .73, .50. Therefore, by equation (10-7) the likelihood of the response vector is

$$.90 * .73 * .50 = .33$$

carried to two decimal points.

Recall that these computations assume conditional independence. In the testing context, this is referred to as *item independence*. For any two items j and j',

$$P(x_{ij} = 1|x_{ij'} = 1) = P(x_{ij} = 1|x_{ij'} = 0). \tag{10-8}$$

The psychological and educational implications of this are not trivial, for it rules out a common testing technique in which a person is asked to read a scenario and answer several questions based on it. In this case, if a person misunderstands the first question the same misunderstanding may influence answers to further questions. The point is discussed further in the comments section at the end of the chapter. Pragmatically, in most testing situations it is possible to construct items that satisfy conditional independence.

The likelihood function is defined for any combination of item and person parameters. For instance, suppose that person i actually was a bit above average, say $\theta_i = 2$. This would change the skill-difficulty discrepancies to 3, 2, 1. The corresponding probability of the response vector would be .226. (If the reader has any questions at this point, I suggest deriving this value.) The point is that the likelihood is defined for any

possible response vector and combination of item and person parameters.

In the development phase test makers find item parameters that
maximize the likelihood of simultaneously observing the response vectors for all examinees. Consider two individuals, i and i^*, with response
vectors x_i and x_{i^*}. Because the response of individuals i and i^* are independent, the likelihood of the two response vectors is

$$L(x_{i\bullet} \bullet x_{i*\bullet}|\theta_i, \theta_{i*}, \beta_\bullet) = L(x_{i\bullet}|\theta_i, \beta_\bullet) \bullet L(x_{i*\bullet}|\theta_{i*}, \beta_\bullet), \qquad (10\text{-}9)$$

recalling that $\beta_\bullet$ is a vector of J item parameters, and does not vary across
individuals.

Generalizing this principle, the likelihood of obtaining the data
from the development phase, where N examines have been tested,
is

$$L(\mathbf{X}|\theta_\bullet, \beta_\bullet) = \prod_{i=1}^{N} L(\mathbf{x}_{i\bullet}|\theta_i, \beta_\bullet). \qquad (10\text{-}10)$$

In order to make accurate estimates of examinee parameters (the $\theta_i's$)
during the subsequent application phase it is important that the difficulty
parameters (the $\beta_j's$) be estimated precisely during the development
phase. The procedure for doing this, called *maximum likelihood estimation*,
is computationally extensive and may require testing of hundreds or
even thousands of examinees. Once this is done the application phase
can be completed with much less effort.

10.5. THE APPLICATION PHASE: ADAPTIVE TESTING

In order to understand how IRT is used in practice, after the develop-
mental phase has been completed, it helps to contrast IRT testing to
conventional procedures. A conventional test will contain J test items of
varying but known difficulty. If testing time is unlimited, each examinee
takes every item. If conventional testing is combined with conventional
scoring, the examinee's total score is determined by adding up the
number of correct items, and then either using this score directly or
converting it to a percentage, or on occasion, converting it to a standard
score.

In timed tests, an examinee has to answer as many questions as
possible within a fixed time limit. Items are usually presented in
increasing order of difficulty, from the easiest to the hardest. The score is
the total number of items correctly solved. It is assumed that people will
solve items quickly if their skill level exceeds the difficulty level of an
item, and conversely, that they will take a long time if the difficulty level
exceeds their skill level. Therefore, people with high skill levels are
expected both to attempt more items and to solve more.

When testing time is unlimited, IRT can be used to change the scoring technique. Instead of simply adding up the number of correct answers, examiners use the maximum likelihood method, but this time with known item parameters. For each examinee, equation (10-7) is used to find the value of θ_i that maximizes $L(x_{i\bullet})$ given the item parameters, β, that were determined in the development phase. The example given to illustrate the estimation procedure (see Section 10.4) illustrates this sort of testing.

IRT analysis is not compatible with conventional time-limited testing without some ancillary assumptions relating the ability-difficulty discrepancy to the time required to solve a problem. However IRT is compatible with a time-saving technique known as *adaptive testing*.

In a paper and pencil examination questions are presented in a fixed order. When an examination is administered by computer answers can be scored virtually immediately, which means that the examiner (program) is gathering a lot of information about the examinee as the examination progresses. This information can be used to choose the most informative questions for each examinee. Let us look at how this works.

Adaptive testing requires two preconditions. The first is that the examination be interactive, so that the examiner can choose the next item based on responses to previous items. The second is that there must exist a very large *item bank* containing items of known difficulty. The first condition is easy to achieve with computer-administered testing. Collecting a large enough item bank is an expensive proposition, for it requires a substantial development phase. The costs can be justified for very large testing programs, such as the SAT, ASVAB, or commercial employee screening systems.[5]

Once these conditions are satisfied adaptive testing is simple. First, ask the examinee several questions of intermediate difficulty, with difficulty parameters near zero. Then proceed as follows.

If the examinee answers about half of these questions correctly, stop, assigning the examinee a skill level of zero. (Remember, zero is the median skill level, not an indication of no skill at all!)

If the examinee answers almost all the questions correctly, present items that have a higher difficulty level. Although there is no theoretical bound on difficulty level, in practice the level should be set at the highest level of interest to the examiner. If the examinee answers almost all the questions incorrectly present new items at a lower skill level, but higher

---

[5] People whose experience is primarily in education may not realize how ubiquitous employee testing is. With the advent of the Internet, it is now possible to test prospective employees online, with the results being analyzed by a centralized computer system. One company that provides employee testing using online tests examines 40,000 people a day. That is approximately one examinee every two seconds.

than level zero. If the examinee answers almost all the questions correctly a second time, set a still higher difficulty level and repeat the procedure.

Difficulty levels are adjusted upward and downward until one is found at which the examinee gets about half the questions right. Because difficulty and skill are measured on the same scale this is the examinee's skill level.

In order for this method to work the amount that the difficulty level is changed, either up or down, has to be progressively smaller at each adjustment, providing that an upper and lower bound has been set on skill level. For example, if an examinee found items at level 0 easy, and then found items at level 1 hard, the next set of items to be presented would have difficulty levels of about .5.

Appendix 10A presents a more precise description of the algorithm. Readers who would like firsthand experience with the procedure can turn to the exercise presented in Appendix 10B.

10.6. MORE COMPLICATED IRT MODELS

In the one-parameter IRT model, all information about an item is summed up in the single-item difficulty parameter, β. There are many situations where a finer description is desired. Two further item characteristics have been considered, *item sensitivity* and *base rate*.

In most cases we want items for which the pass rate increases monotonically with skill level, on the assumption that the more skilled the examinee is, the better the chances are that he or she will give the right answer. However, items may differ in the rate at which the probability of getting the correct answer increases with increases in examinee skill. This is referred to as a difference in item sensitivity. The "perfect" question would be one that was answered correctly by everyone over a certain skill level, and by no one below that level. Conversely, a poor item is one where the probability of obtaining a correct answer rises very slowly with the examinee's skill level. The former item would be said to have high sensitivity, while the latter would have low sensitivity.

The *two-parameter* IRT model provides a measure of item sensitivity. The model adds a new parameter, α_j, so that the ICC function becomes

$$\Pr(x_{ij} = 1) = \frac{1}{1 + e^{-\alpha(\theta_i - \beta_j)}}. \tag{10-11}$$

If α_j is less than one, the item-response function increases more slowly than in the one-parameter model. If α_j is greater than one, the item-response function increases more rapidly than in the one-parameter model. The case α_j equal to one is equivalent to the one-parameter model. This is shown graphically in Figure 10-2, which plots item-response

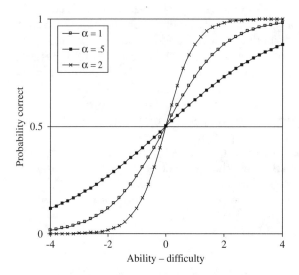

FIGURE 10-2. The effect of varying the α parameter upon the item-response function. Depending upon whether or not the α parameter is greater than or less than one, the item-response function for the two-parameter model is more or less sensitive to changes in skill-difficulty discrepancies than it would be in the one-parameter model.

functions for $\alpha_j = .5$, 1, and 2. In general, one always wants more discriminating models, and so α_j should be as high as possible.

Although the theory applies to any question for which the concept "correct or not correct" makes sense, IRT is most often used to analyze data from multiple-choice tests. If IRT is to be used in conjunction with adaptive testing, this restriction is almost dictated by technology. Given present technology, it is trivial to program computers to evaluate multiple-choice responses, but hard to program them to evaluate open-ended responses. However, multiple-choice examinations have a built-in problem, guessing rates.

If an examinee chooses an answer randomly the probability of correctly answering a multiple-choice item with k alternative answers is $1/k$. However, this is seldom the case, because a typical examinee may not know the right answer but may be able to rule out alternative answers. The problem is illustrated by this hypothetical question.

Tax problem: In a graduated income tax system, the tax rate varies with the level of income. Suppose that there is a 10% tax on the first $25,000 of income, a 20% tax on the next $25,000, and a 30% tax on all income over $50,000. Mr. Jones makes $100,000 a year. How much income tax does he owe?

(a) $30,000
(b) $5.00
(c) $125,000
(d) $22,500.

Answer (d) is correct. Answer (a) is the answer that would be obtained if the examinee erroneously applied the 30% figure to total income. A person who simply refuses to do mathematics could still rule out answers (b) and (c) on the grounds that both figures are ridiculous; no one owes a $5 income tax, and no one is taxed more than is earned. (It just seems that way!) A case can be made that the guessing parameter is more likely to be 1/2 than 1/4.

The example was constructed to make the point obvious. Subtler cases are likely. The three-parameter IRT model provides a way to estimate a guessing rate, c_j, for each item. If a person may get the correct answer either by guessing or by applying his or her ability the ICC becomes

$$P(x_{ij} = 1) = c_j + (1 - c_j)\left(\frac{1}{1 + e^{-\alpha(\theta_i - \beta_j)}}\right). \tag{10-12}$$

Some examples are shown in Figure 10-3 for different values of c_j.

The addition of parameters increases the number of people who must be examined in the development phase in order to obtain stable parameter estimates.

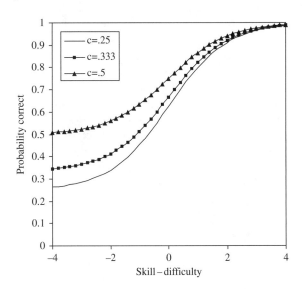

FIGURE 10-3. The item characteristic curve corrected for guessing. ICCs are shown for the case in which the probability of correctly guessing an item is .25, .333, or .5 and the sensitivity parameter α is equal to one for all items.

10.7. MATHEMATICS MEETS THE SOCIAL WORLD: MATHEMATICAL ISSUES AND SOCIAL RELEVANCE

By the time the twenty-first century began, personality, intelligence, ability, and employability tests had become very widely used, and also subject to a great deal of controversy. It is of some interest to look at how these controversies relate to the mathematical basis of testing.

Some people see testing as an important socioeconomic tool. Economically, testing makes possible a better fit of applicants to jobs. The first large-scale use of testing for this purpose was in 1917, when the U.S. Army developed a testing program to deal with its rapid expansion in World War I. After the war, testing was introduced into college admissions, as an antidote to the prevailing practice of selecting students on the basis of social background and attendance at well-known preparatory schools.

Paradoxically, testing has been attacked as a vehicle that promotes social inequality, even though one of the motivations for developing tests was to reverse inequality. The argument is almost always driven by the observation that certain demographic groups, notably African-Americans and Latinos, tend to score below whites and Asians on tests of cognitive abilities. A related, controversial observation is that women, on the average, have lower scores than men on tests involving mathematics and on certain tests of visual-spatial reasoning. The mean differences are substantial: slightly less than one standard deviation unit for the African-American–white contrast, and about half a standard deviation for the male–female contrast. Women, on the average, score somewhat higher than men on tests of verbal skills, but the difference is much smaller than those just cited and has not been a cause of controversy.

Many of the issues involved are not mathematical. They have to do with whether or not the populations in question have all had an equal chance to prepare for the test, and the relative costs of "misses," in the signal detection sense, when a test score is used to reject candidates belonging to different demographic groups. However, there are some areas where mathematical analysis can be used to clarify the issues involved. One is statistical, and so will be treated only briefly (although it is very important). The other is directly relevant to the mathematical models used to construct tests, both at the test battery level, as discussed in Chapter 9, and at the item level, as discussed here.

The statistical issue has to do with the definition of *fairness* (or, to put the issue negatively, *bias*). To some people, a test is biased if one demographic group is consistently given lower scores than another. This definition of bias assumes that the talents required for both the test and performance on the criterion measure (e.g., SAT and college GPA) are equally distributed in each population. To me, this seems to be a suspect way to proceed, for the definition assumes what the answer should be. In order to test for bias as defined in this way, it is necessary to examine the two populations using some measuring system that is felt to be more valid than the test in question. The construction of such a test is outside the scope of mathematics.

A second argument for test bias is that a test may be less predictive for one group than another. The issue here is whether the correlations and regression equations between test scores (e.g., SAT) and criterion measures (e.g., college GPA) are the same for all groups. This question can be dealt with by appropriate statistical analyses. The analyses are more complicated than one might think, and so will not be dealt with here. There is a considerable statistical literature on this topic.

A third argument for test bias is more general because it goes to issues of test accuracy at the individual as well as group level. Furthermore, it is directly relevant to the use of factor analysis and IRT to measure individual performance.

Both factor analysis and IRT assume that every examinee attacks a test in the same manner. Factor analysis provides a model of the relation between scores on tests after the test scores have been assigned. Item response theory provides a model for scoring a test. The two models are connected to each other by regarding the ability level on test j, possibly established by IRT, as a function, g, of a person's ability levels on the K factors that load on the test, given the loadings that the test has on each of the factors. Symbolically,

$$\theta_i(j) = g(f_{i1}, f_{12} .. f_{ik}, .. f_{iK} | w_{ji}, w_{j2}, .. w_{jk} .. w_{jK}), \tag{10-13}$$

where $\theta_i(j)$ refers to person i's ability on whatever trait test j evaluates, the g function expresses that skill in terms of that person's abilities on the underlying factors (the f's), and the w terms refer to the j th test's loading on those factors. The f_i terms vary across individuals but the w terms do not. Psychologically, this amounts to an assumption that every person uses the same strategy to relate his/her "basic" skills (the f_i's) to the compound skill evaluated by test j. While this assumption seems to be reasonably accurate for some skills, there are situations where it is suspect.

To illustrate, suppose that we wanted to construct a test of people's ability to follow geographic instructions, such as instructions about how to go from place to place in a city. The questions used on such a test might read like this:

To go from the Lux Hotel to the Odeon Theatre, turn left on 1st Avenue, walk north to 14th Street, turn west, and walk until you reach the theatre on your left.

These instructions mix "route" directions, such as "turn left" with "surveyor" terms, such as "north." Psychological research has shown that some people follow geographic directions by memorizing sequences of turns and distances (*route* representation), whereas others use verbal directions to develop a mental map of the situation (*survey* representation).[6] It is also well known that short-term memory for verbal material and the ability to deal with mental spaces are basic mental abilities (factors).[7] Depending upon whether one uses a route or a survey representation, the task will draw upon a verbal memory or a spatial factor. Therefore, the function, as well as the factor scores, vary across individuals. Neither the IRT nor factor analytic models allow for this.

This deficiency by no means invalidates current mental test procedures. It does limit the conclusions that can be drawn from them. The tests work well, providing that the examinees more or less agree on the way to attack each problem. If there are substantial individual differences in examinees' qualitative approach to problems the rationales for both classic test theory and the IRT model are suspect.

There is also a more general limit on the use of mathematical models for analyzing intelligence and personality tests. Both factor analysis and the IRT model provide ways of characterizing a test of intelligence or personality, after that test has been developed. Neither mathematical model provides guidance about what items to put on the test in the first place. It is up to the psychologist to conceptualize what to test, and to develop the initial items. Once this has been done, mathematical models can be used to evaluate the result of the original work. Mathematical analysis can identify tests that do not load on underlying factors in the way that the test developer thought they would, and to identify items whose ICC just does not make sense. Such information can be highly useful as tests are refined. Deciding what the content of the test should be is a matter for psychological or educational theory, not mathematical modeling.

APPENDIX 10A. THE ADAPTIVE TESTING ALGORITHM

Several algorithms for adaptive testing are possible. Here is one:

1. Set the current item difficulty level to 0. Go to step 2.
2. Select k items at the current level of item difficulty from the data bank and present them. If the respondent answers $\frac{1}{2}(k \pm e)$ items correctly, where e is an indicator of allowable error, stop. The examinee's skill level is equal to the current item difficulty level. Otherwise go to step 3.

---

[6] See Hunt (2002, Chapter 6) for a discussion of this research.   [7] Carroll (1993).

3. Reset the level of item difficulty according to the following rules:

(a) If this is the first time the item difficulty level has been reset, set the next item difficulty level to K if the examinee responded correctly to more than $\frac{1}{2}(k+e)$ items on the initial presentation, or to $-K$ if the examinee responded correctly to fewer than $\frac{1}{2}(k-e)$ items. K should be chosen to produce very difficult items (i.e., almost everyone gets fewer than $\frac{1}{2}(k-e)$ items correct at difficulty level K) or very easy items (almost everyone gets more than $\frac{1}{2}(k+e)$ items correct at difficulty level $-K$). Set the past level of difficulty to 0. Go to step 2.

(b) If the difficulty level has been reset previously, compute half the absolute difference between the current item difficulty level and the previous item difficulty level. Call this the *adjustment value*. Set the previous item difficulty level to the current difficulty level. If the examinee got fewer than $\frac{1}{2}(k-e)$ items correct at the current level, set the current level to current level minus the adjustment value. If the examinee got more than $\frac{1}{2}(k-e)$ items correct at the current level, set the current level to the current level plus the adjustment value. Go to step 2.

The adjustment procedure is directly analogous to a military procedure called "bracketing," which has been used to direct artillery fire since Napoleon's time. In bracketing an observing officer first estimates the distance between his post and the target (the "range"), and orders that a shell be fired at that range. If the shell lands on the target further fire is directed at the same range until the target is destroyed. If the round lands beyond the target ("over") the officer shortens the range to a value that is almost guaranteed to cause the next shell to short. (If the first shell fell short the observer adjusts the range so that the next shell lands over.) The range is then adjusted by firing a sequence of short and long shells, each time halving the distance between shots that land over and short, until a shell hits the target. Adaptive testing does the same thing, but the target is the examinee's skill level. The difference between the two is that when the artilleryman gets a hit, firing continues until the target is destroyed. When a tester "gets a hit," the examinee goes home.

APPENDIX 10B. AN EXERCISE IN ADAPTIVE TESTING

In this exercise, you will be asked to determine a possible sequence of questions in order to determine the skill level of an unknown applicant.

Figure 10-1 presented the item-response function by showing the probability of a correct response as a function of the discrepancy between

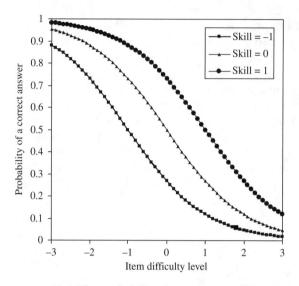

FIGURE 10-4. The probability that an item will be answered correctly, shown as a function of item difficulty level. Probabilities are shown for three skill levels, −1, 0, and 1. The one-parameter model was used to calculate these functions.

examinee skill and item difficulty. An alternative way to display this function is to plot the probability that an item will be responded to correctly as a function of item difficulty, with separate plots for different levels of examinee skill. This is shown in Figure 10-4 for three examinees, one with a skill level of −1, another with a skill level of 0 (the median examinee), and one with a skill level of 1. As would be expected, the probability of getting an item correct drops as item difficulty increases.

Imagine that you are an examiner who knows that one of these three people is being examined, but you do not know which one. How would you proceed in order to identify the examinee? What item would you select first? Depending upon the actual identity of the examinee, would the next item you select probably be more or less difficult than the first? How would you decide how difficult the second item should be? How would you proceed from there on? Is there any chance that you would be trapped on a wrong answer? How would you reduce this chance?

As a further exercise, take one of the curves in figure 10-4 and assume that it is the correct one. Imagine that you have exactly four questions to ask. The first will have an item difficulty level of 0. What are the possible sequences of item difficulty levels for the next three questions, and how likely is each sequence?

11

The Construction of Complexity

How Simple Rules Make Complex Organizations

11.1. SOME GRAND THEMES

The previous chapters have illustrated how mathematical modeling can advance our understanding of behavioral and social phenomena. This and the next chapter are concerned with a slightly different topic, *computational modeling*. What is the difference?

In mathematical modeling, beliefs about a phenomenon are expressed as mathematical statements. These are then further developed in order to understand what the model implies about behavior in the world. Today, computers are often used as part of this enterprise. Either they can be used as tools in order to investigate a specific case, as in the ecological models of predator–prey interactions, or they can be used to connect data to theory, as they are in factor analysis and item response theory.

In computational modeling the beliefs are cast as programs to be executed by a digital computer. The program/model is then run in order to see what it implies. This is called *computer simulation*. Simulation is used as an alternative to mathematical analysis. Computational modeling has two advantages. It is concrete, and it is often possible to program basic beliefs (i.e., the axioms of a model) that are complex enough so that they defy mathematical analysis. On the other hand, computational modeling has important disadvantages.

Simulation reduces to analysis of specific cases. Trends can be seen but proofs cannot be obtained. Paradoxically, some people seem more disposed to trust something that "came out of the computer" than something proven by mathematical analysis, but in fact, the converse should be true. Running computer simulations shows that in the particular cases analyzed certain results were obtained. Mathematical analysis, when it is possible, shows that under given situations certain results will always be obtained.

We will look at two topics in computational modeling. In this chapter, we look at how complex (social) patterns can be formed by the interactions among anywhere from three to a hundred simple agents. Some further motivation is given in the following section. In the next chapter, we look at some attempts to develop computational models of cognitive behavior based on ideas about the organization of the brain.

11.2. THE PROBLEM OF COMPLEXITY

A graduate student from Thailand who was working in my laboratory received an invitation to spend Sunday watching the professional football championship, the "Super Bowl." On the Friday before the game, he asked me to spend a few minutes explaining the rules and strategies of American football. I offered him a swap; I would explain football to him in two and a half days if he would spend a comparable time explaining to me the meaning of all the tales of Krishna. We agreed that the two tasks were impossible, and both of us proceeded in ignorance.

The general principle at work here is that social structures can be pretty complicated. The rules for professional football are simple compared to the rules for constructing sentences in any natural language. Our social rules are so complicated that modern societies have created a lucrative profession, the law, whose practitioners do little but explain the rules to the rest of us.

Social complexity is not the half of it. Living beings, many of whom do not seem to be very smart individually, create complex patterns. Examine the construction of a wasp's nest. (Remove the wasps first!) You will find that it is a marvel of geometric regularity. Coral reefs have the architecture of submerged castles taken from a fantasy movie. For that matter, real castles and cathedrals are pretty complex – but artifacts in general do not begin to be as complex as the structures created by plant and animal life.

Biological organisms are themselves fantastically complicated. We all know, from modern biology, that patterns in our DNA are replicated in messenger RNA, which then provides the instructions for assembling proteins. But wait a minute. What do we mean by "instructions for assembling proteins"? It is easy enough to envisage how the information about structure is transferred from DNA to RNA. That next step, interpreting the structure, is what boggles the mind. I doubt that there is a little elf riding on the ribosome. How does the RNA go about assembling proteins to create structures as different as the brain, the eye, the skeleton, and the reproductive system?

Why is life on Earth so complicated? Two answers have been offered. One, the *intelligent design* hypothesis, asserts that the complexity of the world is in itself evidence that some Intelligent Designer created these patterns, either directly or by implanting the Earth with self-replicating devices whose interactions were sure to produce the complexities that we see about us.[1] The implantation hypothesis is ingenious, because it allows for the fossil evidence. All that the Intelligent Designer had to do was to pick exactly the right combination of initial gadgets, and the complicated structures we see would inevitably follow, leaving a fossil trace along the way. But the Intelligent Designer must have exercised knowledge in order to plant the Earth with the right combination of organisms in the first place.

Virtually all modern scientists (including me!) reject this explanation. Instead, they accept an *evolutionary* hypothesis. According to evolutionary thinking, our present complexity arose from trial and error. What we see about us is the result of 5 billion years of competition and selection. It might have gone some other way – perhaps bipedalism and symmetry aren't necessarily the best way to go, but that is what happened to win out in the genetic competition. "Impossible!" scoff the intelligent designers. To which the evolutionists reply that 5 billion years is an incomprehensibly long time in human terms, and that, possibly excepting a few specialists, we have difficulty grasping how much trial and error could occur since our world began.

Although scientists overwhelmingly reject the intelligent design hypothesis, opinion polls have shown that the lay public does not. One of the reasons seems to be that it is difficult for most people to imagine how randomness could produce complexity. That is where the study of self-organizing systems comes into play. In the last 20 to 30 years a number of models have been developed that illustrate how complexity may be an inevitable outcome of the interactions among entities that follow a very small number of rules. Complexity of the overall structure evolves from the interactions of large numbers of simple agents. The resulting structure may be capable of complicated interactions with the environment, even though the simple ones are not. In this case, the properties of the complex system are said to emerge from the interactions of the simple ones. To the extent that one accepts this argument, the evolution of the present world was thus almost inevitable; there just are not a great many possible worlds.

People who see complexity as emerging from simple interaction sometimes use the ant colony as an example. At the colony level, ants are surprisingly sophisticated devices. The colony locates food, multiple individuals transport supplies back to the colony, the reproductive capabilities of the colony are defended, provision is made for the

---

[1] See, for instance, the op-ed piece by Michael Behe in the *New York Times*, February 7, 2005. Many critics of intelligent design have said that it is nothing more than a disguised version of the Christian creation myth. I disagree. The Intelligent Designer would, of course, be equivalent to a god, but not necessarily to the Christian God. Somehow, though, the conclusion that Wotan could have done it has not increased my own (nonexistent) belief in intelligent design.

development of satellite colonies, and some species even exhibit a form of agriculture, aphid ranching! The individual ant is colossally stupid. The intelligence is in the interaction.

In the 1950s, John von Neumann, the brilliant Hungarian American mathematician, speculated that it would be possible to design self-replicating computers that could construct just about anything. Since that time, the study of how small, simple entities might work together to produce large, complex systems has become a small growth industry, somewhat in the shadows of mainstream science. A great deal of the progress in this field depends upon the use of computer programs to explore the implications of interactions between simple entities.

There is no really good name for this area of study. The term "cellular automata" is sometimes used, but I have yet to see a good definition of just what this means. I have heard studies that seem to me awfully close to examples of cellular automata referred to as studies in "computational demography." The two titles conjure up quite different pictures in my mind. Probably the best thing to do is to describe what we are about. This chapter will deal with ways in which complicated structures or behaviors can arise from the (usually simple) interactions between agents who have not been given any overall plan or direction. That sounds rather as if a home builder simply hired a group of carpenters, plumbers, and electricians and told them to "do their thing," without hiring an architect, foreman, or general contractor. While that probably won't work for home building, it turns out that it does for society building!

The examples we will investigate, and the sorts of models that are studied in the field, fall into two classes: *deterministic* and *stochastic* models. In a deterministic model the implications of assumptions about agents and interactions are absolute; if we could work out all the inter-actions by hand we would find that a certain complex structure must arise from interactions between simple agents. Since it is beyond human capacity to see what the implications of the interactions are, they are investigated by programming them on a computer, running the pro-gram, and seeing what results. The important thing is that there is no random element. The computer is being used solely (but not trivially) as a mechanical device for investigating the implications of the initial assumptions about the agents.

Stochastic models contain an element of randomness. To get some idea of what a stochastic model is, consider what may be the ultimate stochastic phenomenon, the emergence of life on Earth. Current scientific belief is that life began in stages. First, molecules of various substances floated around in a sort of primordial soup, mixed by energy received from the Sun and heat sources internal to the planet. The molecules collided, randomly, until some of them stuck together to form amino acids. Some amino acids, again acting randomly, collided to produce proteins, then single-celled creatures, and eventually here we are!

How likely was this event? We really have no idea. What we do know is that it took about 5 billion years to get here, which provides a lot of time for trying out random designs. About 3 billion of the 5 billion years were probably spent in the initial stage, which raises the interesting question of why there has been a rapid acceleration in the prevalence of complex structures in the last 2 billion years.

How likely is it that there are other planets like Earth, that can produce and support life as we know it? Again we have no idea, but we do know that there are billions of stars and that some of the nearer ones have planets orbiting them. Given the laws of physics, life may be a virtual certainty, somewhere in the universe, even though it is extremely unlikely to occur around any given star.

Now what has this to do with social structures? The argument behind a stochastic simulation is that random interactions between simple agents are likely to, but will not inevitably, produce certain social structures. In order to find out what "likely to" means, either we can determine, analytically, the probability of a given structure or, if the analytic problem is too hard, we can construct a computer program that runs hundreds or thousands of simulations of the random interactions between agents. One book describing this process bore the apt title *The Garden in the Machine*, which nicely describes the logic.[2]

Readers should be warned! Some people have claimed that the study of automata is a method of analysis that will replace conventional mathematics as a tool for understanding the world. Steven Wolfram, one of our leading computer software designers, called his book on this topic *A New Kind of Science*.[3] A reviewer of Wolfram's book made it clear that not everyone agrees.[4] The truth probably lies in between. It may well turn out that the study of automata is useful for understanding some types of complex behaviors and not others.

11.3. CELLULAR AUTOMATA CAN CREATE COMPLICATED CONSTRUCTIONS

The first example is taken from *A New Kind of Science*. It might be thought of as a design for producing abstract art.

Wolfram considered rules for progressing across a gridlike universe. The agent in this case is a single cell on the grid, which can be either "on" or "off," where these terms refer to a state of the grid, usually its color. The rules for turning a cell on or off over time (or space) are determined by the cell's own state and the state of its immediate neighbors, the cells

---

[2] Emmeche (1994).   [3] Wolfram (2002).   [4] Mitchell (2002).

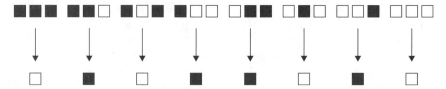

FIGURE 11-1. An example of one of Wolfram's automata, rule 90. The upper row shows eight configurations of the index cell, in the middle, and its two surrounding cells. The second row shows the value of the index cell at the next step.

on its right and left. Call this the *neighborhood* of the cell. Because there are three cells in a neighborhood, the neighborhood itself can be in $2^3 = 8$ different states. Think of the rule for the agent's behavior as a function, and the neighborhood of the state as its input. The function (rule) has a domain of 8 different input states. The value of the function can be either 1 or 0 ("on" or "off") for each of the inputs. Accordingly, there are $2^8 = 256$ possible rules for agent behavior. One of these rules, rule 90 in Wolfram's numbering scheme, is shown in Figure 11-1.

What happens if rule 90 is applied iteratively, 28 times? (The number 28 was chosen solely to fit onto the page.) The rule grows the surprisingly complex structure shown in Figure 11-2. Note that the structure has a self-replicating "fractal" pattern that was not clear from the description of the rule itself.

Why does this happen? Each agent participates in three neighborhoods, its own, in which it is the center cell, and the neighborhoods of the adjacent agents, in which it is either the right- or left-hand cell. The result is that each agent, proceeding using simple rules, influences its own state and those of its neighbors at each step of the process.

Agents that behave in this manner are called *cellular automata*. Wolfram investigated the patterns formed by all of the 256 possible automata defined by three cells. Some of them produced patterns that appeared to him, apparently subjectively, to be "random." (There are statistical tests for randomness in patterns, but Wolfram does not report applying them.) Other patterns had complex structures that differed considerably from the pattern produced by rule 90. To illustrate, Figure 11-3 shows the pattern produced by rule 110.

Wolfram (and several other investigators before him) speculated that (a) any life form can be regarded as a form of computation, and that (b) the computation can be performed by simple automata, working in concert. Scientists who hold this belief argue that explorations along this line will present some deep revelations about life and social patterns.[5]

---

[5] Wolfram's own book (op. cit.) on the topic is immense, albeit quite readable. Emmeche (1994) has produced a more compact discussion of the principles involved, without any mathematical analysis.

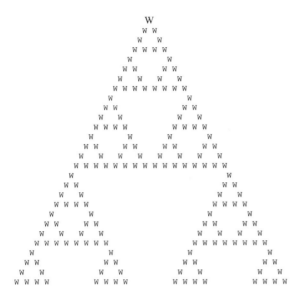

FIGURE 11-2. The structure produced by repeating Wolfram's rule 90 28 times, starting with the large W at the top. "W"s have been used to replace grayed areas for typographical reasons. The pattern has a self-repeating (fractal) structure that was implied by the rule, although the implication is not obvious when the rule is considered alone.

Personally, I must admit to a bit more caution. The various illustrations of how complexity can be derived are fascinating, but I am not ready to assert that these demonstrations go very far toward replacing conventional science. Is this a fad that will fade away, or is it going to make a major contribution to scientific thinking? Stay tuned!

11.4. IS CAPITALISM INHERENTLY UNFAIR?
RECONSTRUCTING A SIMPLE MARKET ECONOMY

Karl Marx said that in an ideal (communist) society, all citizens should contribute to the general wealth according to their abilities, and take from it according to their needs. Free market capitalists claim that this simply will not work. They argue that the only way to motivate people is to reward them for their efforts, including allowing them to invest their capital in a way that will profit them (mostly) and all of us (somewhat). Eduoard Sheverdnadze, the Soviet Union's last foreign minister (and subsequently the president of the Republic of Georgia) said that Marx's ideal was worthy, but that in practice, the Soviet bureaucracy had been unable to make communism work. Capitalism and the free enterprise economy look good, at least on a competitive basis.

```
W
WW
WWW
W WW
WWWWW
W  WW
WW  WWW
WWW W WW
W WWWWWWW
WWW   WW
W WW   WWW
WWWWW  W WW
W  WW WWWWW
WW WWW W  WW
WWW W WWWW  WWW
W WWWWW  WW W WW
WWW  WW WWWWWWWWW
W WW WWWW   WW
WWWWW W  WW    WWW
W  WWWW WWW   W WW
WW W  WWW WW  WWWWW
WWW WW W WWWWW  W  WW
W WWWWWWWW  WW WW  WWW
WWW    WW WWWWWW W WW
W WW   WWW W  WWWWWWW
WWWWW  W WWWW W   WW
W  WW WWW WW WW  WWW
WW WWW  W WW WWW WWW  W WW
```

FIGURE 11-3. The pattern produced by Wolfram's rule 110.

But ... disparity in wealth plagues virtually every free enterprise economy. This can be seen dramatically in the developing countries, where some people do very, very well while the majority of people are grindingly poor. The split seems to occur rather quickly after the free market economy is introduced. The developed states have introduced such mechanisms as progressive income taxation and inheritance taxes at least partly as an attempt to limit gross disparities in wealth.

Some advocates of free market economies argue that disparities in wealth reflect disparities in a variety of talents. Intelligence is not the least of these, and the argument is sometimes called the argument for a meritocracy. The sociologist Linda Gottfredson, psychologists Arthur Jensen and Richard Herrnstein, and the political economist Charles Murray[6] have all observed that there is a positive correlation between indices of intelligence and measures of wealth. These writers believe that the correlation is produced by a causal mechanism: People with high intelligence are said to be better able to manipulate the opportunities of their society; therefore, the disparity in wealth is inevitable and, in some sense, appropriate. Other people, notably the proponents of affirmative action, have argued that no such thing is true. According to them, disparities in wealth arise because some people have a head start, due to

---

[6] Gottfredson (1997); Herrnstein and Murray (1994); Jensen (1998).

initial social privilege, and in particular, access to wealth. From that point on, wealth begets wealth.

This debate will not be settled by computational modeling. Computational modeling does make possible an exercise in microeconomics. We can set up a simple (hypothetical) economy and ask whether or not certain rules of exchange would lead to disparity in wealth, without any assumptions at all about talent or head starts due to inheritance. That is what will be done here.

The model is based on the *yard sale* economic model explored by Brian Hayes in a popular science presentation,[7] which was itself based on some analogies between economics and exchanges of energy between gas molecules. The name "yard sale" is appropriate because the model describes an economy in which N traders meet and swap goods. However, sometimes (randomly) one trader gets the best of the deal. The process is then repeated. Here are the rules:

1. At cycle 0 all N traders have a fixed amount of wealth.
2. At each cycle the traders are randomly paired. Let A and B represent a pair.
3. The traders then each put stakes on the table, equal to the total wealth of the least-wealthy trader. To see the reason for this, consider a poker game where Bill Gates (as of 2006, the second-richest man in the world) and I decide we will wager up to the value of our respective houses. The stakes will never go above the value of my house!

   Let s represent the stakes. Because each person puts up s, the total amount of the transaction is $2s$. Following poker terminology, this will be called the pot.
4. A random number, p, is drawn, ranging from 0 to 1. (I used a uniform distribution in my simulations.)
5. The stakes are then divided, with player A receiving $p \cdot 2s$ from the pot, and player B receiving $(1 - p) \cdot 2s$.
6. The play continues.

What is the expected value of each of these swaps? Let $W_a(t)$ be the wealth of player a on cycle t, while $W_b(t)$ is the wealth of player b. Assume that $W_a(t) \geq W_b(t)$, that is, that player a is at least as wealthy as player b. How wealthy is each player after the swap?

$$E(W_a(t+1)) = (W_a(t) - W_b(t)) + 2p \cdot W_b(t). \qquad (11\text{-}1)$$

---

[7] Hayes (2002b). Hayes, a science writer, makes clear that his model was based on more formal microeconomic modeling done by economists and physicists interested in the economy. I have chosen to use the Hayes version for simplicity of exposition.

The term in parentheses on the right, $(W_a(t) - W_b(t))$, is the amount that player a holds out of the pot; the second term, $2\,W_b(t)$, is the size of the pot; and $2p\cdot W_b(t)$ is player a's expected share of the pot.

The expression for player b is similar, except that b can never hold anything out of the pot. Therefore,

$$E(W_b(t+1)) = 2 \cdot (1 - p) \cdot W_b(t). \tag{11-2}$$

Equations (11-1) and (11-2) refer to the exchange of wealth after p has been determined. What about the *expected wealth*, $E(W_a)$ and $E(W_b)$ that each player could reasonably expect to have as "average winnings" before p has been determined?[8] Since p is the only random variable involved, the two players' expectations are given by the equations, with the expected value of p substituted for p. In a fair game, such as the one in which p is uniformly randomly distributed across the 0–1 interval, $E(p) = .5$. Substituting .5 for p into equations (11-1) and (11-2), we find out that $E(W_a(t+1)) = W_a(t)$ and $E(W_b(t+1)) = W_b(t)$. On the average, each player can expect to retain current wealth, no matter who that player has to deal with.

So, in the long run in this capitalistic society, everyone should be equally wealthy because, as we have assumed at the start, everyone is equally talented (p is not weighted toward any individual). Is that right? No, it is not. Wealth accumulates.

Following Hayes's instructions, I programmed an "economy" to start with just 10 traders and a wealth of 100. Figure 11-4 shows the results after just two cycles. Two or three of the traders seem to be doing pretty well, and a few have less wealth than they began with. Are these temporary aberrations or an omen of things to come?

I then ran the model for an additional 37 cycles, that is, through cycles 3–40. The results are shown in Figure 11-5. There is now a strong concentration of wealth in the hands of one individual, trader 3, who was not the wealthiest trader early in the simulation. Further examination of the figure shows that trader 8, who was a leader after 2 cycles, has virtually no wealth by cycle 40.

One simulation run does not a conclusion make! The simulation contains a random element, the value of p for each trade. It could be that the results in Figure 11-5 (or any other result from just one run of a computer simulation) depend upon the particular random numbers chosen on that run. To take an analogy, suppose that you wanted to find out if a particular coin was "fair" in the sense that it was equally likely to land with the "heads" or "tails" side up. No one would be convinced if you flipped the coin twice and said it was fair only if it landed heads-up

---

[8] See Chapter 2 for a further discussion of the concept of the expectation of a random variable.

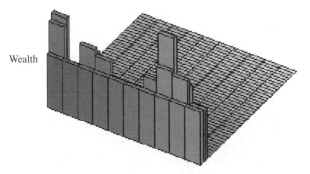

Trader, arbitrarily 1–10

FIGURE 11-4. Distribution of wealth in the yard sale economy over cycle 0–2. The x axis indicates traders, arbitrarily numbered 1–10 from the left. The y axis indicates wealth. The z axis indicates cycle number. Although all traders started with equal wealth at cycle 0, by cycle 2 traders 1, 8, and 9 appear to be amassing more than the average amount of wealth. Traders 3, 4, 6, and 9 also have more wealth than they started with. The remaining traders appear to have "dropped off the screen." In fact, they have less wealth than they started with, and so are "hiding" behind the wall of initial wealth. See, for instance, trader 10. We can "peek around" the wall of initial values to see that trader 10 has lost a small amount of wealth, but is close to where he/she started.

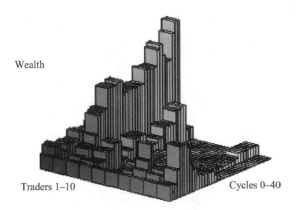

Traders 1–10   Cycles 0–40

FIGURE 11-5. The distribution of wealth over 40 cycles of the yard sale economy. A great deal of the wealth is now in the hands of trader 3, who was not one of the wealthiest traders at cycle 2. In spite of their initially strong start, traders 8 and 9 now have less wealth than they initially had.

once and tails-up once. You would have to flip the coin numerous times, and see if it landed heads-up approximately 50% of the time. The same logic applies to computer simulations whenever the model being tested contains a random element. Numerous simulation runs have to be

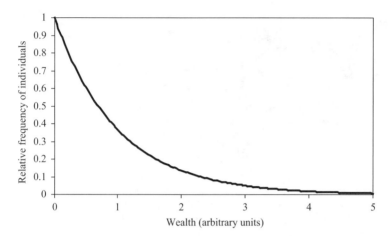

FIGURE 11-6. The relative frequency of individuals possessing more than a certain amount of wealth (in arbitrary units), plotted as a function of wealth.

conducted, to make sure that the results do not depend upon a fortuitous generation of random choices within a particular run.[9]

Hayes did just this. He ran many simulations of the type just described, and then examined how wealth was distributed, on the average, across these simulations. He found that wealth was distributed exponentially, as shown in Figure 11-6. A small number of individuals held a large amount of wealth, many individuals had very little wealth, but, interestingly, there were always some individuals at any level of wealth. In the yard sale economy, there is no break in wealth between the wealthy and the poor; a "middle class" always exists.

How seriously should we take results based on simulations of behavior in an oversimplified economy? Hayes's article evidently struck a raw nerve, for several people wrote to the magazine, *The American Scientist*, protesting. One letter said, and I quote, "This mirrors the rhetoric of reality-challenged left-wing politicians."[10] I rather doubt that this sort of assertion advances understanding. Another objection was more substantive.

Hayes[11] reported that a common objection voiced in both the published (two) and many of the unpublished (number unspecified) letters to the editor was that his model is based on a conservation-of-wealth

---

[9] Computers do not actually generate truly random events. Indeed, it is quite difficult to find an event that is truly random. When a computer program requires a random decision, a number is generated from a sequence of what are called *pseudo-random* sequences. This means that there is very little correlation between the values of any one member of the sequence and the members in front of and behind it. Further restrictions are also required, but going into them would take us too far afield.

[10] Lyman (2002).   [11] Hayes (2002c).

principle. The yard sale economy assumes that the total wealth remains constant; all that happens is a redistribution of it. Most real economies, and especially most capitalist economies, do not preserve wealth. Instead, they create it. To the extent that the new wealth is shared across the entire economy, everyone benefits. As people who defend capitalism point out, in the developed countries people at the bottom of the economic rung, relatively, live quite well by historic standards. While this is emphatically not true of the developing countries, the critics have a point. Many people whom we consider poor today have benefits that, less than a hundred years ago, were provided only to the well-to-do. The critics claim (implicitly or explicitly) that the benefits achieved have largely been the result of investment of capital, and that investment is only possible when some people are rich enough to invest.

Readers who have studied economics will recognize this as a form of the "trickle-down" theory of economics that was espoused by, among others, the Reagan and G. W. Bush administrations. It is true that if the new wealth were distributed equally, everyone's wealth would rise, and the proportional differences would decrease. On the other hand, it could be argued that the assumption of equal distribution is unreal. Capitalists do not invest their money for the public good; they invest it to make more money! If the new wealth were distributed proportionate to investment, there would be no change in proportional inequality, and raw inequality (differences in wealth) would increase even though average wealth might increase.

I do not think that it is useful to present verbal arguments about these results. I (and, for that matter, Hayes) would like to see studies of specific versions of the argument that concentration of capital increases wealth. It would also be useful to explore different assumptions about the relative values of trades. Many current economic models assume that trades are always at exactly the right price, which in the yard sale model means that $p = .5$ in all trades. That seems unrealistic, but letting p have any value from 0 to 1, with equal probability, also seems unrealistic. It might be instructive to explore a model where the value of p varies, but small deviations from .5 are more likely than large deviations.

11.5. RESIDENTIAL SEGREGATION, GENOCIDE, AND THE USEFULNESS OF THE POLICE

In many societies, including our own, sub-groups tend to cluster together. We have "Chinatown," "Little Italy," and many other ethnically homogeneous residential areas. Because passions on this topic can run high, it is a good idea to begin by defining our terms.

Historically, many societies adopted legal sanctions to ensure that like lived with like. To take an extreme, during the Middle Ages the Jewish quarter in the Spanish city of Segovia was literally walled off from the rest of the city. Bringing things closer to home, until the 1950s some American residential deeds had "covenants" attached to them forbidding titleholders to sell to certain racial or ethnic groups. (In the 1950s these covenants were ruled to be illegal.) I think I am correct in saying that no developed country today enforces such rules. Therefore we will not be concerned with them.

What is more difficult to explain is a *pattern of segregation*, in which members of each sub-group in the society cluster together, in the absence of any overt regulations forcing them to do so. It is often claimed that this is because of hidden discrimination, such as realtors being reluctant to show real estate to members of one group. What else could account for segregation?

In an interesting article on cellular automata that appeared, in all places, in the *Atlantic Monthly*, a magazine more known for its literary and social essays than for its mathematics, J. Rauch[12] showed that residential segregation could be produced by a model that assumed only that each person in a sub-group wants to have at least k of their N closest neighbors be from the same group. In other words, people are not prejudiced but do not want to be too isolated. Rauch then presented the results of a computer simulation showing how this minimal assumption of in-group pressure could produce a pattern of residential segregation.

Rauch's work was based on earlier work by the economist Thomas Schelling. Here I will present a formal analysis of Rauch's model, give an example, and then comment on the meaning of the work.

Let a residential area be defined by an $N \times N$ grid, and assume that the grid "wraps around" so that the left edge is considered to be adjacent to the right edge, and the top edge adjacent to the bottom edge. Each cell in the grid represents a residence. Therefore, every residence has eight neighboring residences, as shown in Figure 11-7. We assume that the individual residing in a cell wants at least $k < 8$ of his or her neighbors to be of the same ethnic group. In the case of an unprejudiced individual, one might expect that this person wants $k/8$ to approximate the relative frequency of his or her own group in the population. For example, in the United States, and considering only two groups, "African Americans and Latinos" and "the rest," k would be 2 for African Americans and Latinos, and 6 for the rest, because just under 25% of the population is either African American or Latino (or both).

Rausch only considered the case for two equal-sized groups. He further simplified by considering only the 4 neighbors to the right, left, and up and

---

[12] Rausch (2002). As in the case of the yard sale economy, I have chosen to present Rausch's model, rather than the original work of Schelling and others, in the interests of clarity and explanation.

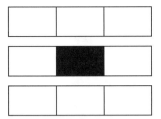

FIGURE 11-7. In a grid neighborhood, each cell has eight immediate neighbors. In Rauch's model, the only assumption made is that the inhabitant of the index cell (shown in black) wants k of the neighboring cells to be occupied by members of the same group.

down. I wrote a simulation extending the model to the more general case of 8 neighbors, while retaining the idea of equal-sized groups.

Here are the rules in my simulation:

1. Begin with each cell occupied, with probability $p = .5$ (equal groups) by a member from group 1. Members of group 2 occupy the remaining cells.
2. For each cell, determine whether or not the occupant is satisfied or dissatisfied. The occupant is satisfied if no more than $8 - k$ of the neighboring cells are occupied by members of the other group. In the examples reported here $k = 4$, saying that no member of a group wants to be in a minority locally.
3. If the occupant is satisfied, do nothing. If the occupant is dissatisfied, pick a cell at random and exchange the two occupants. Mark both occupants as satisfied immediately after the trade.
4. Repeat steps 2 and 3 for c cycles.

The results can be quite striking. The upper panel of Figure 11-8 shows the initial state of the matrix. Groups of 1s and 2s are scattered about. The lower panel of the figure shows the state of segregation after 50 runs of the simulation, starting from the random placement required by step 1. There is now a sharp demarcation of the region into two regions, each occupied by a different group.

To trace the development of segregation, I defined a "homogeneity index":

$$H = \left(\frac{1}{8 \times N}\right) \sum_i k(i), \tag{11-3}$$

where $k(i)$ is the number of same-group neighbors surrounding the ith cell, and N is the total number of cells (100 in my simulation). This index ranges from 0 to 1, with 1 representing the case where only same-group

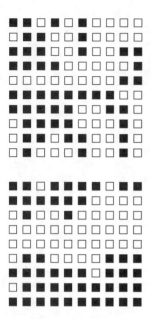

FIGURE 11-8. The results of application of the rules of the segregation model. The upper panel shows the distribution of 43 Group 1 (black) and 57 Group 2 (white) cells randomly distributed over the grid. The lower panel shows the distribution after 50 cycles of the segregation model. The Group 1 cells now approximate a cluster inside Group 2 cells.

members surround each cell. This condition cannot be obtained because there has to be a boundary between groups. In the case of equal-sized groups, the expected value of the homogeneity index for randomly distributed group members is .5.

Figure 11-9 shows values of the homogeneity index across 50 cycles. The pattern is typical of others that I have observed. The index rises rapidly, and then fluctuates around a stable value considerably above the expected value for a random distribution. This indicates that the segregated pattern develops rather quickly. The pattern appears even though (a) each simulated resident only wants not to be in a minority in his or her local neighborhood, and (b) when a simulated resident is moved the next location is picked randomly.

Rausch only considered the case in which there were two groups of equal size. I obtained a bit of additional insight by examining the case in which there is a majority and minority group, with 3 majority group members for every minority member. As before, I started with a random configuration of majority and minority group members. A segregated pattern did appear, but it took considerably longer than in the equal-groups case.

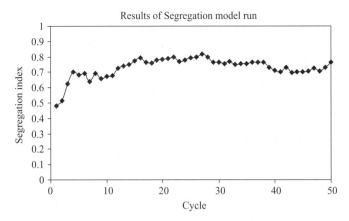

FIGURE 11-9. Changes in the homogeneity index over time in the residential seg-
regation model. The case shown is for the simulation demonstrated in Figure 11-8.
Although the segregated pattern appears, the index does not rise to a maximum.
The average value across cycles 21–50 is .752.

The way that the pattern appeared was interesting. Most of the majority
residents met the satisfaction criterion most of the time. Minority group
members found themselves isolated and moved a good deal. The reason
that it took so long for the segregated pattern to appear is that moves are
random, and so there is a high chance that a minority resident, dissatisfied
with one location, will move to another that is also dissatisfying. If I were
to have programmed a strategy in which a dissatisfied group member
actively sought out other members of the same group the segregated
pattern would have appeared much more rapidly.

Moving outside of the mathematics, it strikes me that in the case
of unequal-sized groups, Rausch's model is more a model of self-
segregation than enforced segregation, or majority "flight." As such, I am
not sure that it applies to residential segregation. But what about the
clustering of ethnic groups that is sometimes noticed in cafeterias,
auditoriums, and other public places?

Rausch also proposed a simulation of a more extreme form of segregation. Suppose that a simulated resident can become dissatisfied to the
point of becoming homicidal! More formally, consider a group 1 member
resident at a particular cell. Assume further that at least one of the eight
contiguous cells is occupied by a member of group 2. In Rausch's
"genocide" simulation, at each cycle the group 1 member, with some
probability, destroyed the group 2 member, who was then removed from
the board. The probability of destruction will be called the *tension*
parameter. The same rules applied for the chances that a group
2 member became homicidal and removed a group 1 member.

Three things determined the probability of destruction: the overall level of tension; the number of group 1 and 2 members in the immediate vicinity – so that a group 1 member was more likely to be "assassinated" if surrounded by group 2 members; and the presence, in the immediate neighborhood, of a third group, C, for C(ops). Group C cells would temporarily inactivate ("put in jail," in Rausch's terms) any group 1 or 2 cell that reached the level of trying to eliminate a cell in another group. This was a local effect; group C cells only controlled those cells contiguous to them. In addition, cells could move if they reached the dissatisfaction criterion.

Rausch gave one example of this pattern and made a few general remarks. If group 1 and 2 were equal in size, segregated regions developed with blank spaces between them. If one group was larger in size than the other, the final result depended upon the number of C cells. In some simulations, the smaller group clustered together but was then destroyed. In others, the smaller group clusters were ringed by C cells that acted as protectors.

As was appropriate considering the journal in which he was writing, Rausch did not give a great deal of detail about the exact rules used in his genocide simulations. Therefore, I have been unable to examine them in any detail. Subsequently, one of my students did develop a simulation of this sort and found a variety of "genocidal" patterns other than those reported by Rausch, although Rausch's patterns were also found.

11.6. IS THIS A NEW KIND OF SCIENCE?

Let's look more closely at Wolfram's claim that this is a "new type of science." The automata models fit the general scientific strategy of hypothesis, followed by deduction. However there is a difference. Newton and Einstein set forth a few principles, and then applied formal algebraic methods to solve them. Newton had to invent a new branch of mathematics, the calculus, in order to do this, but that is a side issue. The important point is that the implications of a few principles were worked out. This method has dominated the physical sciences ever since, and has been amazingly successful. The technique has had less success in the biological and social sciences, where there is more reliance on description than deduction, but the technique is certainly not unknown.

The difference between models based on cellular automata, or upon simple interactions in a microworld, and classic mathematical modeling is that the newer models rely upon computation, rather than explicit algebraic analysis. When computation is applied to a deterministic model, as in the case of Wolfram's (and other) analyses of cellular automata, the computer is not just being used as a fast, accurate, but rather dumb clerk. The act of programming focuses attention upon the process being studied in a dramatic way.

There is an interesting example of this, teaching introductory physics. Physics is traditionally taught in abstract, algebraic form, accompanied by a few demonstrations. Anyone who doubts this is invited to look at one of the summary notebooks published for student review. Perhaps as a result, both teachers and students regard introductory physics as an exceptionally difficult course at both the high school and college level. Andrea DiSessa, a professor at the University of California, Berkeley, developed a different approach.[13] Students were taught to program the movement of "objects" (actually, graphic symbols on a computer screen) in a microworld that obeyed Newton's laws of motion. Prof. John Frederiksen, of the school of education at the University of Washington, has developed a similar program. According to DiSessa, sixth graders instructed in this fashion were able to learn material normally associated with the eleventh and twelfth grade, and beyond.

DiSessa has speculated that the concepts of computation will eventually come to be the basis of our understanding in science, replacing more abstract algebraic models. He further suggests that this breakthrough may result in as profound an increment in our ability to think about scientific topics as the development of algebra did. It is an interesting idea. To the extent that DiSessa is right, the simulation of microworlds will be an increasingly common mechanism for developing theories in all the sciences. The idea is especially interesting when it is applied to the behavioral, biological, and social sciences, where mathematical modeling has been much less successful than it has been in the physical sciences.

Although Wolfram's models and DiSessa's microworlds deal with very different phenomena there is a sense in which they are similar. In both cases the final product, the behavior of the microworld as a whole, is determined by the interaction between agents within the microworld being studied. Furthermore, these interactions are simple and understandable, taken alone. Wolfram's pattern-generation rules are easy to state, and DiSessa's rules for interactions are simply the well-understood mechanical reactions of Newtonian physics. The computer, acting as a very fast, accurate, but unimaginative assistant, works out the implications of all the simultaneous interactions among many agents.

This logic was made explicit in the "parable of the ant," introduced by Herbert Simon, one of the pioneers in the development of computer programs that simulate human thought. Simon asked us to consider the path of an ant, walking across a sandy, grassy area near a beach. The ant's path would be erratic and tortuous, and generally would seem impossible to describe mathematically. Further study of the ant itself would show that the animal obeyed very simple rules about when to go

---

[13] DiSessa (2000).

forward, backward, right, or left when confronted with an obstacle. The complexity of the path was the product of a simple ant, interacting with easily describable obstacles, such as pebbles or trickles of water. The complexity did not come from the agents; it came from their interactions.[14]

In one aspect, Wolfram is certainly correct. This kind of science, new or not, would not be feasible without computers because we would be unable to work out the implications of the interactions between agents. With computers, we can solve problems that would have boggled our minds if we were to attempt to deal with them by paper and pencil.

Having said that, let us look again at the deterministic-stochastic distinction made at the start of the chapter. In those terms, Wolfram's models are deterministic, while the yard sale economy and residential segregation models are stochastic. Does it make any difference?

There is a sense in which any probabilistic model is an expression of ignorance. When two individuals bargain they do not flip coins to determine who will get the best of the deal. People do not decide to move their residences by rolling dice. For that matter, if you flip a coin, whether it lands heads or tails is not determined randomly. The event depends upon the angle at which the coin is held, the torque imparted by your fingers when you toss the coin, the distance to the floor, and myriad other factors. Nevertheless, from the viewpoint of an outside observer (a model maker?), when many coins are tossed a model that appeals to randomness will do a very good job of estimating how many of them come up heads.

Observers of social phenomena are not able to specify all the forces that act upon each individual in a society. It is unlikely that they will be able to do so in the foreseeable future. Therefore models containing some appeal to randomness will be required for a long time to come. I believe that their study will often be quite revealing, for they tell us how likely it is that certain patterns of behavior will be observed, at the macroscopic level, even though we cannot explain in detail what led individual agents to act at the microscopic level.

---

[14] Simon (1981).

12

Connectionism

Computation Connects Mind and Brain

12.1. THE BRAIN AND THE MIND

The mind is the product of the brain. Modern scientists are convinced that all the thoughts in our mind can, somehow, be reduced to physical actions in the brain. Alas, the "somehow" is important. We don't know just how the brain does it. What we think we know, though, is that computational modeling will help. To understand why we have to take a quick look at brains and neurons as physical devices.

The human brain is composed of about 5 billion ($5 \cdot 10^9$) nerve cells, or *neurons*. Neurons are organized into many different functional areas, and the areas into sub-areas. The neurons themselves serve as computing and communication elements, so that you can think of "cables" of neurons transmitting signals from one region of the brain to another. A good example is the optic tract, which transmits signals from the retina of the eye (which is anatomically a part of the brain) to the *primary visual cortex*, which is located in the occipital region, at the back of the brain. However, you are not aware of a scene just because there is activity in the primary visual cortex. What happens next is much more complicated than we want to go into here. Suffice it to say that a tremendous amount of computing, editing, and even inferential reasoning goes on before perception occurs. The "pixel level" picture on the retina gets taken apart, augmented, interpreted, and put back together before you are aware of anything.

We probably know more about the neural basis of vision than we know about any other cognitive system. However, the general remarks about neural computing that apply to vision can also be said about memory, attention, olfaction, touch, hearing, and even emotional arousal. It is all in the neurons, but that is like saying that computing is all in the transistors, resistors, and diodes. We have to give more details.

Progress in modern neuroscience has been facilitated by two huge technical developments. One is the staggering advance in our ability to observe the brain. We can now locate regions of activity in the brain while a person is thinking about something, without penetrating the skull. When it is possible and ethical to plant recording and stimulating devices directly on the brain, we are able to record from individual neurons.[1] As a result, neuroscientists can watch activity rise and fall in different parts of the brain, as people do different cognitive and behavioral activities. For instance, we can look at the difference in activity when a person is asked either to read a word and do nothing else or to read a word and think of a semantic associate, as in "read hammer, think nail."

The advances in brain observations are so well known that terms like "MRI" (magnetic resonance imaging) have dictionary definitions. A second, less publicized advance is the increase in our knowledge of the role of brain chemicals. To understand this, we have to understand a bit about how neurons send signals to each other.

In electrical circuits signals are transmitted directly, in the sense that electricity actually "flows" from one element to another. Neuron-to-neuron transmission is quite a bit more complicated. Neurons are not attached to each other. Instead, they sit very close to (impinge upon) each other, so that chemicals generated by one neuron can be taken up by another. When a neuron is *internally* electrically active it deposits chemicals, called *neurotransmitters*, near the neurons on which it impinges. The neurotransmitters are taken up by the impinged-upon neurons, and if enough neurotransmitters are taken up, the second neuron becomes electrically active.

There are several types of neurotransmitters. This means that neural circuits that are anatomically close to each other may be chemically isolated. We also know that some neurotransmitters facilitate and some inhibit activity in the receiving neuron. And just to make some things more complicated, we also know that some neurotransmitters do not act directly, but rather modulate (increase or decrease) the effectiveness of the facilitating and inhibiting neurotransmitters.

Knowledge of the neurotransmitters has tremendous importance in medicine. Certain gross disorders of the brain can be traced to disruption in the chemical neurotransmission process. This has led to chemical and pharmaceutical therapies for a number of mental conditions. To name

---

[1] Obviously, it would be unethical to expose the brain solely for research purposes. On the other hand, there are situations in which the brain has to be exposed in order to remove tumors or to locate and neutralize a center that is producing epileptic seizures. During such operations it is both appropriate and medically necessary to record the activity of individual neurons, in order to guide the surgical procedure. The information gathered during these medically necessary operations has told neuroscientists a good bit about how the brain works.

only a few, Parkinson's disease, schizophrenia, manic-depressive psychosis, attention deficit disorder, and severe depression are all treated pharmacologically today.

Summing up in a somewhat irreverent manner, we know (or are well on the way to finding out) *where* in the brain things happen when we think, and *what chemical systems* are involved. What we do not know is how the various neural centers achieve their computations, or even what those computations are.

This is where computer simulation comes in. The individual neuron is a very limited computing device. Thought must depend upon the patterns of activity of hundreds, or even thousands and hundreds of thousands, of neurons. It is not possible to understand how these patterns evolve by tracing out the connections of individual neurons to each other. This is hardly feasible, for with approximately 5 billion neurons in the brain, there are 25 billion billion (25×10^{18}) potential connections between neurons. Suppose that all the neuron-to-neuron connections could be drawn on a map. Could anyone understand the map? I doubt it. An alternative that has been taken is to develop computational techniques for studying the sorts of functions that can be computed by abstract networks of idealized neurons.

This effort is known as *connectionism*. It started out as an exercise in showing how networks of "neuron-like" elements could mimic mental functioning. While we certainly do not understand how the brain computes all the thoughts people have, there has been a good deal of progress in understanding some types of thought. As a non-trivial side benefit, research in connectionism has churned out some useful devices. These include automated handwriting analysis (as is done in your personal digital assistant), voice recognition software, and a computerized driver for an autonomous motor vehicle. For some perverse reason, when connectionist computing is used as an engineering tool the technique is often referred to as *neural network* computation, even though the computer science and engineering applications may use algorithms that pretty well destroy the analogy to the nervous system.

This chapter presents the basic principles of connectionist computing. Only a few of the many possible examples will be given. Because the purpose of this book is to illustrate the use of mathematics in the behavioral and social sciences, we will focus on applications in those areas, rather than in biology or engineering. We will also ignore the use of connectionist networks as alternatives to conventional statistics.

12.2. COMPUTATION AT THE NEURAL LEVEL

The first step in understanding connectionism is to understand computation at the level of the neuron. Figure 12-1 shows a cartoon drawing of

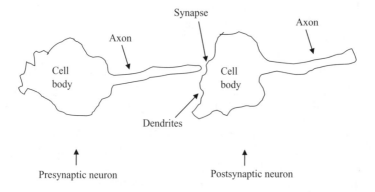

FIGURE 12-1. A rough drawing of two neurons and the connection between them. The neuron consists of a *cell body*, short projections called *dendrites*, and a single long branch called the *axon*. The *synaptic cleft* is the small region between the axon of the *presynaptic* neuron and a dendrite or cell body of the *postsynaptic* neuron. An axon from a presynaptic cell typically impinges on many postsynaptic neurons. Similarly, the typical postsynaptic neuron receives input from many presynaptic neurons.

two neurons. The small space between them is called the *synaptic cleft*. The cell to the left of the synaptic cleft is the *presynaptic neuron* and the cell to the right is the *postsynaptic neuron*.

The gross actions of a neuron are easy to summarize. Metabolic processes within the cell body of the presynaptic neuron produce an electrical discharge along the axon. This discharge is always of a constant voltage, and travels like a wave along the axon. The electrical activity in the axon triggers release of chemicals (neurotransmitters) into the synaptic cleft. The transmitters are then bound to receptors in the postsynaptic neuron. When sufficient neurotransmitters are bound the postsynaptic neuron will discharge its axon, thus contributing to the firing of other neurons.

After a neuron has discharged there is a refractory period of about one millisecond, during which it cannot be fired again. Sensitivity then returns gradually, so the rate of firing will be determined by the quantity of neurotransmitters in the cleft, along with some other factors that are too complicated to explain here. Therefore, the presence of electrical activity in the axon of the postsynaptic cell is only a crude indicator of activity at the synapse. On the other hand, the frequency of pulses in the postsynaptic neuron does provide a reasonable indicator of the amount of presynaptic activity over a brief period of time.

Synaptic connections vary in their efficiency. This appears to be due to changes in the membrane of the postsynaptic neuron. The effect of these changes is to make the synaptic connections between two neurons more efficient if firing in the presynaptic cell is followed by a discharge in the postsynaptic cell. These changes are believed to be the basis of learning at the cellular level.[2]

Connectionist models capture these ideas in an idealized mathematical model of the neuron. We may think of the connections between neurons as defining a mathematical network, that is, a set of N nodes. We also think of time as being quantized, $t = 1, 2, \ldots$, which is clearly an idealization, as we doubt that the nervous system has a mechanism for calling cadence. Let $X(t) = \{x_i\}$ be the set of levels of activity of each of the N nodes, and let w_{ij} be the weight of the connection from node i into node j. The $x_i(t)$ and w_{ij} terms correspond, in a rough way, to the level of activity in the axons and the efficiency of synaptic transmission between neurons i and j.

The weights can be arranged in a matrix, $W = [w_{ij}]$, where

$w_{ij} > 0$ indicates that activity in node i at time t facilitates
activity in j at time $t + 1$

$w_{ij} = 0$ indicates that the two nodes are not connected (12-1)

$w_{ij} < 0$ indicates that activity in node i at time t inhibits
activity in j at time $t + 1$.

The matrix W defines the *network architecture*. This is shown in Figure 12-2 for a simple case where all weights are either 1 (facilitating), -1 (inhibiting), or 0 (unconnected).

Examining Figure 12-2, we see that nodes can be classified into two groups. The *input nodes* (1 and 2, on the left) receive input from some external source. The *output nodes* (3 and 4 on the right) send signals outside of the network. This network does not contain a third class of nodes, *hidden nodes*, which send and receive signals within the network. The role of hidden nodes is discussed subsequently.

To complete the argument we must specify a function that determines activity in an individual neuron as a function of the immediately preceding activity in the network as a whole:

$$x_i(t) = f(X(t-1), W), (12-2)$$

where $X(t-1)$ is the set of node activation levels at time t-1 and W is the connection matrix.

It is useful to define this function in two steps. The weighted inputs from different nodes are assumed to summate. Therefore, the total input

[2] LeDoux (2002).

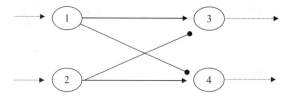

$$W = \begin{bmatrix} 0,0,1{-}1 \\ 0,0{-}1,1 \\ 0,0,0,0 \\ 0,0,0,0 \end{bmatrix}$$

FIGURE 12-2. The upper part shows a network of four nodes. The left-hand nodes are *input* nodes, which receive input (dotted arrows) external to the network. The right-hand nodes are *output* nodes, because their output is directed outside the network. On the diagram, an arrow indicates a facilitory connection, and a line ending in a dot indicates an inhibitory connection. The connections can be specified in the weight matrix, W, shown below the network.

to the jth node at time t is

$$\eta_j(t) = \sum_i w_{ij}x_i(t). \tag{12-3}$$

The *activation function* for a node is the function that relates the weighted input to the output. In general, any function that is non-decreasing in its input could be considered a plausible activation function. In practice, though, only a few have been used. One of the commonest is the *threshold function*,

$$x_i(t) = 1 \text{ if } \eta_i(t) > \theta_i, \text{ 0 otherwise.} \tag{12-4}$$

There is a strong analogy between this function and plausible models of neural activity, providing that we interpret "activity" as referring to a pulse of electricity going down the axon.

An alternative function reflects the idea that an output unit should reflect the magnitude of its input over some range, but that activity should not increase without bounds. A popular way of capturing this idea is to use the *logistic* activation function, which is

$$x_i(t) = \frac{1}{1 + e^{-(\eta_i(t) - \beta_i)}}, \tag{12-5}$$

where β_i is a biasing constant somewhat analogous to a threshold. This equation is not appealing in its algebraic form, but when it is graphed, one can see that it does capture the idea of a transition from inactivity to partial, and then maximum, activity. This is done in Figure 12-3. As the

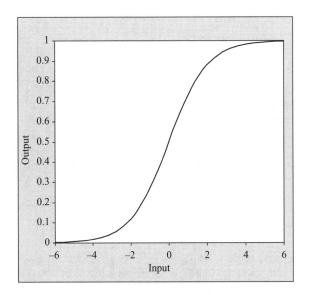

FIGURE 12-3. The logistic activation function with a threshold of zero.

figure makes obvious, low inputs receive virtually no response, then for a while the response is nearly a linear function of the input, and finally the response level approaches a maximum, and only responds minimally to further increases in input.

12.3. COMPUTATIONS AT THE NETWORK LEVEL

We now shift our focus from what functions neurons can compute to what functions networks can compute. In the context of connectionism, a function is a mapping from the set of possible input vectors to the set of possible output vectors. Look back at Figure 12-2, and assume that the nodes have threshold activation functions with a threshold of .01 at each node. The network maps from the four possible input vectors to three possible output vectors. The mapping is

$$
\begin{aligned}
(0,0) &\rightarrow (0,0) \\
(1,0) &\rightarrow (1,0) \\
(0,1) &\rightarrow (0,1) \\
(1,1) &\rightarrow (0,0).
\end{aligned}
\tag{12-6}
$$

Now consider an observer who only knows what the output vector is. If just one of the input nodes was activated, the observer could tell which one it was. However, the observer could not discriminate between the input vectors (0,0) and (1,1).

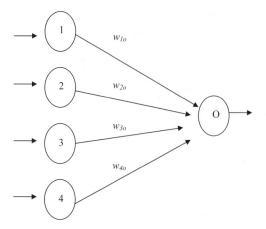

FIGURE 12-4. A connectionist network with one input layer, with the output from the input layers all directed to a single output unit. This is sometimes called a perceptron. The term is used for any two-layer network with input nodes activating one or more output nodes.

To extend this argument, when threshold activation functions are used each output vector acts as a classifier. Suppose that there were many input nodes and only a single output node. This configuration is sometimes referred to as a *perceptron*. The network architecture is shown in Figure 12-4, with input nodes labeled 1...4 (but could be 1 to any large number) and an output vector labeled 0. Instead of showing the weight matrix, I have labeled the arcs from input to output. This network classifies all possible input configurations into inputs that produce a 0 or 1 output.

Classification is important, for a great deal of human thought is based on our ability to classify things as being of a particular type, and then reacting to the type, rather than to the (possibly novel) object at hand. For instance, we can classify a strange animal as a *dog* (or a *skunk*) and react appropriately. Much of connectionist research can be thought of as exploring how (idealized) neural networks can learn and utilize classifications.

The output units of two-layer networks using threshold activation functions, such as Figure 12-4, have a limited ability to classify. If the output node uses a threshold activation function, all that an observer of the output can tell about the input is that a weighted sum of the inputs, $\Sigma_{i=1} w_{io} x_i$, exceeds some threshold value, β_0. If a continuous activation function such as the logistic function (equation [12-5]) is used, the output unit can, in a sense, compute an infinite set of linear classifications, because each value of the output unit indicates that the sum of the inputs to it has exceeded a given amount. Nevertheless, all these functions are linear. What each individual output unit, o, tells the observer is that $\Sigma_i w_{io} x_i$ exceeded or did not exceed some value. The observer has no way of knowing how that sum was composed.[3]

Linear classification is not trivial, for many of the classification problems we face "in the real world" are linear classifications. To take an example discussed earlier, in the context of testing, most university admissions programs give applicants points for having a variety of properties, including good high school grades, high SAT scores, attendance at a high school with a good academic program, involvement in extracurricular activities, and so forth. Applicants are admitted if their point score exceeds a cut point. This is a linear classification scheme, for it does not matter how the applicant got his or her points, just as long as the applicant has enough of them.

Take a moment and think about some other real-life problems that can be treated as linear classification. This should be fairly easy to do. Now, try to think of a few problems that cannot be treated as a linear classification system. This is harder, but it can be done.

The fact that a two-layer network is restricted to linear classification places an important restriction on what a network, as a whole, can do. To understand why, we have to remind ourselves what a digital computer is.

In the theory of computation, a digital computer is (conceptually) a universal Turing machine, which means that, if we disregard practical limits of time and space, a digital computer can be programmed to compute any computable function. At the same time, a computer is "nothing more than" a large device for computing logical functions. The five fundamental logical operations are NOT, AND, OR, IMPLIES, and exclusive or (XOR). The double implication condition, IF AND ONLY IF, is sometimes included in this list, but it is the negation of XOR.

Now consider a perceptron with two inputs, which would be a reduced version of Figure 12-4, with two binary input units; call them x and y. Because the inputs are binary, we can think of them as taking on the values 1, for TRUE, and 0, for FALSE. Which of the five binary logical operators can be computed by such a perceptron?

The unary operator NOT(x) can be implemented by the simple circuit shown in Figure 12-5, by letting the output (right-hand) node have a threshold value less than zero. AND and OR are easily implemented by appropriate weights in the three-unit (two inputs, one output) networks shown in Figure 12-6. As an exercise, try your hand at finding

---

[3] The careful reader may want to object at this point, because the example of Figure 12-4 does appear to contain a non-linear classification. The reason for the apparent paradox is that the example combines two output units. Each of these outputs units, alone, are linear classifiers. The pair of outputs, taken together, can produce a non-linear classification, as they do in the figure.

FIGURE 12-5. A connectionist network that can implement logical negation. Let each unit have a threshold activation function, and set the input unit to 0 or 1. The output unit has a threshold less than zero. If the input unit has value 0, the output value will be 1; if the input unit has value 1, the output value will be 0.

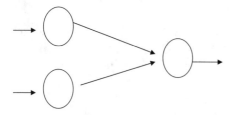

FIGURE 12-6. This simple connectionist network, with appropriate arrangements of weights and threshold values, can compute the logical functions AND, OR, and IMPLIES.

appropriate weights. It is pretty easy to do so. (Implication is a bit tricky, but the problem is solvable.)

What has just been shown is that the logical connectives NOT, AND, OR, and IMPLIES can all be expressed as linear classifications, and hence can be realized in a connectionist system.

The XOR function, "X or Y but not both," is translated to the statement about the inputs, "$x=1$ or $y=1$ but not both." There is no way that weights and a threshold value can be chosen so that the expression "$w_{xo} + w_{yo} > \beta$" is true if and only if "$x=1$ or $y=1$ but not both" is true. Two-layer connectionist systems cannot compute XOR. This is an important limitation, for the XOR computation (and its negation, IF AND ONLY IF) are required in order to compute certain functions.

To bring the discussion back to the social and behavioral sciences, consider the concept of symmetry. Humans are extremely good at distinguishing between symmetric and non-symmetric visual patterns. But symmetry is a form of the IF AND ONLY IF relation, the negation of XOR. A pattern is symmetric if and only if the sub-pattern on one side of an axis of symmetry is identical to the sub-pattern on the other side. Therefore, symmetry cannot be detected by a two-layer connectionist network, making such networks inadequate models of human visual perception.

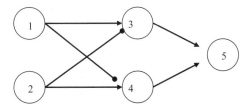

FIGURE 12-7. A connectionist network that computes XOR. The input units (1 and 2) take values 0 or 1. All other use a threshold function with a threshold of .99. Therefore, a node will be activated if and only if the sum of its inputs reaches 1. All links have a weight of either 1 or -1, indicated by arrows or circles impinging on the receiving unit. If just one of the two input units (1 and 2) has value 1, either hidden node 3 or 4 will take value 1. If either 3 or 4 has value 1, the output unit, 5, will have value 1. However, if both 1 and 2 are active, 1 inhibits hidden unit 4 and 2 inhibits hidden unit 3, and so that unit 5 does not receive input and takes value 0. If units 1 and 2 both have value 0, there is no activity in the network, and so unit 5 has value 0.

The XOR problem can be solved by networks with three layers of nodes. Figure 12-7 shows one solution. The middle layer, which has no direct connections to input or output, is called the *hidden layer*, and a node within it is called a *hidden node* or *hidden unit*. The required computations are explained in the figure caption.

This demonstration shows that connectionist networks can compute XOR. Since it has already been shown that a connectionist unit can compute NOT, it is possible to arrange a connectionist network that is a logical combination of XOR and NOT circuits. This is an important result, for one of the basic findings in the theory of computation is that any computable function can be expressed by an appropriate combination of XOR and NOT functions.[4] Therefore any computable function can be computed by some connectionist network, providing that hidden nodes are allowed.

This does not mean that any connectionist network can compute any computable function! Nor does the theorem state how many nodes the network must contain. Once one introduces a limit on the number of nodes or a restriction on the architecture, the number of functions that can be computed drops drastically. This brings us to an important philosophical aside.

12.4. A PHILOSOPHICAL ASIDE

The aside refers to the concepts of Turing machines and computability, and so it may not make much sense to people who are not familiar with

---

[4] This is the theoretical basis for reduced instruction set computing, or RISC, as is found in some computers today.

these ideas. However, these ideas are increasingly widespread. I want to make these remarks for the sake of completeness.

Suppose that it is observed that people make a particular classification. This could vary from being able to recognize an object as being the same object, when seen from different perspectives, to being able to classify dogs into groups named St. Bernard, German shepherd, collie, and so forth. Some of our most complex computations deal with language. Native speakers can classify word strings as being well-formed or ill-formed sentences. Can connectionist networks model such behavior?

The answer "of course they can" is true, but in a vacuous sense. A classification is equivalent to a function, and a connectionist network can be constructed to compute any function that can be computed by a Universal Turing Machine. A more interesting question is whether or not the function in question, which we know people compute, can be computed by a network whose architecture reflects what we know about interactions between different areas of the brain. The more we learn about the brain's functioning as a physical device, the more we are able to constrain the set of plausible connectionist models of psychological phenomena.

My argument depends upon the identity between functions that Turing machines compute and functions that connectionist networks compute. But aren't there functions that Turing machines (and computers, and connectionist networks) cannot compute? And doesn't this mean that neither the computers nor the networks are powerful enough to model human thought? The answers to these questions are "Yes" and "No."

Yes, there are functions that can be defined but cannot be computed, in the sense that a Turing machine computes functions. There is no proof that a human can compute these functions either. Arguments based on intuition and common sense miss the point, for computability here is being defined as, in psychological terms, some stimulus $->$ response mapping. It does not depend upon a person's being able to report why he or she made a response, just upon its being made.

To get a flavor of what is being said, let us look at an undecidable question, which is just another way of saying an incomputable function. No program or connectionist network can be constructed to answer this question, which was put somewhat picturesquely in a Russian book about set theory and computation:[5]

In the days of the Tsar, a certain regimental commander issued the following order: All men in the regiment are to shave. All men who do not shave

---

[5] Vilenkin (1965/1968).

themselves are to be shaved by the regimental barber. The barber must not shave anyone who shaves himself.

Should the barber shave himself?

Can you answer the question? Is there any logical computation that can deal with this question?

12.5. CONNECTIONIST ARCHITECTURES

The simple networks described so far demonstrate that computing modules can be used to construct connectionist networks. The modules themselves do something, but not much. Complicated behavior occurs when the modules are combined in more complicated ways. The form of the combination is called the *network architecture*. Figure 12-8 shows three basic types of architectures. We consider briefly the capabilities of each one.

Network (a) in Figure 12-8 is a *feed-forward* network. In these networks activation of the input leads to activation of the hidden units, which in turn leads to activation of the output units. As has been shown, three-layer, feed-forward systems, if sufficiently complicated in the hidden

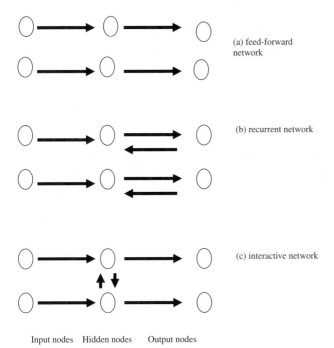

Input nodes   Hidden nodes   Output nodes

FIGURE 12-8. The three basic types of connectionist networks.

layer, can compute any desired mapping from an input vector to an output vector.

Network (b) in Figure 12-8 is a *recurrent network*. In recurrent networks activation may be passed forward or backward. Using a biological analogy, we may think of the state of the input units as the information sensed from the environment, the hidden units as a representation of that information, and the output units as a decision based upon the representation. A recurrent network has a "memory" in the following sense. At any time, t, the hidden units will contain information from the environment, as it existed at time t, and the decision that was made at time $t - 1$. Therefore the hidden units can interpret (more correctly, perform computations on) information about the current state of the environment and the system's interpretation of previous states of the environment.

Networks with recurrent features have been used to build natural language understanding systems. The memory property allows a network to interpret a word differently depending upon the context in which it occurs. The problem is illustrated by the following sentences:

John decided to win the <u>race</u>.
John decided to <u>race</u> to win.

where <u>race</u> is first a noun and then a verb. In the example, the article <u>the</u> must be followed by an adjective or noun, while <u>to</u> is a preposition that can be followed immediately by a verb. A network for interpreting words, presented one at a time, could use recurrent activation to distinguish between <u>race</u> following an article and <u>race</u> following a preposition.

Panel (c) of Figure 12-8 shows the architecture of an *interactive* network. This network now has a memory more than one item back. In fact, the interactive network potentially has an "infinite" memory. (Look back at activation levels and think about nodes that feed into themselves. You should see how an infinite memory would work.) In practice, though, interactive networks are usually constructed so that information about an event dies out over time.

Psychologists have used interactive networks to simulate phenomena associated with short-term memory and learning. The point about memory has already been made. When learning is to be simulated interactive networks provide a way that the system can connect a pattern in one part of the input nodes to a pattern in another, or to patterns that arrive sequentially. Obviously, mammals do this quite well. Many modern theories of the brain assign the role of binding things together to the hippocampus, a brain structure in the medial temporal cortex. Interactive connectionist networks have been used to simulate hippocampal functioning.

Interactive networks have also been used to simulate situations in which the input has to be assigned to just one of several classes. This is sometimes called the "concept recognition" problem. It is an important issue in cognitive psychology, because so much of human thought depends upon recognizing that the current instance is a member of a class, and then responding on the basis of class assignment. That is how we might, for instance, deal with a barking dog even if we had no experience with that particular dog. Are we dealing with a poodle or a pit bull? It makes a difference.

To illustrate how classification works, and in order to show what an actual connectionist model looks like, the next section presents a model to explain an interesting phenomenon in visual pattern recognition.

12.6. SIMULATING A PHENOMENON IN VISUAL RECOGNITION: THE INTERACTIVE ACTIVATION MODEL

In visual detection experiments, an observer sees displays that are visible for a tenth of a second or less. The observer's task is to tell whether a particular character, symbol, or object was present in the display. In the case to be analyzed, the objects are typed letters, for example, "a," "n," and so forth. The experiment runs like this:

> *Instructions: Press a button if the letter "a" is displayed.*
>   *(Wait about 300 milliseconds.)*
> *"letter displayed for a variable length of time"*
>   *observer responds, indicating "a" or "not-a."*

The purpose of the study is to determine the shortest time at which an observer can reliably detect a target letter. Call this *detection time*. Once determined, detection time can then be related to variables associated with the display (e.g., the visual contrast between the display and the target) or associated with the observer (e.g., intelligence, which is associated with short detection times).

In the letter detection task, the target letter may be displayed alone, with flanking letters and symbols, or displayed in a word. Examples are

Alone–	"a"
Flanking symbols–	"$a&"
Word–	"cat."

Letters are detected more quickly when they are displayed alone than when they are displayed with flanking symbols; *detection time* ("a") < *detection time* ("$a&"). This is not surprising, for visually the letter

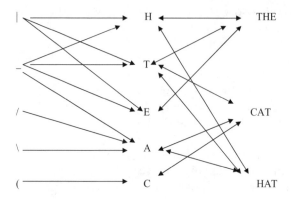

FIGURE 12-9. A simple interactive activation model for letter perception. The model is based on a more complicated model described by McClelland and Rumelhart (1981).

is hidden within the flankers. What is more puzzling, though, is the fact that it takes *less* time to detect a letter when it is presented in a word than when it is presented alone. That is, *detection time* ("cat") < *detection time* ("a"). This is called the *word recognition effect*. Why should letters, which are flanking stimuli, behave differently from non-letters?

In one of the early demonstrations of connectionism, James McClelland and David Rumelhart[6] showed how this could happen. They combined some facts about the visual system, presented in the next paragraph, with a connectionist network based on these facts. First, the facts themselves.

The visual system does not detect letters directly. It detects line and curve segments, things like { /, \, ( ) – }. We have learned that certain configurations of lines and curves make up letters, as in **A**, which is made up of /, \, – in a particular spatial configuration. Therefore, the input to a letter recognizer has to consist of these sorts of letter parts. The second thing we know, because we have learned that this is so, is that certain sequences of letters define a word.

The network shown in Figure 12-9 puts these facts together. The network consists of an input level, which senses letter segments such as "\," a set of letter nodes that act as output nodes, and a hidden level of word nodes. All nodes use the logistic function for activation, and all nodes are connected positively to themselves. This means that they can build up activation over time because their own previous level of activation acts as input to them. There are feed-forward connections from the line segments to the letter nodes. The letter and word nodes are connected interactively; one feeds back to another.

_____

[6] McClelland and Rumelhart (1981).

Because of the interactive architecture, activation will be passed through the network until each node's activation level has stabilized. At this point the network is said to have recognized the letter node with the highest asymptotic activation level. How long does this take?

Initially, letter segments are presented to the network, for example, the letter segments {/, \, – |. C } found in the word CAT. The letter segments pass activation to the appropriate letters. The letter nodes pass activation forward to the relevant word nodes. The word nodes return activation to the letter nodes, so that the letter nodes are now receiving activation from both the input nodes and the word nodes. The result is that the activation levels of the letter nodes will stabilize more quickly in the "letter in word" case than in the case of "letter alone," because selected letter nodes will receive activation both from the input nodes and from the word nodes that are connected to that letter node.

Readers may gain some insight into this process by working through the flow of activation if (a) the letter "A" is presented alone, or (b) it is presented as part of the word CAT.

Interactive activation networks can produce a number of other phenomena related to the word recognition effect. To gain an idea of what these are, the reader should try to find the answer to the following question:

Suppose that a letter is presented as part of a "wordlike" non-word, such as HET or BOT. Does the model predict that a word-recognition effect will be found? Why or why not?

12.7. AN ARTIFICIAL INTELLIGENCE APPROACH TO LEARNING

One of the more popular cartoon strips of the 1990s, "Calvin and Hobbes," dealt with the adventures of a six-year-old boy, Calvin, and his imaginary tiger, Hobbes. In one strip, Hobbes remarked that "people have no night vision, their claws and teeth are a joke, and as for beauty, people don't even have tails." So why does this large, slow, relatively weak, hairless primate dominate the planet? Two reasons stand out: language and a superb ability to learn. Interesting connectionist models of language have been developed, but it would take too long to develop them here. We shall look at some connectionist models of learning.

In biological systems, learning depends upon changes in the effectiveness of synaptic connections, so that nerve elements that used to fire in response to one pattern of inputs now fire to another input pattern. The analogous change in a connectionist network is a change in the weight matrix. But what do we mean when we say that a connectionist network has learned?

If we were training a person or an animal, we would define a set of stimuli, and train our student until he or she gave a desired set of responses, for example, the sound "fetch" plus a thrown stick, followed by the dog getting the stick. One way of training a connectionist network uses the same idea, but "he or she" is replaced by "it." Instead of stimuli, we say "possible input vectors," and instead of response, we say "possible output vectors." The idea is to present an input vector to a network, observe the output vector, note the discrepancy between the desired vector and the vector the network computed, and then change the weight matrix in such a way that on the next presentation of an input vector, the network is more likely to produce the desired output vector. So far, the idea is the same as giving a dog a piece of food when the stick is retrieved, and withholding the food when it is not.

This is the point at which the analogy becomes a bit strained. Connectionist networks are trained by error correction, rather than by reward. The following definitions are intended for a three-layer, feed-forward network, such as the one sketched in Figure 12-8.

Let $D(t)$ be the output vector that was desired in response to input $I(t)$, and let $O(t)$ be the response that was observed. Define the error vector as the difference between these,

$$\Delta(t) = D(t) - O(t). \tag{12-7}$$

The individual elements of the error vector, $(d_j(t) - o_j(t))$ indicate the extent to which the jth output unit missed its desired value.

The reason that the jth output had the value it did was because of the levels of activation of the units $\{x_{ij}\}$ that provided input to the output unit and the weights of each of those inputs. The x_{ij}'s may be input or hidden nodes. The important thing is that they have some connection to the output node, j. This is denoted by the weight $w_{ij}(t)$. Learning occurs when the weights are changed in a way that minimizes $\Delta(t)$. We next examine two algorithms for doing this.

The first rule to be considered, the *generalized delta rule*, applies only to two-layer networks, where the input nodes are directly connected to the output nodes, as in the perceptron discussed earlier. Learning in the perceptron is important, even though the perceptron itself can only make linear classifications, for two reasons. The first is trite; decision rules are often based on linear classification. The second reason is a bit subtler. Understanding the generalized delta rule sets the stage for *back propagation*, a technique that can develop non-linear classification rules.

The generalized delta rule for changing the weight from the ith to the jth node, w_{ij}, is

$$w_{ij}(t+1) = w_{ij}(t) + \alpha(d_j(t) - o_j(t))x_i(t), \tag{12-8}$$

where $0 < \alpha \leq 1$.

In words, the weight unit is changed by an amount that is determined by (a) the extent to which there was a discrepancy between the desired and observed output, multiplied by (b) the level of activity in the input node, and (c) a constant term, α, that determines the amount of change. If α is very low, weight adjustment may take many trials. However, if α is too high, the network may bounce back and forth between weight levels that are either too high or too low.

Suppose that the output was not as great as desired, so that $(d_j(t) - o_j(t)) > 0$. Suppose further that $x_i(t)$ was positive. This means that $x_i(t)$, the input, was in the right direction, in the sense that if the weighted value of the input from i to j, $w_{ij}x_i(t)$, had been higher than it was, the output would have been moved closer to the desired output. Therefore, w_{ij} should be increased. On the other hand, if the discrepancy is negative, $(d_j(t) - o_j(t)) < 0$, weight w_{ij} should be decreased. If x_{ij} had been negative, the opposite change would have been made. If you examine equation (12-8), you will see that it deals with each of these situations appropriately.

Is this a good analogy to learning? Consider a social situation. You are wondering whether or not to go to a movie. Your friend says it is good. You give some weight to your friend's advice. If the movie is even better than you expected you will give your friend's advice more weight in the future. If the movie is bad you will pay less attention to your friend in the future. The same logic is embedded in the generalized delta rule.

It can be proven that, given enough trials, the generalized delta rule will solve any linear classification problem. Because a preceptron cannot compute non-linear classifications, no learning rule can be used to find the weights required to solve such a classification, for they do not exist.[7]

We need a rule that applies to networks with hidden units, for these networks can compute any computable function. The problem is that modifying the weights involving hidden units introduces an added complexity. Another social analogy illustrates the problem.

Most investors rely on the advice of stock analysts. The stock analyst looks at a variety of indicators about firms and general market situations. For instance, a stock analyst might examine a company's financial report; look at the profit, loss, debt, and anticipated earnings in that report; and also consider such more general variables as trends in oil prices, national employment statistics, and proposed government policies. Call these variables, collectively, the "market factors." After examining market factors the analyst issues buy and sell recommendations for several different stocks. Investors examine the

---

[7] Proofs for this statement have been published by a number of authors. Minsky and Papert (1969) present one such proof, in the context of what is often considered to be a definitive statement of the computing capabilities of perceptrons.

recommendations of several analysts, and on the basis of their recommendations, make purchases and sales. The stocks rise, fall, or hold steady, and the investor is appropriately rewarded or punished by the external market.

The stock market example maps onto the three-layer, feed-forward network shown in Figure 12-8. The market indicators play the role of input nodes, the stock analysts are the hidden nodes, and the investors' decisions about individual stocks are the output nodes. The questions are "What weights should the investor place on an individual analyst's recommendations?" and "What weights should each analyst place on the different market indicators?"

These questions have to be answered separately for the different analysts and stocks. One analyst might pay attention to one indicator, while another analyst paid attention to another. Similarly, analysts may differ in their ability to predict different types of stocks. One analyst may specialize in predicting commodity futures (the future prices of the raw materials of the economy, including things like wheat, sugar, and even oil), while another analyst might specialize in technology stocks. A prudent investor would give considerable weight to the first analyst's prediction about, say, wheat futures, but give much less weight to this analyst's predictions about the prospects of a computer company. The second analyst would be treated in the opposite way.

The investor's problem, weighting the analyst's recommendations, is analogous to the learning situation for the two-layer feed-forward system. Therefore, it is not surprising to find that the solution to changing the weights in the hidden-to-output layer is very similar to the solution for the simple network.

The solution for the input-to-hidden (market-to-analyst) weights is a bit trickier. Think first of the social analogy. The analyst will have issued advice about multiple stocks, and some parts of this advice will have been good while other parts will have been bad. The error signal to the analyst, then, should somehow combine the effects of the good and the bad recommendations. The algorithm to be described, *back propagation*, does this.

For the purpose of describing the algorithm let $x_i(t)$ be the activation level of the ith input node at time t, let $x_j(t)$ be the activation level of the jth hidden node and let $x_k(t)$ be the activation level of the kth output node. Let $d_k(t)$ be the desired level of output of this node. The goal is to adjust the input unit to hidden unit weight, w_{ij}, and the hidden unit to output unit weight, w_{jk}. This will be done by determining an error term associated with the output node, using it to adjust w_{jk}, then amalgamating the error terms for all output units in a way that expresses an error term for the hidden node ("back propagating"), and finally using the hidden node's error term to adjust w_{ij}.

Calculating the error term for the output node is straightforward,

$$\delta_k(t) = (d_k(t) - x_k(t)) \cdot x_k(t) \cdot (1 - x_k(t)), \tag{12-9}$$

where the first term on the right-hand side is the discrepancy between the desired and observed output, and the product of the second and third terms is the derivative of the logistic function with respect to its argument. This reflects the level of sensitivity of the unit to changes in input.

The weight from the hidden to the input node is then changed by

$$w_{jk}(t+1) = w_{jk}(t) + \alpha \cdot \delta_k(t) \cdot x_j(t), \tag{12-10}$$

where α is a parameter that establishes the rate of adjustment. Including the $x_j(t)$ term reflects the fact that, for a given level of discrepancy, the amount of change should reflect the level of activation of the hidden unit. In the stockbroker example, a strong recommendation to buy, followed by a loss, would lead to a greater drop in the investor's confidence in the stockbroker than would an equivocal recommendation, followed by a loss.

In order to determine the error associated with the hidden unit consideration has to be given to the error term for all output units, $x_k, x_{k'}, x_{k''}$ that receive input from the jth hidden unit, weighted by strength of the hidden-output unit connection. Let $\Delta(t) = \{\delta_k\}$ be the set of error terms of output units at time t. The error associated with the jth hidden unit is

$$\delta_j(t) = x_j(t) \cdot (1 - x_j(t)) \sum_{\delta_k(t) \in \Delta(t)} \delta_k(t) \cdot w_{jk}(t). \tag{12-11}$$

The input to hidden unit weight is then adjusted to

$$w_{ij}(t+1) = w_{ij}(t) + \alpha \cdot \delta_j(t) \cdot x_i(t). \tag{12-12}$$

Where does all this mathematics get us? To begin with the positive news, back propagation can be used to solve a problem when people do not know the explicit solution! A particularly good illustration of this is the ALVINN project, in which back propagation was used to construct the control program for an autonomous motor vehicle.[8] The control program's task was to receive input from television cameras and output signals to the steering wheel, accelerator, and brake. The interesting thing is how this program was constructed.

At first, the designers attempted to write down the appropriate input-output rules for slowing, turning, and so on. Although the designers certainly knew how to drive, they were unable to anticipate all the

---

[8] Jochem and Pomerleau (1996).

problems that might occur during driving, and hence were not able to develop an adequate list of driving rules. Then they changed their strategy. A human driver controlled the vehicle while automated sensors recorded what the situation was and what the driver did. A connectionist network was then trained to make the same input-output mappings, using back propagation to adjust its weights. The vehicle was subsequently driven along freeways from Pittsburgh to San Diego. The only time that humans had to intervene (besides indicating direction changes) was when the car was on the Los Angeles freeway system.

It is useful to look at projects like this more abstractly, because the abstract analysis shows what can be done with connectionist networks as artificial intelligence devices.

Consider a problem where there exists some very large, but finite, set $I = \{i\}$ of possible inputs, and a (usually much smaller) set of outputs, $O = \{o_i\}$. What is desired is a program that maps from I to O. An error function can be defined for every mismatch (e.g., given a particular i, the wrong o is computed, and the cost of this mistake can be determined). The problem is that the designer does not know, explicitly, what the correct $I -> O$ mapping is. In the driving example, for instance, experienced drivers can give you generalities, but they cannot list, explicitly, what they would do in every possible situation. Therefore, the designer cannot program the $I -> O$ mapping explicitly. What the designer can do is observe examples of specific instances of $i -> o$ mappings and train a connectionist network to mimic them. This is called the *training phase*. In the *test phase*, the network utilizes these weights to compute outputs for a new set of input vectors. If the test phase goes well, the connectionist network can be used as a control program.

Variants of this technique have been used to develop practical control devices. Back propagation has also been used to create psychological simulations somewhat akin to existence proofs in mathematics. Suppose a person argues (as many have) that no conglomeration of simple associations satisfying certain restrictions can learn a particular classification rule. Because connectionist networks are conglomerations of simple associations, showing that a connectionist network that satisfies these restrictions can learn the rule amounts to a counterexample of the assertion.

This reasoning may seem somewhat convoluted, but the technique has been particularly useful in psycholinguistics. We know that children learn languages largely by observation. One of the major questions in psycholinguistics is whether a general "neural-like" computational system could also learn a language by observation. If this is not possible, then some special human-language learning capacity has to be assumed. One way to assemble evidence against the argument that language learning is special is to show, by example, that a connectionist network can learn grammatical rules, such as the rules for constructing the past tense of verbs or rules for sentence construction. The way this has been done is to show the network examples, and use back propagation to find the appropriate weights. Several of these efforts have been quite successful.

An important restriction has to be kept in mind. When back propagation is used to construct a network that mimics human performance, we know, by example, that such a construction is possible. The question of how the brain/mind constructs the network remains open because back propagation is not a plausible model of learning at the neural level. Back propagation, as the name implies, relies on accumulating error signals and passing them backward from one layer of nodes to another. There is no known mechanism in the nervous system that could do this.

If you are using back propagation to construct a neural network to solve some applied problem, the issue of how the network was constructed is of little interest. The important thing is that the network be constructed, not how the construction was done. If you are interested in psychology or the neurosciences, though, the learning mechanism itself has to have a biological justification.

With that in mind, we next look at a connectionist learning mechanism that does have a biological justification.

12.8. A BIOLOGICAL APPROACH TO LEARNING: THE HEBBIAN ALGORITHM

In the 1930s, E. R. Guthrie, a psychology professor at the University of Washington, developed a theory of learning based on the idea that all that had to happen to link two events was for them to occur close together in time. During the 1940s, the Canadian psychologist D. O. Hebb amplified upon Guthrie's ideas and gave them a neurological interpretation. To understand the idea, it helps to look at the basic psychology involved.

Many psychological theories assume that people learn by reward; we repeat those actions that have led to a reward. This idea is at the basis of Pavlov's famous experiments in which dogs learned to salivate at the sound of a bell, because the bell signaled that food was about to be delivered. It was also the idea behind B. F. Skinner's equally famous studies in which pigeons (and rats, and people) learned to peck at a target or pull a lever in order to operate a device that sometimes delivered food pellets. If you think that these experiments do not mimic human behavior, I invite you to visit the slot-machine row at a nearby gambling casino.

Both Pavlov's and Skinner's work emphasized reward as the driving force in learning. If we take an engineering point of view about learning we are led to a somewhat different conclusion. The engineering view is that learning depends upon negative feedback. An organism (or a robot) reacts to a situation, does not do things quite right, receives an error signal, and then adjusts the reaction in order to reduce the error signal. This is the way back propagation works. In the 1960s a considerable number of experiments showed that in certain situations, error correction drives human learning.

Guthrie rejected both the argument that learning occurs through reinforcement and the argument that learning occurs through error correction. He argued that we learn by contiguity. Whenever a stimulus and a response occur in sequence, the bond between them is strengthened. Rewards cause us to continue whatever we are doing, while punishments cause us to change our responses. We learn whatever we practice, but if what we practice leads to good things, we practice it more, and conversely, if what we do leads to bad things, we do something else. Reward and punishment do not participate directly in the learning process, but they do control it indirectly.

Hebb[9] applied Guthrie's ideas to learning at the neural level. He assumed that the bond between any two connected neurons is strengthened whenever the two are simultaneously active. Now suppose that a presynaptic neuron, A, is weakly connected to a postsynaptic neuron, C, and that C is strongly connected to another presynaptic neuron, B. If A and B are simultaneously active, B will be the neuron that causes C to fire, because B is the only neuron that can deliver enough activation to C. However, because A was active when C fired, the efficiency of the synaptic connection between A and C will be strengthened. Eventually, activation of A will be sufficient to activate C.

Hebb's ideas were attractive to psychologists, neuroscientists, and computer scientists, albeit for somewhat different reasons. Psychologists liked them because they offered a simple mechanism to explain Pavlov's and Skinner's findings. From there you can go to almost any theory of learning, including error correction. In addition, as Hebb pointed out, his mechanism provided a way to form classes without explicit instruction. This was important because we know that a great deal of vocabulary learning takes place in this way. To see how this might work, consider how a child might learn the class "dog." It would be sufficient for the child to observe dogs (visually) while hearing adults use the word "dog." There is no requirement that the child say "dog" and then either be rewarded or corrected. In fact, careful observation has shown that adults do not spend much time explicitly rewarding or punishing children for the use of words, but do spend a lot of time illustrating the use of words.

Neuroscientists like Hebb's idea because it explains learning in a neural network solely by local action, rather than requiring back

---

[9] Hebb (1949).

propagation of signals through the network. Some experiments in the 1980s and 1990s strongly indicated that Hebbian learning really does occur. The conclusion was based upon direct observation of modifications of synaptic connections in an animal with an exceptionally simple nervous system, the sea slug (*Aplysia*). It turned out that the slug's nervous system adjusts by Hebbian learning. The results generalize, for individual neurons appear to be much the same across all species, although the organization of neural nets does vary across species. Following this discovery, neuroscientists have made considerable progress in determining what the mechanism is for strengthening synaptic connections as a function of use alone.[10]

Finally, computer scientists like Hebb's model because it is easy to implement, and because it provides a mechanism for *unsupervised learning* by observation, as in the dog example just given. Using the Hebbian algorithm, you can design a connectionist network that picks up statistical regularities in the environment, without any explicit training.

At this point, let us go to the mathematics.

Let x_i and x_j be any two nodes in a connectionist network (without distinguishing between input and output nodes), and let $w_{ij}(t)$ be the connection between these nodes. As before, $x_i(t)$ will be used to indicate the level of activation of node x_i at time t. The Hebbian learning algorithm is

$$w_{ij}(t+1) = w_{ij}(t) + \alpha x_i(t)x_j(t). \qquad (12\text{-}13)$$

The adjustment to weight w_{ij} is proportional to the product of the activity in the sending ("presynaptic") and receiving ("postsynaptic") unit. The result is that large weights will be associated with nodes that are simultaneously active, which is the principle behind Hebb's learning rule. If the network is constructed using an activation function that permits negative values, two units whose activities are negatively correlated over time will tend to have large negative weights; that is, the sending unit inhibits the receiving one.

12.9. THE AUTO-ASSOCIATOR

There are many examples of Hebbian networks to simulate psychological phenomena. One of the simplest is the auto-associator, which demonstrates an interesting primitive memory capacity. What is even more interesting is that in this case, we can prove why it works. I will first illustrate the auto-associator and then prove that it always solves certain problems in learning and memory.

Consider a network of nine nodes and, for simplicity, set α to 1. Let nodes x_1 to x_6 represent "stimulus" nodes, and let nodes $x_7 \ldots x_9$

---

[10] LeDoux, op cit.

be response nodes. In less psychological terminology, we could think of the first six nodes as pictures of people and the last three nodes as their names. The state of the system can be represented by a column vector:

$$x(t) = \begin{pmatrix} x_1(t) \\ x_2(t) \\ x_3(t) \\ x_4(t) \\ x_5(t) \\ x_6(t) \\ x_7(t) \\ x_8(t) \\ x_9(t) \end{pmatrix} \tag{12-14}$$

where $x_i(t)$ represents the level of activation of unit i at time t.

Let $W(t)$ be the matrix of association weights at time t, and initially set all the weights to zero. In order to make everything simple, we will assume that the activation units use the threshold rule with a threshold of zero; that is, $x_j(t) = 1$ if and only if $\eta_j = \Sigma_i w_{ij} x_i(t)$ is greater than zero.

We want the system to "remember names" in the following sense. If the input "picture" is $x_1 = 1$ and $x_2 = 1$, with the remaining input nodes equal to zero, respond with the "name" $x_7 = 1$, and $x_8 = x_9 = 0$. Similar "pictures and names" can be assigned to x_3, x_4, and x_8, and to x_5, x_6, and x_9.

In a learning session, pictures and names are presented in combination. Suppose the first picture is presented. Write the transpose of this, $x(1)^T = (1,1,0,0,0,0,1,0,0)$. We want to add the quantity $x_i(t)x_j(t)$ to the w_{ij} element of W. This can be done in vector notation by

$$W(1) = W(0) + x(1) \cdot x(1)^T. \tag{12-15}$$

In an alternative notation, this amounts to adding the quantity $x_i(t)x_j(t)$ to weight $w_{ij}(0)$.

Suppose we start with the first picture-name combination, $x(1)$. $W(1)$ will have the following values:

$$W(1) = \begin{matrix} 1\,1\,0\,0\,0\,0\,1\,0\,0 \\ 1\,1\,0\,0\,0\,0\,1\,0\,0 \\ 0\,0\,0\,0\,0\,0\,0\,0\,0 \\ 0\,0\,0\,0\,0\,0\,0\,0\,0 \\ 0\,0\,0\,0\,0\,0\,0\,0\,0 \\ 0\,0\,0\,0\,0\,0\,0\,0\,0 \\ 1\,1\,0\,0\,0\,0\,1\,0\,0 \\ 0\,0\,0\,0\,0\,0\,0\,0\,0 \\ 0\,0\,0\,0\,0\,0\,0\,0\,0. \end{matrix} \tag{12-16}$$

Next let $x(2)^T = (0,0,1,1,0,0,0,1,0)$ and $x(3)^T = (0,0,0,0,1,1,0,0,1)$. $W(2) = W(1) + x(2) \times x(2)^T$ and $W(3) = W(2) + x(3) \times x(3)^T$. At this point, the weight matrix is

$$W(3) = \begin{matrix} 1\ 1\ 0\ 0\ 0\ 0\ 1\ 0\ 0 \\ 1\ 1\ 0\ 0\ 0\ 0\ 1\ 0\ 0 \\ 0\ 0\ 1\ 1\ 0\ 0\ 0\ 1\ 0 \\ 0\ 0\ 1\ 1\ 0\ 0\ 0\ 1\ 0 \\ 0\ 0\ 0\ 0\ 1\ 1\ 0\ 0\ 1 \\ 0\ 0\ 0\ 0\ 1\ 1\ 0\ 0\ 1 \\ 1\ 1\ 0\ 0\ 0\ 0\ 1\ 0\ 0 \\ 0\ 0\ 1\ 1\ 0\ 0\ 0\ 1\ 0 \\ 0\ 0\ 0\ 0\ 1\ 1\ 0\ 0\ 1. \end{matrix} \qquad (12\text{-}17)$$

Now to test the matrix. Let the test vector be the "name" of pattern 1, $x(test)^T = (0\ 0\ 0\ 0\ 0\ 0\ 1\ 0\ 0)$, using the transpose solely for ease in typing. The input from this test vector to each of the nodes in the matrix is

$$\eta_j(test) = \sum_i w_{ij} x_i(test), \qquad (12\text{-}18)$$

or in matrix notation,

$$\eta(test) = W \cdot x(test). \qquad (12\text{-}19)$$

The result is $\eta(test)^T = (1,1,0,0,0,0,1,0,0)$. Given the name, the auto-associator reconstructed the picture.

Why does this work? The trick was to construct the original stimuli, the pictures plus the name, so that they were orthogonal. In vector notation, for any two different patterns presented at different times, t and t^* ($t \neq t^*$),

$$x(t)^T \cdot x(t^*) = 0. \qquad (12\text{-}20)$$

Because of the way that W was constructed,

$$W \cdot x(test) = x(1) \cdot x(1)^T \cdot x(test) + x(2) \cdot x(2)^T \cdot x(test) \\ + x(3) \cdot x(3)^T \cdot x(test). \qquad (12\text{-}21)$$

Since $x(test)$ was constructed from a fragment of $x(1)$, the expression $x(t)^T \cdot x(test)$ is zero for all $x(t)$ except $x(1)$. More generally, assume that equation (12-20) holds, and that $x(test)$ is a vector whose entries are all zeroes except that there are k entries where $x_i(test) = x_i(t) = 1$. That is, the test vector contains k of the non-zero entries of $x_i(t)$. Then

$$x(t)^T x(test) = k, \qquad (12\text{-}22)$$

and

$$W(test) \cdot x(test) = x(t) \cdot x(t)^T \cdot x(test)$$
$$W(test) \cdot x(test) = x(t) \cdot k. \tag{12-23}$$

This result will be a vector in which the entries are zero if the corresponding entry of $x(t)$ is zero, and will be k otherwise.

Finally, recall that what we have calculated is the input activations, $\{\eta_j(test)\}$, not the activation levels themselves. However, because the network uses a threshold activation function with a threshold of zero, $x_j(test) = 1$ if and only if $\eta_j(test) > 0$. Given only a fragment of a training vector, the network recreates the entire vector.

The auto-associator is only one of many connectionist networks that can be used to mimic something that, at least superficially, looks like human memory. It is interesting to note that if condition (12-20) is not met, that is, if the training vectors are correlated, then a test vector constructed from a fragment of the training vector will retrieve an amalgam of the original training vector and all training vectors correlated with it. This is at least analogous to the well-known phenomenon of *interference*; people's memory of an experience can be distorted by confusion with similar experiences. This principle is used in connectionist networks based on Hebbian learning to simulate category formation by observation.[11]

12.10. A FINAL WORD

This chapter has only touched on the burgeoning field of connectionism. The advocates of connectionist models believe that they have developed a language to explain how brain mechanisms produce mental action. This may be, but the effort is proving to be much harder than was anticipated when connectionist models were first introduced, in the late 1970s. Interesting connectionist models are being developed today, but we have yet to achieve a full understanding of the brain. Given the complexity of the problem, that is hardly surprising.

Whether or not connectionism will take over all of psychology remains to be seen. At the least, though, it will be an important tool in the arsenal of theoretical psychology, and at the same time a useful tool in industrial applications.

---

[11] See Hunt (2002) for several further examples.

13

L'Envoi

I have been told that an author loses half the readers with every equation. If that is so, and if every person on the globe started to try to read this book, I have a reader left! My thanks and congratulations, lonely reader.

Actually, I am not that pessimistic. It seems more likely to me that you lose half your readers on the first, one-third on the second, and so on. Some hardy souls will persevere. They may even expect mathematics. And we are at the end.

But we do not need to be. I have barely touched the surface of every topic that has been discussed. Specialists in each field may curse me for having given so light a treatment of their topic. Those same specialists may grouse about my having spent so much time talking about things outside of their interests. All I can say to the reader is that if you want to go further, go to the specialty literature. I am not being snooty; I really hope that some readers will want to take these chapters further.

I knew when I started that I would have to omit some topics, for there are so many applications of mathematics in the social sciences – well beyond statistics – that it would take volumes to cover them all. I mean that literally. The series *Mathematical Psychology*, which covered psychology alone, ran to three full volumes ... in 1963! Things have happened in the intervening 40-plus years. A complete treatment of all topics on mathematical applications in the behavioral and social sciences would require a bookshelf. That is more than I am capable of or want to produce.

I particularly regret not covering certain topics, so let me describe them briefly and explain my reason for omission.

Cognitive psychologists have made extensive use of the time it takes a person to do something, reaction time (RT) for short, in order to reveal mental processes. Mathematical modeling has been used heavily in this effort. Much of the work is of very high quality. The problem, though, is that the tasks themselves, what participants in an experiment actually do, are usually not very interesting outside of the theory that generated them. For example, suppose that a participant in an experiment is asked to watch a computer screen while a series of one to six numbers (e.g., 1, 6, 3, 7) appears, one at a time. The participant is then shown the number 4 (or 3) and asked to press a button on the right if the last number was one of the ones shown, a button on the left if it was not. It turns out that the time it takes to press the button is a linear function of the number of digits in the preceding series. That fact, and some related ones, generated a substantial debate over the appropriate mathematical model to describe the retrieval of information from short-term memory. The debate was not trivial, but to someone outside of cognitive psychology it was certainly opaque.

This example illustrates the problem that I had. From the viewpoint of cognitive psychologists, mathematical analyses of reaction times were used, often in an elegant way, to answer questions that arose during the development of theories of mental action. There are excellent reviews of this technical literature, which indeed is a fine illustration of the power of mathematical argumentation.[1] From the viewpoint of an outsider, though, you needed a course in cognitive psychology in order to understand why the question was being asked at all. I made a decision to concentrate on situations where it would be easy for people to under-stand why a behavior was of interest, so that readers could concentrate on the analysis. I know that this ruled out discussion of some very good research, but that was my decision.

This hurt. I have done a fair bit of reaction-time research myself. You will not find it described here.

I also omitted an important field that lies between mathematical modeling and statistics. Beginning in the 1970s, sociologists and econo-mists began to use elegant modeling techniques to explore questions of causality. I am very impressed by these studies, and wish I could have presented it. However, here I faced a problem that was a mirror image of the problem of discussing reaction times. It is easy to see why social scientists want to understand the causal relations among, say, health, economic well-being, and level of education. However, the mathematics involved in causal modeling presume a fairly high level of familiarity with linear algebra and with multivariate statistical methods. As I wanted to address people other than specialists in the field, causal modeling had to go.

Economics makes considerable use of mathematical modeling. One application that intrigues me is a technique known as input-output analysis, which can be used to model the ways in which changes in one aspect of an industrial system will propagate through the entire system.

---

[1] Luce (1986); Townsend and Ashby (1983).

I would also have liked to have presented models based on a mathematical technique known as Markov chains. I did mention the field briefly but did not do very much with it. Why? The examples that I know of require considerable explanation of the field before the mathematical problem can be explained. So, by the same logic that kept me from writing about the analysis of reaction times, I decided not to include models using Markov chains.

I would not be surprised if the third person to read the previous paragraph will think of the example that I could not find! That is the way things go.

Was it all worth it? As I was writing this book I read a letter to the editor of the *American Scientist*. The writer was commenting on the models discussed in Chapter 11, but I think he would extend his comment to everything that has been said here. The letter said: "Economics is an aspect of human behavior. As such, it is no more amenable to mathematical modeling than is such behavior itself."[2]

If my readers agree that the letter writer was dead wrong, this book will be worth the effort it took to write it.

---

[2] W. F. Schreiber (2002), letter to the editor, *American Scientist*, 90 (6): 494.

References

Ackerman, P. L., and Beier, M. D. (2001). Trait complexes, cognitive investment, and domain knowledge. In R. J. Sternberg and Elena L. Grigorenko (eds.). *The Psychology of Abilities, Competences, and Expertise*. Cambridge: Cambridge University Press, pp. 1–30.

Alroy, J. (2001). A multispecies overkill simulation of the end-pliestocene megafaunal mass extinction. *Science*, 292(8 June): 1893–6.

Anderson, N. H. (1996). *A Functional Theory of Cognition*. Mahwah, NJ: L. Erlbaum.

Anonymous. ([1100s] 1959). *El Poema de mio Cid*. Translated by W. S. Merwin. London: Dent.

Arrow, K. J. (1963). *Social Choice and Individual Values*. 2d ed. New York: Wiley.

Ashby, F. G., and Perrin, N. A. (1988). Toward a unified theory of similarity and recognition. *Psychological Review*, 95(1): 124–50.

Bahrick, H. P., and Hall, L. K. (1991). Lifetime maintenance of high school mathematics content. *Journal of Experimental Psychology: General*, 120(1): 20–3.

Barzelon, E. (2005). Sentencing by the numbers. *New York Times Magazine*, January 2.

Beach, L. R. (1990). *Image Theory: Decision Making in Personal and Organizational Contexts*. New York: Wiley.

Bernstein, P. L. (1996). *Against the Gods: The Remarkable Story of Risk*. New York: Wiley.

Carroll, J. B. (1993). *Human Cognitive Abilities*. Cambridge: Cambridge University Press.

Committee to Review Scientific Evidence on the Polygraph (2003). *The Polygraph and Lie Detection*. Washington, DC: National Academy Press.

Crystal, D. (ed.) (1995). *The Cambridge Encyclopedia of the English Language*. Cambridge: Cambridge University Press.

Dardonini, V. (2001). A pedagogical proof of Arrow's Impossibility Theorem. *Social Choice and Welfare*, 18: 107–12.

DiSessa, A. A. (2000). *Changing Minds: Computers, Learning, and Literacy*. Cambridge, MA: MIT Press.

Dodds, P.S., Muhamad, R., and Watts, D.J. (2003). An experimental study of search in global social networks. *Science*, 301(8 August): 827–9.

Egan, J.P. (1975). *Signal Detection Theory and ROC Analysis*. New York: Academic Press.

Embretson, S., and Reise, S. (2000). *Item Response Theory for Psychologists*. Mahwah, NJ: L. Erlbaum.

Emmeche, C. (1994). *The Garden in the Machine: The Emerging Science of Artificial Life*. Translated by S. Sampson. Princeton, NJ: Princeton University Press.

Falmagne, J-C. (1985). *Elements of Psychophysical Theory*. Oxford: Oxford University Press.

Gigerenzer, G. (2000). *Adaptive Thinking: Rationality in the Real World*. Oxford: Oxford University Press.

Gladwell, M. (2000). *The Tipping Point*. New York: Little Brown.

Gleick, J. (1987). *Chaos: Making a New Science*. New York: Viking.

Gottfredson, L.S. (1997). Why g matters: The complexity of everyday life. *Intelligence*, 24(1): 79–132.

Gottman, J.M., Murray, J.D., Swanson, C.C., Tyson, R., & Swanson, K.R. (2002). *The Mathematics of Marriage: Dynamic Non-linear Models*. Cambridge, MA: MIT Press.

Greenwald, A.G. (1992). New look 3: Unconscious cognition reclaimed. *American Psychologist*, 47(6): 766–72.

Gullberg, J. (1997). *Mathematics from the Birth of Numbers*. London: Charles Norton.

Halpern, D. (2002). *Thought and Knowledge: An Introduction to Critical Thinking*. 4th ed. Mahwah, NJ: Erlbaum.

Hammond, K.R. (1996). *Human Judgment and Social Policy: Irreducible Uncertainty, Inevitable Error, Unavoidable Injustice*. Oxford: Oxford University Press.

Hayes, B. (2001). The weatherman. *American Scientist*, 89(1): 10–14.

Hayes, B. (2002a). Statistics of deadly quarrels. *American Scientist*, 90(1): 10–15.

Hayes, B. (2002b). Follow the money. *American Scientist*, 90(5): 400–405.

Hayes, B. (2002c). Reply to letters to the editor. *American Scientist*, 90(6): 494.

Hebb, D.O. (1949). *The Organization of Behavior*. New York: Wiley.

Henley, N.M. (1969). A psychological study of the semantics of animal terms. *Journal of Verbal Learning and Verbal Behavior*, 8(2): 176–84.

Herrnstein, R.J., and Murray, C. (1994). *The Bell Curve: Intelligence and Class Structure in American Life*. New York: Free Press.

Hoffrage, U., and Gigerenzer, G. (1996). The impact of information representation on Bayesian reasoning. *Proc. of the Eighteenth Annual Conference of the Cognitive Science Society*. Mahwah, NJ: Erlbaum, pp. 126–30.

Huillard d'Aignaux, J.N., Cousens, S.N., and Smith, P.G. (2001). Predictability of the UK variant Creutzfeldt-Jakob disease epidemic. *Science*, 294(23 November): 1729–31.

Hunt, E. (1995). *Will We Be Smart Enough? A Cognitive Analysis of the Coming Workforce*. New York: Russell Sage Foundation.

Hunt, E. (2002). *Thoughts on Thought*. Mahwah, NJ: L. Erlbaum.

Hunt, M.M. (1993). *The Story of Psychology*. New York: Doubleday.

Jacoby, L. L., Toth, J. P., and Yonelinas, A. P. (1993). Separating conscious and unconscious influences on memory: Measuring recollections. *Journal of Experimental Psychology: General*, 122(2): 139–54.

Jensen, A. R. (1998). *The g Factor: The Science of Mental Ability*. Westport, CT: Praeger/Greenwood.

Jochem, T., and Pomerleau, D. (1996). Life in the fast lane: The evolution of an adaptive vehicle control system. *AI Magazine*, 17(2): 11–50.

Johnson, W., and Bouchard, T. J., Jr. (2005). The structure of intelligence. It's verbal, perceptual, and image rotation (VPR), not fluid and crystallized. *Intelligence*, 33(4): 393–416.

Johnson, W., Bouchard, T. J., Jr., Krueger, R. F., McGue, M., and Gottesman, I. I. (2004). Just one *g*: Consistent results from three test batteries. *Intelligence*, 32: 95–107.

Johnson-Laird, P. N., and Byrne, R. M. J. (1991). *Deduction*. Hove, UK: L. Erlbaum.

Kahneman, D. (2003). A perspective on judgment and choice: Mapping bounded rationality. *American Psychologist*, 58(9): 697–720.

Kahneman, D. A., and Tversky, A. (1973). On the psychology of prediction. *Psychological Review*, 80(4): 237–51.

Kahneman, D., and Tversky, A. (1979). Prospect theory. *Econometrica*, 47: 263–92.

Klein, G. (1998). *Sources of Power: How People Make Decisions*. Cambridge, MA: MIT Press.

LeDoux, J. (2002). *The Synaptic Self: How Our Brains Become Who We Are*. New York: Viking.

Link, S. W. (1994). Rediscovering the past: Gustav Fechner and signal detection theory. *Psychological Science*, 5: 335–40.

Luce, R. D. (1986). *Response Times: Their Role in Inferring Elementary Mental Organization*. New York: Oxford University Press.

Luce, R. D., and Galanter, E. (1963). Discrimination. In R. D. Luce, R. R. Bush, and E. Galanter (eds.). *Handbook of Mathematical Psychology: Volume 1*. New York: Wiley, pp. 191–244.

Luce, R. D., and Krumhansl, C. L. (1988). Measurement, scaling, and psychophysics. In R. C. Atkinson and R. J. Herrnstein (eds.). *Stevens' Handbook of Experimental Psychology*, Vol. 1: *Perception and Motivation*. New York: Wiley, pp. 3–74.

Luce, R. D., and Raiffa, H. (1957). *Games and Decisions: Introduction and Critical Survey*. New York: Wiley.

Lyman, R. (2002). Letter to the editor. *American Scientist*, 90(6): 494.

MacMillan, N. A., and Creelman, C. D. (2004). *Detection Theory: A User's Guide*. 2d ed. Mahwah, NJ: Earlbaum.

McClelland, J. L., and Rumelhart, D. E. (1981). An interactive activation model of context effects in letter perception: Part I. An account of basic findings. *Psychological Review*, 88: 375–407.

Milgram, S. (1967). The small world problem. *Psychology Today*, 1(1): 60–7.

Minsky, M., and Papert, S. (1969). *Perceptrons: An Introduction to Computational Geometry*. Cambridge, MA: MIT Press.

Mitchell, M. (2002). Doing science: A new kind of science. *Science*, 298(14 October): 65–8.

Murray, J. D. (2001). *An Introduction to Mathematical Biology*. New York: Springer-Verlag.

Narens, L. (2002). The irony of measurement by subjective estimations. *Journal of Mathematical Psychology*, 46: 769–88.

Newman, J. R. (1956). *The World of Mathematics*. Vol. 2. New York: Simon and Schuster.

Parducci, A., and Wedell, D. H. (1986). The category effect with rating scales: Number of categories, number of stimuli, and method of presentation. *Journal of Experimental Psychology: Human Perception and Performance*, 12(4): 496–516.

Peter, L. J. (1977). *Peter's Quotations: Ideas for Our Time*. New York: Murrow.

Ratcliff, R., Spieler, D., and McKoon, G. (2000). Explicitly modeling the effects of aging on response time. *Psychonomic Bulletin and Review*, 7(1) 1–25.

Rausch, J. (2002). Seeing around corners. *Atlantic Monthly*, April, pp. 35–48.

Reich, R. (1991). *The Work of Nations: Preparing Ourselves for 21st Century Capitalism*. New York: Knopf.

Richardson, L. F., and Pear P. (1946). *Psychological Factors of Peace and War*. London: Philosophical Library.

Rubin, D. C., and Wenzel, A. E. (1996). One hundred years of forgetting: A quantitative description of retention. *Psychological Review*, 103(4): 734–60.

Schiffman, S. S., Reynolds, M. L., and Young, F. W. (1981). *Introduction to Multidimensional Scaling: Theory, Methods and Application*. Orlando, FL: Academic Press.

Simon, H. A. (1981). *The Sciences of the Artificial*. 2d ed. Cambridge, MA: MIT Press.

Spearman, C. (1904). General intelligence, objectively determined and measured. *American Journal of Psychology*, 15: 201–293.

Spearman, C. (1927). *The Abilities of Man*. London: Macmillan.

Stankov, L. (1999). Mining on the "no man's land" between intelligence and personality. In P. L. Ackerman, P. C. Kyllonen, and R. D. Roberts (eds.). *Learning and Individual Differences: Process, Trait, and Content Determinants*. Washington DC: American Psychological Association.

Stevens, S. S. (1957). On the psychophysical law. *Psychological Review*, 64: 153–81.

Stevens, S. S. (1966). A metric for the social consensus. *Science*, 151(14 January): 530–41.

Stevens, S. S. (1975). *Psychophysics: Introduction to Its Perceptual, Neural and Social Prospects*. New York: Wiley.

Thompson, R. F. (1993). *The Brain: A Neuroscience Primer*. 2d ed. New York: W. H. Freeman.

Thurstone, L. L. (1927). A law of comparative judgment. *Psychological Review*, 34: 273–86.

Thurstone, L. L. (1938). *Primary Mental Abilities*. Chicago: University of Chicago Press.

Townsend, J. T., and Ashby, F. G. (1983). *Stochastic Modeling of Elementary Psychological Processes*. Cambridge: Cambridge University Press.

Travers, J., and Milgram, S. (1969). An experimental study of the small world problem. *Sociometry*, 32(4): 425–43.

Tversky, A., and Kahneman, D. (1981). The framing of decisions and the rationality of choice. *Science*, 211(30 January): 453–58.

Tversky, A., and Kahneman, D. (1983). Extensional vs. intuitive reasoning: The conjunction fallacy in probability judgment. *Psychological Review*, 91: 293–315.

Vilenkin, N. Y. (1965/1968). *Stories about Sets*. Scripta Technica Translation. New York: Academic Press.

Valleron, A-J., Boelle, P-Y., Will, R., and Cesbron, J-Y. (2001). Estimation of epidemic size and incubation time based on age characteristics of vCJD in the United Kingdom. *Science*, 294(23 November): 1726–8.

Von Neumann, J., and Morgenstern, O. (1947). *Theory of Games and Economic Behavior*. 2d ed. Princeton, NJ: Princeton University Press.

Wagenaar, W. A. (1986). My memory: A study of autobiographical memory over six years. *Cognitive Psychology*, 18(2): 225–52.

Wagner, R. K. (1991). Managerial problem solving. In R. J. Sternberg and P. A Frensch (eds.). *Complex Problem Solving: Principles and Mechanisms*. Hillsdale NJ: Erlbaum, pp. 159–84.

Williams, G. P. (1997). *Chaos Theory Tamed*. Washington, DC: National Academy of Sciences.

Wolfram, S. (2002). *A New Kind of Science*. Champaign, IL: Wolfram Media.

Index of Names

Index of Subjects